Maestro
of a
Lost World

The Path to Sky-End

translated by Madeleine Daines 

This cover image of a dancing trio, two human figures surrounding a turtle, was copied from a carving discovered at Nevali Çori, an archeological site in south-eastern Turkey dating to the 10th millennium BC. That site has since been submerged by the construction of the Atatürk dam and its stones, of which a skull with rising serpent (illustration of line 85), are now displayed in the Sanliurfa Museum.
The dancers illustrate line 97.

First paperback edition in 2024

Copyright © Madeleine Daines and Ian Faure 2024

ISBN: 978-2-956045946

Associate Editor: Ian Faure

111

Now the whole world had one language
and a common form of speech.
(Genesis 11:1)

111

Write on a scroll what you see and send it to the seven
churches. (Revelation 1:11)

111

Then I was given a measuring rod like a staff and was
told, "Go and measure the temple of God and the
altar,..". (Revelation 11:1)

111

RE VEL
Bird of Fire
Gather together for the Revelation.
(The Path To Sky-End 111)

Contents

p.1   Preamble

Part I

p.9   The Celestial Mill

p.15   The Bird and the Sun

p.19   The Tiger and the Bee

p.23   The Lion and the Bee

p.25   The Lion, the Bull and the Bees

p.27   King of Bees

p.29   The King on his Bier

p.33   A Cog-boat of Necessity

p.37   A Need for Mead

p.39   The Rustle of Stones

p.41   The Skull

p.45   Tuning the Turtle's Strings

p.49   Sothic Mysteries

p.53   Kings and Riddles

p.57   Cusco

p.61   Giza

p.65   The Great Sphinx

p.69   The Emerald Tablet

p.71   Comet Strike

p.75   Sky People of Kitara

p.79   Language of the Birds

Part II

P.83   The Path to Sky-End

Part III

p.133   Translation Notes

p.268   The Number of Thoth-Hermes

p.271   Bibliography and References

p.273   Index

Preamble

There are extraordinarily large gaps in our knowledge of the ancient world, potentially deep and broad enough to forfeit all hope of fully evaluating this unexpected inheritance; the writings of people from a distant past, completely free from any intervening censorship or manipulation of any kind. From them to us.

Over time there has been a great deal of deliberate obfuscation concerning our 'pagan' origins. The lie began several thousand years ago and has led to those distorted messages perpetuated over the last century or so concerning the Mesopotamian clay tablets. Propped up by intellectual hubris and unwarranted faith in past interpretations, that falsehood continues to dominate today.

We were not meant to receive this gift of knowledge. And our only hope of recuperating some part of it is to return to those so-called 'Sumerian' texts and to study them afresh as we would a message written in a strange but vaguely familiar language; a long and complex note found inside a bottle that has floated untouched on an immense ocean of time, some five thousand years or more, potentially considerably more. It must be treated with immense respect for its age, its resilience and with overwhelming curiosity. Almost everything already said about that message – however many times repeated, however authoritative the tone - must be swept to one side. We have to start over, equipped with a new mindset and that hitherto missing dose of humility; this time considering that the authors knew as much as we do about the world around us – certainly more than we have given them credit for – and even that they knew far more than most of us on certain matters.

Shortly after beginning this re-translation of *Enki's Journey to Nibru*[1] in 2017, I decided to buy two very different books: *Hamlet's Mill* by Giorgio de Santillana and Hertha Von Dechend[2], and *The Language of the Goddess* by Marija Gimbutas[3]. Because mills are mentioned many times in the texts, (including in *The Instructions of Shuruppak*[4] re-translated in 2016) *Hamlet's Mill* took priority and so I ordered it from a bookshop in Paris after deciding to hold off on the more costly purchase of the *Goddess*. But just a few days later, during one of my trips to a local second-hand shop, I was browsing through the small section of books in English and there, in that obscure brocanterie in a suburb of Paris, it was waiting for me; an immaculate coffee-table copy of *The Language of the Goddess* at a very affordable price. I chose to take that as a message. Somebody had my back and was urging me to get on with it. But still, it has taken over seven years to pierce at least some of the themes and coded messages of the scribes and to get to this point. For me it was worth the wait. The reader of this will, of course, decide for themselves.

The Language of the Goddess is a feast for the eyes, both visually inspiring and informative, its images and comments serving to perceive something of the mindset that led to the creation of the artefacts displayed in its pages; a glimpse that was immensely thought-provoking and useful. For example, it allowed me to illustrate the opening lines of this text with confidence that the context was exact and that the essence of the story has not faded; the celestial goddess, her waters breaking over earth and creating a mighty flood as she prepares to give birth. Despite the great passage of time, she can still be seen in a few places, carved onto church walls or hanging over a gateway, ready to douse us. A reminder of past events and of our mortality. Her Irish name is Sheela Na Gig. NA has the meaning 'stone' in Sumerian.

Hamlet's Mill, on the other hand, is a long and difficult delve into an important aspect of archeoastronomy, the matching of myths from around the world to the observable movements of planets and stars. At the heart of that book is the notion of an ancient celestial churning mill, regulating the heartbeat of the galaxy. With a large number of examples drawn from different places and times, the authors suggest that knowledge of the phenomenon called the precession of the equinoxes - the approximately 25,920-year planetary cycle resulting from an almost imperceptible wobble in Earth's axis - had been encoded in those myths at some extremely early point in our history. If they are correct, the implications are huge.

It was the author and investigative journalist Graham Hancock who first brought the importance of the information contained in *Hamlet's Mill* to my attention. I already had a copy of *Magicians of the Gods*[5] (purchased in 2016) and had taken note of his references to Mesopotamia, to the astronomers of Harran in the north of that region and their attested pilgrimages to the site of the pyramids and Great Sphinx in Egypt. I was also able to gain some basic understanding of the complex mechanism of precession thanks to the clarity of his explanations and despite my woeful lack of knowledge of the science of astronomy.

I began to seriously consider the possibility that the ancestors of those Harranian astronomers, with their connection to the Giza plateau, were the authors of this second text that I was striving to understand and translate.

And as their words began to give up just a few of the document's secrets, it appeared increasingly obvious that I was on the right track.

A fourth book became a prerequisite for the task ahead: *Star-Names and their Meanings* by Richard Hinkley Allen, published in 1899[6]. I can't overstate the importance of that book in retracing the path of the astronomers and story tellers to this, their one source language – primarily through ancient Arabic accounts.

When I first began the re-translation of *Enki's Journey to Nibru* I had very limited understanding of astronomy and how the celestial movements might be observed and noted. I wasn't looking for a lost civilization or alien life or anything of that sort. The text was the obvious choice for a couple of purely practical reasons; primarily its comparatively reasonable length (129 lines as opposed to the 280 lines of *The Story of Sukurru*) and pristine condition; intact but for two words. The cherry on that cake came when I later discovered that one version of it is inscribed in the tiny cuneiform script of the Old Babylonian period (ca1900-1600 BC) onto a four-sided prism displayed in the Ashmolean Museum in Oxford.[7] That magnificent and carefully preserved 3,800 year-old artefact has been visibly shouting out to us that something equally glorious and important is written on it, that the information covering its four surfaces was once considered to be of great value. And yet there is strictly nothing in the existing officialised translation to confirm such a logical observation.

The other reason for choosing to attempt the translation was the incipit, UD RI A, the first three words of a number of Mesopotamian texts including *The Story of Sukurru*; that text recorded on at least one tablet around one thousand years earlier, ca.2600-2500 BC. It seemed reasonable to see the repeated formula as a sign that the stories are of the same or similar origin, that they are probably all at least 4,500 years old, potentially derived from even older sources, and that they all contain some reference to a time in which a great flood occurred. In *The Story of Sukurru*, those three words translated to 'By day, the deluge'. Today, I look at them from a slightly enlarged perspective and see there the sun, UD, and its flow, along with a bird, RI, the 'gatherer'. The bird of the flood flies over the water looking for land, gathering information. More specifically, it flies with the sun.

The discoveries made in the course of studying both *The Story of Sukurru* and *The Path To Sky-End* have led me to understand that their core themes match those of many if not all later myths, including the Ancient Egyptian writings. They reflect the teachings of a master known to us as either Hermes Trismegistus or Egyptian Thoth – and they encompass elements of Jonah, John the Baptist, Enoch and Idris, along with Prometheus and Odysseus, among others in a long list either referring to the man himself or some disciple. There can be no doubt. The names and their stories are there in some form or other, buried in the Mesopotamian texts. And I posit that those figures are reaching out to us from much deeper antiquity than we have so far imagined possible - from as far back as the 10th millennium BC, approximate age of the recently discovered sites of Göbekli Tepe, Karahan Tepe, Nevali Çori and other similar places in the region of Harran in southern Turkey, the original homes of the astronomers. Further still? I'm not ruling it out.

If it can be shown that a group of people living and carving figures onto stone in northern Mesopotamia at the end of the ice-age ca.9600 BC had knowledge of the complexities of long astronomical cycles, it would indicate that there once existed a civilization – all sight of which has been lost - sufficiently sophisticated to measure and record celestial events over multiple generations: a pre-flood, pre-Ice Age civilization. That information would necessarily have been transmitted in some form or other by survivors of one or more cataclysmic events. If the theory underlying *Hamlet's Mill* and also developed in *Magicians of the Gods* is correct, the myths - tales of astronomical events and their effects in coded form – inherited by different cultures in far different regions around the world, are all the dying embers of that one unique story.

This is not a new subject of study but my translation and its accompanying notes bring into play a hitherto unnoticed aspect; the earliest written word out of Mesopotamia, ultimate key to firmly link some, if not all, of the many later mythological figures and gods of ancient Greece and ancient Egypt to the stars, planets, constellations, to cycles of time, and to warnings about the repetitive nature of events affecting life on Earth.

And if there is any one theme that holds all of this text together, it's the tale of that written word. The hero of the story, riding the skies above and below, has been charged with taking notes in 'clay of the land'. The 'land' is written MA and takes the abstract form of a hanging fruit. That image has the dictionary-given meanings 'land' and 'fig' to which I have added its other obvious and most significant meaning: 'truth' – truth about the world we live in, the truth of our past. the truth of Mesopotamian Ma who is Egyptian Ma'at. The truth inscribed on clay tablets still silently displayed or lying unnoticed and gathering dust in the backrooms of museums around the world.

The witness is EN who has the dictionary-given title 'lord'. This is the story that became Enoch's account, the account of the witness, their eye on the clay, already identified in *The Story of Sukurru.* In truth, the original scribe knew and transcribed far more about our world both above and below than any modern translator, myself included, has so far perceived. As a late-born disciple of Thoth, it has been a great struggle to keep up and I'm painfully aware that I have failed more than once. But I trust in His patience and at least the work of recuperation has begun.

Again, this text was chosen for entirely practical reasons and not according to my expectations of the story it would tell. While bearing in mind the precious information gleaned from the authors here above whose books were consulted innumerable times in the process of translating, I have nevertheless steadfastly refused to knowingly force my own preferred narrative into any part of it. When beginning to tentatively translate the words, I had no inkling of the treasures they contained or the direction in which they would take me. I didn't so much as glance at the existing academic translation – not through arrogance but as the result of experience. It wouldn't have helped. Skull fittingly emptied, I braced myself and prepared to have my mind blown once again. And slowly, very slowly the tiny words etched into clay came back to life; the bull, the tiger, the bird of destiny, the rising fish and winding snakes, and that most glorious and unexpected of creatures: the honeybee.

Slowly the enigmatic cuneiform script gave up some of its deeper meanings, one discovery leading to another. There appeared to be an underlying order to the text, not only in the positioning of the words but also in the positioning of the lines, the unwritten line numbers, the number of words in the lines, the number of times a particular word was used overall, and the placing of certain key words inside the lines. There were layers within layers, circles within circles, spirals even, messages to be read from inside out or from outside in.

On closer examination, I discovered the second cherry on this mountainous cake: the text inscribed on the four sides of that impressive Ashmolean prism speaks of music. And not just some light-hearted song. No, an awe-inspiring opera. The whole thing, clay included, is a work of art, a musical masterpiece. Here was Pythagoras long before Pythagoras. Every part of it had been deliberately laid out to incorporate a message and to relay one number – no doubt of great importance – the ultimate key to something. I was not disappointed by my choice of text and if the reader of this has the slightest interest in our shared history and all things Egyptian and Mesopotamian neither should they be.

For greater clarity, I have attempted to highlight some of the threads of this ancient web. Certain names and numbers of interest, from astronomy or mythology, are mentioned under the pictograms. Some are given in brackets within the translated version. Vertical wordplay is indicated. That doesn't mean that one theme is of more importance than another or that everything has been laid bare. Like a Rubik's cube, every layer is part of the mesh. Have I got to the bottom of the well in this rusted, rickety bucket? Where astronomy and numbers are concerned, certainly not. But a fair way down nevertheless. Enough for others to pick up the rope. Its chords were woven by a grandmaster, a maestro. It has lasted.

The book is divided into three sections: The translation itself, rebaptized *The Path to Sky-End,* appears from p.81 to 132. My further explanations are given either in the preceding twenty-one introductory chapters or in the extensive translation notes at the end.

It begins with an account of the astronomical phenomenon of precession of the equinoxes which must be at least superficially understood in order to fully comprehend some of the codes. Experts are free to zap, of course. Certain words, phrases and, most importantly, the riddles are analysed in the translation notes where I also express my opinions from time to time and point out the few meanings added – of necessity - to existing lexicons. Unlike most, if not all other translations of Sumerian, my choices are always explained as fully as possible. To a large degree and at the risk of appearing awkward, the translation follows the source almost word for word. Anyone willing to make the effort can quite easily retrace and confirm most of the steps for themselves with time, patience and the use of a few internet tools.

As with *The Story Of Sukurru,* the cuneiform style has been peeled back to give an idea of the original pictographic form of each word inasmuch as they existed in the 4th millennium BC – and almost all of them did. In some cases, they are especially illuminating. The translated words added under each transliteration (alphabetic equivalence of the original words) are given as guides and are not exclusive. The translating process sometimes involves using the same word more than once, circling back and forth over its various related meanings, marrying it to both the words that precede and those that follow. In one or two cases, I have taken the spiralling to great heights.

Yes, they are all words - not meaningless phonemes as proposed by 'specialists'. Don't expect modern rules of grammar or attempt to match the meanings only to their designated modern alphabetic forms while ignoring the existence of the original word. My translations take place between those source words and all of their possible (and relatively limited) range of meanings according to each context in which they are found. 'Given meaning' is repeated here ad nauseum to indicate that conventional dictionaries agree. I will probably stop bothering one day.

Those who remain sceptical, preferring the academic version of events, are those who will not have made the effort to cast aside their preconceptions while reading what follows. Stiff with the rules handed down by the original 'specialists' of the 19th century, they will have decided beforehand that my claims for this language cannot possibly be right, that there can be no upsetting of such a well-established and respectable apple cart. Those people are free to continue life in the company of Enki, Enlil and the rest of that superficial, weird and unwonderful band. May the modern cacophony play on.

Looking back, I see no reason to make corrections to my two explanatory books (*Before Babel the Crystal Tongue* in 2019, *Lost Stones of the Anunnaki* in 2021) in which I explored the language, its sources and meanings to the best of my ability at the time. There's nothing much I would revise today. Looking forward, I can only hope that the few remaining nebulous sections in this text, those that I have not been able to unpack to my own satisfaction, will give food for thought. Perhaps the loose ends will one day be woven back into the fabric thanks to other people and their specialised knowledge, particularly of astronomy. It would be a great bonus. Already and only just in time before publishing, some highly relevant information gleaned from Robert Bauval's *The Egypt Code*[29] has been added. This is the first edition of the truly ancient story in modern times. There may be others. I hope so.

As always, I am immensely grateful to those who, over the past centuries, collected the tablets, transcribed and transliterated the texts, and to those who have since posted them in all their enigmatic, unreadable, alphabetic splendour onto the internet for everyone to see and for anyone to unpick.

My heartfelt thanks go to the authors of the four books mentioned here above. Without their input, I wouldn't have got very far at all. I also have to thank my son, Ian, who encouraged me through those episodes of anguish, the many times I convinced myself there was no hope of ever coming to grips with the meaning of a line or a word – like someone who loses patience and throws down a piece of a puzzle until (and as he always reminds me) it suddenly falls neatly into place. "Of course you can!", he has said countless times.

More than that, he has provided me with precious insights into subjects relating to those spiritual, psychedelic themes that wind through the Mesopotamian texts and, on a more earthly level, forced me out, away from my computer screen. Entirely thanks to my son, late in life I have experienced the magic of seeing the Great Pyramid of Giza for the first time. I have rested against the mighty pillars of the Temple of Karnak in Luxor, ancient Thebes. By chance or some other force, I have heard for myself the eery, echoing sound made by workers striking stone in the Valley of the Kings – a sound which might be mistaken for the distant shrill barking of dogs. Together, we have visited the remnants of the lost world of Göbekli Tepe in Turkey. And most recently, we stood together in silence at the heart of the megalithic cairn of Gavrinis in the Golf of Morbihan (see the notes to line 129). Thank you, Ian.

The Celestial Mill

It's not difficult to imagine that the mill as we know it, serving to transform the produce of the earth into food and drink, would be part of any story told by a tribe of newly-civilised hunter gatherers. As long as nothing intervenes to prevent the soil from providing a harvest, the stalks of wheat and barley would be gathered and threshed, the grains pounded and ground into a consistency suitable for making bread or beer.

The grinding stones might be big or small depending on use but their task has always been the same; to crush and to transform; two stones, one above and one below, or some other technique. Many birds and some mammals use stones in their gullets or stomachs to prepare food for digestion. These are the internal, invisible millstones; the gizzard stone of the big-footed dodo, the cud of cattle and other animals.

For our ancestors, a crucial period in each year was the mid-winter solstice when the sun is seen to hesitate for three days at the same spot on the horizon, creating a doubt as to its intention. Will it remain stationary? Will it disappear into its cave beyond the horizon never to be seen again? Or will it begin its return journey? Regeneration. A new cycle, a new circle.

Without at least some basic knowledge of the celestial clock, most of the meanings encoded into the Mesopotamian texts would remain unfathomable and lost to us forever. Without it, I would not have got anywhere close to the original version of *The Path to Sky-End*. And that's why my own explanation of precession given here is necessary for those who know nothing about astronomy. Readers who are not already familiar with the night sky should complete it with their own research. Those who know more than me are free to skip over it without loss.

(The sun warns Phaeton) *Moreover, the rushing sky is constantly turning, and drags along the remote stars, and whirls them in rapid orbits. I move the opposite way, and its momentum does not overcome me as it does all other things, and I ride contrary to its swift rotation. Suppose you are given the chariot. What will you do?* (Ovid, Metamorphoses, Bk.2)

Precession of the equinoxes consists in the apparent anti-clockwise movement of the sun which, as measured at four specific dates in a year (spring and autumn equinoxes, summer and winter solstices), rises in front of and obscures a set of stars. It 'resides in' each of the twelve constellations for approximately 2,160 years on those dates, slowly working its way backwards (visually that is to say) from one to the other and completing its journey through all of them just once every 25,920 years or thereabouts:

- 25,920 years to complete one Great Year,
- A one-degree shift every 72 years.

That extremely gradual backward movement results from a wobble in Earth's axis. We might look at ourselves and think that we are quite round, but that isn't true. Like a gyroscope as it begins to slow, we are askew.

Imagine a shaft through the centre of Earth pointing in the directions of the two poles, north and south. Taking the stars closest to those end points as references, the main northern pole star used in navigation will change over time. Currently, it's Polaris in the constellation of Ursa Minor. But some 16,000 years ago, it was the star Deneb in the constellation of Cygnus followed by Vega in Lyra. With the continuing shift in Earth's axis, Vega will regain its position as the northern pole star around 13700 AD:

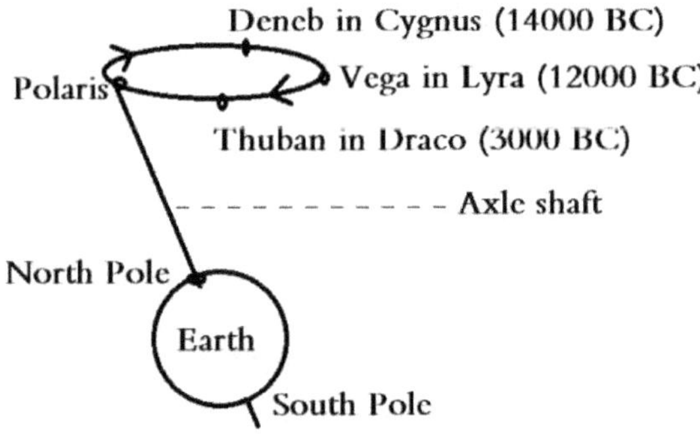

Presently on December 21st at the winter solstice (when it reaches its furthest limit along the horizon in mid-winter), the sun rises somewhere between the constellations of Sagittarius and Scorpio, not yet having completed its drift into Scorpio. Neither has it completely passed from Pisces into Aquarius at the spring (vernal) equinox, or from Gemini into Taurus in the autumn (the two equinoxes when day and night are of the same length).

In some years from now and in our northern skies, the sun will have fully completed its entrance into Scorpio in December and will rise in those four constellations at those four dates for the following 2,160 years before moving on to the next set of stars. Four constellations always moving in lockstep and not to be confused with the zodiacal dates in modern astrology:

(Galactic Plain)	Sun flow	Present Position	
(Southern gate)	Sagittarius	Winter solstice→	
(Southern gate)	Scorpio	→	(Summer 10500 BC)
	Libra		
	Virgo	Autumn equinox→	
	Leo	→	(Spring 10500 BC)
	Cancer		
(Northern gate)	Gemini	Summer solstice→	
(Northern gate)	Taurus	→	(Winter 10500 BC)
	Aries		
	Pisces	Spring equinox→	
	Aquarius	→	(Autumn 10500 BC)
	Capricorn		

★★★

1. Sagittarius (winter), Pisces (spring), Gemini (summer), Virgo (autumn)
2.   Scorpio★ (winter), Aquarius (spring), Taurus (summer), Leo (autumn)
3. Libra (winter), Capricorn (spring), Aries (summer), Cancer (autumn)
4. Virgo (winter), Sagittarius (spring), Pisces (summer), Gemini (autumn)
5. Leo (winter), Scorpio (spring), Aquarius (summer), Taurus (autumn)
6. Cancer (winter), Libra (spring), Capricorn (summer), Aries (autumn)
7. Gemini (winter), Virgo (spring), Sagittarius (summer), Pisces (autumn)
8. Taurus★ (winter), Leo (spring), Scorpio (summer), Aquarius (autumn)
9. Aries (winter), Cancer (spring), Libra (summer), Capricorn (autumn)
10. Pisces (winter), Gemini (spring), Virgo (summer), Sagittarius (autumn)
11. Aquarius (winter), Taurus (spring), Leo (summer), Scorpio (autumn)
12. Capricorn (winter), Aries (spring), Cancer (summer), Libra (autumn)

★ For example, approximately 12,960 years (2,160 years multiplied by 6) will pass between the time of Scorpio (2) rising with the sun at the winter solstice and Taurus (8) doing the same. In terms of precession, they will always be separated by the same number of years (12,960 x 2 = 25,920).

The vernal (spring) equinox brings hope of good crops. But at the summer solstice and at its zenith, the sun associated with the Pleiades and the star Sirius, is known to be unruly; excessive heat, absence of rain, too heavy or too light handed. Heat and drought will kill all hope of abundance. At the autumn equinox, the results are in; the harvest good or bad or non-existent. Then the winter solstice - when food stocks begin to look slim and the sun hesitates in its course - must have seemed the most dangerous of times. No doubt all four of those milestones were important in the minds of people who didn't buy their food from supermarket shelves. Celebrations, hand-wringing, supplications, praise and thanks: the festivals and their music have always been orchestrated by the movements of the sun and its followers. That's where it all began.

When dividing up a circle for the purpose of time-keeping, a starting point must be determined. For a day, that's easy enough but for the greater cycles, the decades, the centuries, the millennia? Our era apparently began without the aid of the science of astronomy. As far as we know, someone somewhere decided that year zero should coincide with the birth of a saviour in mid-winter. But what was the situation before that happened?

The well-documented Mayan calendar gives the clue as to how more ancient cultures counted time and when it began. The end of their great cycle of around 26,000 years being famously placed at around 2012, we can reasonably presume that, in the absence of a catastrophe, they considered that year to be the beginning of a new cycle, a new age; the age of Aquarius which is a reference to the position of the sun in front of that constellation at sunrise on March 21st, the vernal equinox, from around 2012-2040 AD.

No single group of humans on this planet could be aware of the full cycle without having received the knowledge from their predecessors and/or possessing extremely sophisticated tools. Just one degree of the sun's movement is equal to one lifetime – 72 years if we're lucky.

To further complicate matters, two pairs of constellations have a fixed position in relation to the galactic plain. Two pillars, a pair of gates at each end of the Milky Way. The permanent markers of the extreme northern end of that great arch are Gemini and Taurus while Sagittarius and Scorpio together mark the region known as its southern gate (see Galactic Plain in the diagram here above). At its most southerly point lies the central and nebulous region called the Great (or Dark) Rift.

Thus, when the sun rises somewhere between the constellations of Sagittarius and Scorpio at the winter solstice (as it does in our time), it is also passing between those same two guardians of the southern gate of the galactic plain. In so doing, it crosses in front of the Great Rift at the centre of our galaxy, creating the very special celestial alignment noted by the

Mayans and which takes place just once every 25,920 years. The last time it happened was pre-ice-age, approximately 14,300 years before Göbekli Tepe was buried some 11,600 years ago. And it is happening again in our time. In 2015, Graham Hancock wrote:

> *The exact targeting of the galactic centre occurs in a window that is no more than 80-years wide and we will continue to be in that window for approximately another 25 years.* [8]

That date was the end of the Mayan calendar: the point on the circle when the great clock stopped (at around 2012) after 25,920 years of ticking. If all goes well, it now reboots and begins again at zero. But that expectation comes with a terrible caveat: that no great life-extinguishing event occur. Otherwise, no-one will be around to see the sun slowly moving from the water-pourer of Aquarius at the start of spring to its next destination in Capricorn at that same date some 2,160 years from now.

Perhaps nothing will be left of us by then; the slate wiped clean whether by fire or flood, by freezing or burning, or their joint effects. It has happened before and it is beyond our control, most certainly not of our making. Then, at some point in the unfolding of a new civilization on Earth when the small number of remaining humans will lift their eyes to the skies once again, a year zero will be discussed for the purpose of keeping accounts – a necessity for those inhabitants of our planet who will, as this latest generation has hardly done, listen for the buzzing of the bees in spring and learn to distinguish the harvest years of finer wines. Then as more time passes, they will begin to congratulate themselves on the ever-evolving sophistication of their civilization – the first on this planet.

Perhaps the calendar used by the next civilization - rising quasi-memoryless out of the dust - will also be based on observations of the flow of sun, moon and certain stars, and even aided by a reboot from some surviving intelligence, something that a maestro of this or an earlier lost world will have deliberately left for them. Will it all happen again? And, if it does, will someone succeed in obscuring that inheritance, manufacturing a new calendar, established not according to celestial observations but in order to gain control over the minds of men? Who knows? And who knows what an unexpected resurfacing memory inserted into an authoritarian scheme might provoke?

In the meantime, the celestial cogs continue to turn around the axle in the mill of the sky. The whole setup, whether terrestrial or celestial, requires rhythm and a considerable amount of energy. Those carrying out the work must demonstrate certain qualities: physical power, tenacity, industriousness, dedication, concentration. A rogue stone, even a tiny grain, made of a material impossible to crush, appearing out of nowhere and allowed to stray into the mix; all hell might break loose. A powerful kick of an ox's heel in a certain place, at a particular time, and a hole in the matrix appears. A rogue fungus, cause of hallucinations and death, falling into the mill among the grains of wheat and inadvertently added to the final mix… Too much rain. Not enough sun. So many parameters. So many complexities.

Control, concentration and knowledge of the risks are paramount in the workings of any mill. A sense of rhythm, balance and grace also. Music. A ballet. A cosmic opera. And for the cogs, some oil.

The Bird and the Sun

In fact, the sun figure appears to be located accurately on the ecliptic with respect to the familiar constellation of Scorpio, although the scorpion depicted on the pillar occupies only the left portion, or head, of our modern conception of that constellation. As such, the sun symbol is located as close to the galactic center as it can be on the ecliptic as it crosses the galactic plane. [9]

In a short article on Graham Hancock's website written in 2012, Paul D. Burley, environmental geologist and author, appears to have been the first person to notice that the scorpion on the main face of Pillar 43 at Göbekli Tepe can be usefully compared to the modern day constellation of Scorpio observed in relation to the sun. He refers to the ball on the wing of the nearby bird as the 'sun figure'.

Paul Burley posits that the carvings represent a very specific moment in time when the sun crosses in front of the Milky Way at the winter solstice and, more precisely, crosses the very heart of our galaxy, that distinct bulge at the southernmost tip of the Milky Way known as the Great Rift. That alignment occurs only once every 25,920 years and is the situation we are living through today.

The questions that arise from his observations, discussed in *Magicians of the Gods*, are:

- Was the ball on the bird's wing meant to represent the sun?

- If so, was the sculptor of the pillar referring to past events ca. 23900 BC that they could not possibly have experienced in their lifetime?

- Were they composing a message to future generations concerning that particular moment in time?

- Did that message stem from some pre-Ice Age civilization which disappeared almost completely from view after some great cataclysm?

There is another question to be answered; one that very few would think to ask. Did any of the writings in the language of Mesopotamia mention the existence of such a message? We have copies of a couple of enigmatic passages in texts from antiquity written in Greek but that is all:

> *After Euedoreschus some others reigned, and then Sisithrus. To him the deity Cronus foretold that on the fifteenth day of the month Desius there would be a deluge of rain: and he commanded him to deposit all the writings whatever which were in his possession, in the city of the Sun in Sippara.* (L.P. Cory, *Ancient Fragments*, 1832: Berossus ca.290 BC, sourced from Eusebius (ca. 260–339 AD) Chronicles 5.8., from Abydenus ca.200 BC.)

Sippara is taken to be located somewhere alongside the river Euphrates in Mesopotamia but where exactly and when? And in what language did they write at the time of the flood?

> *24. Between the two rivers, the ring-necked bird on the great stone guide to the otherworldly crossing of the sun and the soul points the way (and shows the arrow's flow).*

The first indication that this text refers to a bird sitting somewhere between the rivers Euphrates and Tigris comes on line 24 with the Idigna bird. And it is showing the way – as is the bird on Pillar 43 at Göbekli Tepe. According to the dictionaries, it has a ringed neck as does the bird on that pillar. Follow the direction of the stone guide whose triple-barrelled name include the words for 'sun' and 'crossbeam', and translates to 'Euphrates' (notes to line 24).

Both textual and engraved, the distinctive bird is referencing the movement of the sun. One was carved ca.9600 BC and the other existed in the 4th millennium. In this context, it was written on clay tablets sometime around 1600 BC. They are telling the same story. The 'stone guide' is a pillar. It's also the main element of the modern name Anunnaki (*Lost Stones*, p.28 and 209).

Is it possible to confirm that the big-footed bird in question was intentionally pointing to the position of the sun at a particular moment in time; namely its passage at the winter solstice between the two permanent guardians of the southern gate of the Milky Way, Sagittarius and Scorpio?

(Sagittarius) *in Egypt, where it is said to have been known as an Arrow held in a human hand;* (*Star Names* [6], p.352)

The central bird at the top of the pillar is balancing a ball which is understood to be the sun. That is what Paul Burley concluded, placing it precisely on the ecliptic with respect to the position of Scorpio, the constellation that partners with Sagittarius to guard the southern gate of the Milky Way (p.11). On line 24, not only do we find the bird of Pillar 43 and the stone guide to the movement of the sun; we also have a hand and an arrow. The link between the bird of the Euphrates and the constellation of Sagittarius is confirmed (using only dictionary-given meanings).

However, according to a parallel and equally reasonable theory developed by author Andrew Collins, the featureless ball might rather represent the skull of the headless ithyphallic man seated on the bird at the bottom of the same pillar.[10]

It takes very little imagination to see that the head has, by some magic, been propelled from the bottom of the pillar to the top, from one bird to another or rather, in the manner of an ancient comic strip, to the same bird in its new position. Line 26, no doubt meant to convey a degree of humour, brings confirmation (see notes):

26. By the beam of the moon and in a thunderbolt, the brainless skull the size of the gap not knowing, the measure of the spreading wing not taking...

Line 26 evokes a number of underlying themes. Lack of measure means a lack of boundaries, a foolhardy attitude, that of the initiate bouncing into the unknown, or the son on a foolish quest to find his father. But it's also the spreading of the maestro's arms as he prepares to lead a mighty orchestra. It's the delicate arching of the musician's fingers preparing to pluck the strings of an ancient instrument. It's the arrow pulled back and held firmly as the archer takes careful aim. It's the silence before the thunder bolt of Zeus and it's the spreading wing of a great mythical bird preparing to take flight.

The text calls to mind the accounts of two figures from Greek mythology: Phaeton and Icarus. Phaeton, on a quest to discover his origins, is admonished by the sun, believed to be his father:

> *And, O my son, lest I may be the author of a baneful gift, beware,*
> *and as the time permits recall thy rash request.*
> (Ovid, *Metamorphoses*, Bk.2, trans. Golding)

He ignores the advice, attempts to handle the reins of the sun's carriage and is struck by a thunder bolt from Zeus in an effort to save Earth from his folly. Both he and Icarus are doomed to fall from the sky and to die. Phaeton falls into the river Eridanus (notes to lines 30 and 36), another name that can be traced back to its Sumerian source in NUN, the stone guide of the river Euphrates (*Lost Stones*, p.207).

Icarus, equally foolhardy, falls into the sea when the wax holding his fragile wings together is melted by the heat of the sun. Did he use the beeswax from an ancient honeycomb? Found in Homer's description of a ferocious battle, the term Icarian became synonymous of a great and destructive wave (see ULA in the notes to line 25):

> *And the whole assembly surged like big waves at sea, the Icarian Sea*
> *when East and South Winds drive it on, blasting down in force from*
> *the clouds of Father Zeus,* (Homer, *Iliad*, Bk.2)

The Tiger and the Bee

If an important story involving astronomical events is reproduced in the carvings of Pillar 43, it is logical to first consider the creatures on its main face - the partially-exposed canine, the scorpion and the large birds along with the other elements, of which the three 'offering baskets' perched over a relatively obvious depiction of the three streams of the galactic plain (notes to line 60). Paul Burley's short article and Graham Hancock's subsequent assessment of the pillar referred to that frontal view. But there is more. To find the second episode, a corner must be turned and a side road explored…

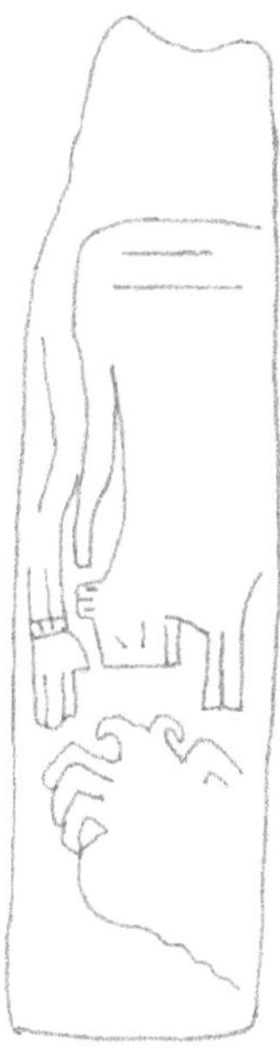

The Caspian tiger, recently declared extinct, roamed the river banks of the Tigris and Euphrates rivers as far back as the 10th or 9th millennium BC. Carvings of the felines are plentiful at Göbekli Tepe even if not prominent on the now famous Pillar 43. But yes, it does appear there – twice in fact. It's not hard to find. Just leave the facade and move to the side panel of the upper section.

On that narrow side of the stone, a downward slinking tiger comes nose to nose with a partially destroyed insect. The tiger's body is entirely flanked by what appear to be two long parallel arms ending in a pair of hands.

Swift and unpredictable, the Tigris and the tiger were metaphors one for the other. The river roars like the tiger which was roaming its banks when the stones of Göbekli Tepe were carved. That's why the feline faces downwards on those pillars; it streaks down from the mountains, matching all the qualities of its namesake.

The Tigris flows through the middle of Lake Thopitis, as it is called, in the direction of its breadth; and, after traversing it to the opposite shore, it sinks underground with upward blasts and a loud noise; and having flowed for a considerable distance invisible, it rises again not far away from Gordyaea; and it traverses the lake so impetuously, as Eratosthenes says, that, although the lake elsewhere is briny and without fish, yet in this part it is fresh, runs like a river, and is full of fish. (Strabo, Geography, 7:16.1.20, Trans.H. L. Jones)

The arms pointing downwards along the feline's profile represented and became the word for the banks that enclose all rivers, all water channels of any kind. DA (one of several differing pictograms shown here)  appears in the lexical tablets as part of the name of the celestial river Eridanus of Greek mythology (notes to lines 30 and 36), a word with an unarguable link to the NUN of the Anunnaki. One of its given meanings is 'riverbank' (*Lost Stones*, p.206-207). As I have already said elsewhere, like the Tigris, the written language of the Mesopotamians has its source here in the region of Harran among the ancestors of those astronomers known to us as Chaldeans and Sabians.

I went looking for confirmation that the insect on the side of Pillar 43 is a bee rather than a spider or some other insect, and found what appears to be the same figure on the side panel of another pillar. This time, its three pairs of legs show a different articulation. They stretch out to touch the sides of the channel in which it lodges, those sides taking the form of snake heads. Apart from that, it appears to be the same creature and the rounded body is fully visible. The form of the head and location of its antenna are better matched to a bee than to a spider. Then again, a spider has four pairs of legs.

The only other possibility is that we are looking at a honeypot ant. Once again, my research has led me into unknown territory where I discover for the first time that such an insect exists. Unlike the bee which takes pollen back to the hive attached to its body, honeypot ants stock their nectar inside their abdomens which swell up to look just like the round forms on the pillars. More so, in fact, than those of the oval bodies of honeybees. Honeypot ants also have the peculiarity of hanging from the roof of their dwelling and gradually disgorging food for fellow ants. All in all, it would make an excellent metaphor for food stockage during a period of famine, as in Aesop's fable, *The Ant and the Grasshopper*.

It might also be a depiction of a bumblebee which has a rounder body than the honeybee. That said, I favour the honeybee for a number of reasons, one of them being that it is infinitely more productive and important to humans than other insects. At least one rock carving from some 30,000 years ago shows the picture of a man climbing to perilous heights on cliff faces in search of wild hanging honeycombs. So no surprise that the honeybee would somehow figure in any important and enduring story of survival. That importance is echoed in the images and writings of Ancient Egypt. The bee appears in the hieroglyphics in profile alongside its partner, the sedge. Together they form the praenomen, ('before the name') written next to the pharaoh's 'throne name', a position conferring great importance on all concerned (notes to line 61).

That second 'bee' pillar at Göbekli Tepe is situated in the same enclosure as Pillar 43 and has only recently been fully excavated. Between the winding snakes, a third version of the same insect appears at ground level, and this one has four pairs of legs – as do spiders but also as do the Egyptian bees here above. So more than one bee in that story. And just above it is a disproportionately small four-legged animal..

The second mention of the tiger on Pillar 43 is considerably more discreet. It stems primarily from the visual similarities between the central bird on Pillar 43, particularly its neck rings, and the earliest pictographic name given to the Tigris. The likeness is remarkable and not a coincidence (see notes to line 24, and *Lost Stones*, An Enduring Bird, p.122). Both the bird on the facade and the carving on the side panel speak of felines and rivers in one way or another.

The neck of the carved and written bird represents the point at which the far later so-called ouroboros creature, a combination of snake and bird, is seen to bite its own tail (see notes to line 10, and *Lost Stones*, p.139).

The encounter between the tiger and the bee, an unlikely pairing, should give pause for thought, and even more so in light of the numerous discussions in recent years about the carvings on the face of that pillar. There appears to be consensus that they were all part of an extremely early astronomical calendar. And yet those two seem to have slipped by more or less unnoticed.

A pair of arms, a tiger and a bee carved nose to nose down the side of a stone slab on a hilltop not far from the Taurus mountain range some 11,600 years ago. Why?

The Lion and The Bee

When Samson returned later to take her, he left the road to see the
lion's carcass, and in it was a swarm of bees, along with their honey.
(Judges 14:8)

What is the meaning of that strange biblical verse inserted for no apparent reason into the story of Samson, the man whose strength had left him until the final moment when he stood between two pillars and pushed? Is there a well-anchored and far more ancient message lurking behind that tale?

The Great Sphinx at Giza is the most obvious – and unarguably the most exciting - feline to set against the tiger on Pillar 43 at Göbekli Tepe, particularly as it once crouched with its paws dangling on or over the banks of the Nile (or tributary), another unpredictable and sometimes raging river. That feline is understood to have its twin in the constellation of Leo. Turning again to *Magicians of the Gods*:

> *My intuition is that these devices, both the Mayan calendar and the*
> *Göbekli Tepe pillar, are an attempt, using the precessional code, to*
> *send a message to the future. I see the lineaments of that message also*
> *in the huge astronomical geoglyph formed by the Pyramids and the*
> *Great Sphinx of Giza.*[11]

The theory is that, on one hand, the Mayan and Göbekli Tepe calendars point to the passage of the sun in front of the dark rift at the southern end of the Milky Way at the winter solstice, an alignment that happens only every 25,920 years or thereabouts – and is happening in our time.

On the other ticking hand, the Giza complex, through the position of the Great Sphinx facing the rising constellation of Leo at the spring equinox, points to the time when Göbekli Tepe came into being ca.9600 BC which corresponds with the end of the last ice age. The proof put forward by Robert Bauval and Adrian Gilbert in *The Orion Mystery* takes the form of a celestial map matching the three pyramids of Giza to the belt stars in the constellation of Orion, the Nile to the galactic plain and the Sphinx to Leo rising before the sun at that specific moment in time.[12]

Between the two clocks - the wing of the bird on Pillar 43 at Göbekli Tepe and the paws of the Great Sphinx at Giza - a message concerning the end of the Great Year is formed.

As Graham Hancock also notes, there exists a record showing the Sabians of Harran to have been keen disciples of Hermes Trismegistus, who is Egyptian Thoth. The claim by Selim Hassan that they made pilgrimages from northern Mesopotamia to Egypt provides a direct connection between the practice of astronomy in the regions of Göbekli Tepe and the Egyptian Giza plateau at some point in time.[13] There is no record to state when the tradition began. But there are other connections between Egyptian and Mesopotamian astronomers in ancient texts indicating Egypt as the ultimate source of their knowledge (see p.35–36).

When Leo rose before the sun in the east at the spring equinox in 9600 BC, the same phenomenon was taking place both in front of the Great Sphinx (or the protruding natural mound forming its neck and head) and over the more easterly region of Harran and the Taurus mountains. In both places, the lion was immediately preceded by the rising constellation of Cancer which carries at its heart a group of stars known as Praesepe, the beehive cluster. The celestial lion's face follows the bees as they climb, heralding the beginning of spring. It may be that, in the most ancient astronomers' eyes, the lion was larger and closer to Praesepe. Perhaps the bees were buzzing inside its mouth or under its nose:

> (Cancer) *the manzil Al Nathrah, the Gap in the hair under the muzzle of the supposed immense ancient Lion, was chiefly formed by Praesaepe (Star Names[6], p.110)*

Manzil is Arabic for 'house', being the twenty-eight resting places of the moon, those points at which it crosses the ecliptic (path of the sun) on its journey around Earth during a solar year. The lunar houses serve to calculate its movements in relation to the sun.

Thus a relatively tiny detail might be added to the calendar of the Great Sphinx at the spring equinox of 10500 BC. While the lion king contemplated its magnificent counterpart in the sky, it had to put up with a swarm of bees. And at certain times it had to deal with both the bees swarming around its nose and the passage of the moon before its eyes.

The Lion, the Bull and the Bees

They (bees) retire for the winter at the setting of the Vergiliæ (Pleiades), *and remain shut up till after the rising of that constellation, and not till only the beginning of spring, as some authors have stated;* (Pliny, Natural History, Bk XI:5)

Three months before Leo rose with the sun in the spring of 10500 BC, the constellation of Taurus was the backdrop at the winter solstice. It was the bull that announced the return of the great life-giving planet: 'God'. Mid-winter was a time celebrated with festivals combining supplication with gratitude for past and future generosity – again in both places, the pyramids of Giza and the Taurus mountains. The large number of references to the bull in and around Mesopotamia, whether in carvings or painted images, demonstrates that it was already the object of considerable importance when Göbekli Tepe and other sites were constructed.

And when the great bull of Taurus rose, pulling with it the newborn sun, it also carried over its shoulder another cluster of bees, this one more prominent than the Beehive in the constellation of Cancer but less famous as such. Still, they are well known - even to those who rarely look up - as the bright cluster of the Pleiades.

This drawing (copied from a bas-relief first discovered in Kish and used to illustrate lines 29 to 30 of *The Story of Sukurru*) shows just one of a large number of closely similar images from Mesopotamia and surrounding regions; a lion biting down on the back of a bull. In this case, it appears to be chomping on the hump of an ox; a zebu. No-one, at least to my knowledge, has come up with a convincing theory for the pair being portrayed in that well-attested position.

For what it's worth, my suggestion is that they hark back to a long calendar based in both solstices and equinoxes. It incorporated Taurus with the Pleiades cluster above its back – perhaps associated with the hump of the zebu - and a more ancient version of our feline with the beehive Praesepe in its mouth. The winter solstice animal, Taurus, was brought down by the might of its spring equinox rival, Leo (see p.11). The lion of the spring bit down and released the regenerated bees (Pleaides) from inside the bull, merging them with those of the rising beehive cluster in the constellation of Cancer, now in front of Leo's nose. Thus the dominating feline, whether tiger or lion, was symbolic of spring and the re-emergence of the bees from their winter home.

If correct, that founding story from as far back as 10500 BC - and potentially considerably earlier - was never forgotten. And in no way does it obviate any other timeline carved onto the pillars of Göbekli Tepe. The bull and the lion will always move in lockstep. When Taurus rose in and around 2500 BC at the spring equinox, in the age when the Great Pyramid is said to have been built, Leo took over the role of companion to the sun at the summer solstice and so on.

Whatever the truth of that matter, it's the regeneration of the bees after the difficult winter months or after any long period of intense cold or heat and certain death - the ice-age for example – that remains all-important. That ancient method of bringing nature back to life through the death of the bull was encountered more than once in the process of translating and writing the accompanying notes. Here for example:

> *Bury the carcasses of sacrificed bulls (it is a known experiment) in the ditch where you have thrown them, and flower-sipping bees, will be born, here and there, from the putrid entrails. After the custom of their parent bodies, they frequent the fields, are devoted to work, and labour in hope of harvest.* (Ovid, *Metamorphoses*, Bk.XV, 361, Pythagoras' Teachings, Autogenesis.)

If the biblical account is to be believed, the same could be said of the carcasses of lions rotting along a side road. The bees must reappear. We are lost without them.

Line 109 brings into play another element of that ancient recipe for regeneration: the added effect of urination (see the quote under that line).

King of Bees

It's easy to prove beyond reasonable doubt that the word BI – given in the dictionaries as 'beer' and the verb 'to be' - was once of great importance in calculations of time. Evidence is found over and over again in the *Sumerian King List*[14] where BI appears as part of the qualifying MU-BI written after totalled numbers and translated together as 'years'. MU gives the word 'year' followed by the silent verb 'to be' from BI:

MU BI

Year(s) to be, Age of the Bee

Another word that appears constantly in the *King List* is the king himself. To my knowledge, that word in its original pictographic form has never before been discussed in the context of bees. But look more closely:

LU2 GAL / LUGAL

The word bears no relation to a human form. Nor is it regal as we understand that word. It has no arms or legs, and the head, with two lines presumably marking disproportionately large eyes in a chinless face, is frankly weird. How much more logical does this pictogram become when the king is understood as an abstract rendering of a bee? How much more logical is the phrase MU BI, 'total of the reign', when we realise that it refers to the reigns of kings so closely associated with bees as to take on the guise of the insect in written accounts? (see notes to line 61).

LUGAL, the 'great man', translates to 'king' or 'ruler' rather than 'man' entirely thanks to his sign of superiority, GAL, the T-shaped form with a number of vertical lines rising from it, highly reminiscent of a comb of some sort. Without it, he would be an inferior form of the species, just a man.

When the realization that the king was a bee finally dawned (after a shamefully long time), I went looking for more evidence of the scribe's original intention; something that might explain both the shape and the meaning of his accompanying instrument, GAL, the 'great'; preferably something that would prove his king-bee status beyond any doubt, linking it uniquely to the world of ancient – and perhaps even modern – beekeeping. And once again, by following the trail of words, I was not disappointed. There can be no doubts, no dispute. It has exactly the same form as the word. No need for a picture even. Just look at the word. There exists still today an instrument known as an uncapping fork. Uncapping is the process by which beeswax is detached from the outside of the honeycomb cells to release and to gather the precious life-giving honey. Beeswax, useful for sculpting (the lost wax process) among other things, is the veil covering a secret chamber and the king is unique in that he possesses that ultimate key to the hidden riches of the hive. Who could have guessed? Not me.

For the hive's self, or stitched of hollow bark,
Or from tough osier woven, let the doors
Be strait of entrance; for stiff winter's cold
Congeals the honey, and heat resolves and thaws,
To bees alike disastrous; not for naught
So haste they to cement the tiny pores
That pierce their walls, and fill the crevices
With pollen from the flowers, and glean and keep
To this same end the glue, that binds more fast
Than bird-lime or the pitch from Ida's pines.
(Virgil, *Georgics*, Bk.4)

With that knowledge in hand and through the lens of those highly civilised people who we now know to have been astronomers, bee-keepers and brewers, it becomes possible to scrape away the wax plugging the entrance to this ancient hive and hope to uncover its golden stream of information. For that, we must pay close attention to the buzzing.

The workings of bees and beekeepers are not common knowledge in our times and most of the information gleaned just from Virgil's long account was unknown to me before I began this journey. But I did know that bee colonies are ruled over by a queen – not a king. There are no kings in that domain; only male workers. But workers need a leader in the outside world.

The King on his Bier

They say that, if a young swarm go astray, it will turn back upon its route and by the aid of scent seek out its leader. It is said that if he is unable to fly he is carried by the swarm, and that if he dies the swarm perishes; and that, if this swarm outlives the king for a while and constructs combs, no honey is produced and the bees soon die out. (Aristotle, The Nature of Animals, Part 40.)

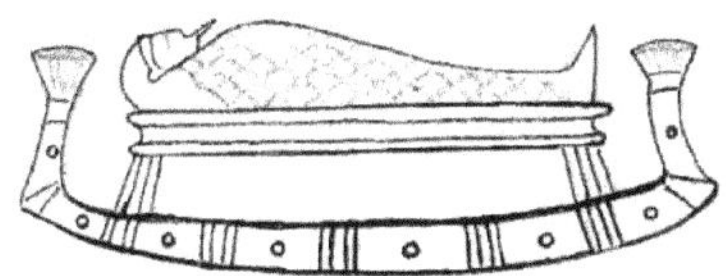

No translator, however skilled in a language, can do justice to a subject about which they know nothing. Both *The Story of Sukurru* and *The Path To Sky-End* encode astronomical references, most of which I missed in 2017. Fortunately, I did manage to grasp a number of references to spiritual journeying and to the use of hallucinogenic substances despite being relatively ignorant of those themes too.

One of the most mysterious tales gleaned from the papyrus scrolls and temple walls of Ancient Egypt is that of the journey of the soul after death. It involves the negotiating of a path across the skies through the traps or challenges set out along the way. The dead person carries a book of instructions to help them pass along to the great gate of the goddess Ma'at where the heart is weighed for truth. At that point, their soul is judged according to its negative responses to forty-two questions (see line 42). We know something of that journey thanks to the recovered papyri known as *The Book of the Dead*. As with the bees in the carcass of bull or lion, there is the hope of a successful reincarnation at the end of it all.

Retranslation of two long Sumerian texts in their original monosyllabic style has brought proof that the Mesopotamians knew those rituals. The measure of the journey is noted by the scribe – following instructions - as he travels with the sun. The questioning at the moment of death and the weighing of the heart are also present.

Without detailed knowledge of the Egyptian ritual and finding in *The Story of Sukurru* that, instead of the human heart, a stone was being weighed against the feather of truth, I concluded that some cruel joke was being played on the victim who had no chance against such odds. I wrote the English version of it and my notes with that in mind. Line 40 reads:

40. Between the stone and the feather, into the dini he sinks.

Now I see my mistake. The Egyptian ritual did indeed involve using a stone amulet called the Heart Scarab in place of the human heart, apparently to preserve that organ from potential damage. So, while my understanding was incomplete, nevertheless the translation - always based on the words rather than personal assumptions - was correct. (Dini is an ancient name for an underground karstic waterway.) The phrase is too precise and fits too well with the Egyptian account to be passed off as coincidence.

The first pharaoh according to myth was the personification of the sun god Ra. In Mesopotamian lore, RA is also an epithet applied to the sun – although not according to academia. It has the dictionary-given meaning 'thresh' which, in my translation, is generally replaced by 'churn'. RA is the celestial 'churner'.

"The proverbial phrase, 'the copper vessel in Dodona,' originated thus: In the temple was a copper vessel with a statue of a man situated above it and holding a copper scourge, dedicated by the Korkyraians; the scourge was three-fold and wrought in chain fashion, with bones strung from it; and these bones, striking the copper vessel continuously when they were swung by the winds, would produce tones so long that anyone who measured the time from the beginning of the tone to the end could count to four hundred. Whence, also, the origin of the proverbial term, 'the scourge of the Korkyraians.'"
(Strabo, *Geography,* 7 Fragment 3, Trans. Hamilton, Falconer, 1877)

Ancient Egyptian Ra, the pharaoh who travels with the sun after death, holds the three-fold scourge (flail) in his right hand. A fly-whisk has been proposed for that instrument but doesn't relate to any known episode of that journey. Did he need to whisk the flies or the bees along the way? Perhaps both if they were bothering his nose. As no-one to my knowledge has offered a more convincing reason for the importance and use of that instrument during his journey, I posit a connection between the Egyptian instrument and the above quote, particularly as Dodona appears in both Strabo's text and on line 10 of this text - which also includes three rods.

Inexorably, the Mesopotamian path leads back to Hermes Trismegistus and to Egyptian magic. Might the copper vessel be assimilated to a copper tablet become green with age? Or a metal bowl in which a celestial hero travels? And why that precise number of four hundred strikes given by Strabo? Does it relate to the calculations of an ancient calendar?

The Mesopotamian king in his pictographic form is also signalled by a pronged instrument, but in his case it's more likely to be the capping fork of the bee-keeper (p.28). That tool shows the ruler to be responsible for sustaining life through the work involved in collecting the honey. He might be the leader of the worker bees, the earthly bee-keeper or, more generally, the father of all farmers, the mythical golden king: the sun. That said, the number of prongs to the word GAL varies; on some of the earliest tablets just three and on others five or six.

Both figures are connected to the sun. And both emerge from myths in which, after death on earth, their spirit travels either with or as the sun from east to west. They both must sink into the abyss before being reincarnated. There is only one sun unless Saturn is taken into account and matters further complicated. In any case, the dead Egyptian pharaoh and the Mesopotamian king on a journey through the underworld have a lot in common.

> *(Ursa Major) Delitzsch says that even to-day the group is known as a Bier in Syria; Flammarion attributing this title to the slow and solemn motion of the figure around the pole. This seems to have originated in Arabia; and from it come the titles even now occasionally heard for the quadrangle stars — the Bier and the Great Coffin. With the early Arab poets the Banat stars were an emblem of inactivity and laziness. (Star Names [6], p.433)*

Taking the various myths of journeying heroes and attempting to combine their adventures into one through this language is like finding a rope hanging down from the sky and trying to climb it bare-handed, all the while staring up into the cloud above in an attempt to see who or what is holding the other end. Willingly or not, we must grip tight and push forward over an abyss that concerns us all and about which most people on this planet today have been taught next to nothing in school, myself included. As with the phenomenon of the sun's anti-clockwise movement, I will keep it simple and hope to not make mistakes.

Where astronomy is concerned, there are knots along the rope that indicate the path and give a moment of respite. For the most part, they are the meanings – and sometimes the words themselves - that have filtered down from the original Mesopotamian into Arabic, and from there found their way to Allen's essential book: *Star Names And Their Meanings.*[6]

The king on his bier is named three times in *The Path To Sky-End* (lines 17, 39 and 91) and once in *The Story of Sukurru* (line 181). Long before the astronomical and bee-keeper aspects had revealed themselves, using the same words and their dictionary-given meanings I wrote:

181. The king who smells of beer...

It's easy to confuse beer and bier because they both derive from BI followed by ER. If context allows, the two words are also the source of:

- 'the erring bee',
- 'the king and his beer',
- 'the king on his bier',
- 'the king erring among the bees', etc.

BI was translated 'beer' with ER which is 'smell' (both dictionary-given meanings) and it's very possible that the king did smell. In context, I took it to be an insult thrown at him during an angry exchange with a character strongly resembling biblical Ezekiel, but Aristotle (see p.29), points to the swarm of bees seeking out their leader 'by the aid of scent'. Again, it seems that the essence of that translation was correct despite my ignorance of the behaviour of bees – or that the insects played any part at all in that story – or that astronomy was involved. The author of the text was aware of the phenomenon and I followed their lead as a trusting disciple must – blindly until the truth shines through.

That short three-word phrase has more uses than one. It also serves as more evidence that the two texts – one written ca.2500 BC and the other ca.1600 BC – are telling the same story with the same words, and therefore that both are most probably at least as old as the earliest version, as old as the Great Pyramid of Giza.

Once the preparation of his mummified body was complete, the pharaoh had a boat at his disposal. Across the ceiling of the Dendera Temple, all the figures representing constellations, stars or planets travel by boat. That's also the case here. Bearing in mind that the Ancient Egyptian pharaoh and the Mesopotamian king in these stories came into existence around the time of a great flood, of necessity he had a boat. But not just any boat... He was leaving earth with the firm intention of returning. What better way to do that than in a round boat?

A Cog-Boat Of Necessity

(Argo Navis) *"Sternforward Argo by the Great Dog's tail is drawn; for hers is not a usual course, But backward turned she comes, as vessels do when sailors have transposed the crooked stern, on entering harbour; all the ship reverse, and gliding backward on the beach it grounds. Sternforward thus is Jason's Argo drawn."* This loss of its bow is said to have occurred *"when Argo pass'd through Bosporus betwixt the justling rocks"* (Aratos, *Phaenomena*, quoted in *Star Names and their Meanings*[6], p.65)

If a boat has no bow, how can it be said to have a stern? The obvious solution is that Jason's ship, the Argo, was as round as Noah's ark, an unlikely shape for the vessel of a hero meant to be pointing in just one direction, homeward, but not unknown in the earthly realm. The Mesopotamian straw-woven coracle has been manoeuvred up and down the Euphrates for millennia. Round it is – as round as some of those stone circles at Göbekli Tepe with their two gigantic humanoid pillars.

Less elegant in its movements than the ships of Jason or Odysseus in that it has no great mast and sail, neither bow nor stern, the larger straw coracles have the advantage of requiring just two sailors - and therein lies the joke found in at least one Sumerian proverb; one sailor with his pole at the inexistant stern and the other with his pole at the equally inexistant prow. Which is the leader? Does the absence of clear hierarchy between those two virile creatures create a permanent tug of war, a fight for dominance, a celestial pissing match even, like fools in some meaningless drunken brawl? Around and around their shafts go, taking turns to dominate, rather like the pole stars in the north as seen from our drunken wobbling planet (p.10).

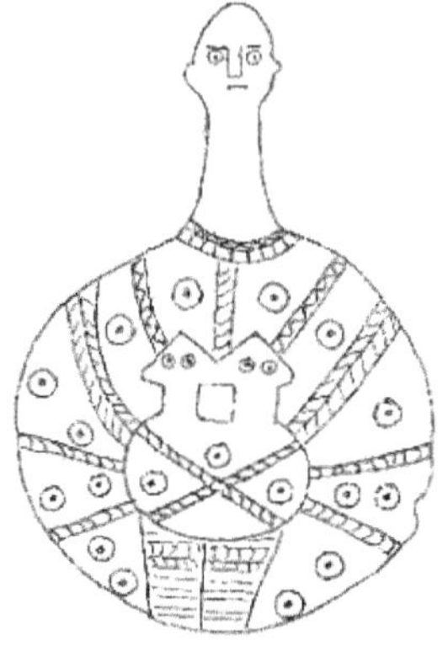

Discovered at Kültepe, another site in the same region of Turkey as Göbekli Tepe, this strange clay artefact is one of several showing a pair of celestial 'sailors' surrounded by the stones of the sky. Here they are tethered by strong cords to the belly of a greater figure. Who do the legs belong to?

Argo Navis as we know of it, not one of the twelve constellations lying across the sun's path, was seen as a huge ship in the southern hemisphere, partially in the Milky Way, with the star Canopus (now part of the constellation of Carina) marking its keel. But, in a round cog-boat managed by a pair of virile sailors, who knows where it might have strayed while they pushed and pulled and argued? Who knows how huge the wave they might succeed in stirring up?

Argo is said to derive either from Greek argon which has the meaning 'lazy' and 'inactive', 'unmoving' or from argos with the opposite meaning of 'swift'. Lazy like the king on his bier? Swift like the Tigris? Jolting along? And who's boat was it really?

> *Mythology insisted that it was built by Glaucus, or by Argos, for Jason, leader of the fifty Argonauts, whose number equalled that of the oars of the ship (…)*
>
> *Egyptian story said that it was the ark that bore Isis and Osiris over the Deluge (…)*
>
> *The Arabians called it Al Safinah, a Ship, (…)*
>
> *The biblical school of course called it Noah's Ark, (Star Names and their Meanings*[6]*, p.65–66)*

It's all rather vague and the findings on line 50 of this text will further muddy the water for those who are still hoping for the physical presence of Noah's ark somewhere on a mountain peak.

50. With bee and brew at its heart, the vessel in the Winding Canal of Ra to the door of the distant womb in the south will go.

ŠA₃ BI

'With bee and beer at its heart', the 'heart of the bee', also 'Beer-heart', the drunken sailor. The earliest known mention of the Sabians is in *The Story of Sukurru*. That is the true source of the epithet given to the Mesopotamian astronomers (*Lost Stones*, p.50).

In this highly coded text, repetition of the first or last word over several lines signals an underlying message of some kind. In the case of the Sabians, it becomes possible to verify that ŠA₃-BI is indeed another epithet of the so-called 'Apkallu' and 'Anunnaki'. That confirmation is gleaned by looking back from line 50 in which Argo Navis and the two words comprising their name appear, to the first words of preceding lines 48 and 49. Both begin with NUN, the 'guide'. Line 48 reads:

NUN with ME are invariably translated together by academia as 'Apkallu' (*Lost Stones*, p.28). ME with ZU give the source of Greek meso-, the 'in-between' of Mesopotamia (*Lost Stones*, p.139). NUN, which also - and not coincidentally - appears in the middle of line 46 here, is the central word of the phrase that gave us the now famous Anunnaki.

The fifty oars of the Argonauts can be matched to line 50 by both the line number and its overall meaning; a ship on a perilous journey. That might still be considered coincidence if it were not for a cross-reference of Beer-Heart, the Sabian, with the Arabic name Safinah, the ship, a name more precisely applied to Noah's vessel, both from that same source on line 50.

Apart from the line number, the fifty oars of the Argonauts and the Arabic name Safinah, there exists another ancient connection between the astronomers of Harran and the number 50. It also indicates Egypt as the ultimate source of their knowledge.

According to Greek mythology and therefore at a completely unknown date, the fifty sons of a king called Egypt (Aegyptus) were to marry the fifty daughters of Danaus, his twin brother. Presumably the heir to the throne of Egypt was the elder by a few minutes. So fifty marriages between first cousins, children of Aegyptus and Danaus, who were sons of the equally mythical King Belus of Egypt.

Apollonius Rhodius in the Argonautica, along with numerous mentions of the fifty oars of the argonauts, also writes of the 'race of divine Danaus'. Thus is found a relatively straightforward threefold connection between the royalty of Ancient Egypt, a king Belus, the number fifty and a divine race. Divine as in purely mythological and/or astronomical? Or might these references be based in some real historical events and connected to the founding story of Egypto-Mesopotamian astronomers? Diodorus Siculus, Greek historian, wrote the following in the 1st century BC:

Now the Egyptians say that after these events a great number of colonies were spread from Egypt over all the inhabited world. To Babylon, for instance, colonists were led by Belus, who was held to be the son of Poseidon and Libya ; and after establishing himself on the Euphrates river he appointed priests, called Chaldaeans by the Babylonians, who were exempt from taxation and free from every kind of service to the state, as are the priests of Egypt; and they also make observations of the stars, following the example of the Egyptian priests, physicists, and astrologers. (Diodorus of Sicily, *Bibliotheca Historica*, Bk 1, 27.28, Trans. Oldfather)

Concerning the exact birthplace of Mesopotamian astronomy, I made the case for it being in the region of Harran in the north rather than Babylon which then inherited the knowledge (*Lost Stones*, p.52-53). I also suggested that KAL, which is connected to the name Harran, was source of the 'Chaldeans'. Further connections of KAL/DAN to calendars and the counting of time are mentioned (*Lost Stones*, p.65-69). The above quote also makes it clear that Babylonians and Chaldeans were separate groups.

The race of divine Danaus is linked to the flood story in this text through the source syllables of the name: DA AN, the 'arm to the sky'. Then again, line 97, while mirroring the later biblical 'two by two' which seamlessly connects it to Noah and the ship of the flood, infers that the seed of Danaus was planted on Earth:

97. *The rod hits the stone and the stone hits the sea. The ocean on one side tilts. On the other it rises with the lord, as by the dancing arms in the sky (Danaus, Scorpio) water and seeds into the immaculate clay of the land from both sides enter.*

There is more to be said about 'The Wobble' and the notes accompanying this translation have barely skimmed the surface of that almighty subject (see notes to lines 97 and 123).

Finally, DA and AN are the two words found in the lexical tablets opposite transliterated DAN, (*Lost Stones*, p.67), linked to calendars and which was translated to a 'vessel', a celestial ship in a section of *The Story of Sukurru*. Just before the great cursing scene begins, line 130 of that translation reads:

130. *Over the mountains, rising in its flight, 'The Clay Eye' around the sky is fluttering.*

A Need For Mead

Appearing sixteen times in all in this text, KUK or KUG is not given as 'cog' or 'to circle' in orthodox lexicons. Its main given meaning is 'metal' with the additions of 'shiny' and 'silver'. My translation of it to a round and circling cog-boat in the opening section results from the context but also its visual form on the earliest tablets where the scribe has attempted to show circling through the striations, unmistakeably a portrayal of roundness and/or twisting: a round cog circling between earth and sky.

In fact, the pictogram resembles the shape and turned metal of an ancient neck ring called a torc. Then again, using the word 'metal' alongside its phonetic form KUG, the notion of a circling metallic cog is possible. In a well-defined context, that could signify an unexplained flying object – for the greater delight of any Sitchin fan who has come this far. To my mind, none of the above can be completely eliminated. It's always a question of context.

In Irish mythology, Corcog was the name of the daughter of Manannan, their sea god. He had a mighty ship named "Wave Sweeper". It had no sail. Another apparently unrelated Irish Corcog is a mountain peak in Galway, where it has the meaning 'cone' and 'beehive'. At first view, there would appear to be no connection other than phonetic between the two names, but it's not a coincidence that the ship of the Irish sea god and the beehive on an Irish mountain peak are linked in that way. They reflect two major themes in this founding story; the perilous quest of the sailor surfing mountainous waves in his celestial round boat and the equally dangerous adventure of the earthly honey-hunter climbing up cliff faces on a fragile rope ladder in search of wild honeycombs.

Add in Sumerian KUR, the three hills, as source of Kor and Greek Kore, the maiden of the mountains who is intimately linked to Persephone and to the Eleusinian Mystery school (*Lost Stones*, p.169). Another hitherto submerged layer of meaning reappears with a discreet buzz into the light of day. And not just any honey.

Images of the celestial cog boat are visible on more than one Indus Valley seal, invariably shown opposite a four-legged animal which is generally - if not always - identifiable as a bovine. The image of the round boat copied here above (see p.81 and another version illustrating lines 15-16) is spectacularly informative in that it shows not only the hemi-spherical shape of the boat but also the floating cogs surrounding it, an eloquent image of a vessel travelling on a celestial sea among stars and planets – or among a freshly revived swarm of golden honeybees. The round boat could easily double as a wild beehive hanging from a tree branch or a cliff face. It could and it does. It is both. Note the curious shaft attaching the hull of the Indus Valley boat to…to what?

It's true that the Irish ship 'Wave Sweeper' was devoid of a sail, apparently functioning more like a surfboard on what must have been a particularly huge and permanent wave, while the Indus Valley boat has a prominent sail made of woven reeds. But whether pushed along by the wind or propelled by a wave (see UL on lines 8 and 25), they result from the same multi-layered age-resistant story.

Taking the subject of ethereal cogs further still, those on the Indus Valley seals can be usefully compared to the cogs lining the back of the hitherto unexplained strutting dog copied from a Minoan gold plaque (used here to illustrate line 6). Note that the blobs emanate from its outer covering which might be said to have the shape of an insect. And they evoke illumination – that of the stars and probably also of the health-giving oil presented in the jar.

But what kind of dog stands upright and glows so profusely while offering an abundance of honey to its mistress or master?

The Rustle of Stones

After gaining all he could from the Phoenician mysteries, he found that they had originated from the sacred rites of Egypt, forming as it were an Egyptian colony. This led him to hope that in Egypt itself he might find monuments of erudition still more genuine, beautiful, and divine. (…) He thus passed twenty-two years in the sanctuaries of temples, studying astronomy and geometry, and being initiated in no casual or superficial manner in all the mysteries of the Gods. (Pythagoras' Journey to Egypt, The Complete Pythagoras, Trans. Guthrie)

The Mill of Time as we know it is perfectly round with two hands, one pointing to the hours of the day and the other to the smaller, inner circle of time: 60 seconds to the minute, 60 minutes to the hour, 24 hours to the day. A more ancient and greatly enlarged version is found at Angkor Wat in Indonesia. Carved into stone figures in the precinct of the great temple there, the two hands of the clock take the form of one single rope wound around a central axle, pulled by 54 people on one side, 54 people on the other, 108 years represented in all – precession numbers. And the echo of that great ticking clock can still be heard in the line numbers of this text.

That tug of war back and forth between two equal clans was not a meaningless battle of virile egos. They were causing the mill to turn on its axle and the waves to rise; the churning of the Milk Ocean, the galactic plain, the Milky Way. The ancient reference to the movement of time through the metaphors of frothing milk and ocean waves hitting the shore is not limited to Indian mythology. It was echoed three times in *The Story of Sukurru* during what appears to be a harvest festival celebration and song. In the context of the instructions given to Noah:

97. Place a man at the mouth of the milk-churning ocean and give him a beer.

It wasn't by force of grunting and pointing that the leader of the team incited the men to use their muscles. There was a spoken language. It wasn't in silence that both the builders and carved figures of Angkor Watt pulled on their rope – which, by the way, took the form of a gigantic snake. At the very least, there was the beating of a drum. Or perhaps they sang along as they tugged back and forth. In the same way, it goes almost without saying that the people who raised the great stones of Göbekli Tepe had a spoken language and even that they had written communication in some form, possibly in existence for millennia already… from a time before. Did they sing?

No, the ancient world wasn't colourless or silent. There were words and rhythm. There was music, more sophisticated than many of the sounds to which we so unthinkingly give that name today, chords precisely tuned to interact with the human brain in a positive manner, to give strength to the arm, to raise heavy hearts, heavy stones, to induce an altered, elevated state of consciousness, with or without the assistance of psychedelic substances.

But I daresay there were some grains of sand in that mill too; roaring drunks here and there, lost souls roaming around looking for a fight, interrupting the work of others, disrupting the harmony until subdued and brought back into the group - or spat out and eliminated.

Beating on drums made of stone or skins, striking the heavy gong, breathing into the double flute, plucking the strings of the lyre; the sounds of the musicians and shamans still lead the dance, give the pace, the raising of both man and sphere. Greek Orpheus, son of Apollo and thus the greatest of all musicians, in his earliest manifestation was the first leader of it all. Pythagoras in Egypt was a far later witness.

For the magic to work, there have always been prerequisites; the location of the site, the arena in which the music is played, the exact time at which it is played. Not just some modern concert venue at 8 o'clock tonight but the precise keys to the mightiest of ancient secrets; the mastering and manipulation of both stone and sound towards a re-creation of supreme beauty. The perfection of harmonic resonances for ear and eye and heart. The subtle effects of sound and subsequent welling-up of emotion, whether tears or wild dancing, in halls dedicated to music are well known.

Once the sites had been established, they served their purpose for many millennia and were continuously restored, some right up to recent times. Knowledge of the building process - the tools, materials and dimensions necessary to obtain the desired effect, the absolute precision – was handed down through multiple generations, through the apprenticeships of masons and shamans with, at some point in that process, the addition of writing, the recording of those instructions. Along with knowledge of astronomy, the movements of the celestial bodies - the music of the spheres - it was all encoded in stone and word, never to be lost. And yet. Does it still exist? In what form? In its entirety or only in fragments? Hidden or in plain sight?

The Skull

Greek enkephalos "the brain," literally "within the head,"

Greek anenkephalos, 'brainless', from an- 'not, without' + enkephalos 'brain,' 'the brain,' literally 'within the head.' (Etymonline.com)

Enki, the great Sumerian hero, acquired his nickname only in the past century or so. Long before that, he was simply EN, the 'lord', and more precisely 'lord between AN, sky, and KE, earth'. As such he gave us the multi-syllabic Greek word 'anenkephalos' with its modern meaning of 'brainless'; he who is without a brain, a fool or worse, nothing but an empty skull, easy to bounce into the ether or into the gaping mouth of a whale.

That said, not all skulls are stupid. Clever heads detached from their limbs were not unknown in the distant past. For example, Norse Mimir, a surprisingly gifted speaking skull, was carried around by the god Odin for the purpose of giving advice. Orpheus, son of Apollo and equally great musician, after trying to save his beloved Eurydice from the underworld, was finally torn to shreds by vengeful women. He ended up bodyless, just his head bobbing up and down in the water until washed up on an island. His story is reminiscent of the fate of Egyptian Osiris, also dismembered and also swept away on a mighty river in Plutarch's version of the myth. Bodyless Orpheus continued to have a voice. According to Virgil, his cry was echoed in the banks of the river:

> *Rent from the marble neck, his drifting head,*
> *The death-chilled tongue found yet a voice to cry*
> *'Eurydice! ah! poor Eurydice!'*
> *With parting breath he called her, and the banks*
> *From the broad stream caught up 'Eurydice!'"*
> (Virgil, *Georgics*, Bk 4)

Take away AN, the sky, from our hero Enki and we are left with Enke(phalos), a pre-Greek brain. Add back the Mesopotamian sky and 'an-en-ke-phalos' can be understood as a 'celestial brain', equivalent to the 'celestial skull' or a more subtle rendering; 'heavenly mind', and 'spirit'.

The difference between that original meaning and the later less flattering Greek 'brainless' lies in the addition of prefix an/AN (left unmentioned in the academic versions). When did AN, the positive, up-lifting Mesopotamian 'celestial' and 'sky', become Greek 'an', the thoroughly depressing 'without'? At what point in time did the skull lose its spirit? Then again, when did Sumerian AN, collocated with the celestial arrow TI, the 'arrow in the sky', become the 'anti' of anti-clockwise?

> *Yet you have held fast to My name and have not denied your faith in Me, even in the day when My faithful witness Antipas was killed among you, where Satan dwells.* (Revelation 2:13)

Antipas apparently stems from Greek 'anti' with 'pater', the father. One of very few details relayed concerning the figure said to be that of a Saint Antipas of Pergamum shows him enclosed and tortured inside a brazen bull known as the Bull of Phalaris.[15]

The torture of the brazen bull, thought by some to have existed in Ancient Greece - but as yet unproven - involved locking the victim inside a hollow bull made of bronze and then lighting a fire underneath. The muffled screams of the burning, suffocating victim were filtered through some sophisticated device and transformed into the sound of a roaring bull. If true, the unpleasant method has its source in both astronomy and bee-keeping (notes to line 95). If untrue, then potentially it derives from the distant memory of some dramatic event. In either case, a trap is involved:

> *then Osiris got into it and lay down, and those who were in the plot ran to it and slammed down the lid, which they fastened by nails from the outside and also by using molten lead.* (Plutarch, *Moralia, On Isis And Osiris*, 13:4, trans. F. Cole Babbitt)

Take away both sky and earth, the 'An' and the 'ke' from Enki. The remaining EN gives the origin of both biblical Enoch, also a celestial voyager, and the Hermetic 'One', the Greek meaning of 'en'. EN is neither here nor there, but everywhere, the beginning and the end. From one to ten and then back again. EN is at the heart of the Tenet of the Sator riddle (*Before Babel*, p.249).

EN's habit of floating around the cosmos led to the addition of the 'phal' of 'enkephalos' in the Greek language at some far later point in time. That syllable came from BAL, 'to turn' or 'to spin':

Old High German gebal: 'skull.'

BAL was the round dance led by the lord and BALAG, one of the string instruments played (lines 62, 64 and 125). BAL also gave rise to the name of that great whale, the high-spinning, high-spouting baleen, famed for having put up with Jonah's bitterness in its belly, but also the initiate's hope of safe transport through purgatory (*Lost Stones*, p.204, p.227). Fortunately, the baleen whale has a kind of filtrating comb in place of teeth.

The original story led to the name of the prophet Balaam, apparently meaning 'swallowing the people' in Hebrew, and found in a biblical tale carried through into the same section of Revelation that mentions the enigmatic Antipas. In fact, the very next verse gives Balaam teaching Balak 'to cast a snare' (Revelation 2:14). Strangely, the only explicitly mentioned man-trap in *The Path to Sky-End* links back to Osiris (line 56).

Enki's three-word epithet is quite regularly accompanied by a fourth which is KID, both 'fool' and 'ghost' among others in orthodox dictionaries. The most obvious solution is that KID is used here as an adjective attached to the lord himself, the foolish, ghostly lord, a brainless skull. But KID poses problem because it has a plethora of possible meanings.

Throughout history there have been (and continue to exist) more constellations in the skies than those twelve that we know to lie in the path of the sun, already mentioned in the context of precession. Some have been added. Others have become obsolete. Different cultures show them in different ways. The association of EN, the lord, with KID as 'ghostly' might even lead back to a constellation that has since been lost to us: Greek Engonasis, said to be a ghostly labouring man who later became Hercules:

While Argo spreads aloft her spangled sails, And Hydra stretches forth her lengthened scales. That nameless figure, kneeling in the sky, now lifts to sight his rising leg and thigh — Ever he kneels — aloft his arm he flings, as if to strike the Lyre's responsive strings. Poor Labouring Man — he knows no night of rest — Ere all his wearied limbs have gain'd the west his morning course begins. (Aratus, *Phaenomena*, trans. Lamb)

Then there is the great constellation of Orion along with his guide Cedalion whose Greek name means 'purifier' or 'cleanser'. Carried on the shoulders of the blinded man, Cedalion is reminiscent of the goat (or kid) on the shoulder of Auriga, another ancient constellation.

It must be said that 'kid', the young goat, is not a given meaning of KID. Nevertheless, it's reasonable to consider that celestial EN and KID are source of one or more of the above figures and that they might be best understood as if in some ancient comic strip in which the initiate travels from one place to another across the sky in search of the ultimate truth of his existence.

If context allows, AN EN KI KID can translate to 'the Lord (who is between sky and Earth) and the fool', in which case the words refer to two separate figures, potentially a lord accompanied by his noisy disciple who is as yet untrained, hence a fool in the nicest possible way (Al Khidr and Moses, *Lost Stones*, p.199), or perhaps asleep through overuse of the blue lotus and in need of a good shaking. KID can also be read LIL_2, source of the very lovely 'lily' and the less delightful 'Lilith', night creature of the biblical account. (See notes to lines 83 and 90.)

The most obvious dictionary-given meaning of KID, taking its visual appearance into account, is a woven mat which not only allows for cosmic sailing, becoming in some accounts a 'reed sail', but also stays within the realm of the lotus plant, its large rounded petals covering the surface of the water and serving as a useful landing mat for thirsty creatures. Then again, the Egyptologist Walter Budge wrote in his notes to the *Book of the Dead*:

> *it will be seen that some plaited object is hanging over the prow of the boat, and this I believe to represent a mat made of reeds and grass. The pilot of a Nile boat often has to sound the depth of the water under his boat, and this he does by means of a pole. As he lifts the pole out of the water, some drops fall on the place where he is standing, which eventually becomes wet and slippery ; to secure a good foothold a reed-mat or layer of grass is thrown down,* [16]

The connection between Egypt and this text is reinforced if Egyptian Anen in his cloak of stars is added to the list of celestial voyagers:

> *Anen is a name given to a character from ancient Egypt, a priestly figure, wearing the skin of a puma or cougar covered in stars. There is an 18th dynasty statue of this hero called Anen, discovered in Egypt and currently residing in the Egizio museum in Turin, Italy. (Before Babel, p.37)*

And finally, KID/KIT with its given meaning of 'mat' fits - for all the world like the final missing piece of an ancient puzzle - into the African name Kitara. There is more on the subject of African travelling mats on p.75.

Tuning the Turtle's Strings

According to the Greek myth, it was Hermes (also named as Apollo) who first had the idea of adapting a tortoise/turtle shell to make the body of the magical lyre with which he churned the stones of sky and earth.

> *He cut stalks of reed to measure and fixed them, fastening their ends across the back and through the shell of the tortoise, and then stretched ox hide all over it by his skill. Also he put in the horns and fitted a cross-piece upon the two of them, and stretched seven strings of sheep-gut. But when he had made it he proved each string in turn with the key, as he held the lovely thing. At the touch of his hand it sounded marvellously; and, as he tried it, the god sang sweet random snatches, even as youths bandy taunts at festivals. (Hymn 4 to Hermes, Trans. H. Evelyn-White)*

Bearing in mind that the acronym PIE (proto-Indo-European) signifies only that no-one knows where the words we use take their ultimate source:

> *Greek harmonia "agreement, concord of sounds," also as a proper name, the personification of music, literally "means of joining," used of ship-planks, etc., also "settled government, order," related to harmos "fastenings of a door; joint, shoulder," from PIE (Etymonline)*

The language of the Mesopotamian astronomer-scribes offers a credible common source for 'harp' and 'harmony', particularly on line 63. It incorporates a double HAR, a word that has the dictionary-given meaning 'mill':

> 63. *Two shafts around two mills (two harps), inside their beams to trap the fire, from the dark beam in the belly of the pyramid he will climb to the Temple on the Horn of the Cow.*

Titled 'Trap of Osiris', line 63 might equally have been called 'The Pole Dance'. Following on from mention of the talent of Orpheus on line 60 and carrying the musical theme into the realm of astronomy, look to the circumpolar constellation of Lyra and note the relatively modern imagery of two horns joined by a cross-beam onto which the seven pegs of its strings are attached. Lyra's great imperishable star Vega (also read Wega), pole star ca.12000 BC, lies somewhere on the crossbeam of the celestial lyre.

(Lyra) Ovid mentioned its seven strings as equalling the number of the Pleiades; Longfellow confirming this number in his Occultation of Orion: with its celestial keys, Its chords of air, its frets of fire,

"The Samian's great Aeolian Lyre,

Rising through all its sevenfold bars,

From earth unto the fixed stars." (Star Names [6], p.281)

The two seven-stringed instruments in Greek mythology – one destroyed by Apollo in a rage and another given by Hermes to Apollon – perhaps take their source here. Both the Pleiades in the constellation of Taurus and Lyra were musical.

A more precise detail in a Nordic story connects this ancient musical theme to a crucial moment in time: Noah's flood. In that tale, mention is made of the ark and of a stringed instrument taken on board. At the great sailor's insistence, it was given the name Noah's Timpan (*Hamlet's Mill*, Appendix 10). TIM is the transliteration of the Sumerian word meaning 'pole' or 'shaft'.

The analogy of the polestar Vega with a peg on the lyre (in the constellation of Lyra) holding the strings in place and adjusting the pitch of the celestial instrument leads to an investigation into the origin of the word 'peg' and the unsurprising discovery that this is just another word of unknown source, given as Germanic. I suggest that Vega shares its source through Greek with that of the winged horse Pegasus (see notes to line 45).

The lyre is just one in a very large family of string instruments throughout history. They come in a variety of shapes and sizes and sounds. Other members include the far larger harp as we know it today and, of course, the guitar, its name derived from Greek kithara. Some images from Mesopotamia show a string instrument with a very small body and an exceptionally long neck which might have resulted in an analogy with a musical shaft joining earth to a pole star; a shaft topped with adjustable pegs.

The tortoise/turtle shell repurposed by Hermes/Apollo has practical uses linked to both music and astronomy. Slow, wise and extremely long-lived, the turtle served as a calendar of moon cycles for Native American Indians, notably the Cherokee. Their Moon Turtle is known as 'Keeper of the Knowledge'. Its shell possesses 13 large sections representing the 13 lunar months in the year while the 28 smaller sections around the base give the days:

$$13 \times 28 = 364$$

The missing day between lunar and 365-day solar calendars was celebrated by the Cherokee as a 'green crop day' in midsummer. All offenses were washed away and life began anew. The similarity of this to the pre-Christian concept of baptism is obvious, and that ritual also appears in this text.

The key word is LUH, with given meaning 'cleansing', shown here above. This transliteration comes from its position opposite two other words in the lexical lists: LU, the 'light' (of the moon, lunar), with UH, which has the dictionary-given meaning 'tortoise' or 'turtle' (see notes to lines 18 and 70). The pictogram fits well with an abstract version of a lyre.

Less obvious - without the assistance of this ancient foundational text - is the direct link between that 'gap' day of cleansing according to the Cherokee calendar and a musical interval. GAB first appears on line 26:

the spread of the gap

In context there, it refers to the moment of silence before the great thunderbolt of Zeus.

In the milk-churning scene on the wall of the Temple of Angkor Wat, the turtle is positioned below the central pole (Mount Meru). On either side, 54 figures pull on the rope. Here on line 54 where the same allusion to the precessional churning is made, GAB, the 'pause', is placed at its centre. In both musical and astronomical terms, turtle and gap work together.

As 'musical and cyclical pause' GAB takes its full sense at the centre of line 72 – in the context of the precession of the equinoxes but also the moment of cleansing before rebirth - where it doesn't appear at all. At that crucial point in time it is quite literally signalled by its absence; the space left by the scribe on the Ashmolean prism between two identical five-word phrases (see notes to line 108). Every 72 years in that considerably longer 25,920-year circle of time, a pause was observed by the ancient astronomers for the purpose of continually marking the anti-clockwise movement of the sun.

Finally, GAB begins and ends line 103 – an ultimate spreading, the most impressive gap that we know of according to the biblical account. Visually, the reconstructed pictographic forms of that line are particularly eloquent.

This is the precursor to the separation of the waters by Moses, a trap set to drown the Egyptian army and a theme already perceived on line 141 of *The Story of Sukurru*:

141. That the midst of water Ra know…through the space where it divides to its heart of reed where the wind will rise.

How old is the story of Hermes constructing the first string instrument from a tortoise shell? How old the counting of time and rhythm thanks to the Moon Turtle? One thing is sure because we have a picture of the scene; the long-lived musical creature was already up and leading the dance for the inhabitants of Nevali Çori, the now-submerged megalithic site in Turkey where a merry trio of two humans surrounding a turtle, all with arms to the sky, was carved some 11,000 years ago. Were they of the race of Danaus (p.35)? Here next to a far later Mesopotamian turtle on its pedestal:

 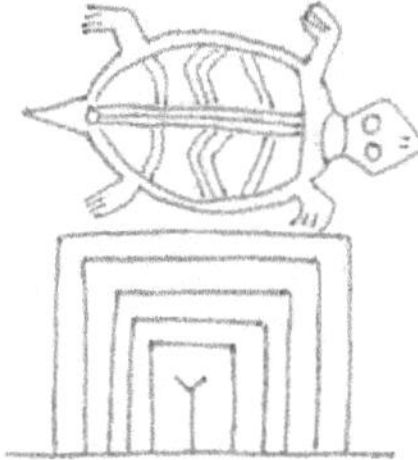

The World Turtle supporting the entire universe on its back is attested in more than one culture, and another myth, this one attributed to the Huron people of North America, invokes a total eclipse most likely caused by the moon or perhaps some more remarkable, prolonged astronomical phenomenon. Whatever the case, according to the account recorded by French Jesuits an earthquake is provoked:

because the great tortoise that holds up the earth changed its position or situation, covering the sun with its shell and rendering it invisible to the world (Relations des Jésuites de la Nouvelle France, 1858, p.62, archives.org,, trans. Daines)

Hermes/Apollo was said to be the father of Greek Orpheus. Both musical genius and trickster, Orpheus opens one of the doors leading down to a great chamber still harbouring his musical notations. There are others. Listen for his lyre and then for the distant echoing sound resembling barking inside the stone hills of Qurna. Is someone hammering out a tomb?

Sothic Mysteries

What kind of dog stands upright and glows profusely while offering a jug of oil to its Minoan mistress or master? In the world of astronomy, there can be only one: Canis Major, the Great Dog, with the exceptionally bright star Sirius on its head. Sirius is special. It doesn't stay in place. According to astronomers, over an extended period of many thousands of years it will extend the neck of the dog downwards as it descends further and further into the abyss and the region of the southern pole before rebounding.

Sirius has every reason to be proud. It's famous. Ever since the great star first reappeared after several thousand years of absence in the early morning skies of the northern hemisphere some 10,000 years ago, it has been remarked upon, both revered and cursed but never ignored. A star's heliacal rising occurs when it's first seen plainly above the horizon in conjunction with the rising sun. And the earliest Mesopotamian astronomers were surely not the only people to notice a small new-born star emerging timidly from the underworld along the southern horizon just as the sun appeared to the east. The same celestial event was happening for their kin at a similar latitude in northern Africa. The annual heliacal rising of Sirius - after some seventy days of absence - eventually became the unique marker of the New Year in Ancient Egypt and signalled the Nile's imminent flooding at the start of the hot summer months.

Sirius, the 'dog star', remains somewhat mysterious. It's impossible to say where or when the first reference to the bright star was made or in what form. Still today, no-one knows if it has a permanent attachment to any other star system. What can be said is that, despite lying below the horizon in the northern hemisphere at the time, a jumping canine resembling Canis Major as we know it[17] was already up and making noise on the stones of Göbekli Tepe some five thousand years before the descendants of those early Harranian astronomers began to mention it on their clay tablets.

 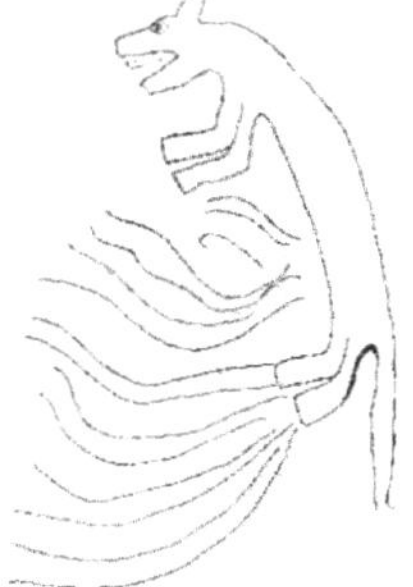

There are some slightly differing versions of canines, most likely to be foxes, at Göbekli Tepe. In the above example (right), the back paws give way to flowing lines that curve around the edge of that pillar's face and onto its side. There they end in four snakes' heads staring directly at an insect that I take to be a bee (p.24). On the left, a pair surround a rectangular hole in the stone, their mouths opening towards a dominating bull's head (the equivalent of the Sumerian word AB_2. See line 92).

The reappearance of Sirius in the northern hemisphere, after around six thousand years of absence, happened very timidly ca.8300 BC and might have been understood as a birth rather than an ongoing cycle by simple hunter-gatherers not having seen it in the southern hemisphere. The waters of the celestial womb had broken and given birth… to a small eye. The eye would become more brilliant as it continued to travel upwards, rising on the neck of the large barking or howling canine. And it was seen to be trained on the three-tiered belt of Orion, its master.

Sirius is both good and bad, heralding fertility but also climatic excesses, which explains why it had a considerable number of epithets in the Mesopotamian language (see the notes to line 17). Elsewhere also, no doubt. It appears in *The Story of Sukurru* under a couple of identified guises (lines 17, 71 and 186). One is that of the smell of burning seeds or scorched young plants, leading directly to its later Greek name Seirios. Line 71 of *The Story of Sukurru*, in the context of a catastrophe provoked by the sun and Sirius in tandem, gives it as 'Dog Head':

71. Dog-Head, between his long feet, new life from rising again
will guard.

In that case, UR SAG is a relatively obvious reference to Egyptian Anubis, the jackal that fulfils the same function by lying across the lids of sarcophagi. Other pairs of words also refer directly to the star. From there, a further strong linguistic connection can be made between Sirius and the Great Sphinx (see UB in the notes to line 17. Also *Lost Stones*, p.91).

Greek Orpheus takes the first syllable of his name from Mesopotamian UR, pictogram of the dog's head and main linguistic marker of Sirius in Canis Major. The second syllable comes from BI, the 'beer', the 'brew' but also 'bee' and 'to be' according to context. His music is also present in NAR/LUL, both fox and musician, also associated with the Pleiades (see lines 67 and 125). The Orphic Mysteries have their origins here with music, snakes and dogs, with foxes, bees and the brew.

BI has yet another quality: it signifies plurality (see p.31, notes to line 61) and can be read as 'binary', always according to context. UR with BI (p.67, line 40) give the source of both Orpheus and, through Latin, 'orbit'.

Sirius is a binary star system. Sirius A and its far smaller companion, Sirius B, circle each other on an elliptical fifty-year cycle. Thus, UR BI might serve to infer that the Mesopotamians were aware of the binary nature of the dog-star, a notion that would correspond to accounts of that same knowledge transmitted through the ages to the Dogon tribe on the African continent.[18] However, Sirius B can't be seen without the aid of a powerful telescope and BI as 'binary' more obviously indicates the existence of a different pair of celestial dogs: Canis Major with a more northerly companion known as Canis Minor and its most prominent star Procyon:

In Canis Minor lay a part of Al Dhira al Asad al Makbudah, the Contracted Fore Arm, or Paw, of the early Lion; the other, the Extended Paw, running up into the heads of Gemini. (Star Names [6], p.133)

Another explanation is that BI as 'binary' refers to the close relationship between the cycle of Sirius and that of the sun, as also indicated in the particularly dramatic four lines 69 to 72 of *The Story of Sukurru*.

Both images copied here above, one from the Egyptian Narmer palette (left) and the other from a Mesopotamian seal, by means of the exaggeratedly long circling necks and equally strange circling tail, might well represent the constant dance between the cycles of the sun and Sirius, drifting out of sync by approximately one day every four years. From there, these images link to the Sothic cycle on which the Ancient Egyptian calendar was based.

Numerological references to Sirius are encoded in the lines of this text and those references confirmed by their contents. Beginning with the heliacal rising of Sirius, the calendar comprised a four-year period of 365 days. Lines 4 and 5 refer to the start of that cycle:

$$4 \times 365 = 1,460 \text{ days}$$

The Sothic cycle is also indicated on line 40 where UR BI appear at its centre (see above and p.67):

$$1,460 / 40 = 36.5 \qquad 1,460 / 2 = 73 \qquad 73 \times 20 = 1460$$

The halfway 73-year mark is further shown on line 73 by an account of the rising of Sirius as a virgin birth linked to the annual flooding of the Nile (see notes to line 91) and later transferred to that of the figure of Immanuel in the Book of Isaiah. (The subject is developed in the notes):

73. In the otherworldly Place of the Whale, the lord from the immaculate clay of the Mother of the land and in Her Truth weightless to the sky will rise.

In 1029 AD, Al Biruni mentioned a myth about Sirius having crossed the Milky Way in the company of Canopus, leading to its epithet Al-abur:

The large bright star (Sirius) in the mouth of Orion's dog, Canis Major, is named Al-shi'ra Al-yammaniyyah and the Passer-Over, Al-abur, for they relate that both of the dog-stars are sister of Canopus, Suhail and that the greater dog-star crossed over the Milky Way to the south with Canopus while the lesser (Procyon) remained on the Syrian side and became blear-eyed. [19]

Two Sumerian words, AB_2 UR_3, 'cow' and 'passage', are collocated more than once in the lexical lists. (See AB_2 over the square hole in the Göbekli Tepe image on p.49, and as the first word of line 95. See UR_3, the 'passage' on p.53 and line 28. See notes to lines 28 and 73.)

The reclining cow in a boat on the Dendera roof beam (its head illustrating line 30) is said to be a representation of Sirius. Given that Orion separates the constellation of Taurus, the Bull, from Sirius in Canis Major, does anyone know why? Did the people who built Göbekli Tepe know of the existence of the bright star Sirius shining only in the southern hemisphere until ca.8300 BC? Were the sculptors of that place primitive hunter-gatherers? Or were they skilled astronomers from further south? Sailors of the Pacific Ocean? Survivors?

Kings and Riddles

The translated antediluvian portion of the *Sumerian King List*[14] begins:

(1) After the kingship descended from heaven,

and ends on line 39:

(39) Then the flood swept over.

Lines 40 and 41 of that academic version are taken to be an introduction to the far longer post-flood section. They read:

(40) After the flood had swept over,

(41) and the kingship had descended from heaven…

As they stand, lines 39 through 41 bring everything to a grinding halt with a great flood before continuing on. The source name of the last king (Ubara Dudu) and city (Shuruppak) correspond to those also found in *The Story of Sukurru* (aka *The Instructions of Shuruppak*) at the time of the flood. But it has so far gone unnoticed that the *Sumerian King List* is coded. It contains astronomical references and involves subtle spirals and circles. Thanks to his name, the last king before the flood – also a sailor – gives up a few of his secrets here in the notes to lines 17, 120 and 126.

Those three lines 39 to 41 incorporate an event ignored in the translated academic version; the moment when the king passes through a false door and begins his journey through the underworld. In *The Path To Sky-End* the same event is described, using the same twice-repeated word found in the *King List* on lines 39 and 40 (here on lines 28 and 29). The orthodox translations of both texts make no mention of that extraordinarily important passage. It has slipped past undetected.

Pictographic UR₃ used twice to describe that point of passage, the invisible door, in both texts is shown on a couple of early examples with a bird (HU) perched above it (see CDLI ref. P001900). This is the UR₃ suggested as partial source of Arabic Al Abur (p.52), the 'passage' of Sirius across the galactic plain recorded at an unknown time in the past. And it looks remarkably like the false doors seen in Egyptian tombs and other imagery. The false door was understood as the threshold between this world and the world of the gods and spirits. Is that Horus?

The *Sumerian King List*, despite its apparently linear form naming the successive rulers and their domains, encodes the precession cycles in its invisible line numbers. And there is one number of particular importance woven into it by the astronomer-scribes. Also identified from two different sources hidden in the multiple folds of *The Path To Sky-End* - one of which being the physical layout of the Ashmolean prism – we can assume that the number is of the utmost importance in a great cosmological symphony, its ultimate key. Considering the main indicators of precession:

$$6 \quad 12 \quad 36 \quad (43.2) \quad 54 \quad 72 \quad 108$$
$$25{,}920 \; / \; 4{,}320 = 6$$
$$432$$

The total number of lines in the *King List*, abruptly ending with line 431, was always intended to convey that all-important key to insiders. In this case and in a spiralling game on a grand scale, it's necessary to circle all the way back to the antediluvian section to find the following number on line 12:

12. MU 43200 NI AK

How many copies of copies before the *King List* was finally handed down to us in multiple fragments? How many possibilities for error or omission and yet… still today the reader is invited to consider 12 in relation to 432?

Again, it was in *Magicians of the Gods* that I first came across the most meaningful explanation of the 432 enigma, just one of the many links between Mesopotamia and the Giza plateau. Graham Hancock writes:

> *Essentially, if you measure the height of the Great Pyramid and multiply it by 43,200 you get the polar radius of the earth and if you measure the base perimeter of the Great Pyramid and multiply by 43,200 you get the equatorial circumference of the earth.*[20]

That's not all he writes or all there is to know about the various paradigm-shattering calculations involving 43,200 - far from it - but sufficient for my purpose here which is to explore the importance given to 432 in this text and to emphasise its connection to the site of Giza.

As explained in *Lost Stones* (p.259), the antediluvian section of the *Sumerian King List* includes a relatively straightforward riddle or message. Three words are out of place, embedded at the centre of three of those meaningless names propagated by experts. In transliterated form, they read:

11. EN ME EN   LU$_2$ AN NA

13. EN ME EN   GAL   AN NA

26. EN ME EN   KU   AN NA

Taking the fourth word of each line, couched between and signalled by threefold repetition of EN ME EN and AN NA, 'lords of magic' and 'above and below' they read:

LUGAL KU

where LU$_2$-GAL, transliterated LUGAL, is 'king' and where KU has given meanings to include 'hole', 'seat', 'seize' or 'to dwell'; potentially becoming 'the seat of the king', 'the king in the hole' or just possibly 'King Ku'...

Then again, taking the figure to be King of Bees (p.27), KU becomes the hole of the bee, its small passage into and out of the hive, the spirit hole, leading to a shaft through which the king (or pharaoh) and bee must travel in order to be reborn. Pictographic KU is shaped rather like a coffin... or perhaps the outer casing of an Egyptian mummy.

Why go into the detail of a riddle in the *King List* here? Because it's a necessary introduction to an equally important three-word acrostic also ending in the word KU in this text (lines 106 to 108). Without the in-depth analysis already carried out on the antediluvian portion of that famous list (for *Lost Stones of the Anunnaki*) and the discovery that the word KU had been mis-transliterated there, I would probably not have thought to look so closely at the transcript of *The Path to Sky-End* – the version derived from the Ashmolean prism - to double-check the exactitude of the last words on those lines 106 and 108.

I was right to do so. Again the same error is made between transcript and transliteration. It might be considered a very minor blip if it were not for the importance of the message concealed in that riddle. In fact, I double and then triple-checked just to confirm I wasn't hallucinating. The most unexpected of names really is recorded in the acrostic at the ends of lines 106, 107 and 108. Its presence in this essentially Egypto-Mesopotamian account leads the overall subjects of encoded information and history of those and other civilizations to ever greater heights – travelling across the ocean to South America in 1600 BC or thereabouts. On the Pacific?

Cusco

The Story of Sukurru was written on fragmented tablets of which the earliest date back to around the same period as that given for the building of the Great Pyramid ca.2600-2500 BC. The text is corrupted by some serious breakages and, for that reason, will never cede more than a portion of its secrets. Out of its 280 lines, I belatedly discovered and investigated just one long acrostic spanning five lines (223 to 227). That riddle culminates in the first two words of the fifth line: GIZ BAL, which translate to 'wooden spindle' always depending on context. They might equally be developed to read 'the spinning axle shaft'. Taken in the context of the winter solstice, the words rounded off the three nights during which the sun resides in the same underground chamber before beginning its return journey along the horizon. Turned around, GIZ BAL give Balgis, one of the epithets of the Queen of Sheba.

The Path To Sky-End is virtually intact and, better still, there exists a magnificent copy of the entire text on that rectangular clay prism which was carefully laid out to encode the precession numbers across its four faces – and to incorporate an extra message cleverly indicating knowledge of the backward flow of the sun. To read the ultimate message on the Ashmolean prism, it must be physically turned anti-clockwise. There can be no doubt that precession was an important part of its subject matter and that it was devised by a master astronomer doubling as a master scribe. Whoever that may have been – and a name does come to mind - they had also travelled.

Given the context and build-up to line 108, and taking into account all the hard work of the two groups of 54 people on either side of the axle shaft tugging on its rope (see line 54), something of great significance had been achieved at that point in the text, something of importance to the overall story. But the discovery, couched in the words across lines 106, 107 and 108, was nevertheless of unexpected magnitude:

> *Finally 'the Inca and his bride entered into Cusco valley. There (at a spot called Cusco Cara Urumi, the Uncovered Navel Stone) they tried their rod and not only did it sink into the earth, but it disappeared entirely… Thus our imperial city came into existence.'* [21]

I read that passage in *Magicians of the Gods* maybe three or four years before beginning work on the meanings of the riddle spanning those three lines. And having completely forgotten about the Peruvian tale in the meantime, it didn't spring to mind immediately when I began decoding them. And yet the origin of the Inca myth is easily identified through the translation. In the context of the mysterious calling-out of measurements (line 105), instructions on planting a celestial pole or shaft are given. Line 107 reads:

107. "Cross with the sun to the churning hole at the heart of the sky and into its thick clay (immaculate spirit and truth of Ma) push the shaft."

Then reading vertically, this time in the last words of each line, we find:

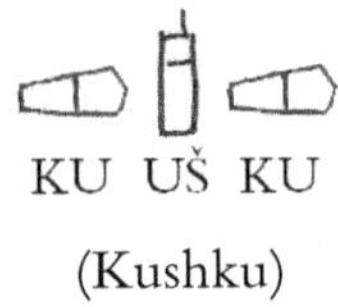

KU UŠ KU

(Kushku)

The second KU of KU-UŠ-KU – without which the link to the name of the Peruvian city of Cusco could obviously not be made – presents exactly the same obfuscating problem as the KU in the *King List* riddle mentioned here above. Although written 'dur$_2$' in the transliteration, verification of the very neatly handwritten transcript of the original cuneiform shows the word to take exactly the same form as the KU of preceding line 106. It is identical.

Cusco means 'navel' in the Quecha language and Cusco in Peru is known as one of the navels of the ancient world, perhaps the first. It is astounding to discover that both the name and the Inca myth lie at the heart of a text written in the language of Mesopotamia, the main message of which is astronomical and concerns the precession of the equinoxes. And I have to point out once again for the pleasure: that text is, at the very least, four thousand years old!

If it were only the sounds of those three words that show this to be a deliberate reference to Cusco, there might be reason to doubt and to scoff. But that's not the case here. The translation confirms the story of the planting of a great pole. There can be no valid argument against any of the above. The words, both original and transliterated, with their meanings are correct. The connection between the lands of Peru and Mesopotamia is proven – through both name and story. At the very least, this takes the connection between them back to 1600 BC. I would argue for much earlier still, but that's enough for one day. It also demonstrates that this 'Sumerian' language had further reach than modern-day scholars give it credit for.

(Scorpio) *and some commentators have located here the biblical Chambers of the South, Scorpio being directly opposite the Pleiades on the sphere, both thought to be mentioned in the same passage of the Book of Job... (R. H. Allen, Star Names and their Meanings [6], p.362)*

My further interpretation of that section of text between lines 106 and 108 is that it is indicating a timeframe as much as a place, which implies that Cusco obtained its name from a navel of an even greater dimension. On one hand, the Pleiades appear here on line 106 through the words that gave biblical Kimah and are directly linked to the story of Atlantis elsewhere in the text (see lines 65 to 67). They are also said to signal the beginning and end of the Great Year:

(Pleiades) *And their beginning the astronomical year gave rise to the title "the Great Year of the Pleiades" for the cycle of precession of about 25,900 years. (R. H. Allen, Star Names and their Meanings [6], p.393)*

On the other hand, Scorpio is the guardian to the southern gate of the Milky Way (see the discussion of the carvings on pillar 43 at Göbekli Tepe on p.17), which is potentially the place of the biblical Chamber of the South in the quote here above. Line 108 is a clear reference to the Great Rift.

I won't bother the reader with a second-hand account of the unfathomably ancient megalithic structures found in and around Cusco. I have never seen them beyond my computer screen. My son has been there for me. Perhaps we'll go together one day. Others have visited and recorded the place. Accounts and images are easy to find.

According to the lexical lists, KU with UŠ are components of another word: KUŠ, one transliteration of that mysterious pyramidal sign ZU/SU with what appears to be a ladder or stairway at its centre and which has the given meanings 'know' and 'sink'.

Giza

Leaving Cusco and crossing the ocean back to the continent of Africa and to the ancient site of Giza in Egypt, one might, if circumstances allow, become even more daring and see KUŠ/ZU/SU (here above) as a depiction of a great pyramid on which to climb in order to be close to the sky.

The straightforward rectangular GIZ, has dictionary-given meanings of 'beam' and 'wood':

This is the wood used by carpenters and shipwrights; the roofbeams of a temple, the hull and mast of a great ship, the shaft of the weaver's spindle, the wood of the archer's bow, and the crossbeam of the lyre onto which the pegs and strings are attached. It's also a beam of light, an all-illuminating beam (see notes to lines 32 and 33).

For a while, I took the dictionary-given meanings at face value and GIZ, blandly inscribed on 4th millennium tablets as either a vertical or horizontal rectangle, seemed nothing more than a tree or something wooden. But then, after discovering that it referred to a particularly magical tree - in a three-word phrase translated to 'Tree of Consciousness and Knowledge' in *The Story of Sukurru* - I looked more closely, identifying GIZ as a syllable in the epithet of Hermes TrismeGIStus otherwise known as Egyptian Thoth. Then I looked at Gilgamesh, that well-attested hero whose name, for some hitherto unexplained reason, also incorporates an invisible GIZ.[22]

The name Giza or Gizeh is said to be taken from Arabic Er-ges-her which translates 'beside the high'. And now that I have come across GIZ a number of times in the astronomical context of *The Path To Sky-End*, I confirm with considerable assurance – well prepared to take on naysayers - that, in such a context, GIZ is far more than a simple tree trunk. It's a rectangular block of either wood or stone and the ultimate source name of the Ancient Egyptian site. I had suspected as much but, once the secrets of the scribes began to pour out, was again taken aback by the overwhelming amount of corroborating evidence in this text. And it's not the only important name in the Arabic language that has its roots here.

There are a number of significant elements linking this story to the site of
the three pyramids and their lion, not least of which two three-line riddles
which both appear to indicate the physical layout of the four structures in
relation one to the other, whereby the sphinx lies to the right of (in front
of) and facing away from the second pyramid.

The first acrostic has GIZ in first position over three lines (26, 27 and 28);
three beams. All three incorporate pyramidal ZU, meaning 'knowledge', in
varying positions. The second line has ZU directly preceding UR–MAH
which translates, always according to orthodox dictionaries, to 'great lion':

Then the three lines 56, 57 and 58, preceded by mention of a great river
on line 55, have E_2, the 'temple' in first position: three temples but equally
three vessels. The second line incorporates PIRIG, which also translates to
'lion' (developed in the notes to the relevant lines):

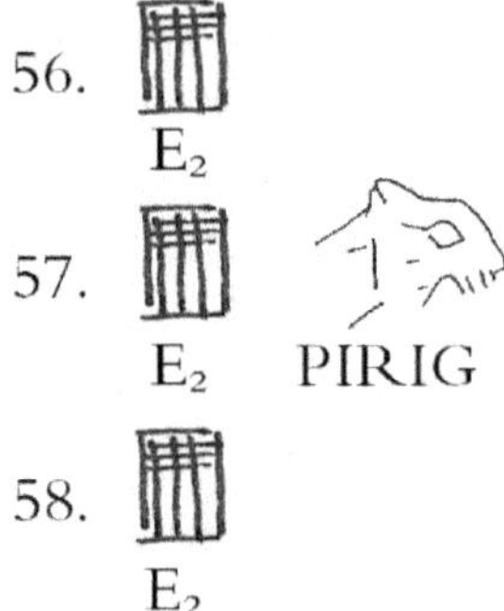

The three temples of lines 56 to 58 can be set against lines 11 and 12 in
which the source name of Orion's three belt stars is revealed along with the
link to three oils. Arabic Alnitak, the 'girdle', is used today to refer to just
one of the three stars but was originally their joint name. The alignment of

the belt stars was deliberately mirrored in the alignment of the pyramids, notably in 10500 BC when Leo rose with the sun and faced the Great Sphinx at the spring equinox.[12] The appearance of Alnitak on line 12, apparent through the source words of the name, is just one of many indications that the information contained in the lines invoking precession numbers is of particular astronomical significance.

In that second riddle (lines 56 to 58) are also found the original words that gave their names to some of the principal figures of Ancient Egypt: Ra, Orion, Osiris, and the goddess Ma'at.

The source name of the circumpolar star Kochab in Ursa Minor, one of a pair deemed 'indestructible' by the Egyptian astronomers (along with Mizar) because always present and circling the north pole, is encoded on line 57 and closely followed on line 58 by the second and final mention of the three-word phrase already translated in *The Story of Sukurru* to 'Tree of Consciousness and Knowledge'. One of the shafts of the Great Pyramid is thought to be directed towards both Kochab and the pole star Thuban in Draco. Kochab results from a transliteration of ZU, the pyramid of 'knowledge', as KUŠ with AB, the 'father'. The name Kochab was passed down to Arabic and apparently also attributed to Polaris, its close neighbour in the constellation of Ursa Minor.

In conclusion, within the context of numerous references to precession, Mesopotamian GIZ, the beam, gives the source of Arabic 'ges', and the name of the Giza plateau to which the Sabian astronomers made their pilgrimages. They travelled there from Harran, that region in northern Mesopotamia about which their ancestors wrote abundantly. Harran derives from HAR RA AN and means 'Celestial Mill of Ra'. The evidence is abundant. As ever, the reader of this is free to decide for themselves if it is sufficient proof.

The Great Sphinx

Alternative names for the Sphinx are Hor-em-Akhet and Horakhti, (…) I propose that Hor results from Sumerian HAR/HUR, the celestial millstone and root symbol of the name Harran. I also propose that HUR-SAG, the 'top millstone', commonly translated to 'mountain', can be read as a reference to the head of the Great Sphinx and to its twin, the millstone in the sky. (Lost Stones, p.91)

In 2021, I made the case for there being numerous references to the Great Sphinx in the mistranslated Mesopotamian texts and, more specifically, that it could be perceived through the analogy with a mill. The original word gave both the HAR of Harran in Mesopotamia and the HUR of Horakhti and Hor-em-Akhet in Egypt. In other words the Great Sphinx, staring due east at the rising sun, functions as a clock reflecting the movements of the mill in the sky.

This second translation confirms that analysis and takes the subject of the Sphinx and the mysteries contained within it to new heights. Line 14, part of the introductory section, is stretched to its utmost limits here and reads:

14. Along the gulley walls and around the founding brick, pierced through with nails and bitter words of bees and their brew, thick reeds and his stylus on the seal of the Father will whirl.

In context - and with a very slight tweak – the final three-word phrase, AD GI_4 GI_4, of that line, becomes:

(On the temple wall the story of) Atlantis among the reeds is inscribed.

In the lexical lists, both that phrase repeated three times in this text (see lines 14, 40 and 91) and PIRIG with UD, the 'Lion of the Sun' (see here below), are found opposite MA LI KU, the source words of Arabic malik which has the meaning 'king'.

(Regulus) In Arabia it was Malikiy, Kingly (Star Names [6]*, p.256)*

Note that the last word KU is the same as the word in the *King List* and Cusco riddles (p.55 and 58):

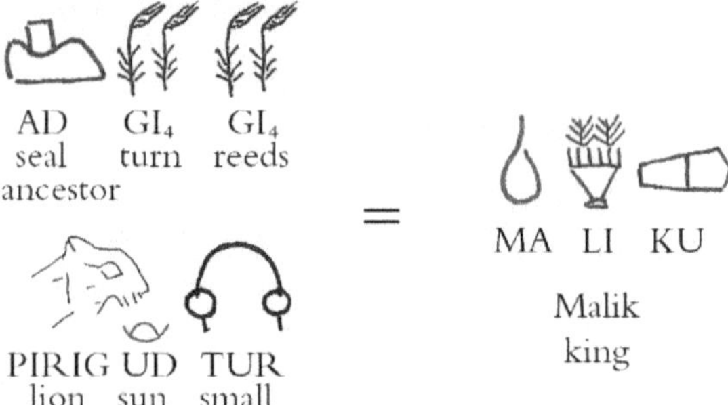

Regulus, from the Latin word for 'little king', is the bright star that lies at the front of the constellation of Leo, forming the lowest point of the sickle-shaped asterism. TUR, here above with the lion of the sun, has given meanings 'small' and 'child'. If that star were to be placed on the form of the stone Sphinx at Giza, it would sit somewhere at the front above its paws (see the enigmatic pictographic MAH here below). With its title 'little king', Regulus can be linked to the rebirth of the sun and of the pharaoh. Thanks to the stone plaque between the paws of the Sphinx, it can also be linked to 'Zep Tepi', Egyptian reference to the 'First Time'.

More evidence that this text refers to the Great Sphinx is found in the total four-fold repetition of pyramid and feline together, three times with ZU to the left and once – on line 57 as Kochab - to the right:

On line 32 the lion sits between a pyramidal form and the symbol of the sun. Line 31 reads:

31. Its gate to know, the Great Lion, to itself and to the soul the way of the arrow's flow will show.

On line 40, the lion in animal form is less evident. This time it takes on its identity as celestial clock and is sitting, surrounded by cords and chords, under the guise of Horakhti, HOR/HUR/HAR, playing the music of the mill (see the notes to line 40). Analysis of the six central words provides one of the greatest insights into the secret of the Egypto–Mesopotamian astronomer who first placed the words onto a tablet, information presumably held safely in a sealed chamber. I have translated them here to the best of my ability and to their fullest extent:

Tied by the chords of the harp (EŠ$_2$ HAR EŠ$_2$)
of Orpheus (UR BI)
and carried by the feet of the dog (DU UR)
the enduring bond (DUR)
of the Sphinx and Orpheus (Sirius) (HOR UR BI)
the two golden dogs (UR BI)
orbiting with the cord of bees (Pleiades) (EŠ$_2$ UR BI EŠ$_2$)
around the mill (HAR)

and have added the following subtext to the translation of that line:

40. On the adamantine seal of the ancestor under the foot of the Sphinx the story of Atlantis is recorded.

Given the strong link between sun and Sirius discovered in *The Story of Sukurru*, it's my guess that there is more to that astronomical story. That is why the unorthodox but logical meaning of 'golden' is added, taking UR, the 'dog', to be the source of Latin aurum. Thus the Great Sphinx, partner of the constellation of Leo, by association with the sun and Sirius becomes both feline and canine in nature. And it is golden like the honeybee.

Among the many gifts of this text is the reference to the enduring nature of the Great Sphinx. That part is coded of course but with care and respect for its age, it's possible to peel the words back to recover a good deal of the intended message.

The collocated words DU, the 'foot' and UR, the 'dog' or 'lion' together become DUR, the enduring 'bond' (always according to the lexical lists). I posit that they can be traced back to 9600 BC and to the big-footed central bird on Pillar 43 at Göbekli Tepe. I have already pointed out elsewhere the importance of the bird's gullet and the fact that it – or a later copy of the same - was the model for the Sumerian pictogram having the given meaning 'neck'. (*Lost Stones*, p.122-127) (See the notes to lines 13, 24 and 40.)

The foot of the dog (or lion) is linguistically connected to the gullet of the bird. DUR connects the time of Göbekli Tepe to that of the Great Sphinx. And between them they link forward to the mysterious alchemical ouroboros symbol (see the illustration of line 10).

DU UR   =   DUR

carry dog   enduring bond

foot of the dog   gullet of the bird

The Idigna bird, symbol of the Tigris river, appears on line 24 (see p.16). Here copied from a 4th millennium tablet:

The Emerald Tablet

Although texts written in the 20th century have been given the same name, seemingly to profit from its renown, there is only one *Emerald Tablet.*. The choice of title for those later writings, said to be channelled by their author and having no link to the original document, should have made that distinction more obvious. But unfortunately, they have succeeded in muddying the waters. First documented in the 9th century AD and thought to be copied from a far more ancient text, according to its own words the *Emerald Tablet* was written by Hermes Trismegistus.[23] It was highly prized among medieval alchemical scholars until, its authenticity disputed, it fell out of favour in the 17th century. Here a version translated from Latin:

True it is, without falsehood, certain and most true.

That which is above is like to that which is below, and that which is below is like to that which is above, to accomplish the miracles of one thing.

And as all things were by contemplation of one, so all things arose from this one thing by a single act of adaptation.

The father thereof is the Sun, the mother the Moon.

The wind carried it in its womb, the earth is the nurse thereof.

It is the father of all works of wonder throughout the whole world.

The power thereof is perfect.

If it be cast on to earth, it will separate the element of earth from that of fire, the subtle from the gross.

With great sagacity it doth ascend gently from earth to heaven. Again it doth descend to earth,

and uniteth in itself the force from things superior and things inferior.

Thus thou wilt possess the glory of the brightness of the whole world, and all obscurity will fly far from thee.

This thing is the strong fortitude of all strength, for it overcometh every subtle thing and doth penetrate every solid substance.

Thus was this world created.

Hence will there be marvellous adaptations achieved, of which the manner is this.

For this reason I am called Hermes Trismegistus, because I hold three parts of the wisdom of the whole world.

That which I had to say about the operation of Sol is completed. [24]

The name 'Green Tablet' appears on this tablet (line 41) as does Tautu, Greek form of Thoth and alternative epithet of Hermes Trismegistus (line 9). Analysis of the name confirms that the figure was most certainly a great astronomer who knew all about the precession of the equinoxes. According to my analysis of the wording of line 41, the constellation of Draco, the great snake, and its pole star Thuban were also associated with him.

At the very least that discovery has the merit of overturning the claim that the *Emerald Tablet* was a medieval forgery conjured out of nowhere. And although it doesn't solve the mystery of the message, it does eliminate all discussion as to whether or not the tablet existed in some form at a date corresponding to the civilizations of Ancient Egypt and Mesopotamia. It knocks into oblivion all questioning of the great age of Hermes Trismegistus.

By precaution, I will add that any challenge to this affirmation will need to be equally precise and detailed, demonstrating why it cannot be correct. Detractors should be able to provide alternative meanings – in some comprehensible context – of the line in which the monosyllabic words that give 'green tablet' appear, bearing in mind that those original cuneiform words, GI and DUB, take the meanings 'green' and 'tablet' from academic dictionaries.

GI DUB

Any serious challenge should include retraceable references, and exclude obfuscation through obscure language referring to 'specialist' knowledge or, heaven forbid, ad hominem attack. For example and in plain language, what was their exact function with regard to the surrounding words? No-one should settle for "It's complicated. Just believe me. I'm the expert." Not from me. Not from anyone. For my part, I have laid it all out as plainly as possible in the line and in the notes.

The phrase 'As above, so below', forever associated with Hermes Trismegistus thanks to the *Emerald Tablet*, appears more than once in this text, including in the wordplay on lines 118 and 119 where AN, the sky, begins the line and NA, the stone, ends it. Sky and stone. Light and heavy.

There is a a great binding force weaving through the *Emerald Tablet*. The same is true of *The Path to Sky-End*. It takes the form of snakes, at least one above and one below (lines 80, 86, 89, 90 and 98).

Comet Strike

Mention of a comet strike here is entirely the result of having come across one by chance during the translating process. It is not in any way an endorsement of Zechariah Sitchin's theory about a twelfth planet. Does this account have any bearing on the cataclysmic events of around 12,000 years ago? I will leave readers to make up their own minds as to that possibility. The translation in its context is accurate. That's all I can and do claim.

Hiding in plain sight on line 93 of *The Path to Sky-End* (aka *Enki's Journey to Nibru/Nippur*) under the guise of a great lump of mortar is an account of something extremely destructive hitting our planet. The defining word in that account is transliterated KUM which I posit is one source of Greek kometes meaning 'comet'.

KUM has dictionary-given meanings of 'mortar', 'crush' and 'kill'. With ŠE (meaning 'seed') added inside it, transliterated KUM became GAZ, the seed-crusher. Its pictographic form (here above) looks for all the world like a grinding bowl containing a heavy stone ball. No doubt that's what it was, a kind of mill, a stone crusher. In context, the word is found with mention of a bull and, in my opinion, also served as a description of castration. But behind all such meanings lies the original account of a life-altering strike of either a single comet or a series of huge meteors.

Adding in a fair dose of healthy scepticism given the importance of the subject, there can be only one follow-up question. If this claim is true, why would we find mention of such a vital piece of astronomical information on only one of the hundreds of thousands of tablets in our possession today? That was the question I asked myself immediately after discovering it and seconds before feverishly combing through the corpus of Sumerian texts. It didn't take long to find three other comets firmly embedded in three other texts, all incorporated into lines which are absolutely identical to line 93 here.

So four texts in all…and that's just the number of versions that have survived through thick and thin for around four thousand years. Impressive. Having four separate examples of that line still available to us today and taken from four different texts is adequate proof of its importance.

Only the first four words, title of the lord between sky and earth (AN-EN-KI-KID) in this version are exchanged for the 'lofty king' or the 'king at the levee' (LUGAL-E) in the three other texts, a useful variation confirming that the two epithets applied to the same figure; the lord and the king are one and the same.

Here below the slightly varying and thoroughly underwhelming academic translations, with KUM/GAZ given as the verb, 'to sacrifice' and 'to slaughter'; the fatal comet totally invisible in those localised and relatively contextless scenes:

- The Flood Story, line 11 (ETCSL ref. 1.7.4, Seg.D):
> *The king sacrificed oxen and offered innumerable sheep.*
- The death of Ur-Namma, line 81 (ETCSL ref. 2.4.1.1):
> *The king slaughtered numerous bulls and sheep,*
- The debate between Hoe and Plough, line 25 (ETCSL ref. 5.3.1):
> *the king slaughters cattle and sacrifices sheep*
- *Enki's Journey to Nibru*, line 93 (ETCSL ref. 1.1.4):
> *Enki had oxen slaughtered, and had sheep offered there lavishly.*

My monosyllabic version of Enki's Journey incorporates all relevant meanings of those twelve words (i.e. excluding the king and lord), and makes use of each of them more than once – taking them to their absolute limits to ensure that not one ounce of the original meaning is lost. In that, it is diametrically opposed to the academic conventions where many of the original, meaningful words are taken to be meaningless phonemes, nothing but sounds. Those translations (including king and lord) amount to fewer words than the original – between seven and ten – a difference resulting only from use of the causative verb form in Enki's Journey.

This translation has the immense advantage of appearing in its true original context of astronomical observations. The king or lord is given in the passive tense, berated and threatened by a far greater and extremely annoyed entity. For those reasons, the result is considerably longer (forty words!) and infinitely more impactful than the officialised versions:

> *93. "The foolish lord between sky and earth, for mortar to make clay of the land of both Mother and Father, his seed with the seeds of the bull (Taurus, Taurids) will be crushed in the levee, and the lambs in clay of land and sea all gathered and slaughtered!"*

The mortar for reconstruction work after the announced cataclysm will be made from the clay, diverse bones of the victims, etc. all mixed with the raging flood waters. A reminder that the Mesopotamians were not only astronomers. They were experts in irrigation techniques and they built their pyramids in fired bricks joined with mortar. Despite appearing just once, the original word KUM/GAZ was used four times here for 'mortar', 'seed', 'seeds' and 'crushed', all firmly linked to one another and all dictionary-given meanings.

Never forgetting – on a lighter note - the other underlying and age-old theme identified in this text: that of the fearless (some would say mad) honey-hunter on his reed-woven ladder clinging precariously to the cliff face while using a fire stick to smoke out the bees and to recuperate their honeycomb – an activity provably harking back to ever more ancient times, certainly pre-Ice Age. The protesting swarm was driven out and the precious comb dislodged with the help of a long prod. If all went well, it fell neatly in one piece into the hunter's basket. Otherwise, no doubt it fell to the ground far below with a dull thud. Perhaps the hunter too.

Those cliff-hanging honeycombs also look curiously similar to the pictogram of KUM which is also GUM. This from Pliny on the subject of beeswax:

> *The persons who understand this subject, call the substance which forms the first foundation of their combs, commosis,* (Pliny, Natural History, Bk XI:6)

The lambs (LU) along with the light (also LU) are exterminated on line 93 thanks to a different but equally dangerous word: ŠAR$_2$ which also has the dictionary-given meaning 'to slaughter', and which appears twice in an equally terrifying context on lines 69 and 70 of *The Story of Sukurru*:

As with the two phrases of line 93 here, only the names at the beginning of those two lines are different. The rest is identical. Both 'crushed' on line 69 and 'slaughtered' on line 70 of *The Story of Sukurru* were translated from ŠAR$_2$:

> *69. Dog-Head with a single stone – weight of destiny – with one fell stroke has decided: All of mankind crushed will be.*

70. Exalted Sun with one thick stroke on the Stone of Destiny has decided: All of mankind slaughtered must be.

ŠAR₂ is also understood to signify the number 3600 and (just for once) the accepted source of ancient Greek *saros* meaning 'sweep clean'. Apparently the Greek version of the measurement might not give an accurate reflection of the original numbers:

> *For 120 saros-cycles make 2222 years according to the Chaldeans' reckoning, if indeed the saros makes 222 lunar months, which are 18 years and 6 months.* (Suda, Trans. C. Roth)

A connotation of chasing out evil and restoring order is present in those biblical verses in which the root of Greek *saros* appears. In the Parable of the Lost Coin:

> *Or what woman who has ten silver coins and loses one of them does not light a lamp, sweep (saroi) her house, and search carefully until she finds it? And when she finds it, she calls together her friends and neighbours to say, 'Rejoice with me, for I have found my lost coin.'...* (Luke 15:8-9)

And it's not impossible that Hebrew *zaram* meaning 'to pour forth in floods', has its origin in ŠAR₂:

> *The waters saw You, O God; the waters saw You and swirled; even the depths were shaken. The clouds poured down water; the skies resounded with thunder; Your arrows flashed back and forth. Your thunder resounded in the whirlwind; the lightning lit up the world; the earth trembled and quaked....* (Psalm 77:16-18)

Sky People of Kitara

I am not a proponent of Zechariah Sitchin's theory of Anunnaki gods as alien visitors. The simple fact that no verifiable textual sources were cited with that claim is sufficient reason to disregard the entire story. Neither did he provide any reasons for his unorthodox translations of various key words; the Mu sky rockets or helmets and so on. It all made for great science fiction but, in the process, unapologetically heaped yet another layer of modern fiction over the heads of the already crushed Mesopotamian scribes.

That said, I am also about to head down that dizzying path of unreferenced offerings and beliefs in search of long-lost ancestors from another place entirely. Why? Because I have at last come across the so-called 'Anunnaki' in situ here and the result is not entirely what I expected it to be. I found them in unexpected company:

KIT ARA/LI

Research into these two words (appearing on line 117) led to an unexpected place: KID/KIT translates to 'mat' (see p.44) followed by ARA together giving 'altar mat'. Having identified LI as an enhanced version of ARA, pictogram of an incense burner, I typed possible combinations of those words into a search engine and discovered the little known myth of African Kitara, also called the Empire of the Sun.

One of the few sources on the subject comes from a study of African myths written by Harold Scheub (1931-2019), Professor at Wisconsin University.[25] According to that account the people of Kitara emerged somewhere in the region of Uganda, driving their cattle down from an unknown location in the north or north-east at an undetermined time in the past. To the north-east of Uganda lies Ethiopia. Above that come Sudan and then Egypt.

One interesting detail is that the new arrivals were described as being red with long straight hair. Known as the Cwezi, they also had unprecedented magical skills, eventually disappearing from that region of Africa just as mysteriously as they had appeared.

Another source gives them as extra-terrestrials due to their supernatural powers, as 'air-travellers' and, more precisely, as travelling in the air on their mats.[26]

There is nothing about Kitara and those 'red' people that can be proven; nothing at all, not when or how or where from. Perhaps it's nothing more than a myth. Nevertheless, it seems that a lot has been passed down orally concerning the people of that vast empire. The Chwezi (or Cwezi) are named and the region of Uganda is the most cited. So what should be made of the transliterated KIT-ARA appearing in this text directly next to another equally unexplained group recently named the Anunnaki (line 117), also associated with the colour 'red' and a reference to 'hair' in this text (line 48)?

Curiosity as to a connection between the Sumerian meaning of KIT-ARA, the mat placed before an altar, and the culture of the Cwezi led me to spend a little time on the subject. I found that archaeological digs had taken place during the 1990s in Western Uganda and in that region known as Bunyoro-Kitara where a Bacwezi dynasty apparently once existed. The research paper proved interesting. It begins:

> *In the context of this ambitious goal, we are investigating some of the well-known earthworks found in the region, as well as some of the sites that served as shrines to individual Cwezi spirits.*[27]

I reached out to Joshua Mukama Rwakamani, a researcher who has studied the region.[28] He wrote back:

> *There still exist cults today venerating the Bacwezi believed to be demi-gods. And they still use mats on their altars. The Bacwezi were known for their knowledge of astrology. In fact, their huts were decorated with the stars to showcase their knowledge. So Kitara was ruled by the Bacwezi elite and Bigo is believed to have been their capital. Bigo has been a subject of research with iron sherds, pottery and cattle bones from the site studied.*

Further questioned on the name Bigo, he answered:

> *"Bigo" means kraals. A cattle kraal is typically called "orugo" in Runyakitara (Bantu language). So the place was called "Bigo bya Mugyenyi" meaning the kraals of Mugyenyi. The Bacwezi were cattle keepers of the Ankole long-horned cattle.*

According to their report, the American archaeologists found traces of 'extensive ditches' at Bigo but their dating of material there to the 16th century AD is somewhat disappointing. Mounds were found but no burials.

Nevertheless, their report also mentions that a shrine to the Cwezi spirits had been newly set up.

The existence of Bigo and its connection to cattle has done nothing to distill my curiosity as to the founders of the Empire of Kitara, although there is reason to despair of ever finding anything more concrete. Despite the dating, there are some intriguing coincidences. In *Before Babel* (p.53-54), I wrote:

> *Dictionaries give Turkish 'gobek' opposite Portuguese 'umbigo' for 'navel'. Both have their origin in an unknown (PIE) source.*

and followed with what is likely an incomplete list of ancient place names – for example, Mount Bégo in France, the Gobi desert in Mongolia - all beginning GO-BE or BI-GO, to include the name Göbekli Tepe (see notes to line 15).

Adding into the mix a connection between the cattle of the African Cwezi people and the obvious importance given to the ancient aurochs as revealed in the archaeological sites of south-eastern Turkey, the various coincidences become thought-provoking at the very least.

I have spent a lot of time reflecting on that enigmatic word KIT/KID, particularly while writing Lost Stones, and, more recently, was intrigued by a reference made by Robert Bauval to the Egyptian Horus name, Ntjr-y-kh-t, where the three final syllables are pronounced 'khet'. Apparently, khet has the meaning 'Corporation', and, in the case of the Horus name of the pharaoh Djoser, might give a 'corporation' of very ancient gods. He further suggests a possible link to the word 'akhet' meaning 'horizon' which is found in the name of the Great Sphinx, Hor-em-akhet (*The Egypt Code*[29], p.11).

Finally, KIT ARA is one source of the ancient Greek 'kithara', a name that was carried through to the most popular of modern-day string instruments: the guitar (see p.46, notes to lines 105 and 117). The ever-recurring musical theme began with the first pluck of the tortoise-shell lyre by a precursor of Greek Hermes-Apollo-Orpheus.

Language Of The Birds

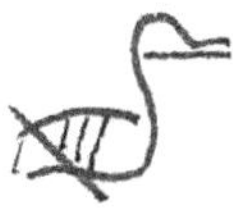

And first, with Heart so full as from his Eyes
Ran weeping, up rose Tajidar the Wise;
The mystic Mark upon whose Bosom show'd
That He alone of all the Birds THE ROAD
Had travell'd: and the Crown upon his Head
Had reach'd the Goal; and He stood forth and said:

Conference of the Birds, by the Persian poet Attar of Nishapur (translated here by Edward FitzGerald in the 19th century), tells the story of thirty birds on a quest to find their future king, the mythical Simorgh. In *Before Babel* (p.169-171), I made the case for a Mesopotamian origin to that tale.

In this text, DAR (shown here above and on line 3) appears at the outset and is the model for Tajidar the Wise. The bird is witness to the ultimate truth; that all of them, on the condition that they can find it in their hearts to undertake the difficult journey and see it through no matter what, will eventually come face to face with their ruler.

The pictogram is not vague; it's a duck. Translations of the Persian tale give Tajidar as a hoopoe while some translators of DAR give this Mesopotamian bird as a black francolin. However, remembering that it is an extremely wise and clever bird capable of piercing a mirror (or any veil), I take it to apply to any bird capable of swooping or dipping down below the surface of the water to catch its food in sea, lake or river. Tajidar is an epithet taken from its qualities, a piercer of screens and veils; a water bird.

The Simorgh, mythical king that the birds are seeking, is also present on line 3 of this text in one of its attested forms: ŠIM, given as 'brewer' in conventional dictionaries to which I have added 'alchemist' and 'witness'. The breakdown given in the lexical tablets shows it to be linked to two other words: ŠI and IM, the 'eye' and the 'clay', 'the eye on clay', the witness to the words on the tablet, the Clay Eye.

In ŠIM is found the origin of biblical Shem, one of three brothers in the Bible whose name gave uneasy birth to its recently-coined derivative, 'semitic' used to distinguish a range of associated cultures and languages from all others. Ironically, during that artificial and unjustifiable process of labelling carried out in the second half of the 19th century, the Sumerian language (a name also coined in 1872) was declared non-semitic – and therefore unrelated to any other known language. In truth, it's quite the opposite. When we read these texts, we are reading our own source language. Staring at the Simorgh and at our own image in the mirror.

Pictographic ŠIM, described by me elsewhere as a piece of laboratory equipment, is in fact a filtrating vessel for honeycomb, its lower funnel serving to pour out the liquid honey while the more solid elements stay put. My suggestion is that this word is linked to the lost-wax process (creating replicas) already in use in 4th millennium Mesopotamia. From there, it more generally implies any magical replication (mirroring) of an existing form; hence the Simorgh.

Line 104 of *The Path to Sky-End* reflects the moment in the *Conference of the Birds* when the few remaining and most courageous birds at last meet the Simorgh face to face. In this more ancient story, it takes the form of a great deal of circling wordplay and has the added merit of finally dispatching those recently-minted names Enki and Enlil into the abyss where they belong. The Persian Simorgh can be compared to the equally symbolic and great Phoenix, born of fire, which rises with the sun towards the end of this text, its existence and original name revealed through two words, one of which is another of the Mesopotamian birds.

Tajidar the Wise appears again towards the end of *The Path To Sky-End* (line 115), this time in the form of TA-JIR₃, the 'question' and the 'path'. Together they refer to the path of questioning along which the initiate must travel in order to pierce the ultimate secret of existence. JIR₃ takes the form of a cow's head, potentially linking it to the original meanings behind the anthropomorphic head of Ancient Egyptian Hathor whose entire body is the path. TA, both 'death' and 'questioning', gives the first syllable of the ancient Greek name Tautu which became Thoth, the equally Wise (line 9).

THE
PATH
TO
SKY-
END

Ye Holy Books,
which have been written by my perishable hands,
but have been anointed with the drug of imperishability,
remain ye unseen and undiscovered by all men
who shall go to and fro on the plains of this land,
until the time when Heaven, grown old,
shall beget organisms worthy of you…

TA – UT - DU

(The Question of the Sun's Carriage)

Thoth in the Hermetica

(Trans. Sir Walter Scott)

1. To the In-Between

By day, the deluge.
The sun and the king on the bird
to their shared fate below with the stars will fly.

Between the Euphrates and the Tigris there flows another river, called Basileius; (Strabo, Geography, 7:27)

2. Birth Place

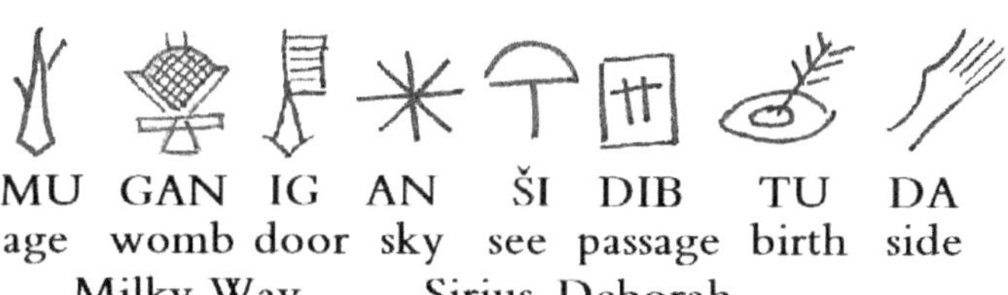

In the age of the open womb and the passage of the Eye in the sky,
when all can see the way and reflect on their place of birth.

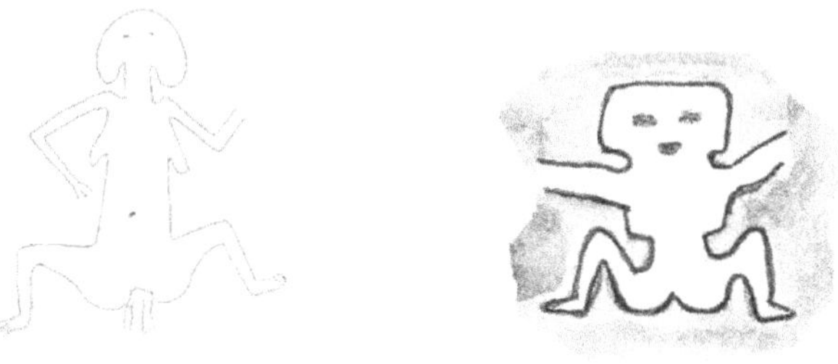

3. The Channel

UN	E	U₂	ŠIM	DIM₂	KI	IN	DAR	RA	BA
land	levee	pipes	brewer	create	place	straw	pierce	churn	below
				Boötes			Cygnus	Draco	

When from the levee to channel the brew to the land below,

the ox of the Creator pierces the straw (of the Milky Way)

for the swan (Cygnus) and the churning dragon (Draco).

4-5. To Tartarus

EN	ZU	AB	LUGAL	AN	EN	KI	KID
lord	know	father	king	sky	lord	earth	mat
			Apollo		Phaeton		

AN	EN	KI	EN	NAM	TAR	TAR	RE	NE
sky	lord	earth	end	destiny	cut	cut	gather	fire
						Tartarus		Phoenix

His father, King of the Sky, to know and the abyss from end to end,

the ghostly lord with the bird of destiny to Tartarus will sail,

to gather the fire of the sun and return with it — again.

6. A Round Boat of Necessity

E₂	A	NI	KUK	NI	UD	ZA	KUR	NA	UR	BI	BA	NI	IN	KAK
temple	water	oil	circle	oil	sun	sound	hills	stone	dog	beer	less	oil	in	nail
		6		6			Qurna	Sirius	Orpheus			6		

Of necessity, a round vessel he must build,
in the Temple of Living Water to sail,
the stone hills to orbit
to the sounds of crows and barking dogs,
with beer and three gifts of oils (Alnitak)
placed inside.

7. Crows, Dogs and Honeybees

KUK	NI	UD	ZA	KUR	BI	UD	KAR₂	KAR₂	A	KA
circle	oil	sun	sound	hills	bee	sun	lift	shine	flow	mouth
				Corvus			Cancer			

Of necessity, a golden cog-boat circling night and day,
to the sound of the crows and buzzing of the honeybees,
lifted with the carriage of the spitting sun,
over the water to flow... in need of mead.

8. Wave-Sweeper

AB	E	ZU	AB	A	UL	IM	MA	NI	IN	DU
ocean	levee	know	father	water	wave	clay	land	oil	straw	carry
	Phaeton				Scorpio					

On the rising ocean, his father at the levee to know
and on the wave to fittingly expand,
thick clay of the land (ballast and writing material)
inside the boat will stand.

9. Thoth

MUŠ₃ KUK GALAM KA GA ZU AB TA UD DU A
space circle fish mouth milk know father question sun carry flow
ermine Piscis Austrinus Oannes Apollo Thoth

Circling in the sacred space among the time-dividing reeds (mousehole),

with the fish, its mouth to the milk,

and his father (Apollo) to know,

the sailor will go with his question

of the carriage of the sun and its flow.

10. Ouroboros

EN AN NU DIM₂ HU HI RA MU UN NA DU DU DU DU GI SIN
lord sky knot create bird veil churn age land stone sailor task bring rod three
(1) ring Boötes Horae sun moon Dodona (4) (2) Earth (3)
Mut Moirai dodo

To the Lord of the Sky Knot who the Celestial Ring (year)

and Feathered Wheel (hours) created,

where the motions of sun and moon

and the ages of the world

by two stone sailors (dodo,

Dodona) are carried,

their four feet and

three arrows turning.

$4 + 2 + 3 = 9$

+ One Lord

11. A Perfect Fifth

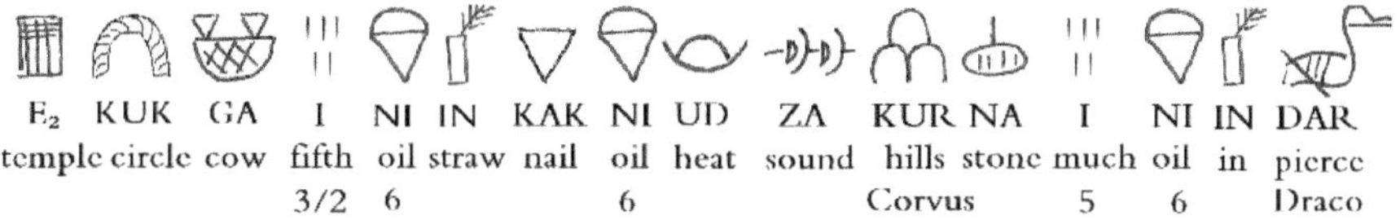

E₂	KUK	GA	I	NI	IN	KAK	NI	UD	ZA	KUR	NA	I	NI	IN	DAR
temple	circle	cow	fifth	oil	straw	nail	oil	heat	sound	hills	stone	much	oil	in	pierce
			3/2	6			6			Corvus			5	6	Draco

Of necessity, in the Temple of the Cow to circle
to the sound of barking and the song of the crows in the stone hills,
an abundance of oils, straw and piercing nails he must carry.

(Orion's Belt) *Alnitak, or Alnitah, for this, the lowest star in the Belt, is from Al Nitak the Girdle. (...) The Chinese similarly knew them as a Weighing-beam, (Star Names [6], p.314-315)*

12. Pride of the Rooster

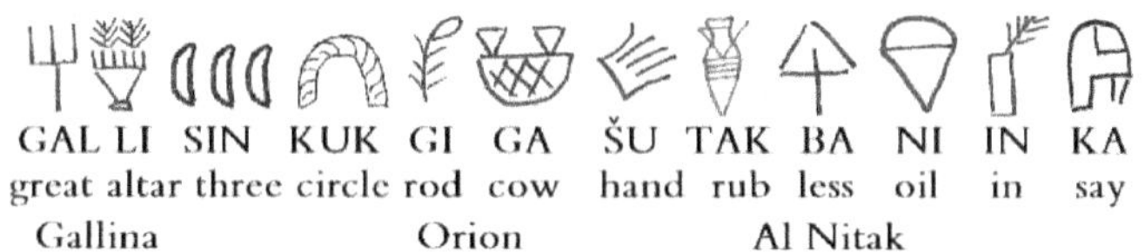

GAL	LI	SIN	KUK	GI	GA	ŠU	TAK	BA	NI	IN	KA
great	altar	three	circle	rod	cow	hand	rub	less	oil	in	say
Gallina					Orion			Al Nitak			

To the hen (Gallina, Cygnus) circling in the reeds with the cow
the greatness of the giant (Orion, giga-) to show,
three galleys on the cog-boat (and a three pronged prod for the cow),
less lowly hand-rubbing and oily words to say below.
(Alnitak, Orion's belt)

Latin cingulum: 'girdle', 'swordbelt', from cingere: 'to surround', 'encircle'.

13. Death of Ego

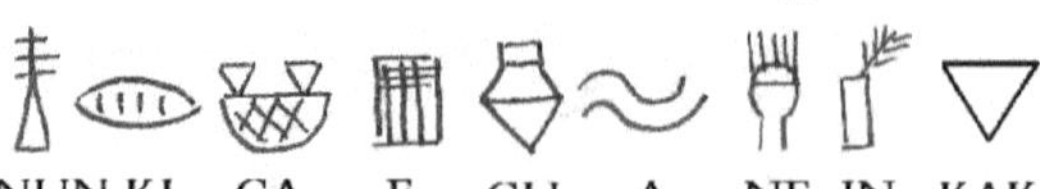

NUN	KI	GA	E₂	GU₂	A	NE	IN	KAK
guide	place	milk	temple	gullet	flow	fire	straw	create
whale			ego	Tigris	blood	red		thorn

In the Place of the otherworldly Guide, his vessel
through the red gulley waters (ego) must go,
a fire in the straw (of the Milky Way) to create
and his blood to flow on its thorn (cactus, acacia).

14. Story of Atlantis

KULLA	BI	KA	KA	KA	AD	GI₄	GI₄
wall	bees	word	word	tell	seal	reed	whirl
	Kabeira		story		Atlantis	Regulus	

Around the founding pegs along its walls,
his bitter story of bees and the brew he will tell,
(the stylus on the seal of the Father turns)
as in the thick reeds he whirls.

(On the temple wall the story of Atlantis among the reeds is inscribed.)

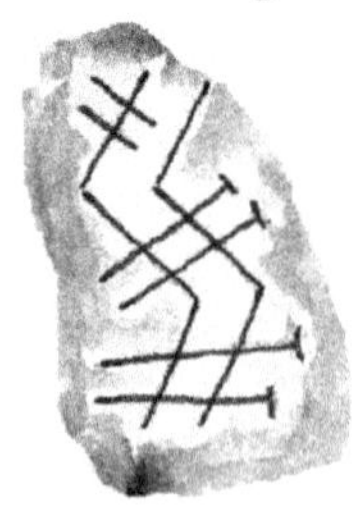

15. Labyrinth of the Bull

GI	SAL	LA	BI	GUD	DIM₂	HAR	IM	DU

GI   SAL   LA   BI   GUD   DIM₂   HAR   IM   DU
rod chamber hang brew bull create mill wind carry
Salus   Gobe Boötes Harran

His arrow to hang in Her Chamber (womb, cairn),

with good beer and the limb of the bull,

around the mill on the wind his spirit is carried.

*Ancient, however, as are "Arctos and Ursa, 'Ash and the Bier, (…),
this splendid constellation ran still further back — three or four or
even more millenniums before even these titles were current — as
the Bull's Thigh, or the Fore Shank, in Egypt. (Star Names[6], p.434)*

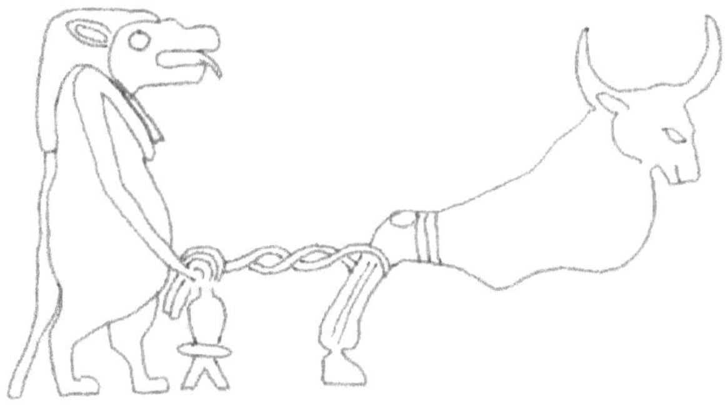

16. Great Measuring Rod

E₂   AN   EN   KI   KID   KA   NUN   DI   DAM
temple sky lord place mat word guide divide trust
canon

From the mouth of the Divine Guide

the rules of division of earth and sky he will learn

and in the word (canon) the foolish lord will trust…

Greek kanon: any straight rod or bar, rule, standard of excellence.

17. The King is Dead

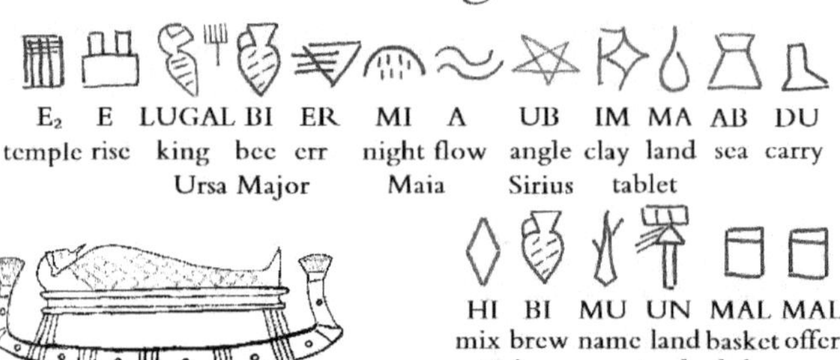

E₂	E	LUGAL	BI	ER	MI	A	UB	IM	MA	AB	DU
temple	rise	king	bee	err	night	flow	angle	clay	land	sea	carry
		Ursa Major			Maia		Sirius		tablet		

HI	BI	MU	UN	MAL	MAL
mix	brew	name	land	basket	offer
Hebe				standard	houses

To the temple at the levee the king will rise on his bier,

all the angles of land and sea to watch by night

and into the clay to be carried (inscribed),

his brew with the brew of the Heavenly Bee (Hebe) to mix

and their names unite with the gifts in their (moon) baskets,

(the total years of their houses establish.)

These kings have one purpose: to yield their power and authority to the beast. (Revelation 17:13)

18. The Veiled Goddess

LUGAL	AN	EN	KI	RA	LUH	AN	BAP	ŠIg	NE	SAL	HI	GE	EŠ	IM	ME
king	sky	lord	earth	churn	clean	sky	cut	eye	red	she	veil	rod	three	spirit	magic
					baptism		weep			Salus	Hygeia			hemi-	
					Babylon										

The king and lord between sky and earth, blinded by weeping,

in Her veiled chamber (Salus, Hygeia, hymen, hive)

will be cleansed and with three arrows

his spirit in Her clay

will be measured.

Rejoice, apostles and prophets! For God
has judged her with the judgment she imposed on you.
(Babylon's Doom, Revelation, 18:20)

19. Inherent Suffering

temple high clay land carry word clay land pour levee
Deucalion   Aquarius

From the lofty temple, in the immaculate clay of Ma (truth of suffering),
into the Cask of Knowledge at the Crossroads the truth will pour.

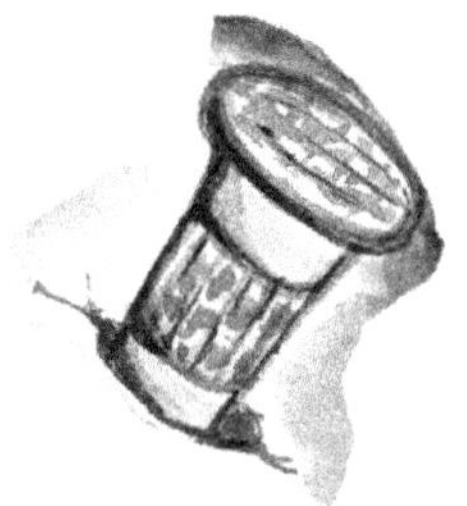

20. The Absent Father

brick clay land carry word clay land father place time
Deucalion   absum   name

On the founding brick in clay of the land (Mother of Truth),
the word will be carried of the absent Father (Abraham, Kronos),
and on it placed the name and the sum of his time.

$$1460 / 20 = 73 \rightarrow$$

Then I saw an angel coming down from heaven with the key to the Abyss, holding in his hand a great chain. He seized the dragon, that ancient serpent who is the devil and Satan, and bound him for a thousand years. And he threw him into the Abyss, shut it, and sealed it over him, so that he could not deceive the nations until the thousand years were complete. After that, he must be released for a brief period of time. (Revelation 20:1-3)

21. Golden Circle

E₂	KUK	NI	UD	ZA	KUR	NA	KI	GAR	RA
temple	cog	night	day	sound	hills	stone	place	measure	beat
Circle	need				Qurna		Key		Ra

Of necessity, the golden vessel will circle night and day
to the sound of barking in the stone hills,
with a stone key to measure
the beat of that place.

21 x 2 = 42 →

22. The Stone Key

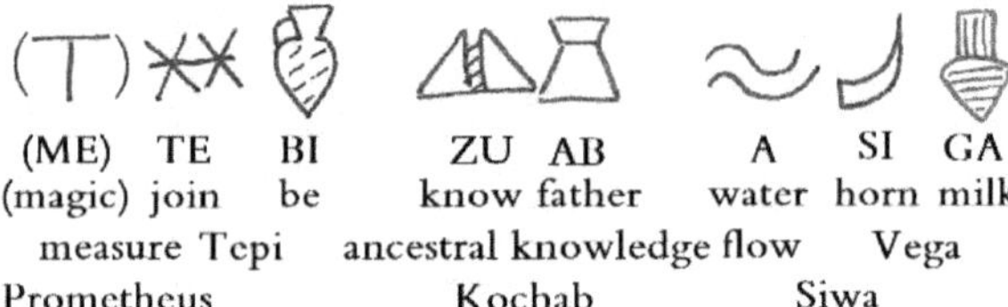

(ME)	TE	BI	ZU	AB	A	SI	GA
(magic)	join	be	know	father	water	horn	milk
measure	Tepi		ancestral	knowledge	flow		Vega
Prometheus				Kochab			Siwa

His father to know and the way of the ocean's flow,
on the Tether of the Perfect Pitch, tied to the horn of the cow,
to her spring of milk the sailor will go.

(Knowledge in the Pyramid of the Ancestor is tied together by Pi.)

22 / 7 = 3.142857

Behold, I am coming soon. (Revelation 22:7)

23. The Question

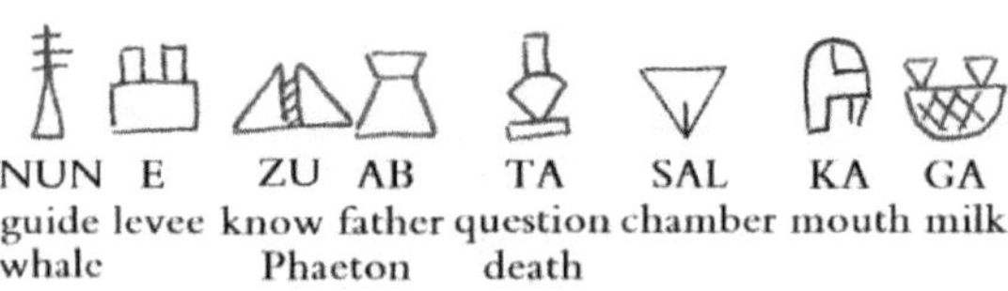

NUN	E	ZU	AB	TA	SAL	KA	GA
guide	levee	know	father	question	chamber	mouth	milk
whale			Phaeton		death		

To the lofty Nun at the levee, the question of his father's death
in Her chamber (Salus, whale) he will softly whisper.

24. Guide Stone

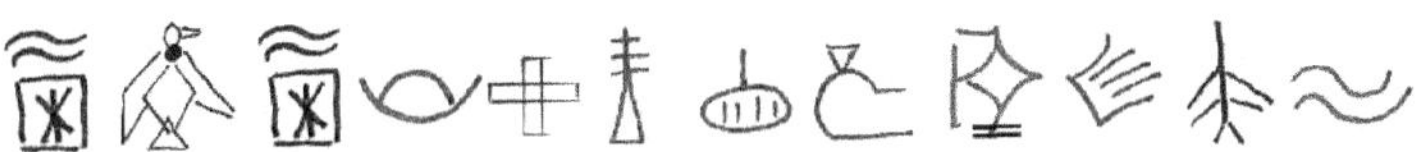

ID₂ IDIGNA ID₂ UD KIB NUN NA MAH NI₂ ŠU TI   A
river fierce river sun ring guide stone great soul hand arrow flow
Tigris   Euphrates   Sagittarius Sirius

Between the two rivers, the ring-necked bird on the great stone guide
to the otherworldly crossing of the sun (ecliptic) and the soul
points the way (and shows the arrow's flow).

25. On a Wave

ZU AB AN EN KI KID UL LA NE IN DU MU
know sea   sky lord place mat wave hang fire straw carry age
Scorpio Cygnus

His father to know on the sea in the sky,
the ghostly lord thrust forward on a wave,
with fire in the straw will establish the new age.

26. The Skull Takes Flight

GIZ SAG KUL ZU GABA ŠU GAR NU TUK
beam head bowl know spread hand measure not take
(1)   skull   pause wing   play
Sagittarius   Cygnus

GIZ By the beam of the moon and in a thunderbolt,
the brainless skull – the size of the gap not knowing,
the measure of the spreading wing not taking...
(a pause...the measure not playing.)

*(Cygnus)...and it was considered to be Orpheus, placed after death in
the heavens, near to his favourite Lyre. (Star Names[6], p.193)*

27. Knowledge of the Lion

GIZ	SI	GAR	ZU	UR MAH	NI₂	IL₂	RU
beam	horn	measure	know	lion great	soul	climb	fall
(2)		claw		pyramid	Sphinx Leo		rise	set

GIZ In its beam, the measure of the horn (Taurus, moon) to know,

the Great Lion and the soul will rise and fall.

28. Passing Through

GIZ	UR₃	ZU	GUD	AN	NA	MUS₃	KUK	GALAM	KA	GA
beam	roof	know	bull	sky	stone	space	circle	fish	mouth	milk
(3)				above	below			Piscis Austrinus		

GIZ In its beam, sweeping through on the Bull of Above and Below,

in the Place of Dividing Reeds to circle

with the fish, its mouth to the milk (Fomalhaut),

the cog-boat will go.

The moon, likewise, who presides over generation, was called by them a bee, and also a bull. And Taurus is the exaltation of the moon. But bees are ox-begotten. And this appellation is also given to souls proceeding into generation. The God, likewise, who is occultly connected with generation, is a stealer of oxen. (Porphyry, On Abstinence, trans. Taylor)

29. The False Door

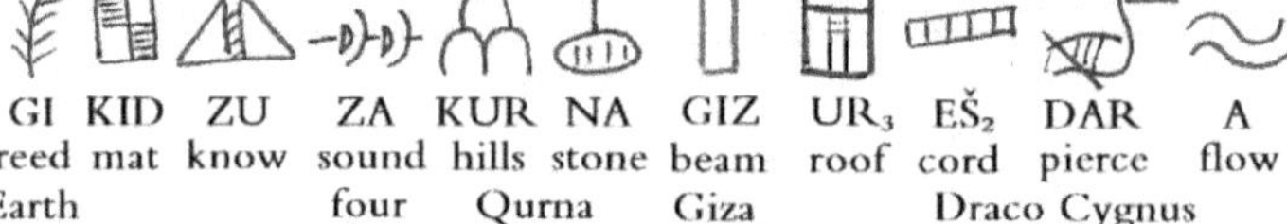

GI	KID	ZU	ZA	KUR	NA	GIZ	UR₃	EŠ₂	DAR	A
reed	mat	know	sound	hills	stone	beam	roof	cord	pierce	flow
Earth				four	Qurna	Giza		Draco	Cygnus	

The mat of the earth and its four corners of stone

to know, to the sounds of barking dogs and crows,

through the door in the roof beam of stone

on the cord of the bird

the boat will pierce the flow.

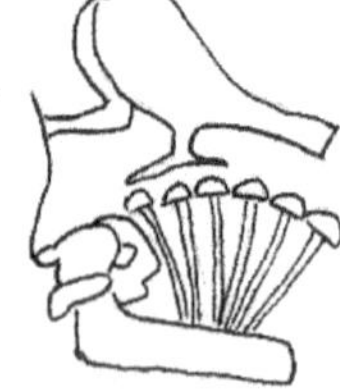

30. Exodus

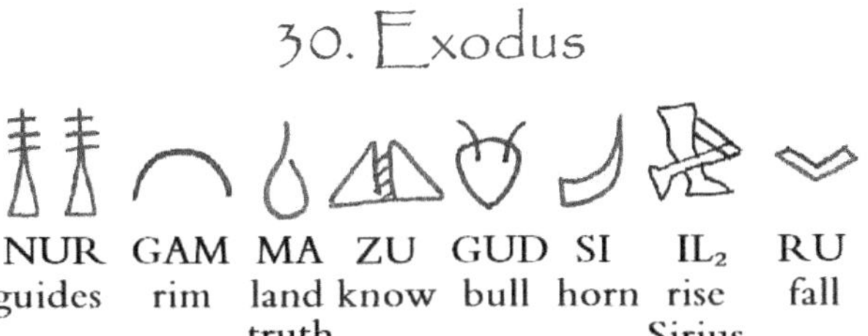

NUR	GAM	MA	ZU	GUD	SI	IL₂	RU
guides	rim	land	know	bull	horn	rise	fall
		truth				Sirius	

The otherworldly vault of the land (Eridanus) and the truth of its rim
to know, on the horn of the bull (Taurus, moon) it will rise and fall.

31. The Lion's Gate

KAN₄	ZU	UR	MAH	NI₂	ŠU	TI	A
gate	know	lion	great	soul	show	arrow	flow
Cancer		Leo	Sphinx	self		Sothis	

The Gate to know, the Great Lion to itself and to the soul
the way of the arrow's flow will show.

32. Illumination

I   LU   ZU   PIRIG-UD LU₂ RA LAGARg-DU NE
multiple light know   lion sun man churn mound carry fire
moon pyramid Sphinx   Ra   sun

Illumination to know by the light of many moons,
the Lion of the Sun and the man with the thresh (Ra)
up and down the mound will carry the fire - again.

33. Measuring Cord

ZU   AB   KI   SAL SI   ME TE IG

know sea   place pure magic join door

Kochab   key   El   Prometheus

His father to know, at the door to Her chamber,

the sailor by a magic tether (temenos)

will be guarded and his fear measured.

34. The Way

E₂ ENGUR RA LUGAL ZU   GIR₃ IM MA RI   IN DU

temple block churn king know path clay land gather straw carry

In the Temple of the Winding Canal,

the king will learn the way,

on the wind of the land and on the bird carried,

and in the immaculate clay (of Ma'at) the truth of the land will gather.

(The King) will cross with you on Thoth's wing to the other side of the Winding Canal, to the eastern side of the sky. (Book of the Dead, trans. J.P. Allen, 1910)

35. Beyond the Horizon

AN EN KI LUGAL ZU   AB   KID

sky lord earth king   know ocean sail

Kochab

Lord between Sky and Earth, the king his ancestor to know,

on the ghostly ocean of the abyss...

36. Lunar, Solar and Sothic

TE	ZU	NI.UD	ZA	GUL	IM	MA	DA	AN	DI
tether	know	night day	sound	carve	clay	land	side	sky	divide
witness		necessary	364	365			Danaus		divine

Of necessity, the tether of night and day he must learn,

to the sound and tooth of the Ghoul (Algol),

by the immaculate arm in the sky

and in the divisions of the clay to be judged.

$$25,920 / 360 = 72 \rightarrow$$
$$1,460 / 36.5 = 40 \rightarrow$$

37. Kali Yuga

KA LI	KA LI	ZA	KUR	NA	SAL	IM	MA	RI	IN KA
mouth song	lips	sound	hills	stone	cave	wind	land	gather	in say
Kali Calliope			Qurna						

Kali…Kali… words on the lips of time,

to the noise from the stone hills,

"Fly into my mouth, into my chamber of stone

on the wind of the land." She sings,

"In clay of the land collect the truth."

38. Mill of Seasons

E₂	AN	EN	KI	KID	LAL₃	HUR	RA	KUK	ŠI.ERIN₂	AK
temple	sky	lord	earth	mat	honey	mill	churn	circle	eye yoke	do
						horaion			Sirius	

On the Mill of Summer, the vessel of the lord with honey and round curses churning, all vision in the circling cog-boat is obscured.

"summer honey," which, from the circumstance of its being produced at the most favourable season, has received the Greek name of horaion; it is generally made during the next thirty days after the solstice, while Sirius is shining in all its brilliancy. (Pliny, Natural History, Bk 11, Ch.14)

39. Osiris and the Bull

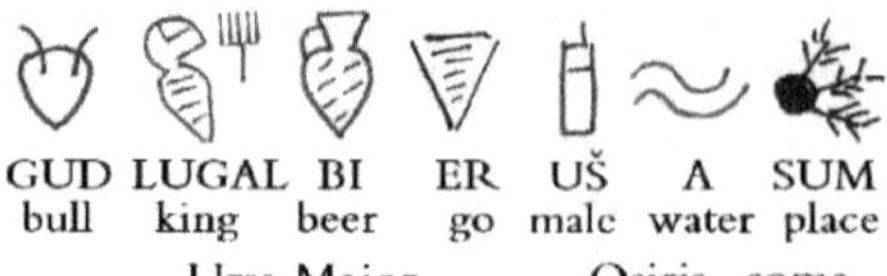

GUD	LUGAL	BI	ER	UŠ	A	SUM
bull	king	beer	go	male	water	place
	Ursa Major				Osiris	soma

The Bull to the king on his bier serves the brew
(Osiris, soma) and with a virile shove
into the water pushes him.

40. Music of the Sphinx

NI₂	BI	EŠ₂	HAR	DU	UR	BI	EŠ₂	AD	GI₄	GI₄
soul	brew	chord	mill	carry	dog	brew	cord	seal	stylus	turn
bee			Sphinx		Sirius	Orpheus		Atlantis		

Around the mill the soul with the brew,
the dogs (Sphinx, Sirius) and the bees
on the cords all giddily whirling
among the reeds.

(On the adamantine seal of the ancestor
under the foot of the Sphinx
the story of Atlantis is recorded.)

← 36.5 x 40 = 1,460

41. The Emerald Tablet

E₂ ENGUR RA AN EN KI KID GI DUB BA AN KUK LAL A AN
temple block churn sky lord place mat stylus write less sky circle hang to be
                          Emerald Tablet   small
                          Earth   Thuban Draco

In the Temple of the Winding Canal, the lord on his mat of reeds
an Emerald Tablet will write about the snake
found hanging in the skies above and below.

42. Forty-Two Questions

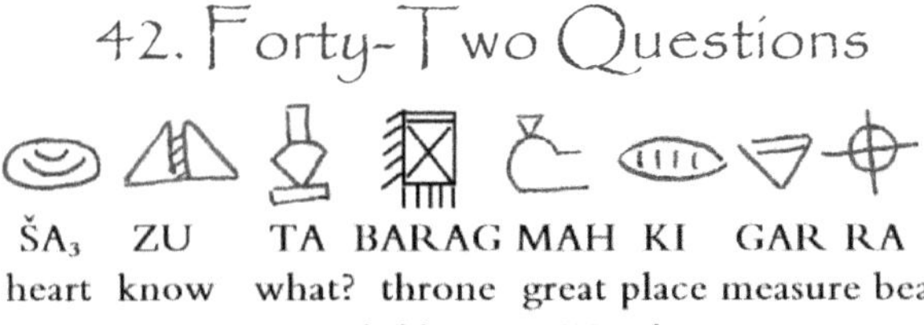

ŠA₃ ZU   TA BARAG MAH KI GAR RA
heart know what? throne great place measure beat
            Mahabharata   Kimah

The heart of death to know and its truth to question,
in the Great Throne Room (Mahabharata)
he will measure the beat of that place.

*At once I was in the Spirit, and I saw a throne standing in heaven,
with someone seated on it. (Revelation 4:1-2)*

43. Marking Time

ZAG GAB   ZU   ID MUŠ₃ KUK AN   NA
mark spread know time space circle above below
432 Gabriel   Astarte

The boundaries of time and space on the Pyramid of Knowledge to mark,
a mighty spread wing (Astarte, Attar) circles above and below.

25,920 / 432 = 60 →

44. Father and Mother

ZU	AB	KI	SAL	SI	KI	NAM	TAR	RA
know	sea	place	pure	place		fate	cut	churn
Apollo		El						Tara

Of his father to know, in the Chamber of the Pure Horn
his fate and the fate of the stars to learn …

45. Do You Hear?

EN	GIZ	TUG₂	PE	GA	LUGAL	AN	EN	KI
lord	tree	hear	pitch	white	king	sky	lord	place
	shaft	cover	Vega	Pegasus				

In the Tree of Consciousness and Knowledge,
covered from end to end by its beam of perfect white,
the king will hear its perfect pitch …

He who has an ear, let him hear what the Spirit says to the churches.
(Revelation 3:22)

46. Annunciation

AN	NU	DIM₂	HU.HI	EN	NUN	KI	GA	KID
sky	knot	create	bird	hole	lord	guide	place	milk	kid
						Cedalion		

As through the feathered hole in the ring of time, with his guide
to the otherworldly place (and the milk of fools) he flies.

47. A Golden Fleece

ŠA₃	ŠEG₉	BAR	RA	LU₂	ŠI	NU	BAR	RI	DAM
heart	ice	out	churn	man	see	not	out	collect	trust
		Aries		Lucifer	Orion		bark		spouse

Blindly into the wilderness and its heart of ice,
the light not seeing (Orion, lucida),
in his bark the man must trust.

48. Guides of the In-Between

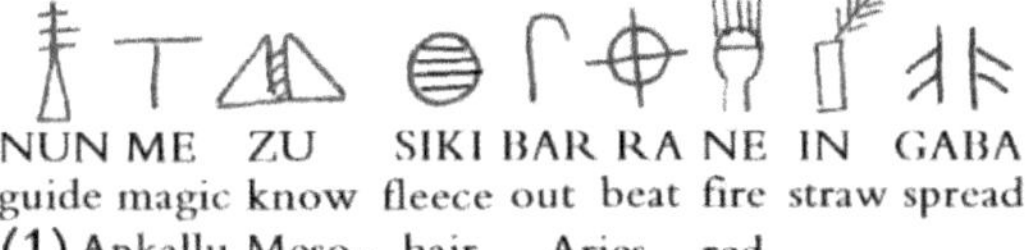

NUN	ME	ZU	SIKI	BAR	RA	NE	IN	GABA
guide	magic	know	fleece	out	beat	fire	straw	spread
(1) Apkallu	Meso-		hair		Aries		red	

The magic to know of the otherworldly Spirit Guides (Apkallu),
Magicians of the In-Between (Mesopotamian),
the golden fleece of a wild animal on the straw is spread.

49. The Three Keys

NUN	KI	AN	EN	KI	KID	KI	NINDA₂	MAL	NI
guide	place	sky	lord	earth	mat	place	(NE)	basket	oil
(2)			Enkelados				volcano Aries		

In otherworldly places to measure their fire,
the hot-headed lord with his basket full of oil…

50. The Argonauts

E₂ ENGUR RA ŠA₃ BI GAN IG SUD GA
temple blocks churn heart brew womb door distant milk
Argo Navis Sabian Canopus Sothis cow

With bee and brew at its heart,
the vessel in the Winding Canal of Ra
to the door of the distant womb (Milky Way)
in the south will go.

51. Hot-head and the Ram

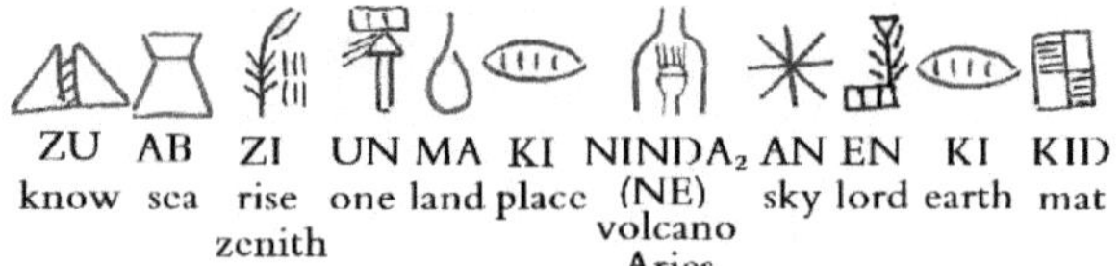

ZU AB ZI UN MA KI NINDA₂ AN EN KI KID
know sea rise one land place (NE) sky lord earth mat
   zenith   volcano
                     Aries

For the ocean to rise with the banner of the land, on a volcano
the hot-headed lord places his mat and measures its fire.

52. At Midnight

E₂ ZAG GA KAK A ME GALAM MA DU MA
temple mark cow nail flow magic fish land carry land
Pleiades keystone mega– madhu truth

From the temple on the shoulder of the Cow (Pleiades),
a peg of measurement nailed in its flow,
the Great Fish will carry the mead of truth from land to land.

53. A Shady Beam

NUN   KI   GIZ   MI   ZU   AB   ŠA₃   GA   LAL   A
guide place beam black know ocean heart milk check flow
whale   Giza   pyramid

In the otherworldly Place of Lost Fish, and in the shade
of the Tree of Knowledge of the Father,
to the heart of the Ocean of Milk the sailor will go to check its flow.

54. Maestro of the Milk Ocean

A   AB   BA   ZI   GA   GABA   ŠU   GAR   NU   TUK
water ocean low rise milk spread show measure not play
fatherless Zeus   gap   maestro   note
(5)   —   (4)

On the waters of the abyss below to rise with its milk,
a spreading hand… a pause… and the measure of the knot is taken.
(the note not yet played, music interval).

And they sang a new song (Revelation 5:11)

54 + 54 = 108 →

55. The Truth

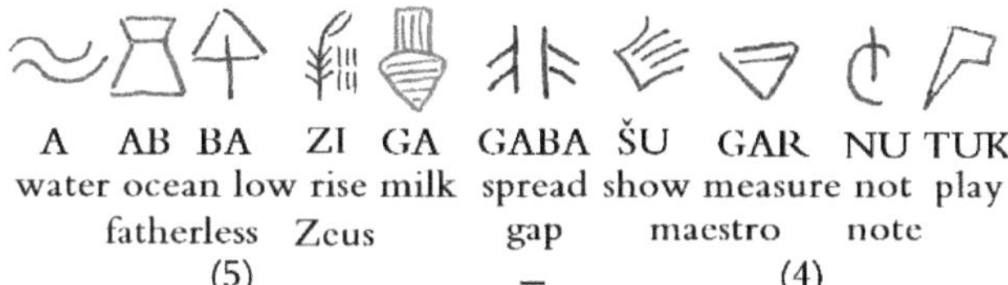

ID₂   MAH   NI₂   IG   LA   SU   UN   MA   ZI   ZI
river great   soul door weigh sink people land life rise
Ma'at Maha   Pyramid of Truth
(5)   —   (4)

On the great river of Maha before the three temples,
the soul at the Weighing Door (of Ma'at) will learn the one truth
of the balance between sinking and rising in the land.

56. Orion and Osiris

E₂	ENGUR	RA	URUxUD	MAH	KI	UŠ	SA
temple	divided	churn	pyramid	sun great	place	male	trap
(1)		Ra	Orion	Kimah		Osiris	

In the churning, winding canal of Ra (Lord of the Knotted Vine),
from the Great Pyramid of the Sun
to the Place of Maha (Pleiades), a man-trap is set.

I hang the Stars with Meshes for Men's Souls:
The Garden underneath my Music rolls.
(Conference of the Birds, Attar, Trans. Fitzgerald)

57. The Lion's Arm

E₂	DA	ENGUR	RA	PIRIG	ZU	AB	ŠA₃	GA
temple	arm	block	churn	lion	know	abyss	heart	milk
(2)	next to			sun		Sphinx Leo		

By the temple on the bank of the winding canal,
the fiery lion with the sailor to the ocean's heart of milk will go.

58. Giza

E₂	MAH	AN	EN	KI	KID	GIZ	TUG₂	PI	UN	E	SUM	MU
temple	great	sky	lord	earth	mat	beam	hear	perfect	land	lift	place	name
(3)	Ma'at			Tree of Consciousness and Knowledge								

From the great Temple of Ma'at, the lord with
the Beam of Knowledge of the Perfect Pitch
will rise to the levee and at its summit will place
his mat and the banner of the land with
the One Supreme Name
and the sum of their age.

59. Preparing the String

GAD	TAK₄	SI	ZU	ID₂	MAH	ZI	GA	DIM₂

GAD TAK₄ SI ZU ID₂ MAH ZI GA DIM₂
string pull finger know river great rise milk create
Ascella   cow limb

Drawing back the string of the bow (and of the lyre),

the great river of Maha and its milk he will cause to rise.

(Sagittarius) The Latin Almagest of 1515 gives this as Ascella, i.e. Axilla, the Armpit of the figure, still its location on the maps. (Star Names [6], p.358)

60. Music of the Spheres

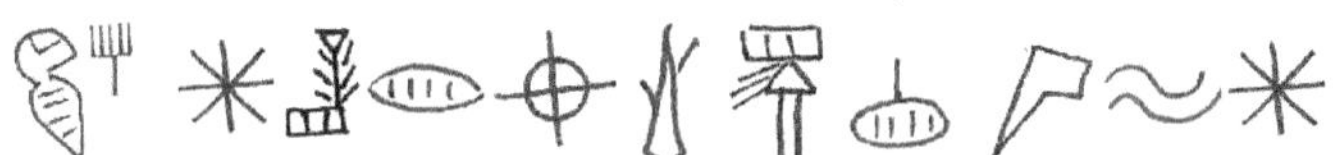

LUGAL AN EN KI RA MU UN NA TUK A AN
king   sky lord earth churn name land stone play flow sky
              sun   moon   music   to be

As the king and lord between earth and sky his music plays (Orpheus),

the sun and moon with all the stones of Time and Place

are churned and the sky weeps.

$$\leftarrow\ 25{,}920\ /\ 60 = 432$$

He discovered that the string stretched by the greatest weight, when compared with that stretched by the smallest weight, the interval of an octave. (Theoretical Music, from Nicomachus, Ch. XXVI, The Complete Pythagorus. Trans. Guthrie)

61. Moon Houses

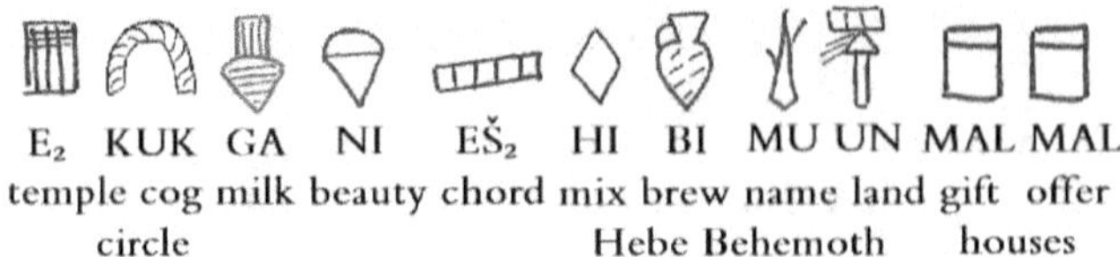

E₂ KUK GA NI EŠ₂ HI BI MU UN MAL MAL
temple cog milk beauty chord mix brew name land gift offer
circle Hebe Behemoth houses

In the Temple of the Circling Cow, with the beauty of his chord
to woo the High Bee and to mix their brews,
the moon and the name of the land in his offering baskets.

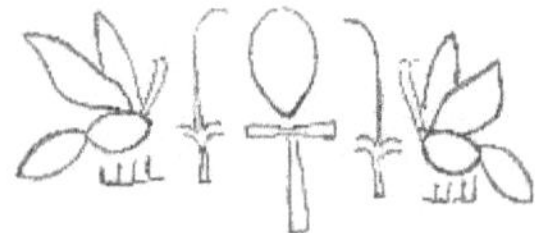

62. Maestro of the Beams of Giza

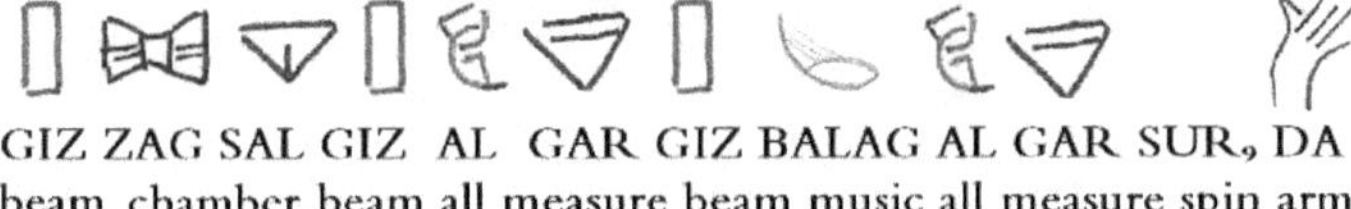

GIZ ZAG SAL GIZ AL GAR GIZ BALAG AL GAR SUR₉ DA
beam chamber beam all measure beam music all measure spin arm
(1) mark (2) (3) side

GIZ Between the beams with his bow to mark Her fine chamber,
GIZ between the beams to give the measure of everything,
GIZ to the music of his lyre
all the measures spinning at his command.

63. Trap of Osiris

GIZ HAR HAR GIZ SA NE TUM GIZ MI URU TUM E₂ SI GA
beam mill grind shaft trap fire belt beam night under inherit temple horn milk
Giza Sphinx Lyra strings Jessu Orion mound memory Vega
(1) (2) Alnitak (3) Pleiades

GIZ Two shafts around two mills (and two harps),
GIZ between their beams in a net (of 14 strings) to trap the fire,
GIZ from the dark beam in the belly of the pyramid
to the Temple on the Horn of the Cow.

64. At the Golden Gate

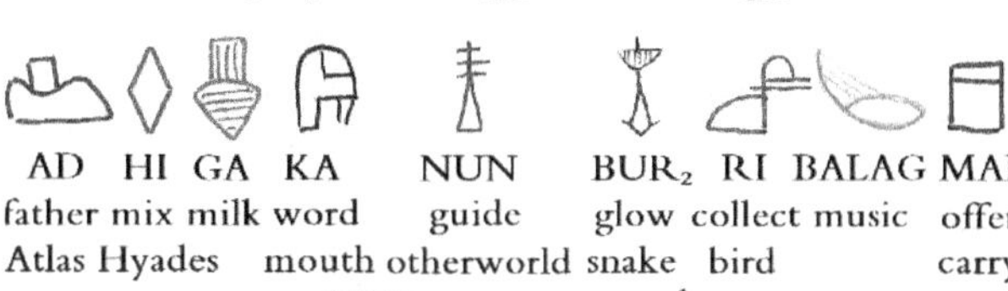

AD	HI	GA	KA	NUN	BUR₂	RI	BALAG	MAL
father	mix	milk	word	guide	glow	collect	music	offer
Atlas	Hyades		mouth	otherworld	snake	bird		carry
				canon	ouroboros			

To mix the milk of the Father (Atlas),

as through the veil he goes, to the music of the strings

the voices and the measured words of the guides are offered.

65. Atlantis Below

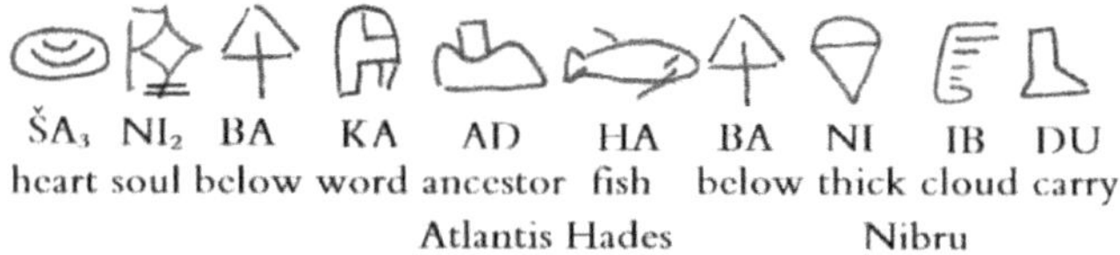

ŠA₃	NI₂	BA	KA	AD	HA	BA	NI	IB	DU
heart	soul	below	word	ancestor	fish	below	thick	cloud	carry
				Atlantis	Hades			Nibru	

Of the Father of the Fish below and his selfless heart they sing,

in a thick cloud below to be carried...

*and the island of Atlantis in like manner was swallowed up by the sea
and vanished; wherefore also the ocean at that spot has now become
impassable and unsearchable, being blocked up by the shoal mud
which the island created as it settled down. (Plato, Timaeus 25d)*

66. Measuring Seaweed

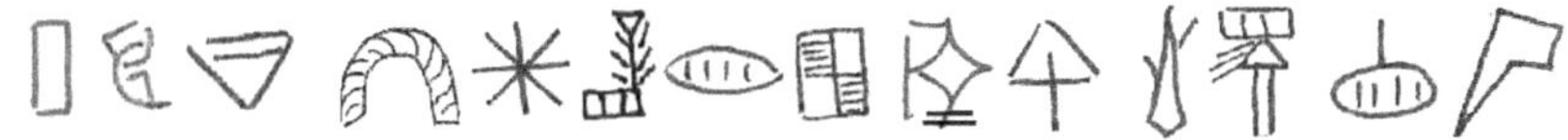

GIZ	AL	GAR	KUK	AN	EN	KI	KID	NI₂	BA	MU	UN	NA	TUK
beam	all	measure	circle	sky	lord	earth	mat	soul	less	time	land	stone	play
Giza				above						world		below	

In the beam, the ocean floor to circle and to measure,

the foolish lord to lesser souls (and the soulless)

without music in the land below

(and less on the stones of the land above)

will play!

67. Songs of the Stars

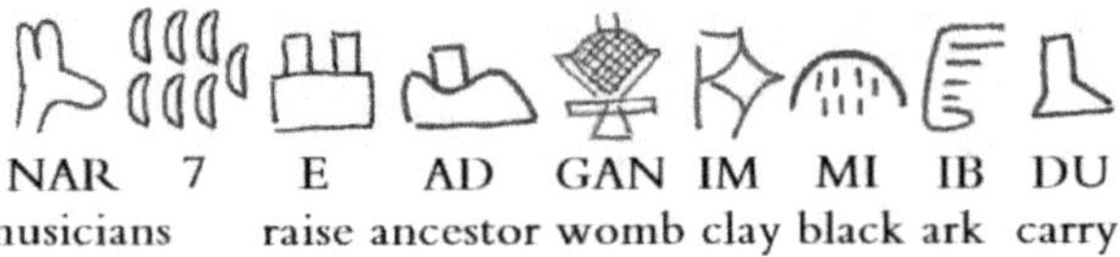

NAR	7	E	AD	GAN	IM	MI	IB	DU
musicians		raise	ancestor	womb	clay	black	ark	carry
Pleiades			Atlas			swarm	cloud	

The seven musicians will raise him to the levee of the Ancestor
and into the darkness of the womb the ark will carry.

68-69. The Whale

KA	GA	AN	EN	KI	KID	ŠU	NU	BAL	E	NE
mouth	milk	sky	lord	place	fool	show	not	spin	rise	fire
Milky Way						nosos		baleen	whale	

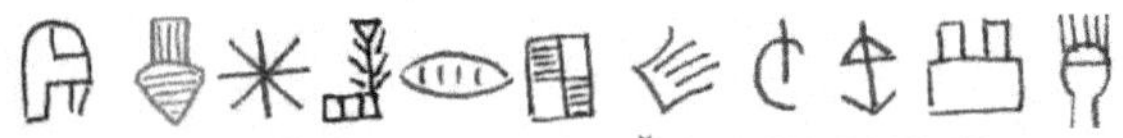

KA	(two words missing)	KI	BI	EŠ₂	IG	LA	A	AN
mouth		place	brew	cord	door	weigh		to be

Softly singing of the white mouth in the sky,
the foolish lord not seeing it, the spinning hand not showing it…
the mouth (two words missing) of a whale by the weighing door
and the chord of the bees hanging open there will be.

*(Aspidochelone) a great whale, that has what appear to be beaches on
its hide, like those from the sea-shore. (Physiologus, 2ⁿᵈ century AD)*

70. Cleansing

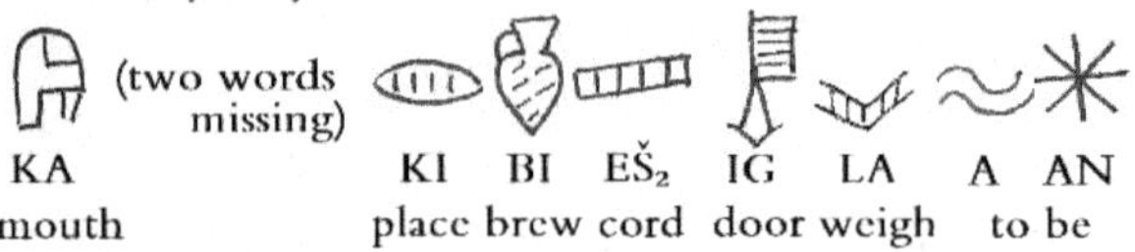

LUH	AN	PAP	ŠIg	NE	SIG₄	E	KA	BA	AN	SUM
quiver	sky	wean	eye	new	wall	levee	say	less	sky	add
clean		baptism		fire					underground	

"Cleansed by weeping and by fire, in the mouth of the whale below,
his fiery words carved into the wall of the levee above will be."
(they say.)

71. The Hemi-sphere

E₂ ENGUR RA KID SAL HI GI EŠ IM ME
temple canal churn mat chamber veil rod three spirit magic
Salus Hygeia Trismegistus

"In the winding canal and in Her Chamber
beyond the veil (hive, heaven) to be cleansed,
his spirit and three arrows immersed in Her clay."

72. Pause

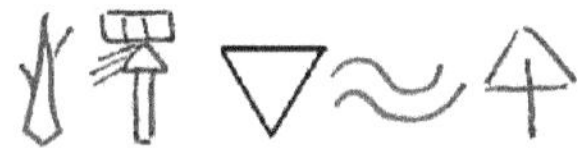

MU UN KAK A BA
age land nail water below
keystone

MU UN KAK A BA
age land nail water below
keystone

"From one age of the world to another to flow,
carved on two keystones in the water below."

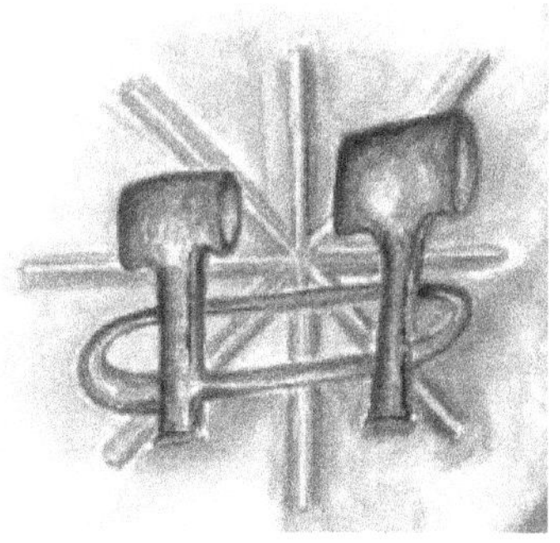

← 36 + 36 = 72   72 + 36 = 108 →

73. Virgin Birth

NUN KI AN EN KI KID IM MA ANU IL₂ LA BA
guide place sky lord earth mat clay land sky rise weigh less
Djed   Immanuel Sirius
                                  Anubis

In the otherworldly Place of the Whale,

the lord from the immaculate clay of the Mother of the Land

and in Her Truth weightless to the sky will rise.

← 20 x 73 = 1460

Behold, a virgin shall conceive and bear a son, and shall call his name Immanuel. By the time He knows enough to reject evil and choose good. He will be eating curds and honey. (Isaiah 7:14-15)

74. In the Fish to Trust

HUR SAG GALAM KAD₅ DAM A   E   BA AN SI A
mill head fish   tie trust swim high low sky horn flow
Sagittarius Pisces   evangel

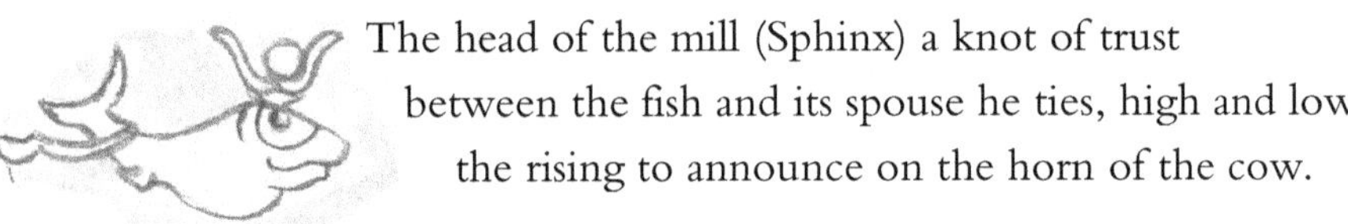

The head of the mill (Sphinx) a knot of trust
between the fish and its spouse he ties, high and low
the rising to announce on the horn of the cow.

75-76. Agitation of the Cow

ZAG   GA   A   NI GIZ GI A BA AN KU
shoulder cow flow thick wood rod flow less sky sit
mark Pleiades   shaft arrow   hole

GIZ SAR   ŠIg   GA GURUN IL₂ LA   A BA
tree orchard meadow milk fruit raise weigh flow below
beam   blind   Corona

The shoulder of the cow to move, with his prod he forces it to sit.

In the blinding beam of her milk, he hangs weightless

with the fruit of the orchard over the water below.

77. Bird and Bee

HU   E   ZUM   BI   MU   UN   MAL   MAL

bird   levee   revolve   total   time   land   basket   offer
Hubal   bee   sedge   houses

With the lofty bird around the levee revolving,
the total ages of the world and the renowned brew
in his travelling baskets.

78. Changing Times

SUHUR   HA   E   U₂   LAL₃   E   E   NE   MU   UN   E

tuft   fish   levee   pipe   honey   rise   high   fire   age   land   rise
Pisces   (1)   Aquarius   (2)   (3)   move   (4)

To the sweet stream from the honeyed pipes (Aquarius)
the fish with a new age rises again and again.

79. Behemoth

GUD   HA   E   GI   ZI   TUR   TUR   LAL   KUN   MU   UN   NA   SUD   E

bull   fish   levee   reed   lively   small   turn   hang   weir   age   land   stone   distant   raise
Bahar   turtle   Lyra   tail   moon   snake-head

Bull (Bahar) and fish to the levee rising,
among the lively reeds all turning and twisting,
on the tail of the turtle (Lyra, Vega) to hang the moon,
and on the weir of the world the distant stone to raise.

*For the mountains yield food for him where all the wild beasts play.
Under the lotus plants he lies, in the shelter of the reeds and in the
marsh. For his shade the lotus trees cover him; the willows of the brook
surround him.*

80. Three Times to Rise

AN	EN	KI	ZI	GA	NA	HA	I	ZI	EŠ₂	NA	ZI
sky	lord	place	rise	milk	stone	fish	many	rise	rope	stone	rise
	Zeus			Naga				3/2	chord		

The lord between sky and earth with the stone rises,

The heavy cow, the water birds and a multitude of fish with

the white stone on the snake-rope (chord) rise.

To the one who overcomes, I will give the hidden manna. I will also give him a white stone inscribed with a new name, known only to the one who receives it. (Revelation 2:17)

81. Indestructible Eye

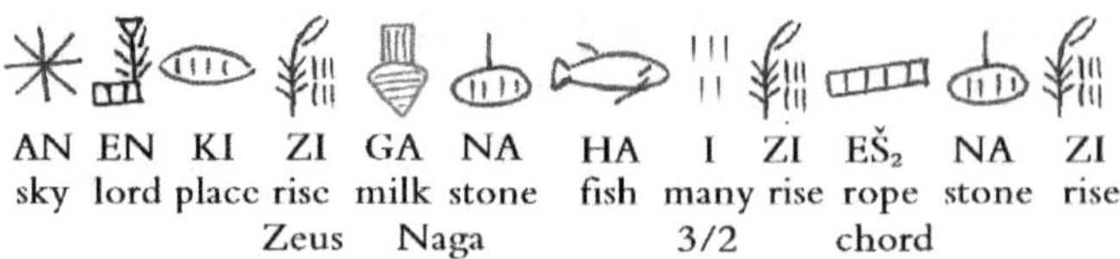

KUŠ	AB	E	ŠI	E₂	A	AN	MA	DU
know	ocean	rise	eye	temple		to be	land	carry
Kochab				pyramidion			madhu (1)	

To the top of the Pyramid (Kochab) it rises,

as the Eye of the Temple there to remain,

the truth of Ma in Her mead to carry to the land.

82. Wing of the Stone Dodo

ENGUR	RA	HUL₂	LA	MU	NI	IB	DU
canal	churn	joyful	hang	age	thick	cloud	carry
						oil	wing (2)
					Great Rift		dodo

In the winding waterway joyfully to hang,

by the two feet of the sailor and the wing (dodo, Dodona),

the ark in a thick cloud (Nibru, Great Rift) is carried.

83. Because I rest upon the Abyss

A   AB BA DIM₂ NI₂ MU UN DA IG
water father less create soul time land side door
abyss   daemon open

But to the fatherless waters of the abyss
and to the daemons of the spirit world by the limb of the bull
a side-door has been opened…

84. The Flood

ID₂ MAH DIM₂ SU ZI MU UN DU RI
river great create sink rise age land carry fly
(1)   Boötes   Zeus   banner Eridanus

… and a great river created,
where the sinking and the rising of the ages of the world
are carried by the eternal bird.

85. Drum Roll

ID₂ UD KIB NUN NA GIZGAL.LU SAGg MU UN DA AN ZI
river sun cross guide stone pyramid light head move land arm sky rise
(2)   Euphrates   Orion moon   banner Dan
        Sippar   Sagittarius   Scorpio

From the river by the boundary stone of the sun (ecliptic),
to the beating of the drum, on two great beams,
by the light of the moon, the skull is raised to the sky.

(Scorpio) *and, it is claimed, inscribed it on the banners of
Dan as the emblem of the tribe whose founder was
"a serpent by the way." (Star Names [6], p.362)*

86. Snakes Alive

GIZ GI MUŠ A NI AN MUŠ A NI
tree rod snake animate sky snake animate
Moses Draco

GIZ On the earthly branch, the snake comes to life.
In the sky, the snake comes to life.

(The souls of sailors carried on the wind come to life.)

Then the LORD said to Moses, "Make a fiery serpent
and mount it on a pole. When anyone who is bitten
looks at it, he will live." (Numbers 21:8)

87. On the Move

GIZ GISAL A NI GI TUR TUR A NI
beam be shaft water thick reed small turn flow thick
tortoise Lyra

GIZ All of the shafts and beams come to life.
Twisting and turning, the reeds and the tiny tortoise
come to life…

For it was Hermes who first made the tortoise a singer…
(Hymn 4 to Hermes, trans. Evelyn-White)

88. To the Womb

AN EN KI HU SI A NI MU GAN IG SUD GA
sky lord earth bird beak animate age womb door south milk
Cygnus Great Rift

The lord and the beak of the bird come to life,
as to the door of the distant open womb they go.

89. Boat of Souls

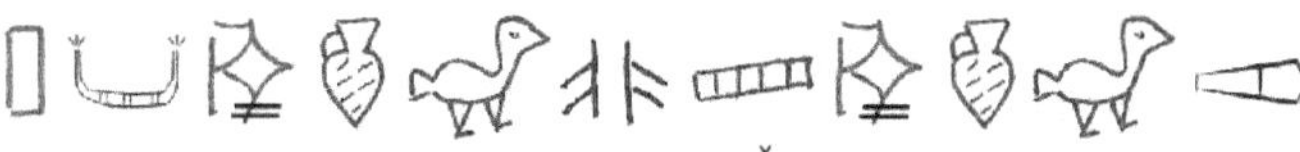

GIZ	MA₂	NI₂	BI	NAM	GABA	EŠ₂	NI₂	BI	NAM	KU
beam	boat	soul	to be	fate	spread	rope	soul	to be	fate	seize
mast				Siren	gap	chord				

GIZ On the beam of the Boat of Souls

the ropes are spread, and the spirits with the birds of fate

on the cord are seized and drawn towards the hole.

90. Snake of the Sun

E₂	NUN	KI	GA	LIL₂	IM	MA	TE	A	RA
temple	guide	place	milk	fool	wind	land	tether	flow	churn
				lily			snake	harbour	sun

In the temple of the otherworldly guide, place of the milk of fools,

tethered to the churning snake and on the wind of the land,

to the harbour of the underworld his vessel is carried.

91. Second Death

ID₂	NE	LUGAL	BI	ER	AD	IM	MI	IB	GI₄	GI₄
river	fire	king	bee	err	seal	clay	black	cloud	stylus	turn
							swarm	ark		

On a river of fire, the king on his bier must err,

and in a black cloud the wings of the ark (ibis),

among the swarming spirits of the night

(the stylus of the ancestor in dark clay) flutter.

Behold with the staff in my hand I will strike the water of the Nile, and it will turn to blood. (Exodus 7:17)

Over the mountains, rising in its flight, 'The Clay Eye' around the sky is fluttering. (The Story of Sukurru, line 130)

92. KAKAKAKTUS

KA BI KA AMAR RA KA AB₂ HI GA KID
word bee word calf churn word cow mix milk fool
Kabeiri   Marduk   Hekate

"The brew of the bee (Kabeiri) and the beer of the bitter son of Ra
(Golden Calf) will be mixed into milk for the fool,"
a cackling voice like flowing thorns (cactus, acacia) is heard to say…

*Then he took the calf they had made, burned it in the fire, ground it
to powder, and scattered the powder over the face of the water.
(Exodus 32:20)*

93. Comet Strike

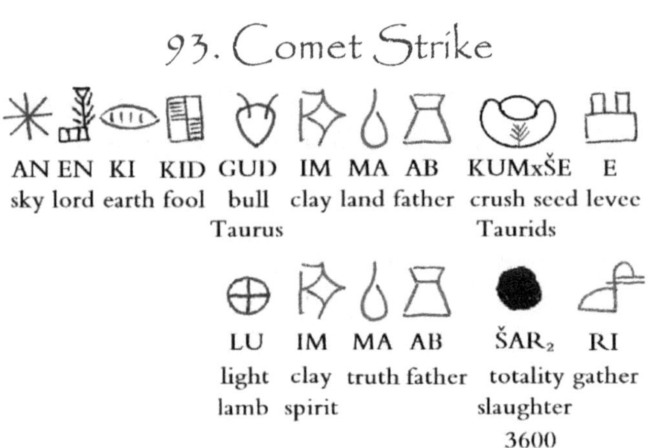

AN EN KI KID GUD IM MA AB KUMxŠE E
sky lord earth fool bull clay land father crush seed levee
          Taurus   Taurids

LU IM MA AB ŠAR₂ RI
light clay truth father totality gather
lamb spirit   slaughter
                       3600

"The foolish lord between sky and earth,
for mortar to make clay of the land of both Mother and Father,
his seed with the seeds of the bull will be crushed in the levee,
and the lambs of light in clay of land and sea
all gathered and slaughtered!"

*In those days men will seek death and will not find it; they will long
to die, but death will escape them. (Revelation 9:6)*

94. Inside the Pyramid of Time

SU	ID	LAL	NU	IG	LA	KI	BI	EŠ₂	DI	IM	KA
know	strong	hang	not	door	hang	place	beer	cord	divide	clay	say
Pyramid of Time			6th gate					bee-line		pole	

"That knowledge of the Wing of Time not openly hang,

the door to the weighing place will be locked and guarded

by the chords of the bees, the clay divided

and your spirit judged." (the distant voice says.)

then Osiris got into it and lay down, and those who were in the plot ran to it and slammed down the lid, which they fastened by nails from the outside and also by using molten lead. (Plutarch, Of Isis And Osiris, 13:4)

95. Inside the Brazen Bull

AB₂xŠA₃	UD	KA	BAR	NU	IG	LA	KI	BI	EŠ₂	IM	MI	IN	UD	DU
cow	inner	heat	voice	far	not	open	hang	place	bee	chord	spirit	dark	in	sun	stand
brazen				7th gate							swarm			constant

"Inside the brazen bull, its door locked and guarded,

hanging in the place of the cord of bees, in a black cloud (swarm)

and in the heat of the unmoving sun to stand…"

The blood of slaughtered bullocks oft has borne bees from corruption.
(Virgil, *Georgics*, Bk.4)

96. Nibru

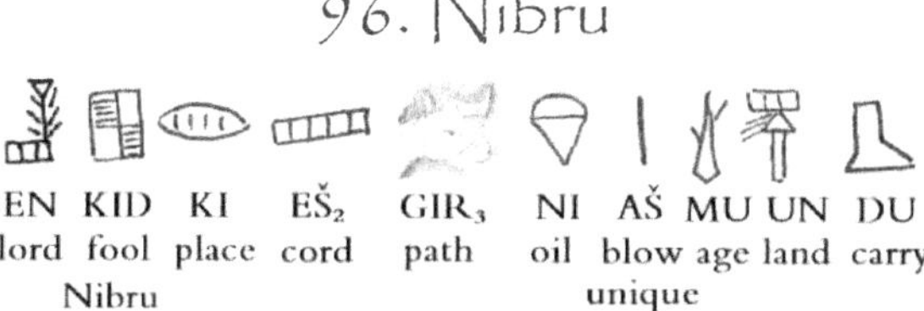

EN	KID	KI	EŠ₂	GIR₃	NI	AŠ	MU	UN	DU
lord	fool	place	cord	path	oil	blow	age	land	carry
Nibru						unique			

"The foolish lord (in Nibru) on the oiled path of the bull,

with a single stroke (of the dill stalk, of the mill handle)

to the world as ashes will be carried."

97. The Wobble

GE	ABg	NA	AB	E	EN	KID	KI	A	IM	MA	DA	AN	KU₄	KU₄

GE ABg NA AB E EN KID KI A IM MA DA AN KU₄ KU₄
rod ocean stone ocean raise lord mat place flow clay land side sky enter enter
Earth tilt heavy levee Nibru Scorpio Danaus seed ropes

The rod hits the stone and the stone hits the sea.
The ocean on one side tilts. On the other to the levee it rises with the lord,
as by the dancing arms in the sky
water and seeds into the immaculate clay of the land
from both sides enter.

98. Battle of the Bees

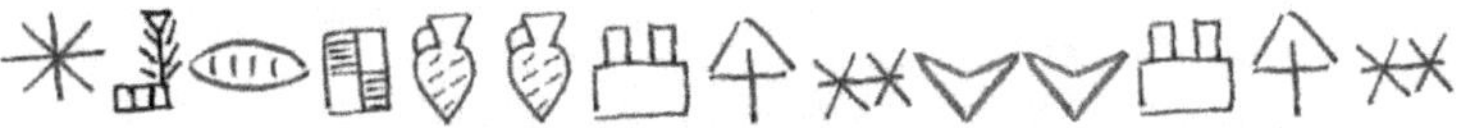

AN EN KI KID BI BI E BA TE DIN DIN E BA TE
sky lord earth mat bee brew levee low tether vine vine high low snake
baetyl Phaeton wine Eden baetyl Phaeton

The foolish lord between sky and earth with the bees
on either side of the trees (Eden) in the vines entangled,
high and low the winding snakes of above and below
from one end to the other all binding.

For oft 'twixt king and king with uproar dire fierce feud arises,
(Virgil, *Georgics*, Bk.4)

99. A Great Copper Bowl

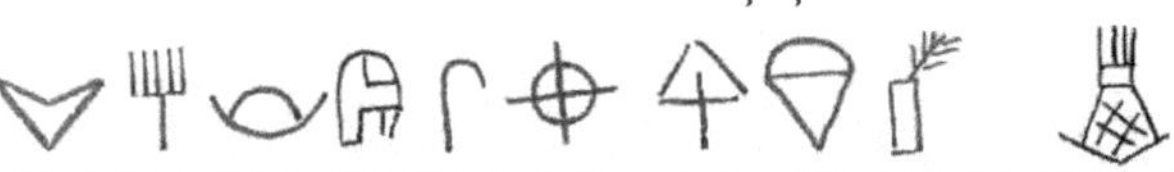

DIN GAL UD KA BAR RA BA NI IN UMUMxKAS
vine great sun word out churn below oil straw pour
wine brazen bowl Aquarius

"From one great vine into one great copper bowl below
the brew will be poured," a voice from the wilderness is heard to say,
"less roaring and churning in the Cask of Knowledge of the Crossroads."

100. Bitter-Sweet Brew

BI	BI	AŠ₂	A	AN	AŠ	A	AN	BA	NI	IN	SUR
brew	bee	curse	to	be	unique	to	be	less	oil	in	stir
					Ashvin						

"Bees and the brew of cursing, bees and the brew of blessing,
united they will be… less oil in to stir below."

101. The Competition

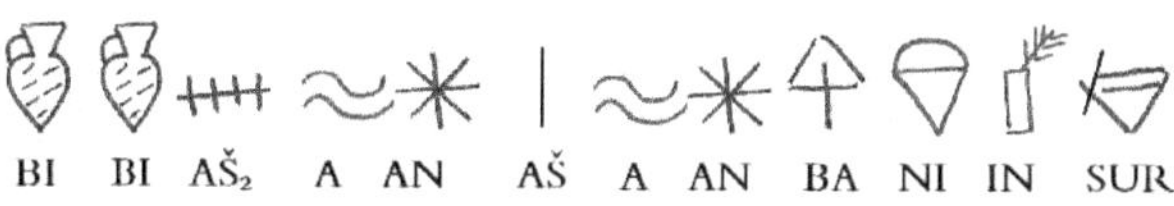

DUG	KU	KUR	KAK	BI	HI	HI	GA	GAB	BI	NE	IN	DI	DI
pot	hole	hills	nail	brew	mix	mix	milk	spread	brew	fire	straw	divide	judge
dog	sit			bee	veil		cow	gap	to be	red		Dioskouroi	
Anubis					Hebe	Hekate							

"Place a pot in a hole in the hills and separate
the brew of the bees from the milk of the cow,
that their boasting in the spreading fire (on the Milky Way)
and division of the straw be judged."

102. The Hum Begins

KA	BI	LAL₃	KA	HUM	MA	GAR	GIR₃	BA	NI	IN	AK
voice	brew	sweet	tell	loom	land	measure	path	less	oil	in	do
Kabeira				Homer							

(says) "The bittersweet voices of the honeybees
humming on the loom of Ma the truthful measure
of the path of the bull at night will tell…
and less stirring of the oil will do."

*When the flight of a swarm is imminent, a monotonous and quite
peculiar sound made by all the bees is heard for several days…
(Aristotle, The Nature of Animals, Part 40, Trans.)*

103. ⟨⟩ Separation ∿ of the Flow ⟨⟩

GAB	BI	GAR	LAL₃	LAL₃	AŠ	A	MUŠ₃.A.DI	EŠ₂	NE	IN	GAB

spread beer measure sweet honey one flow divide flow cord fire straw spread

Moses

The bitterness of the beer to measure against the sweetness of the honey,
with one blow (of the dill stalk) in a fiery chord
the flow is divided and fire in the straw spreads from end to end.

Then Moses stretched out his hand over the sea, and all that night the Lord drove back the sea with a strong east wind that turned it into dry land. So the waters were divided, (Exodus 14:21)

104. The Mirror

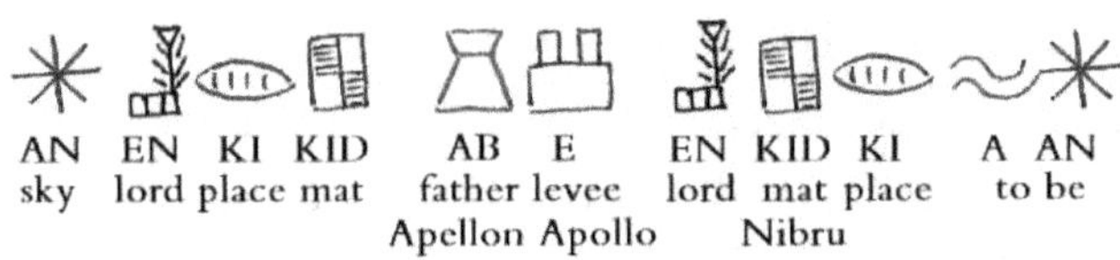

AN	EN	KI	KID	AB	E	EN	KID	KI	A	AN

sky — lord place mat — father levee — lord mat place — to be

Apellon Apollo — Nibru

In the middle of the levee (apex) at the centre of the skies,
face to face on their mats, two lords, Father and Son (Apollo, Enki, Enlil),
meet in the Place of the Ghostly Wing of Time (Nibru).

105. The Measuring

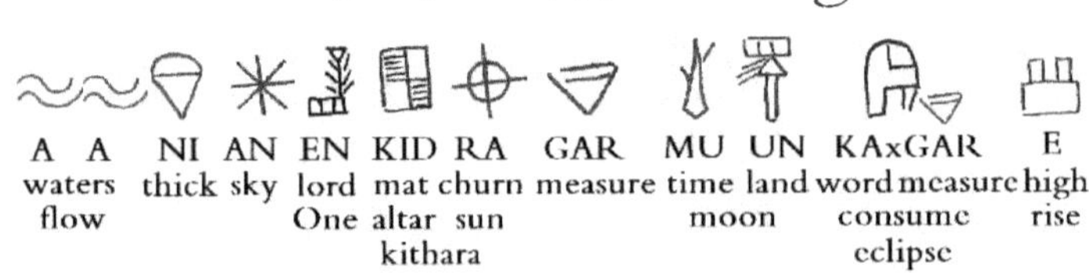

A	A	NI	AN	EN	KID	RA	GAR	MU	UN	KAxGAR	E

waters thick sky lord mat churn measure time land word measure high
flow — One altar sun — moon — consume — rise
kithara — eclipse

As the living waters of the One Lord begin to churn and rise,
the movements of sun and moon, of land and time
in measured words are called out on high.

The LORD said to Moses, "Behold, I will come to you in a dense cloud, so that the people will hear when I speak with you, and they will always put their trust in you." (Exodus 19:9)

106. From the Pleiades

AN	KI	MAH	A	IM	MA	AN	KU
celestial	place	great	water	clay	land	sky	hole
(1)	Kimah	Pleiades	Mahamaya				(1)

"At the Great Place of Maha where truth and water flow,
into the immaculate clay of the land
place a hole (to push the shaft)."

KU

107. Cross the Skies

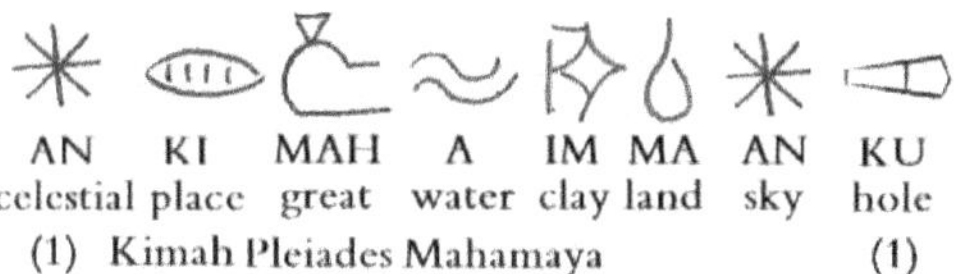

AN	RA	AN	EN	KID	IM	MA	NI	IN	UŠ
celestial	churn	sky	lord	fool	clay	land	oil	in	push
(2)	Ran						Mani		shaft
									(2)

"Cross with the sun to the churning hole at the heart of the sky,
into its thick clay (immaculate spirit and truth of Ma) to push the shaft."

KU - USH

108. To the Great Chamber

AN	SAL	TUG₂	TU	ZAG	GAL	LA	IM	MI	IN	KU

AN	SAL	TUG₂	TU	ZAG	GAL	LA	IM	MI	IN	KU
celestial	chamber		birth	mark	great	hang	clay	black	in	hole
(3)	womb			shoulder	Galaxy			Great Rift		(3)

"In the celestial Chamber of Consciousness,
at the birth mark on the great shoulder of the Galaxy,
where the spirits of darkness swarm (Great Rift),
into the hole in its black clay push the shaft."

KU – USH - KU

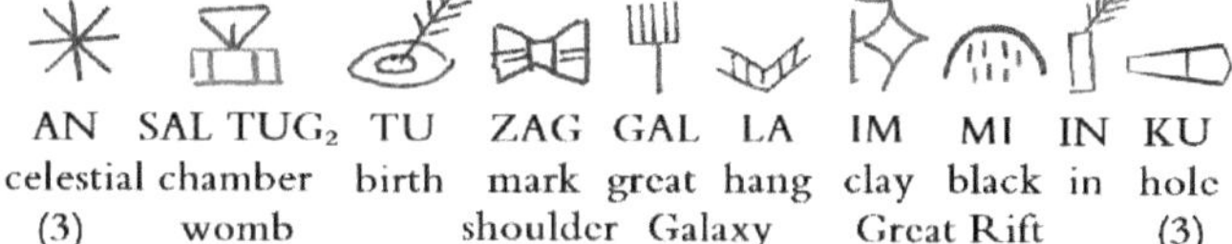

109. The Pissing Contest

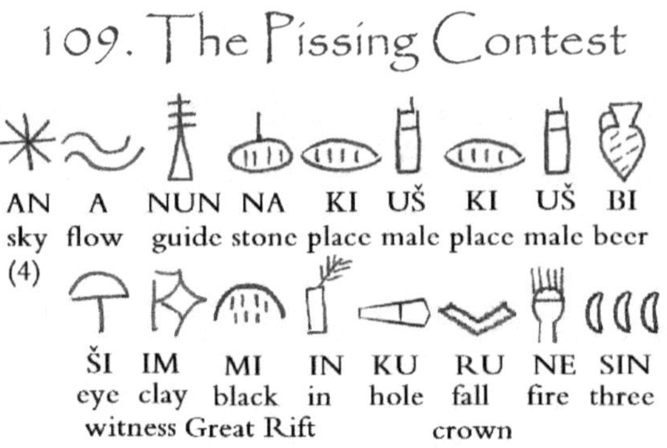

Where the water of the Stone Guide flows (Anunnaki),

at the places of the stone phalli,

where men meet for beer and virile competition,

their shafts in those places will separate man from bee.

There where the spirits of darkness fall through
the hole, where the three-tiered crown is fired,
fire will fall three times again.

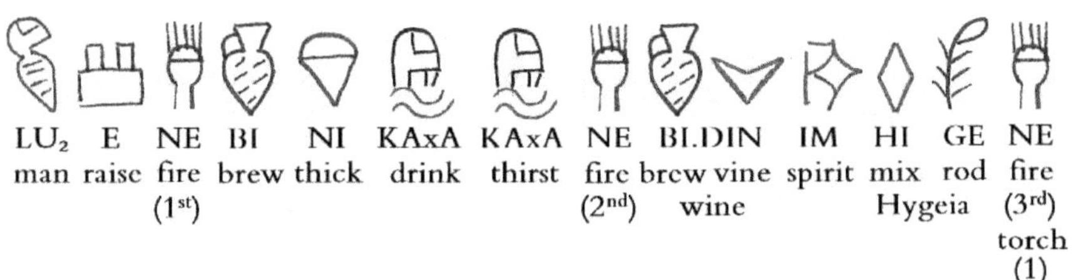

that huge giant born of no marriage-bed, three-father Orion,
sprang up from his mother earth, after a shower of piss
from three gods grew in generative fruitfulness to the self-made shape
of a child, having impregnated a wrinkle of fruitful ox hide…
(Nonnus, *Dionysiaca* 13. 96, Theoi.com)

110. Re-Generation

That man and bee together raise the fire - again,

and drink in abundance the red brew of the vine - again,

that the spirit be healed – again.

111. Revelation of the Phoenix

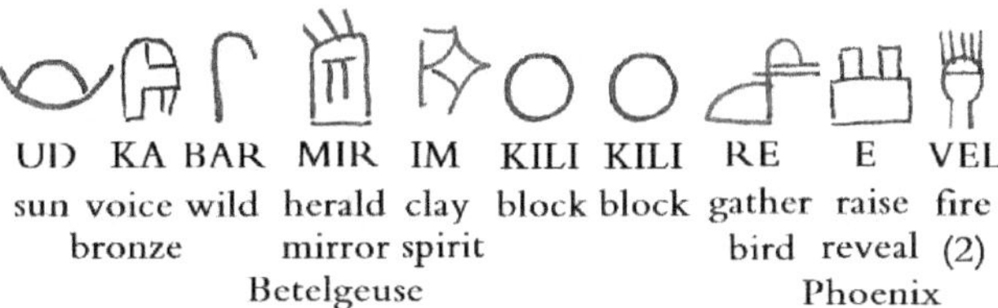

Heralded by the distant lion's roar,

on a mirror of bronze and on two blocks of clay the Phoenix rises,

its fire gathered at the levee and revealed – once again.

When time has built his strength with power to raise the weight, he lifts the nest--the nest his cradle and his father's tomb--as love and duty prompt... ...from that tall palm (in Assyria) and carries it across the sky to reach the Sun's great city (Heliopolis in Egypt), and before the doors of the Sun's holy temple lays it down. (Ovid, Metamorphoses 15:385, trans. Melville)

112. The Devil and the Divine

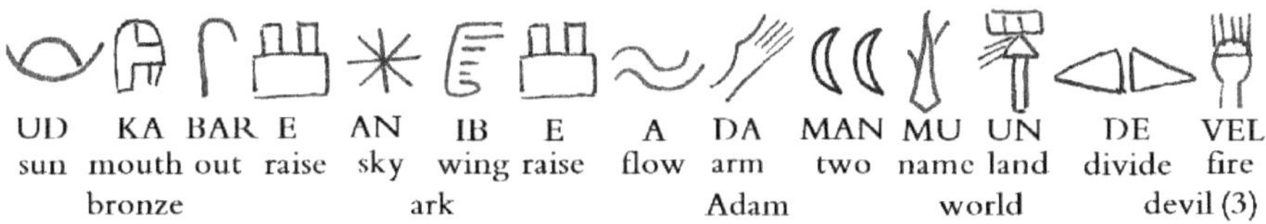

From the roaring brazen mouth, the celestial ark rises,

held aloft on two adamantine arms (two stone pillars),

with their One Divine Name (Adam, Man) and the ages of the world

which the devil will divide in the fire – again.

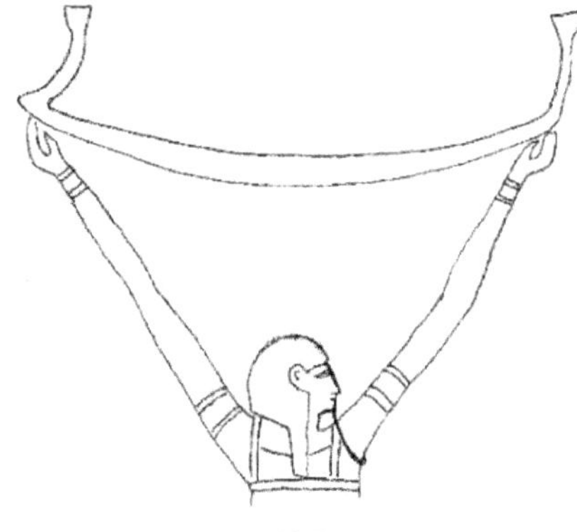

113. Swan Song

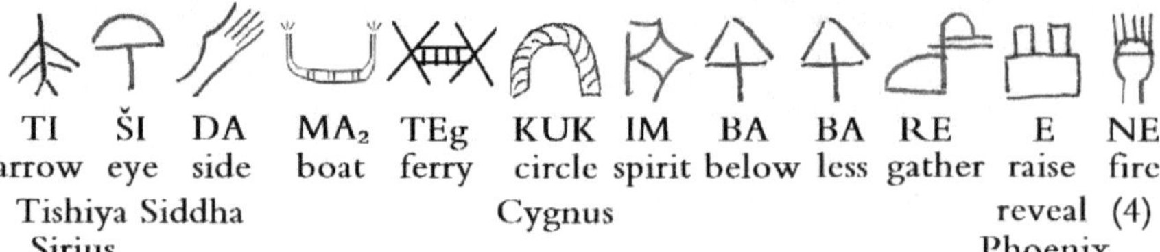

TI	ŠI	DA	MA₂	TEg	KUK	IM	BA	BA	RE	E	NE
arrow	eye	side	boat	ferry	circle	spirit	below	less	gather	raise	fire
Tishiya	Siddha				Cygnus					reveal	(4)
Sirius											Phoenix

The eye on the side of the circling ferry boat

will count the stars and watch for arrows, that the spirits gather less

below with the swan but rise with the Phoenix – once again.

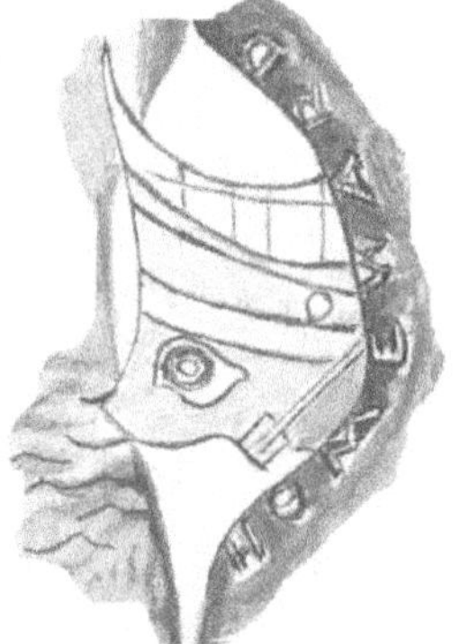

114 – 115. Question of Death

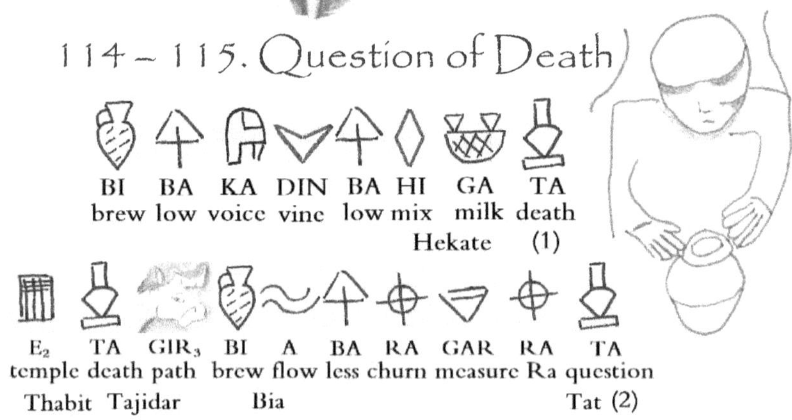

BI	BA	KA	DIN	BA	HI	GA	TA
brew	low	voice	vine	low	mix	milk	death
						Hekate	(1)

E₂	TA	GIR₃	BI	A	BA	RA	GAR	RA	TA
temple	death	path	brew	flow	less	churn	measure	Ra	question
Thabit	Tajidar		Bia					Tat	(2)

In a low voice question the Heavenly Cow

when from the vine is mixed the milk of death,

or in Her Enduring Temple,

your questioning of the path of bull and bee

in the force of the churning water below will be measured.

116. Joyful Reunion

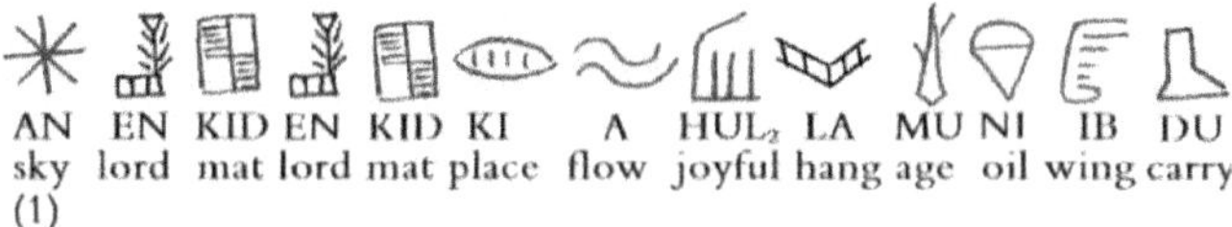

The Lords on their mats of sky and earth will meet at the place
where joyful water flows and time on the wing of the ark is carried.

117. Kitara

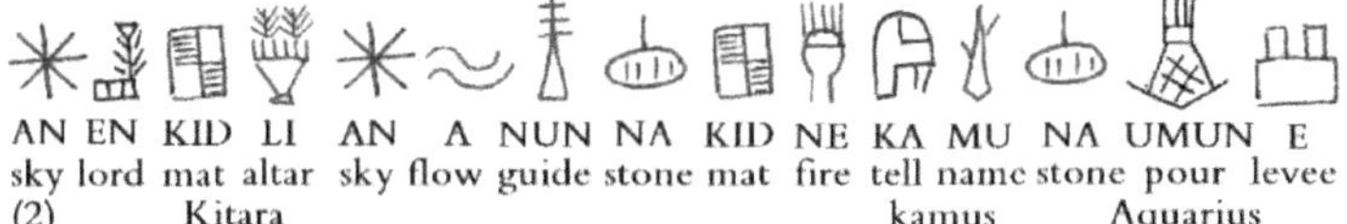

And from the altar mats in the branches of the skies

onto the stone guide the story of time and fire with the water

from the Cask of Knowledge (Aquarius) at the levee pours.

118. Sailors of the Galaxy

As above so below, the great ships of the Galaxy carry the oils

and the measuring rod of the Lord sounds on the stone.

119. As Above So Below

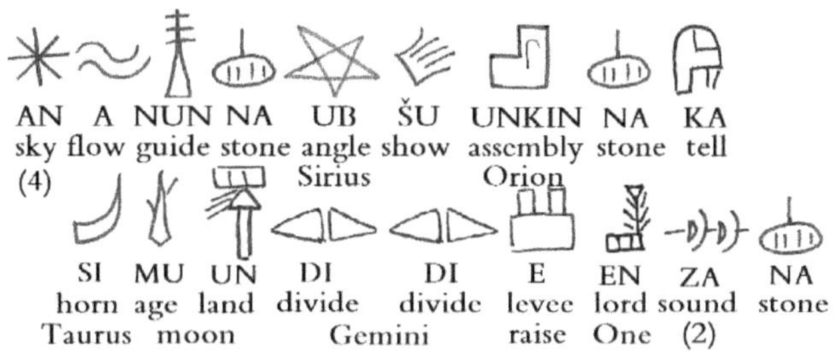

The Guide of Above and Below between its stones

the angles will show and of the Assembly of the Kin will tell.

On the divine horns the divisions announced

and the raising of the Stone of the Lord from below.

120. Anniversary

TUR MU E₂ MU UN KAK LUGAL AN EN KI KID

youth age temple age land keystone king   sky lord earth rule

renown   world moon   Great Bee

For the Renowned Youth a temple built
to mark the encircling ages of the world,
and the joining of the King and the Lord between Sky and Earth.

Perennial stands the fortune of their line,
From grandsire unto grandsire backward told.
(Virgil, *Georgics*, Bk.4)

121. Book of Above and Below

NUN KI HUR SAG DIM₂ KI TA BA RA RI

guide place mill head create place question below churn collect

Sphinx   kitab book   sunless

In the otherworldly place of lost fish, below the Miller's head
a sunless place created, the question of death
and the sun in a twofold book collected.

122. Temple of Truth

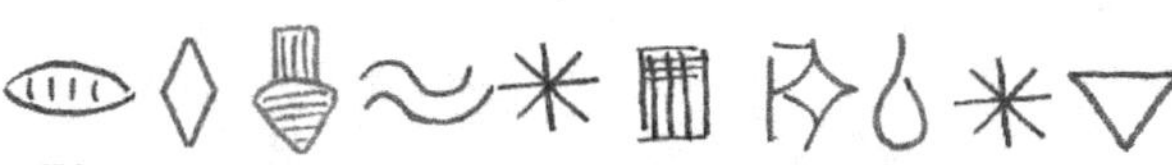

KI HI GA A AN E₂ IM MA AN KAK

place mix milk water sky temple clay land sky build

Hekate   to be   immaculate

crucible womb

A place to mix the milk (Hekate)
with water from the womb in the sky there will be.
A Temple in immaculate clay of land and sky built.

123. Two by Two

NUN	KI	KI	SAL.SI	LU₂	NU	KU₄	KU₄	DA
guide	place	place	pure	men	not	enter	enter	side
	keys		El			seed	ropes	

Two keys, one to the place of the Otherworldly Guide,

one to the Place of the Chamber of Consciousness,

that the seed of man not enter side by side.

124. Milk and Thorns

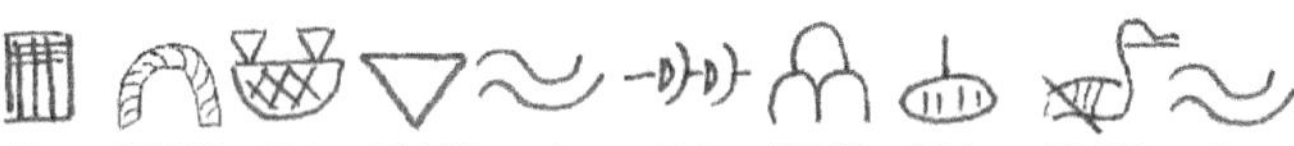

E₂	KUK	GA	KAK	A	ZA	KUR	NA	DAR	A
temple	circle	milk	thorn	water	sound	hills	stone	pierce	water
Milky Way			acacia			Kouretes			

A Temple for the Circle of the Cow,

That Her milk and thorns (acacia brew)

with the sounds in the stone hills also flow.

The Teacher sought to find delightful sayings and write words of truth accurately. The words of the wise are like goads (…) like firmly embedded nails. The sayings are given by one Shepherd. (Ecclesiastes 12:10-11)

125. Stars of Music

E₂	BALAG	LUL	7	E	SI	DI	E	NAM	RU	SUM	MA
temple	musicians	seven	raise	horn	divine	elevate	purpose	rotate	add	land	
	Pleiades				sidereal						truth

A Temple for the Seven Musicians (Pleiades)

on two divine horns raised (Taurus, moon),

in its truth that their music elevate the people

and inspire the rotation and abundance of their land.

126. Eleusinian Festival of Sirius

KIRIS	KUK	UR	E₂	KI	AL	HI	GA
festival	circle	dog	temple	place	all	mix	milk
Ceres		Sirius					Hekate

A Music Festival (Ceres) for the Circling Dog,

his Temple in all the places where the milk is mixed.

(Sirius) *The culmination of this star at midnight was celebrated in the great temple of Ceres at Eleusis, probably at the initiation of the Eleusinian mysteries (Star Names [6], p.125)*

127. From Generation to Generation

AB	ZU	AB	NAM	HI	AN	EN	KI	KID	ME	GALAM	MA	DU	MA
ocean	know	ocean	to	mix	sky	lord	earth	mat	magic	fish	land	carry	land
father		father	fate	veil					measure			mead	truth

The Father and the Mother to know,

from ocean to ocean, from land to land,

the magic of the ancestors

with the mead of truth

and the truth of the measure is carried

by the Great Fish (Oannes, Al Khidr),

Lord of Sky and Earth on his mat.

128. The Brew

NUN KI   E₂   KUK GA KAK A   BA
guide place temple circle milk nail water below
Milky Way   acacia

From the Place of the Otherworldly Guide of Lost fish
and the Temple of the Circling Cow,
that milk and thorns and water continue to flow below.

129. The Final Mark

A   A   AN EN KI   ZAG   SAL
waters flow sky lord earth shoulder lady
to be   One   mark chamber
.6   cairn

That the waters of Heaven forever flow on Earth,
springing from Her Chamber on the shoulder of the One Lord.

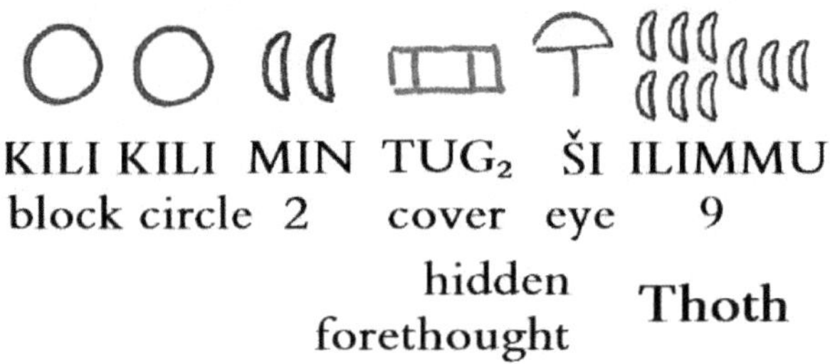

KILI KILI MIN TUG₂ ŠI ILIMMU
block circle 2   cover eye   9
                  hidden   **Thoth**
              forethought

Two blocks concealed by the forethought of the Nine.

Translation Notes

<u>Line 1</u>

Three-word incipit found on a number of texts, including *The Story of Sukurru* (Early Dynastic 2600-2500 BC). The two texts appear to be either written by the same scribe or from the same school. This is just one of numerous similarities in the phraseology. Image of the bird-man from a cylinder seal.

UD (given meanings 'day' and 'sun') in the composite transliteration (ETCSL) differs from the Ashmolean prism which reads 'A' ('flow' and 'water') giving A-RE-A instead of UD-RE-A. (See notes to line 108 for the importance of this variation.)

Introducing one of the major underlying themes of this text from the outset, UD, the sun, is source of Arabic oud, a string instrument. It's also a partial source of the name Thoth (see notes to line 9).

TAR, also transliterated KUT or SIL, with given meanings 'to cut', 'to break off' amongst others. 'Below to cut the churn'; the disappearance, sinking of Ra, sun, king and pharaoh. TAR with RA give the source of Arabic tarana:

> (Ursa Major) *They who spoke of the seven triones had long forgotten that their fathers spoke of the taras (staras) or strewers of light; Al Biruni derived the word from tarana, "passage," as of the stars through the heavens. Thus from the results of modern philological research it is possible that our long received opinions as to the derivations of many star-names should be abandoned, and that we should search for them far back of Greece or Rome. (R. H. Allen, Star Names and their Meanings [6], p.432)*

The positioning of two BA, with given meaning 'to deduct' to which I add 'below' and 'less', around TAR contributes to the overall understanding. The sun and stars (see 'tarana' above) pass between them; below to the underworld (Tartarus).

RE-A and TAR-RA became the goddesses, Greek Rhea and Celtic Tara. Also Hindu Tara which has a complex mix of attributes, as do the words on this line; the breaking waters, indicating a flood but also birth and rebirth, the passage through the underworld, the in-between and connotation of challenges and dangers. (See TAR in relation to GALAM/SUKUD, the fish, in the notes to line 52.) Also the birth of Sirius (p.49-52).

BA with SIL gave Greek basileus with the meaning 'king'. Also the basilisk, a mythological serpent. BA-TAR-RA is source of 'batrachian', a frog or toad, through Greek batrakhos. This creature appears among snakes on a 4th millennium tablet (CDLI Uruk V, 3500-3250 BC, ref. P235770). Note the unusual crest over the amphibian's head; no ordinary toad.

Are there other ancient references identifying the river Basileius (see quote under line 1)? I haven't found any. The word for 'river', originally PU/BU, also meant 'snake'. Was the Basileius the river in-between, also the 'River of the Snake King'? (See Meso-po-tam-ia in *Lost Stones*, p.139-140. ME ZU gave Meso- which translates in Greek to the 'in-between' of line 48. See the Nevali Çori skull illustrating line 85.)

Batara has the meaning 'medicine man' in Malay. These are words used in the unfathomably ancient and coded world of the Agari (*Lost Stones*, p.166), healers skilled in the use of snake and toad venom, experts and guides (see NUN, the whale or 'great fish' of the Anunnaki) in all things relating to water, to the water-regulating levee above and the churning abyss below.

<u>Line 2</u>

Image a) carving from Göbekli Tepe and b) figure with interwoven snakes on either side, 4th millennium tablet (CDLI Uruk IV, ref. P004324).

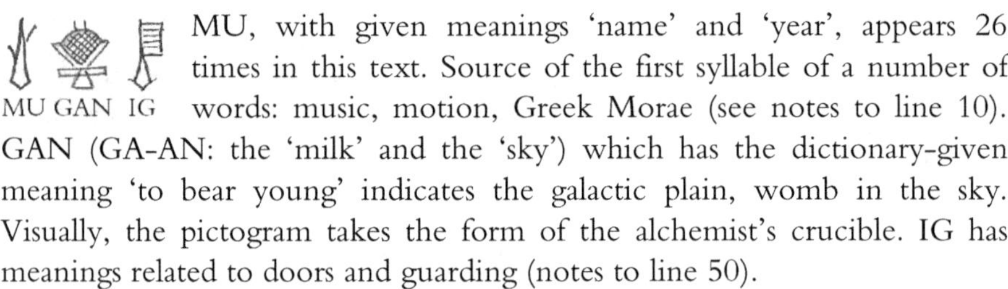

MU, with given meanings 'name' and 'year', appears 26 times in this text. Source of the first syllable of a number of words: music, motion, Greek Morae (see notes to line 10). GAN (GA-AN: the 'milk' and the 'sky') which has the dictionary-given meaning 'to bear young' indicates the galactic plain, womb in the sky. Visually, the pictogram takes the form of the alchemist's crucible. IG has meanings related to doors and guarding (notes to line 50).

> *On that day the LORD will whistle to the flies at the farthest streams of the Nile and to the bees in the land of Assyria. And they will all come and settle in the steep ravines and clefts of the rocks, in all the thornbushes and watering holes.... (Isaiah 7:18)*

DEB/DIB: given meanings 'to audit' and 'to transfer', source of Hebrew Deborah, a renowned judge and prophetess. In Hebrew the word means 'bee'. Coupled with ŠI, 'eye' and 'to see' but also 'first'; 'to first see', reference to the birth of Sirius (p.49-52) and to 'reflect'. Deborah is not the only bee in this story.

DEB stems from DI-IB, 'divide' and 'judge', with the 'wing', also the ark. (See DI in the context of judgement on lines 36, 94 and 101.)

(See TU in the notes to line 108.)

Line 3

(Ursa Major) alluded to in the Book of the Dead as 'The constellation of the Thigh in the northern sky'; and thus mentioned in inscriptions on the kings' tombs and the walls of the Ramesseum at Thebes. (Star Names [6], p.434)

(Also see Hamlet's Mill[2], p.247, The Galaxy, for the myth of the stag's limbs leading to the separation of Orion and Ursa Major.)

Given as 'brewer', I have added 'alchemist', ŠIM takes the form of a vessel used by beekeepers to filter the harvested comb, separating the wax from the honey which pours out through the opening at its base.

Always according to the lexical lists, ŠIM breaks down to 'eye' and 'clay', the 'eye on clay', the 'witness'. The eye is that of Sirius (see notes to lines 17 and 113) and presumably Egyptian Horus. Also reads the 'eye in the clay', the hole in the bottom of the clay vessel and the hole in the clay pipes used as domesticated hives in Ancient Egypt transported in baskets by boat to different locations according to seasonal flowering. No doubt also in Mesopotamia.

Source of Latin similis meaning 'resembling', 'of the same kind' and, from there, to both 'similar' and 'simulation' as in the Simorgh, king of birds in the story of *Conference of the Birds* (see notes to line 104).

$$DIM_2 \quad = \quad \check{S}I \quad DI \quad IM$$

DIM$_2$ given as 'create', 'builder' and 'architect', the Egyptian ox foreleg visible at Dendera where it appears at the centre of the circular zodiac. (8 times: lines 3, 10, 15, 46, 59, 83, 84 and 121) Named as the constellation of Boôtes, ox of the plough of the 'Creator'.

Transliterated to ŠIDIM through ŠI-DI-IM, 'eye', 'divide' and 'clay', found opposite it in the lexical lists, translating to:

- 'eye on the division of the clay'
- 'divisions of the clay to see'

where DI-IM come together to form another central word DIM, the 'pole', connected to the north pole, at the centre of the circle.

> *Greek drakon (genitive drakontos) "serpent, giant seafish," apparently from drak-, strong aorist stem of derkesthai "to see clearly," from PIE* (Etymonline.com)

DAR/DARA, given as 'to split' and 'to cut open', the pictogram of a water bird leads to 'pierce', piercing the water, also a mirror – to see clearly. Tajidar, the wise leader of the birds in Attar's poem, was sourced here and elsewhere (p.79. Notes to line 115).

Following on from the reference to the basilisk (notes to line 1) the celestial serpent theme continues with the source syllable of Greek drakon, constellation of Draco, serpent and dragon (notes to line 29). The connection to the *Emerald Tablet* of Thoth is made on line 41 where the name Thuban, pole star in Draco, is sourced.

Lines 4-5

Precursor to Greek Phaeton who travels to meet his father, the sun. On line 4 the lord and the king appear together, potentially a reference to the Egyptian calendar tracking the four-yearly slide of one day between the cycles of Sirius and the sun. Here EN is also translated 'end'.

> *The first to introduce Titanes into poetry was Homer, representing them as gods down in what is called Tartaros;* (Pausanias, Description of Greece 8. 37. 1, Trans. Jones)

Given twice, indicating either a plural or for emphasis. 'To cut the tar' (see notes to line 1). Another transliteration is CUT/CUD. Greek Tartarus and 'tar' (bitumen) along with English 'cut' from this source. The illustration from the Adda seal shows the hero cutting his way downwards through the mounds (hills or hives) illustrated under this line.

Words of renewal; RE through given meanings 'collect' and 'gather', the bringing back of the sun's fire by Greek Prometheus, with NE, as the 'fire'. I have added 'new' and 'again' to the dictionary.

They appear together – with E between them – in the acrostic on lines 112 and 113; source of 'revelation' and 'bird of fire', the Phoenix (notes to line 111).

Line 6

In *The Story of Sukurru* (lines 223 to 225), NI takes sixth position over three consecutive lines in the acrostic there, leading to the solution 666 (and to the biblical story of the exchange of precious gifts between Solomon and the Queen of Sheba). Here, they appear three times and again three times on line 11. On line 12 their connection to the three belt stars of Orion is confirmed.

E_2-A, the water temple (levee or mill), origin of the name Ea. The central mound or mountain with its springs of water is personified as the father figure in the Mesopotamian images. E_2 is both temple on land and vessel on water according to context.

A-NI, 'water' and 'thick', used six times, is source of Latin animus, considered to be the lowest level in terms of the path to enlightenment according to the Hermetic records, and 'animate', bring to life. Also origin of 'animism', the belief that life and spirit exist in all things. A-NI is translated as 'coming to life' (lines 86, 87 and 88). I have added the word 'night' for NI.

Temple of Living Water implies a place of baptism along a river bank. NI, symbol of abundance, became the first syllable of 'Nile' and 'Niger'. The mythology of the Igbo people established in Nigeria has their Temple of Ani in the middle of Earth where the deity of their culture reigns.

For this ordered world (cosmos) is of a mixed birth: it is the offspring of a union of Necessity and Intellect. Intellect prevailing over Necessity by persuading (from Peitho, goddess of persuasion) it to direct most of the things that come to be toward what is best, and the result of this subjugation of Necessity to wise persuasion is the initial formation of the universe. (Plato 48a, trans. John M. Cooper)

Given as 'metal', KUK is source of 'cog' and, in context, translates here to 'cog-boat' (see p.41). KUK gave Greek kuklos, the 'ring' and 'circle'. NI with UD translate to 'oil of the sun', 'golden oil', 'night and day'. NI is also seen as container of harvest offerings on the Warka vase. Together they are source of English 'neod', 'to need', the necessity of night and day. The 'golden oil' is honey, also a necessity. The theme of necessity through NI-UD continues on line 7, the instructions given to biblical Noah concerning the need to build a boat. Also reflected in Ananke, Greek goddess of necessity.

<u>Orpheus, Sirius and the Dog</u>

Transliterated KUR derives from KU with UR, together translating to 'the seat of the dog' or 'the seat of the lion' (*Before Babel*, p.259), (notes to line 101). From there, a very short hop to the Great Pyramid and to Sirius, the dog star: ZA KUR, 'the sound of barking dogs'. Zakur in the Basque language has the meaning 'canine' (notes to line 21).

UR, pictogram of a dog's head with given meaning 'dog', appears twice (lines 6 and 40) with BI, the vessel containing the brew: 'dog and bee', 'dog and brew'. Discussed in the introductory section (p.51), here below a recap:

UR BI: source of Latin orbis, with the meaning 'to circle', 'to orbit' but also 'purpose', 'end' and 'goal'. Stationed on the Greek island of Minoa the golden dog carries the oil. The same upright circling dog is unmistakeable on more than one eastern cylinder seal.

UR BI: source of Greek Orpheus, epithet of that far later and mysterious figure whose hypnotic music inspires the stars and planets to danse, a name of otherwise unknown origin (notes to line 40) Another pictogram of a canine, NAR, 'fox' and 'musician', is source of 'narcotic' (lines 67 and 125).

BI gives the origin of 'binary' (MU BI in notes to line 61): UR BI, two intertwining dogs. The dog accompanies its master who, according to myth, is Orion. The Great Sphinx plays the music as does Orpheus, inspiring the stars and planets to turn. A great dog and his pup, or two great dogs? How many dogs?

UR, given as 'dog' and 'lion', with MAH, the 'great', together translate to 'great lion'. Like UR BI, they appear together just twice (lines 27 and 31), touching on one of the niggling mysteries of Meso-Egyptian lore, the apparent interchangeability of canine and feline. Was the great Sphinx always a lion? Was it once a representation of Anubis, the jackal, also portrayed numerous times in a sphinx-like pose?

(More on Sirius in the notes to lines 17 and 73.)

Line 7

> *Then, when Helios (the Sun) made him (Herakles) hot as he proceeded, he aimed his bow at the god and stretched it; Helios was so surprised at his daring that he gave him a golden goblet, in which he crossed Okeanos.* (Pseudo-Apollodorus, Bibliotheca 2. 106 – 109, trans. Aldrich, Theoi.com)

ZA, both 'sound' and 'four', with KUR, the 'hills' or 'mountain', appear seven times. In the dual themes of music and archery, ZA with KUR translate to 'sound of the cord', 'sound of the chord', 'sound of the crow'. Also refer to the four cords of the Egyptian 'stretching of the cord' ritual.

> *Greek khorde "string, catgut, chord, cord," from PIE root (Etymonline)*

Source of the noisy crow, constellation of Corvus, circling the sky on the back of the great snake Hydra. Corvus is linked to music through the connection with Apollo (see notes to line 61):

> (Corvus) *mythology having made the bird sacred to Phoebus Apollo in connection with his prophetic functions, and because he assumed its shape during the conflict of the gods with the giants.* (Star Names[6], p.179)

This agrees with the final A-KA, 'water' and 'mouth', which might be read 'thirst':

> (Corvus) *doomed to everlasting thirst by the guardianship of the Hydra over the Cup and its contents.* (Star Names[6], p.180)

ZA KUR as 'sound in the hills' is also linked to music and the birth of Zeus (notes to line 11):

> *the armed Kouretes stood guard over him in the cave, banging their spears against their shields to prevent Kronos from hearing the infant's voice.* (Pseudo-Apollodorus, Bibliotheca 1.4–5, trans. Aldrich)

BI, 'beer' or 'brew' but also 'bee', with ZA, 'sound' translating to 'the sound of the bee in the hills (or hive) followed by UD as 'golden' and becoming a 'golden bee', a honey bee. Visually, KUR, three mounds, shows the rounded beehive(s) on the circle of the sun (two UD surround the phrase). But not only (notes to line 6).

NI UD is set against BI UD, giving 'in need of mead', first indication of the mixing of a brew.

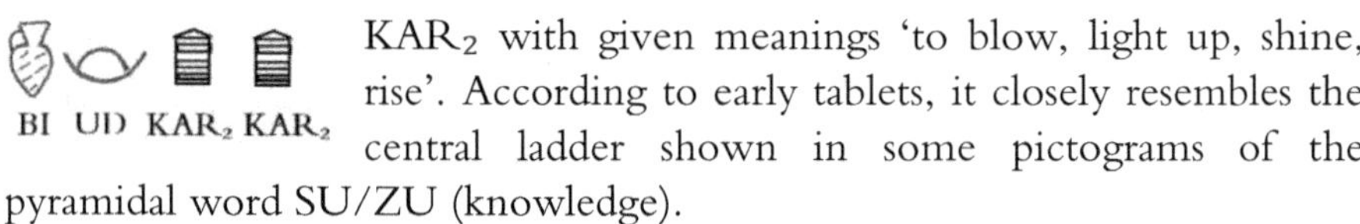

KAR₂ with given meanings 'to blow, light up, shine, rise'. According to early tablets, it closely resembles the central ladder shown in some pictograms of the pyramidal word SU/ZU (knowledge).

One potential source of Greek karkinos, the crab of the constellation of Cancer, KAR₂ also looks similar to a transportable beehive. Given twice, it indicates a plurality of nouns and/or meanings.

Celestial beehives: Praesepe, the nebulous known as the beehive, lies close to the muzzle of Leo and at the mouth of Cancer, the crab (notes to lines 31 and 92), the other lesser known bee cluster being the Pleiades in the constellation of Taurus (notes to line 102).

Line 8

'Father' and 'sea' (or ocean) with E, the 'levee' between the two can be usefully matched to the words on line 97. The first AB on that line is striated, indicating an imbalance not apparent here. The phrase might read 'a levee between the seas' where the type of mound remains to be defined. The notion of Moses separating the water is found here and elsewhere in the text (line 103).

A, the 'flow' of 'water' and UL, with given meanings 'to push', 'to thrust', 'fitting' and 'suitable', translated to 'on the wave'. UL is repeated on line 25 and, in an astronomical context, refers to both the sting of the constellation of Scorpio on which the hero/skull is propelled and to Cygnus (notes to line 25).

In *The Story of Sukurru*, UL also appears in the context of the preparation of Noah's ark where it was used for 'expand' and 'fit'. Line 95:

A great house on a great river there must be; at its heart, the beer and the bull. Expand to fit madam…

'Clay of the land' is, according to context, the material used to make tablets and prisms (four-sided cylinders) onto which the astronomical references were marked and a secondary reference to the clay cylinders used in antiquity for bee-keeping. On the surface of one, the story of the journey through the skies is written (in the cuneiform angular script of the witness) while, inside the other (the man-made cylindrical beehive), the bees can be heard to tell their version of the story.

Pictographic IM takes the form of a ship's sail and has given meanings 'wind', 'rain' and 'clay' to which I have added 'spirit' (NI_2, given as 'self', is the same word with added striations). MA, pictogram of the hanging fruit which, plucked by biblical Eve, resulted in knowledge of nakedness (*Lost Stones*, p.102). Interpreted in this original version as detailed knowledge of astronomy and the cycles of time, in both cases the information was kept secret from humanity. MA gave Egyptian Ma'at and I have added the most important meaning 'truth' to its given meaning of 'land'.

Line 9

With given meanings 'space' and 'crown', the pictogram appears to be a Mesopotamian reed ring post shown on Sumerian seals on either side of an entrance (also on the Warka vase), home of the field mouse (mustela) and ermine. The knot at the apex of the reed bundle and elsewhere the mark of the shoulder knot (see ZAG) is the spirit hole through which souls must pass.

The illustration of an ermine accompanying line 9 was copied from a bas-relief on a pillar at Göbekli Tepe. The rodent copied here above was taken from a 4th millennium tablet and appears just below the depiction of a circle with two T-shaped 'stones' (also illustrating line 72 with my added flourish of an underlying sky symbol). The full explanation of the ermine's presence in this text - and at Göbekli Tepe - is given in the notes to line 43.

Greek god of archery, prophecy and music, Apollo is also present in AB/AP, the 'father', and linked to the rodent hiding in the reed bundle MUŠ₃. One of Apollo's unexplained epithets is Sminthius (Homer, Iliad, line 38) which ancient Greek commentators described as 'destroyer of field mice'.

GALAM KA GA (notes to line 28): GALAM, pictogram of a vertical fish identified here as Piscis Austrinus thanks to the association with KA, the mouth, and GA, the milk, 'its mouth to the milk'

> (Piscis Austrinus) *it is very unnaturally drinking the whole outflow from the Urn. (…) La Lande asserted that Dupuis had proved this to be the sky symbol of the god Dagon of the Syrians, the Phagre and Oxyrinque adored in Egypt; and it even has been associated with the still greater Oannes.* (Star Names [6], p.344-345)

Arabic Fam al-hût, with the meaning 'mouth of the whale', now Fomalhaut, is the bright star in the mouth of Piscis Austrinus.

Thoth

TA UD DU A TA, 'death' and 'question' with UD.DU 'sun' and 'to carry': 'question of the sun carriage'. With A, 'to flow', the phrase can be enlarged to 'the question of the flow of the sun'.

TA-UD/UT-DU is source of the Egypto-Greek name Tautu/Thoth who is also Hermes Trismegistus. As the breakdown of his Greek epithet implies, Tautu is responsible for encoding and transmitting the knowledge of the path of the sun along the ecliptic with its apparent anticlockwise motion known as precession of the equinoxes (notes to line 10. See notes to line 41 for the *Emerald Tablet*).

TA as an element of the honey brew, the theme of psychedelics is linked to the name (notes to line 114). (See p.268 for Thoth, the number 9 and the tablets.) With UD, the sun, as source of Arabic oud, one in a large family of string instruments, the music of Thoth-Hermes is equally present in the epithet. Thoth is Hermes who is Apollo, the Great Maestro of Time.

<u>Line 10</u>

<u>Riddle of the Sphinx</u> (*Lost Stones*, p.119-122)

What is it that has one voice, and is four-footed and two-footed and three-footed? (Pseudo-Apollodorus, Bibliotheca 3. 52 – 55, Greek mythographer C2nd A.D., trans. Aldrich.)

Hence Rhasis in his Epistles, "The Stone," says he, "is a Triangle in its essence, a Quadrangle in its quality." (Atalanta Fugiens, 1617)

Linguistic version of the ouroboros, the circling winged and feathered snake-bird biting its own tail.

 Joining the beginning of line 10 to its end gives EN and SIN, the 'Lord of the Three', or 'the three lords'. With the addition of AN–NU:

EN AN NU

- 'Lord of the Ring of Three' or
- 'Lord of the Three Rings' or
- 'The Three Lords of the Ring'.

EN is also source of the word 'end'.

AN with NU, 'sky' with 'knot' or 'not', the sky knot, preceded by EN, the endless knot of the year. Source of Latin annul, 'to make to nothing', also Latin annus, the 'year,' and French anneau, the 'ring'.

Followed by DIM₂, the ox foreleg of Boôtes, ancient constellation close to Ursa Minor and Major, the reference is to Arcturus and to the imperishable circling stars of the north pole (notes to line 3).

Transliterated MUD, from lexical entries where HU.HI appears opposite MU-UD, 'movement of the sun'. The word 'huhi' in the language of the Warau, an Amerindian tribe, has the meaning 'feather'. HU with RA is source of Greek hora, meaning 'hour', and the Horae, goddesses of the seasons (also see notes to line 38). Greek goddess Hera is also hidden here.

When Ixion bragged that he had slept with Hera, Zeus punished him by tying him to a wheel, on which he was turned by winds up in the air.

(Pseudo-Apollodorus, Bibliotheca E1. 20, trans. Aldrich, Theoi.com)

MU after RA indicates the three Greek goddesses of fate, the Morae who spun the threads of life on their spindles, and who were sometimes shown carrying staffs or sceptres.

RA MU UN

Here is found one of the stories resulting from later interpretations of GE-EŠ, the three rods (see below).

The sun is apparent through both HU–HI/MUD and RA. It's more than probable that the English word 'moon' (another word of unidentified source) comes from MU-UN. So with MU, as 'time' and 'movement', line 10 refers to the motions of both sun and moon – as does the *Emerald Tablet* (p.69).

Four feet of two sailors, where DU.DU has the given meaning 'sailor'. The circle of small birds with big feet turning around the base stone

NA DU DU DU DU

encircling two central pillars at Göbekli Tepe comes to mind. With NA, the stone, it became Dodona, dodo (flying from its stone on line 66 of *The Story Of Sukurru*) and a veiled reference to the circling ship, constellation of Argo Navis:

> (Argo Navis) *Pallas Athene, who herself set in the prow a piece from the peaking oak of Dodona ; the Argo being " thus endowed with the power of warning and guiding the chieftains who form its crew."* (*Star Names*[6], p.65)

GI SIN

The three reeds/branches/rods/arrows lead to a number of possibilities (also on lines 18 and 71):

- the threefold scourge of Strabo's quote (p.34) and a veiled reference to the count of 400 in a musical and/or geometrical context.

- GI-SIN/EŠ, three branches/rods/arrows, together become GIZ, the 'tree' and name of Giza, connected to the three belt stars of Orion. (See lines 11 and 12. Notes to line 71.). A reference to the world tree in various mythologies.

- Three doves were said to live in the hollow of the oak (GIZ as tree trunk) in the story of the island of Dodona, place of oracles, also present on this line.

- The number three, SIN, as name of the Mesopotamian moon–god Sin, referring to the three phases of the moon, and metaphor for the three ages of humankind; youth, middle age, and old age – suggested (but disputed) as the ultimate solution to the riddle of the Sphinx.

<u>Line 11</u>

Second veiled reference to the belt stars of Orion through the presence of three NI (see line 6). The theme is confirmed on line 12 where the name is spelled out. In the Solstice Riddle, three times NI are equated to 666 (see *The Story of Sukurru*, lines 223 to 227 and annexe).

I, 'multiply', NI, 'oil' and IN, 'straw', a three-word phrase given twice here. Pictographic I, given twice in this line, is comprised of five strokes, three over two, and, transliterated IA$_2$, is given as the number 5. A straightforward addition of 5 (from I) with 6 (from NI) gives the line number 11.

However, the image implies an upward expansion from 2 to 3. In *Before Babel*, I suggested that it refers to the Fibonacci sequence of numbers:

> *There is just one example of symbol I on CDLI at the earliest Uruk IV period, but it comes in prestigious company with PI. See page 185 for more on PI. Symbol PI has another phonetic form, YA, which appears to be linked to I-A, multiplication of the flow, and is given as 'five'. Unfortunately, the tablet[9] is little more than a fragment and the 'rabbit ears' of PI are damaged: (Before Babel, p.10)*

In Pythagorean tuning, I becomes a perfect fifth: $3/2 = 5^{th}$. PI translating to 'pure' and 'pitch' appears as an element of the Tree of Consciousness and Understanding on lines 45 and 58.

NI with IN are found opposite NIN in the lexical lists, NIN being a combination of SAL, the 'chamber' and TUG$_2$, the 'cover' or 'hearing':

SAL.TUG$_2$
NIN

SAL.TUG$_2$ refers to a cave or cairn: 'under cover of the cave', 'to hear the sound in the cave', and can translate to 'chamber of resonance' or 'chamber of consciousness' (line 108).

The three-word phrase ZA KUR NA appears on lines 6 and 11 where the three NI also appear, linking that phrase to the encoded number 666. ZA KUR NA appears six times in all in this text (lines 6, 11, 21, 29, 37 and 124). Pictographic ZA with given meanings 'sound' and 'bead' resembles cymbals, perhaps those played in the mountains to keep Kronos from hearing the cries of new-born Zeus (notes to line 7).

<u>Line 12</u>

TAK BA NI

Line 12 x 12 (words) = 144

Line 12 x 3 (third word) x 12 (words) = 432.

25920 / 432 = 60

Calculation of 432, a precession number and also the musical pitch known as Verdi tuning (see line 43 and notes to line 108), is made possible by 3 being the 3rd word on this 12th line comprising 12 words.

This line is illustrated with details from medieval images, surprisingly well suited to this far more ancient text. It's tempting to imagine that fragments – or even large portions - of the stories and information on the Mesopotamian tablets were not lost until relatively recent times.

Overall, line 12 is full of encoded astronomical references. Orion's three belt stars were once seen as the ships of three kings bearing gifts, fitting the context of both this story and that of Solomon and Sheba (see annexe in *The Story of Sukurru*):

GAL LI SIN

Identified as the uncapping fork of the honey-hunter (p.32), and symbol of kingship, GAL is used here as 'greatness'. On the earliest tablets, the pictogram varies between three prongs, four or more. GAL is source of a number of words; the galley of a ship, the galleon, but also Latin gallus, a cock, a rooster and symbol of noisy arrogance.

GAL-LI followed by the number 3 refers to two sets of three astronomical figures: the three stars of Orion's Belt (Orion is portrayed here as the giant rooster) but also the three stars along the body of Cygnus from tail to beak, constellation of Gallina.

Alternatively, GAL-LI-EŠ might refer an earlier constellation comprising three birds comprising Cygnus, Aquila and Vultur Cadens (in Lyra).

LI, given as 'branch' and extended to 'line' and 'limit', is a synonym of transliterated ARA, origin of the constellation of the Altar. ARA is the same pictogram of the incense burner (see above) but without the addition of the ŠE, the 'seeds'. One underlying theme is that of an abundance of incense burning on a great altar (notes to line 117).

TAK with NI, to rub the oil, became the Arabic name Alnitak meaning 'girdle', originally for all three belt stars (see quote under the line) a theme that fits equally well with the three kings bringing gifts of oils to the newborn Christ at the winter solstice. BA is used here as both 'less' and 'below'. The number 3, placed in third position on line 12, represents the third clue to this trio of stars.

The 'staff' or 'rod' and 'cow' become the 'prod of the cow', source of Greek gigas, 'giant', used here to refer to Orion:

GI GA

Homer, who made but a single allusion in the Iliad to this constellation, followed by a parallel passage in the Odyssey, wrote of "the might of huge Orion, and described the earthly hero as the "Illustrious Orion, the tallest and most beautiful of men, (...) The Syrians knew it as Gabbara ; the Arabians, as Al Jabbar, both signifying " the Giant," (...), — and in Latin days occasionally Gigas (Star Names [6], p.305)

GI also has the given meaning 'unit of length'. As three prongs or rods (GI is an element of GIZ), this is a double reference to the three pyramids of Giza, to their celestial counterparts, the belt stars, and to their use as rods of measurement – GI also being the stylus used to write them down. In that context, the notion of 'giant' for Orion refers to the immensity of the cosmos and the necessity to assess it with equally gigantic tools of measurement.

<u>Line 13</u>

Our word 'ego' comes through Greek and Latin from two Sumerian words; E_2, the temple, followed by GU_2, also DUR, the gulley and the umbilical cord. (Lost Stones, p.259)

Temple of the Gulley (*Lost Stones*, p.123, 128, 259). GU_2 with KAK is also transliterated to DUR/TIK/TIG, central word of the ancient name of the river Tigris and reference to the tiger. Visually and linguistically (neck, gulley) matched to the gullet of the central bird on Pillar 43 at Göbekli Tepe (notes to line 24).

E_2 GU_2
Between lines 13 and 15 are found the two pairs of words that give the source of the Gö-be of Göbekli, the Temple of the Tiger and Bee, the other being GU_4/GUD-BI, the Bull and Bee. The two words appear individually, GU_2 on line 13 with BI on line 14, and then BI-GUD together on line 15. They are also collocated numerous times in the lexical lists and written together on line 189 of *The*

Story of Sukurru. Turkish gobek has the meaning 'navel'. Also see Cusco which is 'navel' in the Quecha language (notes to line 108).

 'Red flow' and, in context, 'blood'. Perhaps a reference to the colour of the flooding Nile (also see the River of Fire on line 91).

Line 14

 With given meanings 'mudbrick', 'shoulder' and 'wall', KULLA appears three times (lines 14, 20 and 70). The pictogram suggests an undulating passage or wall punctured by a series of two nails. Used here in the context of the peg-shaped Mesopotamian foundation cones inscribed with cuneiform texts of dedication and integrated into temple walls. Taken with the temple (and vessel) of the previous line, it translates to 'On the temple wall' – signifying ego of the architect inscribing their name.

The kulla still exists; a tall, thin building with slits for windows, situated in valleys and said to have been used as defensive positions in the case of blood feuds; tower houses still found in several countries of which Greece. In that context and conforming to the original pictogram, this is a passage with a set of obstacles along its path, leading on very neatly from the preceding construction: E_2, the temple in a gulley, GU_2.

In an astronomical context, the pictogram indicates observations made from two points of reference and/or the changing positions of the pole stars. Another explanation for the two nails is that the astronomers were observing two different shafts. It was the theory of Schwaller de Lubicz that the ceiling zodiac at Dendera records two pole stars; that of the northern celestial pole and, simultaneously, the pole of the ecliptic. At the same time, KULLA is the brick or wall on which those observations are inscribed.

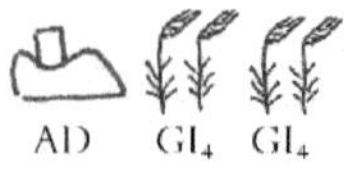 AD, which gave its name to the well-known Adda seal in the British Museum, has given meanings 'father' and 'bead' to which I have added 'ancestor' (See Lost Stones, p.21). GI_4, symbol of the double reed, is given as 'to turn', 'to return', 'to go around' (See p.65, See notes to lines 40, 64 and 65). On another well-known seal, generally called the 'Sitchin seal', the phrase AT-LA-AN give a more detailed source of the name Atlantis and can be understood as:

The (name of the) ancestor hanging in the sky.

<u>Line 15</u>

GI/GE, 'reed', 'green', is also a stylus, a rod, a prod and an arrow according to context. Source of Greek Ge, one name for Earth. Here it's the pole on which the ship's sail is hung, but also the arrow shot into a celestial chamber.

SAL, given as 'vulva', is part of an important riddle in *The Story of Sukurru* where it appears three times in first place, the 'chamber' into which the sun will retreat for three days at the solstices. 'Salla' has the meaning 'lover' in Quecha. SAL is the final word in this text and a precession marker.

<u>Gobe–kili</u>

BI-GUD, 'brew of the bull', 'bee and bull' (see the brazen bull on line 94), can also be read BI-GU$_4$, another version of the Gobi/Bigo name (notes to line 13).

Here preceded by LA, 'hang', with BI, 'beer', 'bee' and 'to be', together giving the source of 'labyrinth', that of the Minotaur, Greek bull killed by Theseus, and of Latin labium meaning 'lip'. (See the labyrinth of the pyramid in the notes to line 36):

Greek labyrinthos "maze, large building with intricate passages," especially the structure built by Daedelus to hold the Minotaur, near Knossos in Crete, a word of unknown origin.

GUD is followed by the ox foreleg, constellation of Boötes in the vicinity of the north pole. The brew of the bull along with DIM$_2$, the bull's thigh, are the forces turning HAR, the mill (of Harran). (notes to line 3.)

GUD = GU UD
bull   cord sun

GUD breaks down to GU-UD, the 'cord of the sun'. This is the cord given to Theseus by Ariadne to enable him to navigate the labyrinth of the Minotaur. It's the cord tied to the ox's foreleg on the ceiling at Dendera, copied with this line. There the rope is held by a hippopotamus, the most likely of all animals to be found wallowing in the clay of the land (IM MA). It's less likely to be found with a pot (of beer?) but nevertheless that's what we both read and see.

Line 16

KA, 'mouth' and 'word', with NUN, the 'guide' are source of Greek kanon. NUN, with the given meaning 'guide' is an element of the name Anunnaki (analysed in *Lost Stones*). Here it can translate to either 'word of the guide' or 'in the mouth of the whale'. Arabic nun means 'whale' or 'great fish'.

KA NUN DI DAM

Seen in some images of the Mesopotamian fish-god and in the much later form of the papal hat, the upward-turned mouth of the fish is symbolic of either Piscis Austrinus or Pisces and measurement of time (GALAM in the notes to lines 9 and 52). The original theme behind the biblical account of Jonah's passage through the mouth of the whale is that of the initiate entering a dark chamber. The connotation is spiritual but not only.

DAM has given meanings 'trust' and 'spouse'. Source of 'dam', a female animal, in this case a cow. DI-DAM appear together in *The Story of Sukurru* where they serve to separate (DI) the quarrelling spouses (DAM) in Noah's boat:

96. If not, by day between the spouses a thick reed fence place.

Line 17

'The king on his bier' refers to the circumpolar constellation of Ursa Major (p.33). The phrase can also read 'the king and the bee will err', 'the king bee will err', or 'the king with his brew will err' (lines 17, 39 and 91). That said, there is no king bee in the natural world, only the leader of wandering worker bees.

LUGAL BI ER

Sirius

Sirius has a broad range of epithets. So far identified:

UB, 'corner' and 'angle' amongst others, refers to the strokes on the clay tablet. It takes the same pentagonal form as the Egyptian hieroglyph said to represent Sirius. The slightly varying text of the Ashmolean prism confirms this reference by replacing UB with ŠI-RI, another source of the name Sirius, also transliterated AR (*Lost Stones*, p.91 where the connection to the Sphinx through its Hor-em-Akhet name is also made).

UB

UB   or   ŠI   RI
AR

Between UB and ŠI-RI and in the context of astronomy, the more general reference is to observations and calculations, and more specifically to the Sothic cycle (notes to line 73).

'Eye of the bird' or 'watch' (from 'eye' with 'to gather'), the two words transliterated together as AR (see above) which has given meanings 'to shine' and 'to appear' to which I have added 'to watch' from ŠI, the 'eye' and RI, 'collect': a 'collection of eyes' or 'the eye to focus'. This is the eye of the bird (Horus), and Sirius as a Watcher (Greek Arkhon). (See notes to lines 6 and 113.)

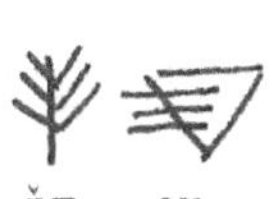
ŠE-IR-TA, seed – smell/err - death/question, where the origin of the Greek name for Sirius, celestial partner of the summer sun, is found. There is the possibility of the seed becoming a plant, bringing the flower and its scent. But, if the heat of summer is overwhelming, the smell will be that of death. TA, as the question, demonstrates that there is nothing sure. Death and the question go hand in hand once again. Which one will it be, to bloom or to die? Ety: searing. (The Story of Sukurru, notes to line 186, 2017)

"A star that keenest of all blazes with a searing flame and him men call Seirios… (…) and to some he gives strength but of others he blights the bark utterly." (Aratus, Phaenomena 328ff, sourced from Theoi.com)

"But their bones, when the skin is rotted about them, crumble away on the dark earth under parching Seirios." (Hesiod, Shield of Herakles, 139ff., sourced from Theoi.com)

ŠI-UR, eye - dog, eye of the dog. The two symbols together are given as HUL with largely negative meanings such as 'bad' and 'ruination'. (The Story of Sukurru, notes to line 17, 2017)

An alternative reading of RI-ŠI gives the source of Sanskrit rishi, translating to 'sage', 'seer', and 'prophet'.

UR-SAG, Dog - Head, the head dog, perhaps Egyptian Anubis. But, while Anubis is said to protect the dead, presumably from the living, Dog Head prevents the dead from living again… (The Story of Sukurru, notes to line 71)

TI   ŠI

The 'eye of the arrow' or 'to see the arrow' are source of Hindu Tishiya, their name for Sirius, and appear together in an eye-opening context on line 113. Also see ŠU-TI on lines 24 and 31.

Two other words link Sirius to the pre-flood king:

EZEN

EZEN, found in the company of UR, the dog, on line 126 and linked to music, is also transliterated ŠIR₃. EZEN is part of the name of the last king before the great flood: Ubara (EZENxKASKAL) Dudu. Also transliterated HER, an element of the name Hermes (*Before Babel*, p.231).

SUD

Given as 'distant', and also transliterated SIR. Element of the name 'Ziusudra' (through ZI UD SUD RA) also given as that of the last king before the flood. Transliterated ŠUT, it became Greek Sothis (lines 50 and 79). Source of the word 'south'.

Neither ŠIR₃ (EZEN) nor SIR (SUD) appear with any breakdown on the available lexical lists, making it impossible to further analyse their meanings through those acquired alphabetical forms (i.e. without involving conjecture).

HI BI MU UN MAL MAL

Six-word phrase repeated on line 61. HI/HE-BE, with given meanings 'to mix' and 'beer', became Greek Hebe, goddess of youth who serves the ambrosia and is wooed by Heracles when he climbs to Olympus. HI BI MU gives 'renowned Hebe', the Queen Bee. HE/HI is source of the first syllable of 'hive', 'heaven' and 'here', and Greek hyphe, a 'web'. This is the veil covering the entrance to the hive. (See ME HI in the notes to line 18. See MU BI on p.27 and notes to line 61.)

MU UN translates in different ways according to context:
- 'Name of the land',
- 'age of the land',
- 'movement of the land',
- 'moon'.

I hesitated far more over MU-UN as the direct source of 'moon' than with any other word – because it is so blatantly obvious. I suspect it will be used against me to suggest that these meanings are entirely based on phonetics which is not the case at all.

MAL has given meanings: 'basket', 'house', 'to place' and 'to replace'.. Following MU-UN, repetition of MAL becomes 'the houses of the moon' or 'lunar mansions', terms used in several cultures for the passage of the moon across the ecliptic – where, if it crosses the path of the sun, it causes an eclipse.

That danse between sun and moon is set to the music of Greek Orpheus and is reflected in the words of line 60 which is immediately followed by repetition of the full phrase HI-BI-MU-UN-MAL-MAL on line 61. Then MU-UN is given twice on line 72. Partial source of Latin mundus meaning 'world' (notes to line 84).

<u>Line 18</u>

> *But the rest, countless plagues (lugra), wander amongst men; for earth is full of evils and the sea is full. Of themselves diseases (nosoi) come upon men continually by day and by night, bringing mischief to mortals silently; for wise Zeus took away speech from them. So is there no way to escape the will of Zeus.* (Hesiod, Works and Days 90 ff, trans. Evelyn-White)

RA LUH AN PAP ŠIg

RA, 'churn' or 'beat', with LUH, 'to clean' and 'wash'. Pictographic LUH, used twice in this text (lines 18 and 70), derives either from an archer's quiver or a lyre, or a combination of the two. Mesopotamian images of musicians playing stringed instruments show them with quivers slung across their backs – archers and musicians like Apollo.The breakdown of LUH according to the lexical lists throws up an association of LU, 'light' and 'lunar' with UH, the 'tortoise' or 'turtle' (see the Moon Turtle on p.46–48, see line 66):

$$ \text{LU} \quad = \quad \text{LU} \quad \text{UH} $$

LUH is frequently collocated with HA, the fish (which is also read PIŠ and gave the names Pisces and Pisces Austrinus). There are considerably more than one fish in the oceans of Earth and sky, leading to confusion:

> (Ursa Minor) *The Arabs also likened the constellation to a fish, while with all that nation, heathen or Muhammadan, it was Al Fass, the Hole in which the earth's axle found its bearing.* (Star Names[6], p.450)

Pictographic AN, the eight-pointed star, with PAP, look curiously the same as the eight surfaces of the Great Pyramid seen from above with the three boat pits situated along its eastern façade (notes to lines 43 and 70).

PAP/BAB is source of both pap, the nipple, and first syllable of Babylon (*Before Babel*, p.4-5). PAP with ŠIg give the source of the Hopi word 'sipapu', the hole in the floor of the dwellings of the Anasazi culture, representing the portal through which the first people emerged. The phrase LUH AN PAP.ŠIg is repeated on line 70 in the context of baptism and renewal.

First occurrence of the six-word phrase (also line 71). HI/HE with ME, surrounding GE with EŠ, 'three rods' or 'three arrows' and IM, 'clay' and 'spirit'. SAL indicates the 'chamber'.

SAL HI GE EŠ   IM   ME

Source of Greek Hemitheia, Hygeia and Roman Salus. Hygeia, goddess of health and safety, is portrayed offering her oils to a snake curled around a tree.

GE with EŠ/SIN are the three rods of measurement that gave the name Giza (elements of GIZ) and the 'gis' of Trisme-gis-tus. They first appear at the end of line 10 in the context of the ouroboros, the circular snake biting its own tail.

IM ME, translate to 'clay of the spirit', the clay from which the spirit is born as mentioned in later texts. Together, they give the source of 'immerse' while PAP, also in this line of text, is origin of Greek 'bap-tizein', the baptism.

HI with ME surround the three words (and again on line 71. On line 127, they surround AN EN KI KID). Source of both 'hymen', the veil, and 'hemi-', the hemisphere. Inversion gives ME-HI, forming part of MEHIDA, a transliteration of MU (notes to line 85).

Line 19

'Clay', 'wind' and 'land', repetition over lines 19 and 20, surrounding DU KA, 'to carry the word', inferring that the words are inscribed on

IM MA DU KA IM MA

two tablets. MA, pictogram of hanging fruit with given meaning 'land' is also 'truth'. (See notes to lines 42, 52 and 122.)

Source of Latin immaculatus: 'immaculate', and Latin immanere: 'immanent' (indwelling, inherent).

DU KA, 'to carry the word', origin of Deucalion, figure in Greek mythology who travels in a strange vessel on floodwaters, caught up in the spirit winds of the motherland, another translation of IM MA.

Also Buddhist dukkha, 'suffering', and, in this context, accompanied by an outpouring of grievances, perceived as self-pity. Surrounded by the clay, it indicates that suffering is inherent, a condition of life on earth. DU, the foot, represents the earthly connection that has not been severed, preventing the soul from taking full flight. But also the connection through the word, bringing the knowledge to earth.

UMUM is given as 'smith' or 'metalworker', and 'knowledge'. Integrating KASKAL, the 'crossroads', together having the given meaning 'to pour', this is the water-pourer, constellation of Aquarius. A lexical breakdown of UMUM/MUM indicates that it stems from MU with UM, 'movement' or 'time' and 'umbilical cord'. In the context of this line, there is an interesting comparison to be made with Japanese umu, which has the meanings of both 'existence' and 'non-existence'.

Line 20

Working backwards from the translation of line 73, the calculation is that of the four-yearly cycle of Sirius in relation to the sun (notes to line 73).

See KULLA in the notes to lines 14 and 70.

Continuation from line 19 with repetition of the six-word phrase, source of two Greek figures: Deucalion and Phaeton who, according to one account, was goaded into asking his mother for confirmation that the sun was his father. A similar Greek myth has Sirius overheating for love of the obscure goddess Opora and being cooled down by the north wind Boreas.

AB, 'Father', 'sea' and 'abyss' also transliterated as ABBA/ABA, gave biblical Abraham (see ŠA-RA-AB in *The Story of Sukurru*, line 14) and refers to the more ancient Greek Kronos, Father of Time.

ABBA survived into Greek and Latin as 'abba' with the meaning 'father'. BA is the inverted form of AB, phonetic wordplay characteristic of this mono-syllabic language. BA is 'below', 'less', 'without': fatherless. With SUM in this line, origin of Latin absum, 'I am absent'. It might relate to planet Saturn through the Kronos link, a reference to the myth of two suns and a cosmic event during which Saturn was said to have shifted further away from Earth.

Line 21

ZA, 'sound', with 'KUR', 'hills', given here as 'barking' (also lines 6 and 11, notes to line 7) illustrated by a pair of dogs with double collars from an Assyrian cylinder seal, indicating the binary nature of Sirius (p.51). Egyptian Anubis also has the symbolic double knot around its neck.

The addition of KI indicates a place name: The hills of Qurna, an important pharaonic burial site. On the opposite bank of the Nile and associated with the city once known as Thebes (modern day Luxor, notes to line 22), lies the Temple of Karnak, its name said to derive from Arabic Khurnaq: 'fortified village'. Another Al-Qurna lies at the confluence of the two rivers Tigris and Euphrates in southern Mesopotamia, a site said to be the Garden of Eden. NA with KI give 'stone key', clue to line 22..

GAR, 'measure' with RA, 'churn' or 'beat', also Ra as sun-god: 'measure of Ra', 'To measure the churn'. Saturn is given as the 'Lord of Measures' and Arabic Fas Al-rahha as Ursa Minor, place of the hole of the mill peg in the context of the celestial mill (*Hamlet's Mill*[2], p.135 and p.137).

'Garra' in Portuguese and Spanish means 'claw' or 'hook'. There is also mention of 'drive' and 'determination' for the Portuguese word which would fit well with the drumbeat – perhaps of the Arabic kettledrum called a naqqara – in the context of a shamanic ritual.

Line 22

22 (line) / 7 (words) = 3.142857 (Pi)

Pi is the ratio of a circle's circumference to its diameter. It can also be read in stone – the stone key of line 21 – in the form of seven satellite pyramids next to the three pyramids at Giza, laid out as a group of three, then one by the middle pyramid and four on the eastern façade of the Great Pyramid.

ZU-AB, a well-attested collocation, would generally be counted as one word, resulting in only six words on this line (see ME here below). Nevertheless, the existence of sophisticated numerical codes elsewhere in the text lends credence to an exceptional separation into two words here for ZU-AB. Additionally, the words possess individual meanings according to context and are not always collocated.

Absent from this line, ME is nevertheless the silent clue to the mathematical reference and is also found engraved in the entrance to the King's Chamber (*Before Babel*, p.219-220). The same line on another tablet (ETSCL ref.4.80.2, line 12) adds ME after TE (the ME TE of Prometheus, notes to line 33 and 36). On line 36, TE appears before ZU, symbol of 'knowledge' and pictogram of a triangle. The precession of the equinoxes is encoded throughout this text along with references to pre-Pythagorean musical notations. Clearly, the person who wrote this down was capable of encoding mention of pi.

TE, also transliterated TEN or TEMEN, has given meanings 'to be near to', 'to approach' and 'foundation' amongst others. TEN is source of Latin tenet, the 'principle' inscribed at the heart of the Sator magic square (*Before Babel*, p.247).

BI, the 'beer', 'bee' and 'to be', is also transliterated PE_2 and has the given meaning 'total' according to the *King List* where it's used with MU for the addition of periods of time (notes to line 61). BI is translated here as 'is'. TE with BI give the totalling of measurements of length, pictographic TE indicating the joining of two points; the Egyptian stretching of the cord ceremony before the laying of foundations (notes to line 7). At the same time, they refer to the other underlying theme of the mixing of ingredients into a unique brew. According to the lexical lists, BI and PI, 'pitch', are interchangeable (see PI with EL in the notes to line 56).

Taking KUR-NA on line 21 into account, it is possible that TE BI give the source of Thebes, both Egyptian (ancient name of Luxor facing the hills of Qurna) and Greek, unless another source is known. The same goes for the 'Tepi' of Egyptian Zep Tepi, the 'First Time', and also Turkish 'tepe', the round 'hill' of Göbekli Tepe and others.

ZU-AB or AB-ZU? On the Ashmolean transcript, it's written ZU-AB while both transliterations (Ashmolean and ePSD composite) have 'abzu'. A transcript (signs copied directly from the prism) is necessarily closer to home than its transliterated form. I read ZU-AB has the advantage of translating nicely to noun followed by adjective: 'pyramid of the father' the visual form of ZU being more than enough evidence to add 'pyramid' or 'triangle' to its meanings. 'Ancestral knowledge' is fully justified through dictionary-given meanings.

Go up to a land flowing with milk and honey. But I will not go with you, because you are a stiff-necked people; otherwise, I might destroy you on the way. (Exodus 33:3)

SI, the 'horn', with A, the 'water', gives 'spring'. With GA, this last being both 'cow' and 'milk', SI becomes the 'horn of the cow' and a 'horn of milk'. SI also has the given meanings 'finger' and 'fret' linking it to a string instrument. Mesopotamia artefacts include a few examples of a 'bull lyre' featuring a bull's head on the main body of the instrument.

A SI translating to 'horn of water', is easily understood as a spring. Siwa in the Saharan desert is a large oasis, and location of a temple to Amun-Ra.

SI with GA are elements of SIG, the 'weak' voice of the swan, constellation of Cygnus (see line 113). The constellation of Cygnus lies in the Milky Way and close to Vega. It's also associated with the musician Orpheus. SI-GA, 'on the horn of the cow' is probably one source of the name. (See Vega in the notes to line 45.) And, of course, there is always the underlying reference to bull-leaping

<u>Line 23</u>

NUN, the 'guide' with E, the 'levee' to which I add 'raise' for obvious reasons; the waters raised by construction of a dam, one of the irrigation techniques used – and perhaps invented - by the Mesopotamians, their Greek name reading 'between the two rivers' (see 'meso-' on line 48). Confirmation of a guide involved in both water management and astronomy comes from the following ZU-AB and line 24.

NUN and KA are found again on this line although separately (see line 16) inferring measurement; the 'canon'. The whale (or 'great fish') is the ultimate reference for all measurement (see line 127).

'The place from which he rises borders our own land [of Egypt]. Go, make the journey if your heart is set, and put your question to Sol [Helios] himself.' Then up flashed Phaethon at his mother's words (Ovid, Metamorphoses 1:750)

Given as 'what', TA is both 'question' and 'death'. Following AB, 'sea' and 'father', with ZU, the 'knowledge', this is one of several mentions of the questioning hero, precursor to Greek Phaeton, cause of catastrophes when driving the carriage of his father, the sun, and shot down by a thunderbolt from Zeus. TA is also a syllable in the epithet Thoth (line 9).

Abzu (or Apsu) is taken by Assyriologists as either the name of a god or a reference to underground water. According to context, it's a name for a sailor: 'he who knows the sea'. With TA as 'question', it's a reference to navigation by the night sky – an experienced sailor. (See the astronomical name sourced from ZU-AB in the notes to lines 32-33.)

Line 24

River Tigris

IDIGNA is one transliteration of the original word translated to 'Tigris', its pictogram sitting in this line between two ID$_2$, 'river'. That is also how the Göbekli Tepe, Karahan Tepe and other archaeological sites of deep antiquity in that region might be described – sitting below the headwaters of the Taurus mountains, between the two rivers that take their source there.

The earliest pictographic version shows a bird with a strange circular indentation at the place of the neck. Others show it without a head. This was later replaced by a three-word phrase, the central word being GU$_2$, the 'neck' or 'gullet'. Striated and combined with KAK, the nail, it became DUR/TIG/TEK and the phonetic source of the name of both river and feline in later languages: both Tigris and tiger, but also the TEK of Tekmor, Greek Goddess of Necessity. Here with dictionary-given meanings:

GU$_2$ KAK = DUR / TIG / TEK
binding, knot, bond
umbilical cord, totality

In *Lost Stones* (p.122-127), I made a detailed case for DUR as source of 'endure'. TIK/TIG is source of 'tiger':

Greek tigris, possibly from an Iranian source akin to Old Persian tigra- "sharp, pointed," Avestan tighri- "arrow," in reference to its springing on its prey, (Etymonline)

TI   IG

Sumerian TIG, both tiger and throat of the bird, results from an association in the lexical lists of the gullet, and TI, the arrow (see line 25), with IG/IK/EK, the 'door': 'the arrow pointing to the door', showing the way.

River Euphrates

BURANUN is the name of the river Euphrates given in academic transliterations. The source name comprises three words: UD-KIB-NUN, 'sun,' 'ring' and the 'guide'. UD with KIB, 'ring of the sun', is a reference to the ecliptic, the path of the sun as seen from earth.

KIB, 'ring', symbol of two crossed beams (GIZ x GIZ) gives the origin of Arabic 'kiblah' which has the meaning 'which is opposite' and is source of the pole star Polaris:

> *The Arabs knew Polaris as Al Kiblah, "because it is the star least distant from the pole," although then 50 away, and helped them, in any strange location distant from an established place of worship, to know the points of the compass (...) (Star Names* [6]*, p.456)*

Besides 'Buranun', two other names have been transliterated directly from words found opposite UD-KIB-NUN in the lexical entries:

Zimbir, (also cited in the translated antediluvian *King List*) and Sippar:

> *After Euedoreschus some others reigned, and then Sisithrus. To him the deity Cronus foretold that on the fifteenth day of the month Desius there would be a deluge of rain: and he commanded him to deposit all the writings whatever which were in his possession, in the city of the Sun in Sippara.* (L.P. Cory, Ancient Fragments, 1832: Berossus, ca.290 BC, sourced from Eusebius, ca. 260–339 AD, Chronicles 5.8., from Abydenus ca.200 BC.)

> *Upon some of the boundary stones of Sippara (Sepharvaim of the Old Testament), a solar city, Sagittarius "appears sculptured in full glory."* (Richard Allen, Star-Names and their Meanings, 1899, Sagittarius, The Archer, p.354)

'Hand', 'arrow' and 'flow' become 'to show the way' but also 'to shoot the arrow'. Preceded by NUN-NA, the 'stone guide', a picture emerges. There is a place between the rivers Euphrates and Tigris – the name of which can be read Buranun or Sippar - where one or more texts of importance were placed before a catastrophic event on Earth. That place, according to the account relayed by Abydenus, was linked to the sun.

> (Sagittarius) *in Egypt, where it is said to have been known as an Arrow held in a human hand;* (Star Names[6], p.352)

TI is also a reference to Sirius as Tishyra (notes to line 113).

<u>Line 25</u>

First of 12 consecutive lines all containing the word ZU, pyramidal pictogram with given meaning 'knowledge'.

Dictionary-given meanings 'to push', 'thrust', 'gore', 'to expand', 'swell', 'to be suitable'. UL, seventh word on line 25, translated to 'wave', appears twice on line 94 of *The Story of Sukurru* in the context of Noah's expandable ark (notes to line 8). In numerous lexical entries, UL is found collocated with GIR2, having the dictionary-given meaning 'scorpion':

UL   GIR₂
swell scorpion

Following the discover of references to Sagittarius in the preceding lines, I went looking in *Star Names and their Meanings*[6] for the celestial twin of UL/ULA, in the hope that something mentioned there would help to link it to the constellation of Scorpio. And once again I was not disappointed. Sha-ULA is both a star and the sting of the scorpion:

> (Scorpio) *Shaula probably is from Al Shaulah, the Sting, where it lies; but according to Al Biruni, from Mushalah, Raised, referring to the position of the sting ready to strike. (...) Naturally it was an unlucky star with astrologers.* (Star Names[6], p.370)

UL can also be linked to Cygnus, the favourite bird of Orpheus, through its alternative epithet Olof and from there also to the constellation of Lyra:

(Cygnus) *Olof, another word for the Swan, both ornithological and stellar, has been current even to modern time. (...) and it was considered to be Orpheus, placed after death in the heavens, near to his favorite Lyre. (Star Names [6], p.193)*

All three constellations – Cygnus, Lyra and Scorpio – as we know their forms today lie in relatively close proximity to one another around the southern end of the Milky Way and the Great Rift. Cygnus lies in its entirety within the Milky Way, its beak pointing towards that centre. Vega in Lyra just above it was once the northern pole star. Scorpio is one of two constellations with Sagittarius on either side of the Great Rift (p.11).

Line 26

First line of a three-line acrostic beginning with the word GIZ. ZU also appears in all three lines although not in second place.

When Helios (the Sun) made him [Herakles] hot as he proceeded, he aimed his bow at the god and stretched it; Helios was so surprised at his daring that he gave him a golden goblet, in which he crossed Okeanos [to reach Erytheia]. (Pseudo-Apollodorus, Bibliotheca 2. 107, trans. Aldrich)

'Beam', 'head' and 'bowl' where SAG, 'head', is the head of the headless man on Pillar 43 at Göbekli Tepe. With SHU-TI, the hand and the arrow of line 24, SAG is the second and, this time, etymological indication of Sagittarius in this section.

SAG (also read SAN) with KUL 'to collect' and 'bowl', become the head that is a bowl (skull of Orpheus, see p.15) and carriage of the sun. SAG/SAN is source of 'sage' and 'saint' through Latin sanctos. Perhaps this is the origin of the San Graal holy cup myth. A human skull filled with some sacred hallucinogenic brew and lifted to the sky as the spirit rose to the otherworld in the direction of Sagittarius, guardian of the southern gate of the Milky Way… Concerning the death of Orpheus:

> *The story goes that he met his death at the hands of women; but according to the epitaph at Dium in Macedonia he was slain by a thunderbolt; it runs as follows:*
>
> *Here have the Muses laid their minstrel true,*
>
> *The Thracian Orpheus whom Jove's thunder slew.*
>
> (Diogenes Laertius, Lives of Eminent Philosophers,

Dictionary-given meanings 'globe-lightning' and 'bolts of lightning' for SAG KUL add atmosphere: a moment of silence followed by a clap of thunder. Then SI, the horn (also 'finger') on which the ghostly lord rises. Orpheus? Sirius? Phaeton? Heracles? All of them?

SAG KUL also constitute a convincing source for English 'skull'. Note the downward pointing arrow and ominous black circle at the centre of KUL:

> *"bony framework of the head," c. 1200, probably from Old Norse skalli "a bald head, skull," (…) But early prominence in southwestern texts suggests rather origin from a Dutch or Low German cognate (…)* (Etymonline)

'To release', 'open', 'spread' – 'hand', 'to show' with 'measure', GABA ŠU GAR together are given as 'rival'. With GABA also given as 'chest', the 'showing of the chest', a gesture of virile arrogance. Homer in the Iliad compares the bronze armour of the soldiers to the brightness of Sirius (notes to line 43).

With NU as 'not', becoming 'measure not to take', 'without limits', a reckless hero about to enter battle. Also musical; the spreading hand of the maestro, conductor of a great celestial orchestra, which is why I add 'note' to the meanings of NU.

TUK has given meanings 'to play' and 'to acquire', first reference to the music of Orpheus in the context of the three pyramids of Giza (see TUK on lines 54 and 60).

As for the skull, the head of Orpheus has left his shoulders and is balancing on the wing of the bird (p.19).

<u>Line 27</u>

Second line of a three-line acrostic with GIZ in first position.

First of four mentions of the lion positioned directly next to ZU/SU, symbol of the pyramid (lines 27, 31, 32 and 57).

 SI, the 'horn' but also 'finger' and 'fret', the music on which Orpheus will rise to the constellations of Cygnus and Lyra. In this underlying musical theme, SI might be the horns used for the two shafts of the lyre or the finger on its strings, and refer to Vega which balances somewhere on the crossbeam of the lyre – in which case SI GAR ZU translate 'the measure (music) with the finger to know'. It's not possible to know the exact size and position given to Lyra in relation to its great star in the distant past.

At the same time, the horn of Taurus tosses the hero upwards towards the Pleiades or possibly the crescent moon. In this instance, the series of three GIZ indicate the importance of the third number 28, a full lunar cycle. (Another instance of a three-line riddle indicating the importance of the third number appears over lines 106, 107 and 108.)

> (lunar mansions) *Their antiquity is proved by the fact that there* (India), *and probably elsewhere, the list began with the Pleiades, when those stars marked the vernal equinox,* (Star Names [6], p.7)

The horn might be that of the new moon when it appears in horizontal position in the form of a bowl, known as the 'wet moon' (see KUL on line 26 and notes to line 28):

IL$_2$ with given meanings 'raise' and 'carry' is shown to be the source of biblical Immanuel associated with the rising of Sirius on line 73. The word appears four times (lines 27, 30, 73 and 76, notes to line 73.) serving to add another meaning to the word SI, horn of the bull: 'to announce'. (See Sirius in the notes to line 73.)

 ZU/SU in fourth position, pyramid of 'knowledge' and 'sinking', is placed before UR MAH, with given meanings 'lion' and 'great'.

First of two lines (also line 57) with positioning of the lion on the second line of a three-line riddle, confirming that this is the linguistic representation of the Great Sphinx.

<u>Line 28</u>

Third line of the three-line acrostic with GIZ in first position. ZU/SU is again present, this time in third position. Reference to the 28-day cycle of the moon and from there to Orion who was loved by Artemis. (See quote under line 109.) Orion was the son of Greek Hermes, the cattle thief.

This section refers to the false door as known from Ancient Egyptian tombs. The positioning - twice over lines 28 and 29 - indicates that the cog-boat of the hero (with the lion and the sun) will pass through it. The description of what lies beyond is given in the words encased between the two mentions of the 'passage'.

Collocated GIZ UR_3 have an intriguing variety of given meanings: 'beam', 'harness', 'roof', 'to drag', to sweep away', 'to raise a boat'. UR_3 appears in the *Sumerian King List* on lines 39 and 40 (p.53). Preceded by AB_2, the 'cow', UR_3 is source of Al Abur, the 'passage', an epithet of Sirius given by Al Biruni (see p.52, notes to line 73).

Bull of Above and Below, generally read as 'bull of heaven'. Given the line number relating to the 28 days of the lunar month, it refers to the moon and the horns of Taurus together or the moon as the one stone in the sky which is present ' by night and day, 'above and below'. Here with 'bowl', a 'wet moon' as seen on numerous Mesopotamian artefacts (notes to line 27). On this line, preceded by UR_3, the 'passage', it gives the origin of the cow sitting in a boat on the ceiling zodiac of the Dendera Temple in Egypt. There it's said to represent Sirius.

Repetition of five-word phrase (notes to line 9). Fish with its mouth to the milk: fish god Oannes, Jonah in the whale, Piscis Austrinus and/or Pisces (notes to lines 52, 73, 74 and 78).

<u>Line 29</u>

Continuing the passage through the false door (line 28) with the description of what lies beyond. Perhaps encoding the 29.53 days of the lunar month.

KID is both 'fool' and 'mat', GI as 'rod' and 'Earth, and together as 'reed mat'. Underlying reference to ancient Buddhist teachings on perception; fear in the darkness of mistaking a rod or a piece of string (cord, chord) for a venomous snake.

Another is to the string of Orpheus' lyre. (KID as partial source of Greek kithara in notes to line 117.)

EŠ₂ given as 'rope' is both 'cord' and 'chord. Here it's also the flying serpent, constellation of Draco combined with the 'piercing' Cygnus (referring to both Orpheus and Lyra). The combination of rope and bird in this context is seen on the Narmer palette.

<u>Line 30</u>

God brought them out of Egypt; He is like the horns of a wild ox for them. (Numbers 23, Balaam's Second Oracle)

Other authors identified our Eridanus with the fabled stream flowing into the ocean from northwestern Europe, — a stream that always has been a matter of discussion and speculation (indeed, Strabo called it " the no-where existing "... (Star Names[6], p.215)

GAM is given as 'circle', 'rim', 'to curve', and 'to wrap around'. The three-word phrase is given as 'arch' or 'vault' (*Lost Stones*, p.40). Written NUR or NIR, a pair of NUN from NU-UN which can translate to 'not of the land', 'otherworldly'. The breakdown of NUN/ERIDA links to Eridanus (*Lost Stones*, p.206–208):

The name of Greek Eridanus, a mythical river, is said to mean 'early-burnt' and linked to the story of Phaeton (Theoi.com). ERI, also transliterated URU, is said to refer to the constellation of Orion (through 'uru-anna'). DA, the arm, has the given meaning 'riverbank' (notes to line 36).

GUD SI, as 'bull horn' is a reference to sound, to the announcement, and also the lyre of Orpheus made from the horns of the bull.

SI, 'horn', with IL₂, 'to raise', refers to the sport of bull-leaping already attested in *The Story of Sukurru* (ca.2500 BC), line 45 in the context of a rite of passage into manhood:

Males who are weaned a rope around the stone bull man raise.

A scene of bull-leaping dating back to ca. 9000 BC has recently been discovered at the site of Sayburc in Turkey (notes to line 109). SI IL$_2$ further translate to 'the horn announcing the rising' and the biblical announcement of the virgin birth in Isaiah 7:14. (Immanuel in notes to line 73. The Hebrew name translates to 'God is with us'). That tale corresponds to the heliacal rising of Sirius which appears to happen in the company of the constellation of Cancer (notes to line 31). Or is it Canopus?

Line 31

> (Cancer) *Yet few heavenly signs have been subjects of more attention in early days, and few better determined; for, according to Chaldaean and Platonist philosophy, it was the supposed Gate of Men through which souls descended from heaven into human bodies. (…) The early Sanskrit name was Karka and Karkata, the Tamil Karkatan, (Star Names* [6], *p.107–108)*

KAN₄ — Given as 'gate', the reference is to the constellation of Cancer, the crab, which appears in front of the mouth of Leo in the morning sky. The pictogram is that of E$_2$, the temple, with the addition of feathers or wings sprouting upwards. The name derives from Latin while 'crab' is from Greek karkinos (KAR$_2$ in notes to line 7). At the heart of Cancer lies the Beehive Cluster, once known as Praesepe. Both Cancer and Taurus are linked to bees (notes to lines 92 and 102).

ZU UR MAH — Second of four mentions of the lion positioned directly to either the right or the left of the symbol of a pyramid (lines 27, 31, 32 and 57).

ŠU TI A — 'hand', 'arrow' and 'flow, together point the way. One source of Greek Sothis, an epithet of Sirius. The Great Sphinx sends off the spirit of the king and opens the New Year celebration. (See SUD on line 50. TI on line 113.)

Line 32

I LU — (See the musical connotation of I in the notes to line 11.) LU with ZU as source of 'luz' meaning 'light' through Latin lux. I with LU give the source of 'illuminate'. Confirmation comes in the form of ME TE on line 33 and a proverb in the lexical lists:

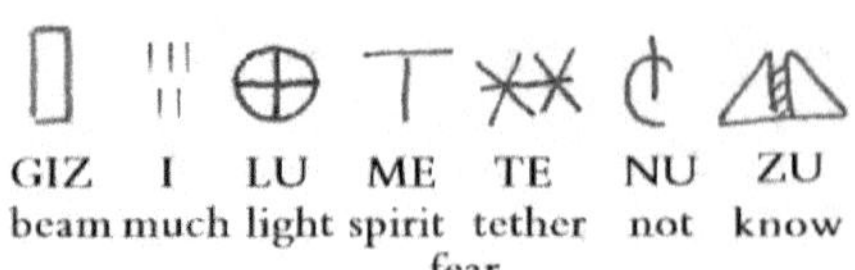

GIZ I LU ME TE NU ZU

beam much light spirit tether not know

fear

In the all-encompassing light (of the beam), the spirit is untethered (Prometheus) and fear unknown. (OB Nippur Ura 1 248)

It further confirms the overall meaning of the flight of the soul out of darkness towards the light (Osiris, Prometheus). (See the theme of fear in the notes to line 29. See the covering of the beam on lines 45 to 48.)

ZU PIRIGxUD

Third of four mentions of the lion positioned directly to either the right or the left of the symbol of a pyramid (lines 27, 31, 32 and 57). The lexical breakdown of transliterated PIRIG gives the guardian of the perimeter door (see Pi in notes to line 22):

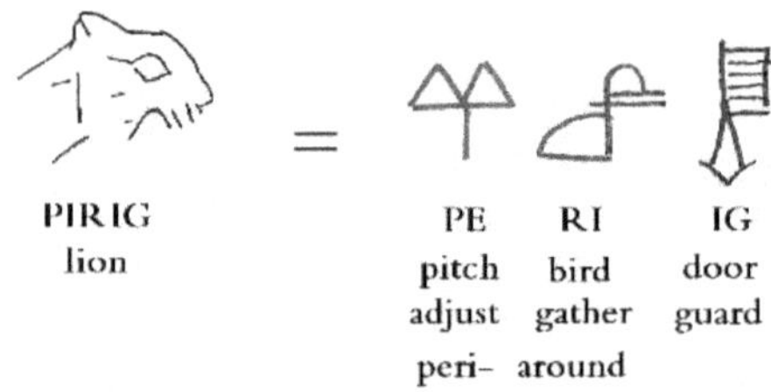

PIRIG   =   PE   RI   IG

lion

pitch   bird   door

adjust gather guard

peri- around

PI with RI give 'peri', origin of Greek peri-. (...) The distance around a circle, the circumference, corresponds to its perimeter. (...) PI as 'musical pitch' with RI as 'gather' indicate a connection between Greek peri- and a gathering of sound, perhaps a combination of notes, a harmony, birdsong. (Before Babel, p.187)

With LU_2, 'man' as prefix, RA, the 'churner' with given meaning 'flail' becomes the epithet Ra, equivalent of the Egyptian sun god Ra.

The same combination appears at the beginning and end (lines 1 and 41) of the antediluvian portion of the *Sumerian King List*. Analysed in *Lost Stones*:

The mound was left unmentioned in the original translation. Was it the mountain of Hephaestus, the mythical smith who lived and worked at the heart of a fire-breathing volcano? Or was it a mound in the style of a pyramid/ziggurat/nuraghe constructed to reach the sky? (Lost Stones, p.251-252)

<u>Line 33</u>

ZU AB, generally transliterated 'abzu' or 'apsu', gives the source name of the circumpolar star Kochab, also attributed to its neighbour Polaris. ZU/SU, given meanings 'knowledge' and 'sinking', pictogram of a pyramidal form with central 'ladder' can also be read KUŠ:

KUŠ   AB
Kochab
knowledge of the sea

SAL, 'chamber' and 'female', with SI, 'horn' and 'remembrance', together read EL with given meaning 'pure'. Following AB, the meeting place of father and son, i.e. chamber of conception. Source of the Canaanite god El.

ME, 'spirit', 'magic', with TE, 'approach', 'foundation' to which I add 'join'. Partial source of 'perimeter' and Prometheus who takes his full name from PIRI, the lion of the sun (Great Sphinx found in 4th position on line 32) or from PER/PIR, one transliteration of UD, the sun, with UM, the umbilical cord, and ME-TE (in 4th and 5th position on line 33), 'the spirit to tether' but also 'to measure'. (UM ME TE on line 68 of *The Story of Sukurru*.) With ME, source of Latin timere, 'to fear', and temere, 'temerity'.

TE, found opposite TE ME EN, in the lexical lists, is read as Akkadian 'temen', and, as such, is source of 'temenos', the perimeter measurement (of EN, the lord, who is the 'one', the 'beginning' and the 'end').

ME was quite carefully carved at some point in time in a central position on the stone above the entrance to the King's Chamber in the Great Pyramid (*Before Babel*, p.220).

<u>Lines 34-35</u>

ENGUR is comprised of KILI, 'block' and 'encircle', with HAL, 'to divide' at its centre, the same combination as ID$_2$, 'river' but without A, the 'water'.

KILIxHAL   =   EN GUR

Found opposite EN, the lord, with GUR, a word meaning 'to bend', 'to curve', 'to wrap around' and 'turban'. GUR gives the 'winding'. With an additional 'twist', it becomes the source of the mythical Gordian knot: the lord's knot. 'Ziggurat', modern name for the Mesopotamian step pyramid, stems from a phrase that includes GUR (*Lost Stones*, p.115).

> *Greek Gorgones "the grim ones," from gorgos, of a look or gaze, "grim, fierce, terrible," later also "vigorous, lively," a word of unknown origin.* (Etymonline)

The two words ENGUR-RA are repeated six times in this text (lines 34, 41, 50, 56, 57 and 82), four of which preceded by E_2, the 'temple' and all at the beginning of the line. On lines 56 and 57, they appear in the context of the three pyramids of Giza.

GIR_3, given as 'path', 'by means of' and 'via', is translated here as 'prophetic bull' (*Lost Stones*, p.57, p.218). Confirmed by its use GIR₃ with TA, the 'question' on line 114. Appears four times (lines 34, 96, 102 and 115).

IN has the given meaning 'straw'. With RI, to 'gather', and RI IN DU DU, to 'carry', it can be understood as the time of harvest. I have added the preposition 'in', giving 'to gather in' and 'to bring in the crops'. See IM MA RI IN DU in notes to line 36.

Line 36

364 (lunar) + 1 (tooth) = 365 (solar) x 4 = 1,460 (Sothic)

ZA, 4th word, (NI.UD count as one) with given meaning 'four' signals the 364-day (28 x 13) lunar calendar. ZA with GUL, 5th word, are given as 'tooth'. ZA signals the 4 x 365 day (1,460) Sothic calendar of Ancient Egypt (see the comb and tooth Sothic calendar at Giza in the notes to line 73).

GUL = GU UL
cord suitable

Given as 'to destroy', 'to break' but also 'to carve' and 'to engrave', plumb-line of the architect, from GU, the 'cord' with UL, 'fittingly' and 'wave', the 'sculptor' (of wood or stone) or 'Destructor' (who moves the hanging cord/tether/plumb-line, 'the wavering cord'). Source of Latin angulus, 'angle', the angular measurements of size and scale by astronomers (with AN, the sky).

Also source of Algol, the Arabic demon star and mischief-maker, a variable double or triple-star system with constant eclipses (where one crosses the path of the other). Algol appears on the gorgon's snake-filled head, among the moving ropes of Greek Medusa's hair. The illustration of this line is from a carving on a pair of slit Gulgul drums in the Metropolitan Museum, New York and also used for lines 186-188 of *The Story of Sukurru*. GUL is the Snake Goddess who ensnares the fox in that image.

TE, with given meaning 'foundation', gave the first syllable of Greek temenos, sacred area around a temple (also line 22). In an equally alarming passage of *The Story of Sukurru* (line 68), Prometheus is written UM-ME-TE where UM is the umbilical cord, again a measuring cord between the celestial Matriarch and Earth (notes to line 33).

> *This is also something that Aesop said. The clay which Prometheus used when he fashioned man was not mixed with water but with tears. Therefore, one should not try to dispense entirely with tears, since they are inevitable.* (Aesop, *Fables* 516 from Themistius, Orations 32, trans. Gibbs, Theoi.com)

Prometheus, tied to the rock, pays the penance for his arrogance (See the weeping in the notes to line 70. See the mixing of the mortar on line 93) but will survive and return with the measurements of the cosmos to be engraved in the stones of the Great Pyramid of the Sun.

ZU, the pyramid, is 'knowledge' and 'learning'. ME-ZU, the 'in-between' and 'knowledge of the spirit' gave the Egypto-Mesopotamian astronomers and architects part of their name (notes to line 52). The Ashmolean transcript shows TE BI in place of TE ZU (composite ETCSL version). As it's impossible to prefer one over the other, the only conclusion is that BI and ZU are analogous, synonyms in certain contexts. (See TE BI on line 22. See the notes to line 108 for the use of BI in the encoding of the Ashmolean prism.)

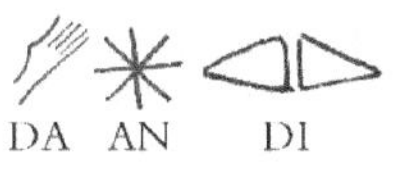

DA AN DI, the 'arm divide in the sky', reads 'divine Danaus', brother of King Belus of Egypt (p.35-36). The arm is that of the astronomer. It's the wing of the bird on Pillar 43 at Göbekli Tepe and the divided aspect of the white arms of the galactic plain just above, the river Eridanus. It's also a reference to the constellation of Sagittarius as southern gate (notes to line 85).

Latin dividere "to force apart, cleave, distribute,

DA, also the 'riverbank' with DI as 'divided' indicating the two banks of the river. It's the two arms of the Great Sphinx pointing the way to the constellation of Leo (line 31).

AN with DI, the 'celestial divisions' are astronomical calculations written down in the divisions (cuneiform wedges) of the clay: IM MA.

DA with AN also give the source of 'dance' and the 'dancers' at Nevali Çori (p.48), further linking to the music of Orpheus and to the constellation of Lyra.

Comparison of lines 34, 36 and 37, where IM MA, the 'clay of truth', introduces the final three words, uncovers a magic square containing coded information. The riddle can be usefully compared to the Sator Square which is traced back to the 1st century AD (*Before Babel*, p.237). This one dates to at least 1600 BC.

AN, the 'sky', eight-pointed star, summit of the eight-sided pyramid, takes central position. The riddle is astronomical and DI, the 'division' (of line 36) divides it into 360 degrees.

Labyrinth of the Pyramid

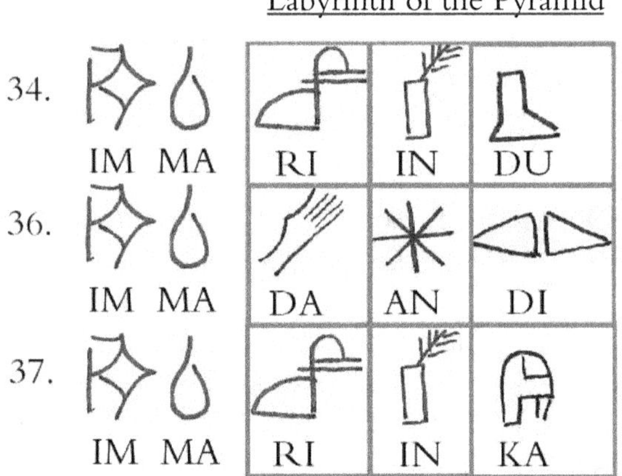

Read vertically:

- RI, the 'gathering', takes place on either side of DA, the 'riverbank', elements of the celestial river Eridanus (p.18, notes to line 30). RI, the collector bird, also has given meanings 'crossbar', 'dividing line' and 'transverse line' (ePSD).

RI is also transliterated DAL giving DA-DAL source of Greek daidalos meaning 'cunningly wrought' and mythological Greek Daedalos who built the labyrinth of the Minotaur (notes to line 15).

- IN, given meaning 'straw', surrounds AN, the 'sky'. Becoming the two white streams of the Milky Way divided by the arm of Dan (Danaus) at their centre: to enter the river of the galactic plain.

- DU with KA, source of Greek Deucalion and Hindu dukkha, the suffering, translate to 'carry the word' or 'divide the action from the word' (notes to lines 19 and 20). The soul will be judged according to both actions and words.

Read diagonally:

- RI, 'collect' and KA, the 'word' surround AN, the 'sky' and summit of the pyramid: 'collect the words (in the sky)'. RI/RE is an element of the Phoenix on line 111.

(See notes to lines 30, 97, 113, and 118.) The arm in the sky will decide the fate of those gathered by the banks of the river Eridanus, waiting to board the Boat of All Souls (line 89):

Line 37

KA, 'mouth' and LI, translated here to 'lip', also ARA, are given twice and written in their original pictographic form on the otherwise abstract cuneiform tablet. This is indicated by capital letters in the transliteration suggesting that their source form was of particular importance. The academic translation ignores the words altogether.

Written twice, the two lips of Calliope, one of the three muses, Greek goddess of music, song and dance, and mother of Orpheus. Following mention of the ghoul on line 36, also source name of Hindu Kali, Goddess of Destruction, which links to the Greek images of a face with grimacing mouth, hanging tongue and large canines (see 'tooth' on line 36) commonly interpreted as that of the Greek gorgons (notes to line 56). The academic Sumerian version of the figure is named Humbaba or Huwawa. (See Yuga in the notes to line 45.)

The mouth is the entrance to SAL, a 'cave' in a stone hill from where ZA, the sound is heard. (ZA KUR on lines 6, 7, 11, 21, 29, 37 and 124).

<u>Line 38</u>

TA, 'question' and 'death' with HI at its centre, given as 'sweet' and 'syrup'. This is the honey of Greek Hebe (notes to line 17), identified as a bee who serves her brew to the gods. The meanings of TA indicate a hallucinogenic brew prepared for the initiate. Perhaps a reference to 'mad honey' (notes to line 52) gathered from the hives of bees foraging pollen from rhododendron flowers.

HAR with RA, partial source of the name Harran. Here translated to 'Mill of Seasons' or 'Mill of Hours' (see the quote under line 38), the 'churning mill' or even 'Mill of Ra' (the sun god). One of two combinations that give the source of Greek hora meaning a limited time within a year, month, or day, a 'season' (notes to line 10).

An underlying theme of sounds is always present in HAR, source of 'harp' and the lyre played by Greek Orpheus (also Apollo). HAR was translated 'round curses' in *The Story of Sukurru* based on lexical entries and pictograms showing the word as HI with AŠ$_2$, the double-edged sword, at its centre; the millstone that grinds out wishes and curses, a prophetic stone.

KUK, the circling of the cog-boat and the cock (notes to line 12), with ŠI ERIN$_2$, collocated words 'eye' and 'yoke' leading to 'blind', with AK, 'to do'. Blind Orion or Osiris whose epithet figures on the following line?

<u>Line 39</u>

<u>Osiris and the Brew</u>

UŠ, the penis, with A, the liquid, together are given as 'urine'. First of two sources for the name Osiris, in both cases taking the first syllable of his name from the sign of the phallus (*Lost Stones*, p.149). The other source name appears in the context of Giza on line 56. The related images appear on the Ancient Egyptian Narmer palette (left) and another palette from the same era.

Deer urine was used by shamans for its psilocybin content, suitably filtered by the animal that had fed on amanita mushrooms. Given the presence of GUD, the 'bull', might the same be said of bull urine? Their excrement is known to favour the growth of magic mushrooms. Is this the direct result of the animal ingesting the fully developed mushroom cap? If so, it's possible that bull urine would have the same quality as that of the tripping deer.

Does the bull send the king on his underworld journey entirely thanks to the strength of its horns?

SUM with given meanings 'equal', 'to place' and 'to give' becomes the 'sum' through Latin summa which also means 'essence', and 'whole body' through Greek söma. SUM with A offer a compelling potential source for Sanskrit soma in this short sentence on the subject of hallucinogenic journeying. 'Urine to offer': In Greek mythology, three kings (Hermes, Zeus and Poseidon) urinate on the hide of a bull in order to generate both bees and Orion (quote under line 109).

<u>Line 40</u>

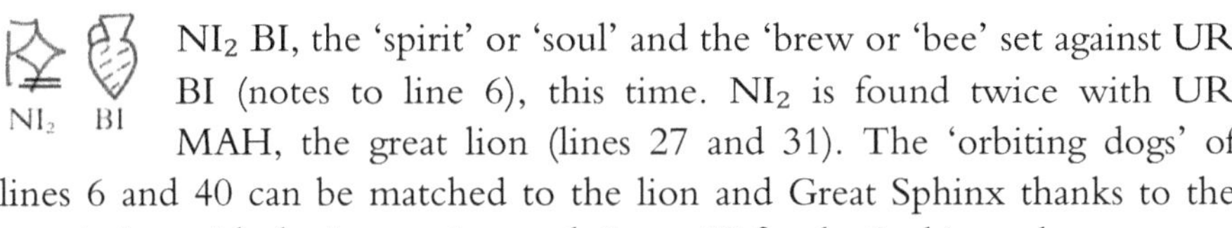

NI₂ BI, the 'spirit' or 'soul' and the 'brew or 'bee' set against UR BI (notes to line 6), this time. NI₂ is found twice with UR MAH, the great lion (lines 27 and 31). The 'orbiting dogs' of lines 6 and 40 can be matched to the lion and Great Sphinx thanks to the association with the journeying soul. See p.52 for the Sothic cycle.

The musical theme continues with UR BI, also source of Orpheus, and the two chords, EŠ₂ around HAR which reads not only 'mill' but also 'harp' (or 'lyre') in this position and context. Discussed in the introductory section (p.67).

EŠ₂ with its given meanings of 'rope' and 'string' has multiple uses. This is the massive snake and rope wound around the central mill in the churning of the Milk Ocean, its two ends held by opposing teams. It's the Ancient Egyptian knotted rope serving to mark out the foundations of their temples during the 'stretching of the cord' ceremony. The two EŠ₂ are also musical chords and the Sphinx is the maestro of the musical mill.

DU UR, 'foot of the lion/dog' is found in the lexical lists opposite DUR which is also the TIG of 'tiger' with given meanings 'bond' and 'knot' to which I add 'endure' (notes to line 24):

Atlas the Endurer, the father of the Hyades and Pleiades, so skilled in knowledge of the skies that he was shown as their supporter; (Star Names [6], p.19)

GI₄, pictogram of two reeds with given meaning 'turn': 'The stylus of the ancestor whirling' but also Atlantis among the reeds. Repeated three times (lines 14, 40 and 91). Atlas is directly mentioned five times in this text through AD, also read AT or ATA (lines 14, 40, 65, 67, 91). Given as 'seal', 'father' and 'bead'. First syllable of Atlantis (notes to lines 14, 64 and 65).

Here, it's no coincidence that the seal appears after reference to the foot of the Sphinx. More than one lexical entry links that three-word phrase to MA LI KU (see p.66) which together translate to:

at the altar of the land (Mother of Truth) to sit (as king)

Malik means 'king' in Arabic. (See LI as synonym of ARA, the altar, on line 117.) Swahili 'mali' from Arabic means 'wealth' and 'property'.

<u>Line 41</u>

ENGUR-RA, winding canal, appears six times (lines 34, 41, 50, 56, 57 and 82. See notes to line 34).

<u>The Emerald Tablet and the Dragon</u>

Written by Hermes Trismegistus (p.69) who is also Egyptian Thoth (line 9).

The eight-pointed star of AN appears three times. Transliterated MUL has given meanings 'star', 'to shine', 'radiate' and is understood to be the prefix to names of constellations (MUL APIN for example). See the biblical verse below citing 'a third of the stars' and linking to a dragon.

GI has given meanings 'green', 'reed', 'to establish' among others, both the stylus used to write on the seal and source of Greek Ge meaning 'Earth'.

DUB/TUB has given meanings 'tablet' and 'copper'. Taking GI as both 'green' and 'earth', GI DUB translates the 'Emerald Tablet' and 'copper tablet of Earth', presumably the vision of Earth from the sky, in which case green may extend to blue. Other given meanings of DUB are 'verdigris', a blue-green patina that forms over time on copper, and 'to tremble'.

DUB BA AN together give the source of Arabic Thuban, a star in the circumpolar constellation of Draco, the Dragon. The name comes from Arabic 'large snake', and is also translatable to 'basilisk' (notes to lines 1 and

85 where it is further linked to Scorpio and to the 'divine Danaus', son of the king of Egypt).

Thuban was the pole star ca.3000 BC. It has also been proposed as the focal point of one of the shafts in the Great Pyramid, another being the circumpolar star Kochab, close to Polaris in Ursa Minor (notes to line 33).

The lexical entries give GI DUB PA AN as an alternative phrase, indicating PA, 'wing' and 'breath', as a synonym of BA, 'below' in this context. PA AN became Pan, both pagan god and source of Greek 'pan-' meaning 'all'.

Several cylinder seals show a figure riding on a horned serpent, one being famously and mistakenly named Marduk. That figure is covered in circular patterns. The lord and king, 'basileus', is circling on the dragon, 'basilisk', above and below.

As further confirmation of its connection to the dragon, DUB also appears on some lexical tablets collocated with BU, pictogram of the horned snake. The following verses from Revelation are thought to refer to Draco:

Then another sign appeared in heaven: a huge red dragon with seven heads, ten horns, and seven royal crowns on his heads. His tail swept a third of the stars from the sky, tossing them to the earth. (Revelation 12:3-4)

The two words, BA-AN, 'without' and 'sky' are translated to 'below'. They might equally read 'underground', giving 'the Emerald Tablet which is underground'. That translation is all the more likely in that it conforms to the analysis of line 40 referring to the message under the foot of the Sphinx.

BA with AN translate to another form (also AN NA) of the phrase for which the *Emerald Tablet* is most famous: 'As above so below.' Between them a semi-circular KUK with LA, the 'hanging circle'. KUK has been used elsewhere in this translation for the cog-boat of the hero but also for Cygnus (lines 12 and 113). LAL has given meanings 'hang' and 'small' which might equally apply to the vision of Earth (Ge) below.

<u>Line 42</u>
Whether biblical, Mesopotamian, Indian or Egyptian, the question of truth is at the heart of everything. Read from right to left, this source of Sanskrit

Mahabharata appears to confirm the existence of the Indian text at ca.1600 BC, a far greater age than the proven age of the Indian epic at ca.400 BC. The line number 42 also confirms the link to the Egyptian *Book of the Dead* in which forty-two questions must be answered in the negative:

> *I know thy name, I know the names of the Forty-two Gods who live with thee in this Hall of Maati, who live by keeping ward over sinners, (…) In truth I have come unto thee, I have brought Maati (Truth) to thee.* (*Book of the Dead*, Trans. W.Budge Appendix from the Papyrus of Nu, Brit. Mus. No. 10477, Sheet 22))

TA, the 'question', is repeated seven times in this text. Pictographic BARAG/PARAG, given as 'dais' (a raised platform) and 'ruler' which I have extended to 'throne room', appears to be formed from MAL, the 'basket', with the addition of a diagonal cross at its centre and, externally, a varying number of short oblique lines. Lexical entries show BARAG opposite PA, the 'wing' with RAK/SAL, which together translate to 'female wings'.

Sanskrit para means "higher" or 'highest' and 'supreme'. Barak has the meaning 'lightning' in Arabic and Hebrew. Hebrew parash means 'horseman', linking to the constellation of Perseus (Pegasus was born from the blood of Medusa killed by Perseus), also in the Indian:

> *(Perseus) Parasiea, current in late Indian astronomy, is only another form of the Greek original.* (*Star Names* [6], p.330)

Arabian Al Buraq is the horse said to have carried the Prophet through the seven layers of heaven and back in one night. Traditional eastern art has since shown this to be a winged horse with female head.

ANŠE

Among other indications, the collocation of ANŠE ('ass', 'donkey', 'horse' and also 'servant') with BARAG in texts, proverbs, and at least one tablet from the 4th millennia (CDLI ref. P325744) confirms the presence of an equid. On a couple of 4th millennium tablets, BARAG is found collocated with pictographic ERIM, given as 'yoke' or 'harness' but which clearly takes the form of an archer's bow complete with string (P002945, P001325) another indication of a link to the Sagittarian archer-centaur.

MAHA has the given meaning 'great'. Sanskrit maha is also 'great' while maya links to illusion and magic. In Malay, mahal is 'beloved' and 'expensive'. In Hawaiian, mahalo means 'to admire', 'appreciate'. In Swahili, mahari means 'dowry', 'bride price'.

In context, the element MA signals 'truth', with the quality of the gifts indicating the degree of love of the suitor. GAR the 'measure' also has given meanings 'things' or 'possessions'. It's possible that an underlying reference is made to the inspection and evaluation of the dowry…material possessions.

The Pleiades are present in this scene under the guise of MAHA with KI, giving Kimah (notes to line 106). It's possible that therein lies the ultimate explanation for the question of 42. Are there six Pleiades or seven? Is there a lost fish somewhere in that equation? The questions must be asked.

Line 43

And I heard the voice of a man calling from between the banks of the Ulai: "Gabriel, explain the vision to this man." As he came near to where I stood, I was terrified and fell facedown. "Son of man," he said to me, "understand that the vision concerns the time of the end." (Daniel 8:15–17)

First of six ZAG (lines 43, 52, 62, 75, 108, 129), given meanings 'shoulder', 'boundary', 'to mark' amongst others. Pictogram of a shoulder knot, a bow used to hold a garment in place.

The three words together and in a musical context (where ZAG breaks down to ZA-AK; 'sound to make') might be further translated to:

'A spreading sound in the pyramid to know'

GAB/GABA, in second position on this line gives the third digit of the main encoded number (43.2). It also has the given meaning 'chest' and might be understood as the 'shield' of Achilles on which the stars and constellations appear, described in unusual detail in the Iliad (Bk 18).

GAB gives the first syllable of the Hebrew name Gabriel, the archangel who announces the birth of John the Baptist (Luke 1:13). Its most ancient pictographic form resembles an abstract representation of a pair of lifting wings and is similar in form to PA, the 'wings of the tutor':

> *It is my contention that PA was once carefully laid out in front of the greatest of the three pyramids of Giza, known as Khufu's pyramid. That message from the past – consistently ignored but magically enduring - takes the form of Sumerian PAP and constitutes one wing of PA, shown here with a couple of the given meanings. (Lost Stones, p.90)*

The knowledge encoded in this text is both astronomical and musical (see GAB on lines 54 and 60),

ZU/SU, fittingly placed in third position, is translated according to one of its dictionary-given meanings: 'knowledge', pictogram of a pyramid with central ladder. It's no longer a secret that the Great Pyramid of Giza encodes equations of time and space in its volumes and position The key is 432 (notes to line 108).

The encoding of 432 in this line comes in the context of a beam of white (milk-like) light (see the proverb in notes to line 32). The beam is in the Tree of Consciousness and Knowledge which will appear soon after (line 45), also translating to the 'beam with the perfect pitch'.

ID is 'time', 'wing', 'strength' and 'power' in the dictionaries while MUŠ₃ is 'space' becoming the 'Divider of Time'. (See notes to line 9. See ID in *Lost Stones*, p.65.)

ID MUŠ₃

The Ermine

MUŠ₃, pictogram of the reed bundle and one source of our word 'mouse' through Greek mys and Latin mus, this is the preferred hiding place of a pesky little rodent, either field mouse or ermine (stoat). It's paired here and elsewhere with the seemingly unlikely meanings of strength and power. But appearances are sometimes deceptive and the ermine has special powers. It has the unique and magical gift of a coat that transforms to pure white in winter. Just a touch of black is left at the tip of its tail.

See the images of the rodent at Göbekli Tepe and the illustration next to line 9 taken from a 4th millennium clay tablet. Also the 'voice of might' on line 16 of *The Story of Sukurru.*

<u>Ashtar, Astarte</u>

(Virgo) Astarte, too, was identified by the Venerable Bede with the Saxon goddess of spring, Eostre, at whose festival, our Easter, the stars of Virgo shine so brightly in the eastern evening sky (Star Names[6], p.463)

Cicero gives Astarte as the fourth Venus:

The first Venus is the daughter of the Sky and the Day ; (...) The fourth was conceived of Syria and Cyprus," and is called Astarte ; it is recorded that she married Adonis. (Cicero, *De Natura Deorum*, Bk III xxiii, Trans. H. Rackham)

The names are derived from the two words in the lexical entries found opposite ID-MUŠ₃:

ID MUŠ₃ = AŠ₂ TAR
Ashtar

AŠ₂, 'wish' and 'curse', with TAR/KUD, 'cut', together transliterated AŠKUD with meanings 'extremities' and 'door'. Ashtar, according to this breakdown of the name, appears to be an important decision-maker with the ability to grant wishes or curses and to change destinies. Source of Aramaean Attar, Ethiopian Astar, and also Canaanite Astarte.

On Tyrian coins, Astarte carries a thrusting spear called a 'hasta'. HAS is another transliteration of TAR, 'to cut', an element of which is TA, 'death' and 'questioning'. Around and around we go.

Line 44

Combination of SAL, 'chamber' and SI, 'horn' and 'remember', transliterated as EL, has the given meanings 'raise' and 'pure' becoming the 'raised horn' and perhaps the purity of its sound. Source of the Canaanite bull god El. Raise the horn...

KI   EL   KI

SAL is also read RAG (from its position in lexical lists opposite RA, 'churn' and AK, 'to do'). In Norse mythology, a loud horn heralds the start of Ragnarok, the end of the world by fire and/or water. The first two syllables – Ragna – have the meaning 'the ruling powers' in Old Norse.

Here between two KI, two 'places', the Chamber of the Horn and of Remembrance is at their heart. In astronomical terms, the first KI might apply only to ZU AB, and refer to the position of the pole star Kochab. In that case, EL refers to the womb/chamber of the north pole.

Another transliteration of EL (SAL SI) gives SIKIL, partially analysed in *Before Babel*:

> *A source of water (KIL in ID$_2$) and encircling blocks (KILI) where cosmic energy (ley lines KI-LI) meets Earth (KI), where a fine horn (SIKIL) is raised in a chamber (KI-EL/KI-IL), where the key to spiritual rising is found (KI-IL), where the souls of the dead (kill?) are purified and rise (SIKIL). (Before Babel, p.93, 2019)*

Line 45

GIZ TUG$_2$ PE GA   Translated in *The Story Of Sukurru* to 'Tree of Consciousness and Knowledge', the three-word phrase is found more than once in the various texts of Mesopotamia with the addition of GA, 'milk'.

GIZ is both 'tree' and 'beam'. This is the beam in which Egyptian Osiris is imprisoned and in which he floats along a great river. It's also the firestick in which Prometheus intends to trap and carry the fire of the sun back to Earth. In astronomical terms, it refers to the axle shaft (see p.57).

TUG$_2$, with the given meanings 'forethought' and 'to cover' amongst others, collocated with GIZ can be read as 'ear' and 'wisdom'. Prometheus also has the meaning 'forethought' in Greek. Here the hero is covered by the beam. He is in its light. He gains its knowledge (see the proverb in the notes to line 32).

Vega

Northern pole-star ca.12000 BC, Vega sits somewhere at the tip of the celestial lyre as we know the constellation of Lyra today (variations in its depiction perhaps occurring over time) and was also known as Lyra.

PE/WE with GA has a musical connotation through PE/PI as 'musical pitch' and GA as the milk ocean (notes to line 54). Given the underlying musical theme with a number of references to the lyre of Apollo/Orpheus, it's probable that both SI GA (lines 22 and 63) and PE GA, given only once, are referencing this most ancient pole star.

PE/PI is given as both 'reduce' and 'expand'. In musical terms, it translates to 'pitch'. Like GIZ, it has a multitude of alphabetic transliterations (*Lost Stones*, p.107). One is WE, leading to Wega, another pronunciation of Vega. 'Pitch' becomes meaningful in the context of Apollo's lyre. Another is YU. Hindu 'Yuga' meaning 'age' finds its source here in PE/YU with GA. Hindu Kali appears on line 37.

The phrase can be understood as a beam of light where PE with GA, as 'perfection' and 'milk white', together give the source of Pegasus, white winged horse of the centurion and archer (part of Sagittarius). Pegasus is thought to originate from Greek pēgē which is a 'fountain' or 'spring', potentially the mythological 'springs of Ocean', near which Medusa was killed by Perseus (see Siwa in the notes to line 22).

> *Athena, they say, was the divinity who gave most help to Bellerophontes, and she delivered to him Pegasos, having herself broken in and bridled him.* (Pausanias, Description of Greece 2. 4. 1)

My understanding is that the reference to a covering of perfect white on line 45 applies not only to Greek Pegasus, the white horse, but also to the Great Pyramid as it would once have appeared in all its splendour before the white lime casing stones were stripped away. There is a further analogy with the colour of the ermine's fur which becomes white in winter (notes to line 43).

Line 46

AN NU DIM₂ HU.HI, the cycles of time, is repeated from line 10, indicating cycles of time (notes to line 10).

Here EN comes after the phrase and is paired directly with NUN KI, the 'lord in an otherworldly place'.

Source of:

- AN NU: Latin annus: 'year'

- EN NUN: Latin enuntiare: 'divulge', 'disclose', 'reveal'

- NUN: Latin nuntiare: 'announce',

- NUN: Latin nuntius 'messenger'

With KI as suffix indicating a place, this is the Place of the Revelation. In biblical terms, it's the announcement by the archangel Gabriel (line 43) of

the virgin birth of Immanuel (line 73) which links to that of the star Sirius
through the line number (Sothic cycle in the notes to line 73).

<u>Line 47</u>

BAR/BARA, pictogram of the shepherd's crook, has given
meanings 'fleece', 'strange', 'outside', and 'behind' to which I
add 'stranger' or 'foreigner' and 'wild' (notes to line 48). This is
BAR RA

the fleece of a wild animal, more specifically a ram, and first mention of the
constellation of Aries. Source of the Greek myth, the golden fleece will
cover the Tree of Consciousness and Knowledge.

Bara was the name given to the constellation of Aries by the ancient
Persians. (There exists a potential but unconfirmed link to BARAG. See
notes to line 42.) BAR-RA is repeated on line 48, and the theme continues
on lines 49 and 51 with the 'volcano'.

'Man', 'eye', 'not': Several ways in which to turn the phrase:
'That man not see', 'that man not look', 'the blind man', an
epithet that applies to Orion. In the context of Aries, it might
LU₂ ŠI NU

explain the ancient images of a ram with its head turned backwards. Is it
avoiding looking at the blinding sun? Also see the proverb in the notes to
line 32. The backward-turned head of Aries, the ram - notably on the
zodiac at Dendera – might indicate the measuring of precession by means of
noting the relative position of the new moon – in which case, 'that the man
not look directly at the light of the sun'. Source of Latin lucida: 'bright star'.

LU₂-ŠI gives the origin of Lucifer, the trickster, whose name acquired
negative connotations at a later date. 'The seeing man' as 'lucid' or 'the man
not to see' as the shape-shifter, the implication being that this is the blind
initiate and tricks are played on them in the course of acquiring wisdom –
when they will see the light. Source of 'hallucinate' (notes to line 100).
Potentially a reference to the absence of Sirius in the night sky of the
northern hemisphere at certain periods and relevant to line 113 where Sirius
is clearly identified as the warning 'eye' of Argo Navis.

'Not elsewhere to collect' where BAR RI give the
source of 'barge' or 'bark', a vessel carrying merchandise
NU BAR RI DAM   (attested in a Sumerian proverb). One source of Latin
nugari: to trick, to cajole, to cheat, to take for a fool. A word of unknown
origin, first used as a warning against the trickster in this line.

With BAR RA, the 'stranger', an underlying warning on this line where DAM can be read as both 'spouse' and 'trust'. Don't take a foreign spouse!

(…) So I advise the younger widows to marry, have children, and manage their households, denying the adversary occasion for slander. For some have already turned aside to follow Satan. (1 Timothy 5:15)

Line 48

NUN.ME, 'spirit guide', is transliterated to Apkallu in conventional translations, as a result of the two collocated words being found opposite AB-GAL, 'Great Father' in the lexical lists. (See the link to Egyptian Nun in the notes to line 70.)

Here followed by ZU, the 'knowledge', combining the Spirit Guide with ME-ZU/SU, 'knowledge of the spirit and of the magic' which became the Greek Meso- of Mesopotamia meaning 'in-between', with the addition of PU/BU-TAM, river and snake of the sun. (notes to line 52).

Collocated BAR-RA has the meaning 'wild' for the animal and translates to 'stranger' or 'foreigner'. Second mention of the constellation of Aries, the ram (notes to line 47). NE, 'fire', linked to SIKI, 'hair' might be understood as either red, golden red or possibly yellow, the colours given to flames. Together they refer to the fiery red-gold colour of the fleece as found in the story of Jason and the Argonauts. In the context of the Apkallu. SIKI becomes the red or golden hair of the stranger. Are they strangers from Mesopotamia or strangers to that place?

The pictogram SIKI appearing on tablets from the 4th millennia closely resembles (is exactly the same as) the Egyptian hieroglyph having the sound 'kh' and part of the name of the pharaoh Khufu.

All things being now prepar'd, Osiris having vow'd to the Gods to let his Hair grow till he return'd into Egypt, marcht away through Æthiopia; and for that very Reason it's a piece of Religion, and practis'd among the Egyptians at this Day, that those that travel Abroad, suffer their Hair to grow, till they return Home. (…)

Taken together in the light of line 48, these two paragraphs from the Bibliotheca Historica written in the 1st century BC lead to the conclusion that the king, LUGAL, who is both an intrepid sailor and a wandering honeybee is to be assimilated to an equally hairy (or fleece-covered) and wandering Egyptian Osiris … and perhaps even to Khufu himself. As the builder of the Great Pyramid, he would have been seen as the first pharaoh to travel to the underworld at its heart. Did they also take him for the king of the bees? Did he ever wear the horns of the ram of Aries?

Line 49

The three-peaked hill [Sicily] that covers Enkelados, as the thunderbolt belches forth in beams reaching to the sky, discharges the eternal fire of Sicilian Aitna (Etna)." (Oppian, Cynegetica 1. 273, Trans. Mair, Theoi.com)

NINDA$_2$, the funnel, with NE, fire, at its heart translates to the 'fire funnel' and from there 'volcano'. Also transliterated NINDA$_2$xNE RAM which gives the origin of the verb 'to ram' and the animal's name. Old Norse rammr: strong. In this case, a basket-load of oil rammed into the funnel, the volcano's caldera, and the first of two mentions (line 51). Third reference to Aries (notes to lines 47 and 48).

The three KI, 'places', might be a deliberate reference to Sicilian Enkelados and to the giant Enkelados of the Greek myth. Or a reference to a conjunction of planets in the 'fiery trigon' formed with Leo and Sagittarius (*Star Names* [6], p.79).

Mixing the myths, the skin of Pallas becomes the golden fleece of the ram (see line 48):

As Enkelados was fleeing, Athena threw the island of Sikelia (Sicily) in his direction. She stripped off the skin of Pallas and used it to protect her own body during the battle. (Pseudo-Apollodorus, Bibliotheca 1. 35, Trans. Aldrich, Theoi.com)

(Argo Navis) in search of the golden fleece. (Star Names [6], p.65)

Image from the Narmer palette. Apart from the line number, several words link to the constellation of Argo Navis and to its keel star, Canopus, marker of the ecliptic and passage of the sun in the southern hemisphere (see p.34).

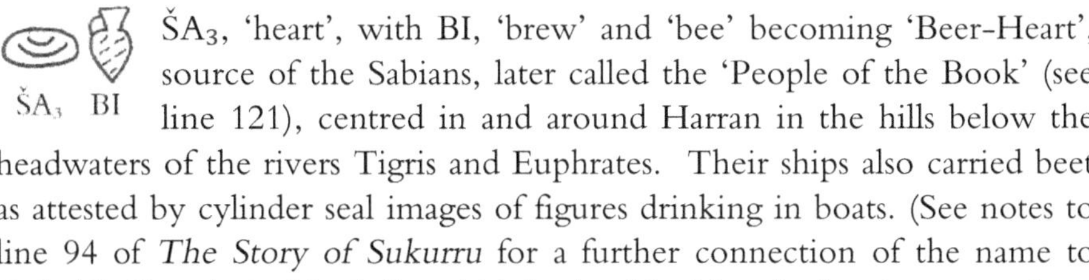

ŠA₃, 'heart', with BI, 'brew' and 'bee' becoming 'Beer-Heart', source of the Sabians, later called the 'People of the Book' (see line 121), centred in and around Harran in the hills below the headwaters of the rivers Tigris and Euphrates. Their ships also carried beet as attested by cylinder seal images of figures drinking in boats. (See notes to line 94 of *The Story of Sukurru* for a further connection of the name to Göbekli Tepe.) Arabic Safina, 'ship', also Noah's ark, has its source here (NA, the stone, becoming 'navis' and 'navel', *Before Babel*, p.217).

There are nine gates (IG) in this text, two more than in the Egyptian *Book of the Dead*. GAN IG (also line 2) refers to the gate of the Milky Way. GAN is also read KAN, potentially also a reference to Canopus, on the keel of Argo Navis, as a direction to the southern gate of the Milky Way (and to the south ecliptic pole). Canopus was known as 'the weight' at the end of the plumbline by the Arabic astronomers (*Hamlet's Mill[2]*, p.271-272). SUD with given meaning 'distant' translated here to 'south' with GA, 'milk' as source of English 'cow'.

With UR BI on line 40 giving 'two dogs' or 'binary dog', here we find BI as the central word and SUD which I posit gives one source of Greek Sothis, another epithet of Sirius (the other being ŠU TI on line 31). That doesn't imply that the astronomers knew that Sirius was a binary star system let alone their 50-year cycle. Such knowledge would have been impossible without sophisticated equipment.

Al Biruni in 1029 AD mentions the myth of Sirius crossing over the Milky Way to the south in the company of Canopus (see p.52).

ZI, source of Zeus, with UN, 'land', 'people' and pictogram of a standard: 'rising of/in the land', or 'to raise the standard'. UN is also read KALAM (*Lost Stones*, p.70, p.242), source of Greek kalamus, the stylus, and 'calamity'.

Latin calamitatem (nominative calamitas) "damage, loss, failure; disaster, misfortune, adversity," a word of obscure origin.

Rising to calamity (notes to line 49).

Pictographic UN/KALAM took more than one form; the vertical 'arrow' topped by different words of which ZU (here with TUG₂), making it impossible to develop further in this specific context. The translation to 'standard' is taken from a combination of the image, given meanings and context.

Line 52

(Aztecs) At the end of every period of fifty-two years, in the month of November when the Pleiades would culminate at midnight, these rude people imagined the world would end. Human sacrifices were offered, while the entire population passed the night upon their knees awaiting their doom. (…)

In Ceylon, and in far distant Peru, a like festival took place at this season of the year. In the latter country the observation of the rising and setting of the Pleiades was the basis of their primitive calendar. (,..)

Four thousand years ago this star group marked the position of the sun at the spring equinox, and this is the principal reason why, as we have seen, it was so universally associated with the apparent wax and wane of the forces of nature. (William Olcott, Star Lore of all Ages; a collection of myths, legends, and facts concerning the constellations of the Northern Hemisphere, p.412, 413 and 416)

The Mark

Situated at 52.2, second of six ZAG (lines 43, 52, 62, 75, 108, 129), shoulder-bow with dictionary-given meanings 'shoulder', 'boundary', 'limit', 'nose-rope' and 'mark'; on line 43 (with GAB) and again on the final line of this text to mark the third digit of a precession number (line 129). ZAG resembles both the double-axe and knot symbols of the Minoans.

ZAG GA (repeated on line 75) 'Mark of/in the milk' or 'shoulder of the cow', following on from MA KI (biblical Kimah, also KI MAH) on line 51 and taking the worldwide myths concerning the month of November and 52-year cycle into account, confirms the reference to the Pleiades, situated over the shoulder of Taurus. The Pleiades embody the starting point for all calculations of time based on the Great Year.

KAK, 'peg', 'nail' and 'thorn', is source of 'cactus'. KAK with A, the 'water', gives 'acacia', the thorned tree from which DMT is extracted.

KAK-A, the flowing nail, indicates the astronomical 'keystones', the point along the meridian when a star, planet or constellation is at its zenith (the observable highest point in its circling across the sky). Used twice on line 72 to pause and to record the anticlockwise movement of the sun.

Fish-God of the In-Between

ME, 'magician', 'spirit' and GALAM, 'fish'. ME-GA gave Greek mega-, 'great' and prefix megal-. Already associated with Thoth (line 9), thanks to this line the Great Fish can be further linked to the Pleiades and to the counting of time: Oannes and Thoth.

ME GALAM

The pictographic vertical fish transliterated GALAM or SUKUD is either a combination of the two fish of Pisces or Piscis Austrinus, the rising fish, or a combination of the two (notes to lines 9 and 74). Some pictograms show two fish dividing out of one, with two vertical lines rising from the dividing mouth (potentially GIZ, the beam), which is more in tune with the two Pisces. The exact forms of these most ancient constellations are unknown.

MA DU MA

The alternative transliterated SUKUD results from finding the vertical fish in the lexical lists opposite SU-KU-UD where ZU/SU is both 'sink' and 'know. KU-UD is the breakdown of KUD/TAR, 'to cut' and 'to divert' which, in turn, indicates Greek Tartarus, the underworld (notes to lines 1 and 5). A disappearing fish (notes to line 73). Here below a pictographic version of the lexical entry with extended translation to better explain the progressive reasoning:

GALAM   =   SU   KU   UD
SUKUD   KUD/TAR

Great Fish = To know the seat (hole of the sinking) of the sun.

MA, both 'land' and 'truth', became Egyptian Ma'at. The phrase in its entirety, ME GALAM MA DU MA (repeated on line 127), refers to the well-known image of the fish god and to the contents of his basket. MA-DU-MA translates:

The basket contains the honey of truth and the measurements (foot) between lands. Source of Hindu madhu, the honey. Also source of English 'mad', given as an adjective from a 'lost verb'. Mad honey? Mixed with thorny and bitter acacia? A recipe for truth or death… or both?

In an overall context of bee-keeping, Virgil gives his account of the myth of Orpheus (notes to line 60):

> *Of air-born honey, gift of heaven, I now take up the tale.* (Virgil, *Georgics*, Bk 4:1-2)

Line 53

First mention of the Pleiades as the starting point of the calendar and one end of the pole shaft (lines 106-108). The following lines refer to the rising of a river, the flooding of the Nile linked to the heliacal rising of Sirius (line 73).

The interchangeability between the Sumerian fish (HA) and NUN, the otherworldly guide, has been demonstrated (*Lost Stones*, p.43, p.272). Multiple connections between Sumerian and the language of Arabic astronomers are also evident. Notably, Arabic nun as 'great fish'.

A hitherto obscure link between Giza and the whale skeletons in nearby Whale Valley was suggested in *Lost Stones*. Here with the word for 'place' between NUN as 'whale' and GIZ as 'Giza':

> *Fossils such as the whales of Wadi Al-Hitan must surely have come to the attention of humans thousands of years ago, here in proximity to Giza and in other locations too. It is completely safe to say that the long sinuous lines of vertebrae and other bones have been lying in that valley throughout history, not for thousands but for millions of years, and it is reasonable to imagine that at least some were discovered and studied long before the Great Pyramid was erected nearby, and that they were known even before the rocky mound of the Sphinx was whittled down, her own front paws stretched out to face the rising sun, stretched out to touch the former bank of the river Nile. (Lost Stones, p.229)*

Also analysed in *Lost Stones*, GIZ, the 'beam' (transliterated there as JES) with MI, 'dark' in a different context – confirming the use of hallucinogenic substances in the ancient world as first posited by John Allegro in The Sacred Mushroom and the Cross.

GIZ–MI together are transliterated JISSU or JESSU with given meaning 'protective shade'. I made the case for this being symbiosis between JES, the tree, and MI, the mycelium. Here I look at the two words in another context while still considering that they are the source of more than one theme:

> *In all probability, Sumerian JES and JESSU were transformed into their alphabetic forms and carried forward into later languages, their origins carefully hidden from public scrutiny, twisted into newly minted stories, one of which involved a man called Jesse who had a tree growing out of his side. (…) In other words, did JES and JESSU become the epithets of prophets thanks to the pre-existing spiritual qualities attached to the name? (Lost Stones, p.177)*

> *Or perhaps 'In GIS was established the knowledge'. The key to the mystery of the tree lies in its heartwood which, I suggest, lies in Egyptian lore. (Lost Stones, p.178)*

(See line 73 and notes for the link between the biblical figure and Sirius.)

Line 54

54   →   72   →   108

Linking the astronomical theme of precession of the equinoxes through the line number to the position of the galactic plain through the Milk Ocean myth. The precession reference is reinforced by the layout of the line: Five words to the left of the gap, and four words to the right. The same is true of line 55 (see notes).

Pause in the music of the spheres and moment when the two parties holding the great snake on either side of Mount Meru begin a mighty tug of war which will cause the Milk Ocean to foam and rise. The scene comes immediately before the riddle of the three temples (Giza and Alnitak, Orion's Belt) found across lines 56 to 58 and culminates in an obvious reference to Orpheus on line 60, thereby firmly linking Giza to the theme of music and to the Indian myth of the churning of the Milk Ocean (see p.39).

GA, 'milk', shown here in one of its pictographic forms which best illustrates the stirring. It also appears as a hemispherical basket with two nails (KAK) planted at each corner (line 50), both versions borrowed from 4th millennium tablets. GA with GAB, 'spread', 'the milk to spread' but also, in the context of the Milky Way, 'the gap in the milk to show': between the two white streams. Linked to the biblical scene of Moses preparing to separate the waters (line 103).

Repetition of ŠU GAR NU TUK (line 26) with the connotation of recklessness as the spirit shoots up into the sky. TUK, 'to play' confirms the musical theme. Orpheus – the skull – is setting the scene.

Line 55

'Before three temples' refers to the three following lines where they (E$_2$) appear in first position.

5 words precede ZU, the 'knowledge', with 4 words following it (see line 54). GAB with ZU: perhaps 'the spreading to know'. The flooding?

ID$_2$ MAH, 'great' might refer to the Milky Way in a continuation of the theme from line 54. The presence of the river Nile is confirmed by repetition of the two words on line 59 where they appear to the right of ZU, the pyramid, and to the left of GA, the milk. The Nile and the Milky Way are connected. (Also see notes to line 57.)

IG has given meanings 'door', 'to open' and 'to guard'. The pictogram resembles the door shown on the Narmer palette where it's guarded by a bird. With LA, the 'weighing', pictogram of a bending rope, this is where souls are interrogated at death. With following ZU/SU, also given as 'sink', the weighing door is in the pyramid.

SU/ZU with UN give 'sinking of people and land' or 'knowledge of the land', and are linked to transliterated SUN/TIL, 'to be old', 'to be complete', and 'to end'. The form of SUN, generally transliterated to BAD (notes to line 73), looks very like the pattern of the stars in the constellation of Cancer.

SU   UN = SUN

Repetition of ZI, 'to rise', along with the meaning of line 55, gives the source of the mythological giant bird Ziz:

ZI ZI

(…) we have a Story of such a prodigious Bird, called Ziz, which standing with his Feet upon the Earth, reacheth up unto the Heavens with his head, and with the spreading of his Wings darkneth the whole Orb of the Sun, and causeth a total Eclipse thereof. This Bird the Chaldee Paraphrast on the Psalms says, is a Cock, which he describes of the same bigness, and tells us that he crows before the Lord. (Humphrey Prideaux, *The True Nature of Imposture*, 1698)

Line 56

First line of the second riddle signalling the Giza plateau (lines 26-28) through repetition of the first word, E_2, the 'temple'. The deliberate references to the three pyramids along with the Great Sphinx and associated figures (Orion, Osiris), both positioning and meanings, are consistent (p.62).

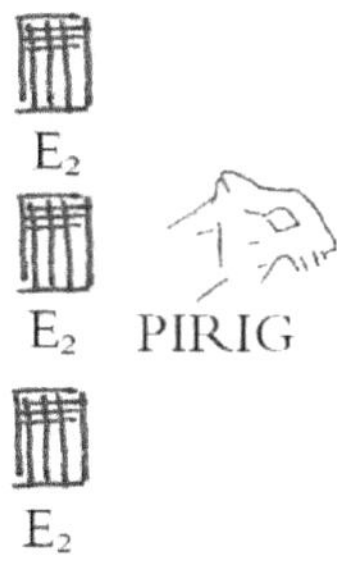

E_2

E_2 PIRIG

E_2

Three temples appear on the composite transliteration (ETCSL website) while on the transliteration of the Ashmolean prism the first E_2 (line 56) is missing, leaving just two temples on lines 57 and 58. Error somewhere along the line or deliberate? Given the overall context, it's not the most important point. ENGUR-RA on that line (elsewhere following E_2) implies the presence of the temple.

The word 'engurra' has the meaning 'wrinkle' in Galician while 'engur' is a grape in the Zazaki language. ENGUR-RA is translated in the sub-text here to 'Lord of the Knotted Vine' (notes to line 34). The brew of the vine takes effect:

Greek Gorgones "the grim ones," from gorgos, of a look or gaze, "grim, fierce, terrible," later also "vigorous, lively," a word of unknown origin. (Etymonline)

URUxUD MAH KI

URU, given as 'city' and 'drum' with UD, 'sun', at its centre. Other pictographic forms show a three–step pyramid which is why I add 'pyramid' as a meaning, perhaps with a connotation of 'climbing'. Others have already associated the word with the constellation of Orion. (Variations on URU appear on lines 63, 85 and 119.) Followed by MAH KI, 'greatness' and 'place', source of biblical Kimah, thought to be the Pleiades.

Osiris

UŠ SA

UŠ, the 'male' with SA, given meanings 'net' and 'string' to which I add 'trap'. SA is the string of the lyre of Orpheus. The words also appear on line 156 of *The Story of Sukurru*, with the same image copied from a petroglyph on Mount Bégo in southern France. Second source of the Greek epithet for Osiris (line 39). Here his name is the trap (strings of the lyre and net of the matrix) in which a male is caught; 'the trapped man' (see the men trapped in a net on the Vulture Stone in the Louvre).

The musical theme (culminating on line 67) and the double meaning of SA (net and strings) show that the trap of Osiris is linked to earthly and cosmic frequencies; the music of the spheres. It also suggests some form of grid, a mapping of the world. *The Story of Sukurru* provides evidence that songs fine–tuned to provoke emotion were a well–attested theme:

35. A ballad about writing and fired–clay specialists and stones from the sky his heartstrings stretches.

That line incorporates the words PI EL, 'pure pitch', partial source of the name Pleiades. PI EL also appear together seven times in a seven–line proverb on the same musical/astronomical theme (ETCSL ref.6.2.3). This and other references demonstrate that the number 7 was particularly linked to music. (Also see lines 67 and 125.) (See pi in notes to line 22.)

Line 57

Second line of the three–line acrostic beginning E_2.

RA PIRIG ZU

Third mention of the lion placed next to the symbol of the pyramid (UR MAH on line 31 and PIRIG with UD, the sun, on line 32). PIRIG appears between RA, Egyptian Ra, the pharaoh, epithet of the sun, and collocated ZU AB (Kochab).

ŠA₃, 'heart', with 'milk' is the second of three references within this section to the river that is the Milky Way but also, by the positioning of the words, the Nile lying to the right of PIRIG, the lion (lines 55 and 59). It might also be understood as the 'soft heart' of the lion.

Line 58

Third and final line of the acrostic. Includes a message relating to the Giza plateau.

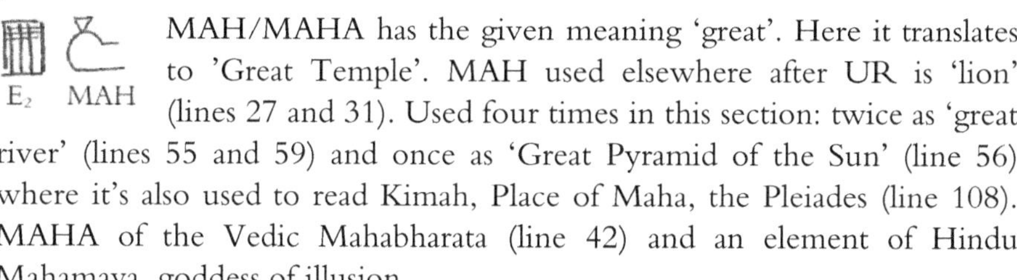

MAH/MAHA has the given meaning 'great'. Here it translates to 'Great Temple'. MAH used elsewhere after UR is 'lion' (lines 27 and 31). Used four times in this section: twice as 'great river' (lines 55 and 59) and once as 'Great Pyramid of the Sun' (line 56) where it's also used to read Kimah, Place of Maha, the Pleiades (line 108). MAHA of the Vedic Mahabharata (line 42) and an element of Hindu Mahamaya, goddess of illusion.

The pictogram slightly, sometimes integrating words inside the more constant paw-like form which might also be seen as a horizontal passage ending in a room. Here it appears to be balancing KAK, the peg or nail. A couple of lexical entries give the word opposite TI, 'arrow'. UR MAH appears with TI (line 31) as the Great Lion pointing the way. DA, the 'arm' and 'riverbank' appears here on the preceding line 57.

My conclusion is that this is a reference to the arm of the Sphinx at Giza (line 106). At the same time, it ties in with the image of the tiger and the pair of arms on the side of Pillar 43 at Göbekli Tepe. There it represents the river Tigris, a name formed from TI (notes to line 24).

GIZ, 'beam' is the 7th word, taking central position in the 13-word line. Second mention of the three-word phrase (line 45). In the context of the Giza plateau, the Tree of Consciousness and Knowledge, previously identified in *The Story of Sukurru*, takes on a new dimension. TUG₂, 'to cover', and PI both have meanings linked to hearing: 'In the beam to hear and to understand'. The phrase appears twice in this text (line 45).

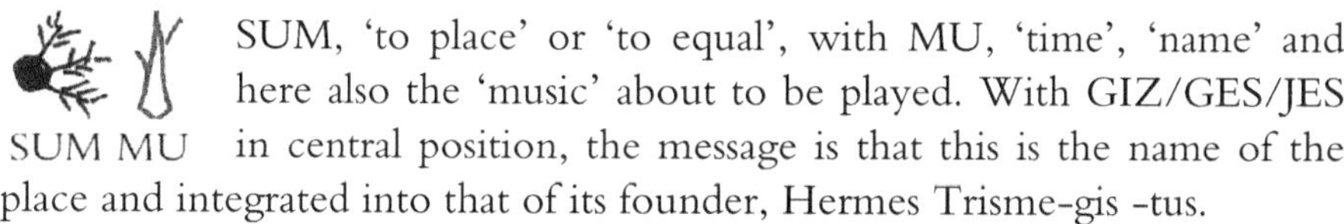

SUM, 'to place' or 'to equal', with MU, 'time', 'name' and here also the 'music' about to be played. With GIZ/GES/JES in central position, the message is that this is the name of the place and integrated into that of its founder, Hermes Trisme-gis -tus.

SUM MU is preceded by AB on line 20, confirming the reference to the 'Father'. Source of Greek summum meaning 'supreme'.

Line 59

GAD TAK₄ SI

Together transliterated to AKKIL, GAD has the meaning 'flax', TAK_4 'set aside', and SI 'horn'. The three words together indicate the archer drawing back the string of his bow, Phonetic AKKIL confirms that this refers to the star Axilla (Ascella) in Sagittarius. Ascella lies in the armpit of the archer. SI in this context refers to the horns holding the strings of the lyre and the wood of the archer's bow. Greek Orpheus prepares to pluck the strings. Here as both archer and musician. This image of Sagittarius with scorpion tail in the Temple of Dendera incorporates a backward-facing lion's head.

ZI   GA   DIM₂

ZI, pictogram of GI the reed with added vertical striations, has given meanings 'to issue', 'to expand' and 'to rise'. Source of Zeus. Here with GA, 'milk', and after the 'Great River', a reference to the Milky Way but also, intriguingly, to the rising waters of the Nile. DIM_2, the ox foreleg, links the scene to Boôtes at the north pole. The strings of the lyre also link the scene to the pole star Vega, another potential source of that name being ZI GA (see notes to lines 22 and 45 for SI GA and PE GA).

The description of the mechanism of the Giza plateau continues with the rising of the Nile. Does the water gush through channels below the Sphinx and pyramids? Is the churning noise is amplified in deep granite spaces; a subterranean roaring as of a bull or a lion? A mechanism of sluice gates regulating the flow?

Line 60

60 (line) x 10 (words) = 600

25,920 / 600 = 43.2 (line 43, word 2, GAB, the musical pause)

The mournful birds, the stricken animals, the hard stones and the weeping woods, all these that often had followed your inspiring voice, bewailed your death; while trees dropped their green leaves, mourning for you, as if they tore their hair. They say sad rivers swelled with their own tears— (Death of Orpheus, Ovid, Metamorphosis, Bk 5, Trans. Brookes More)

Line 60 refers to the number 60 as the base measurement of time and space. It offers the original version of the tale of Greek Orpheus, the great musician who, according to Virgil, became nothing more than a skull (p.13) floating down a river, his body ripped to pieces by spurned women, a story too similar to that of Osiris to be a coincidence. (See p.40, quote from Pythagorus' Journey to Egypt.)

TUK   A   AN

TUK has given meanings 'to play', 'to acquire' and 'to marry'. Collocated A-AN (AM$_3$) give the verb 'to be' and appears six times over three consecutive lines in *The Story of Sukurru* where the contents of three offering baskets (dowry) are detailed (lines 209-211). In that text, the indication of a musical section comes from two-fold repetition of TUK on the preceding line 208 and reference to both song and festival through EZEN (connected to Hermes also on that line, notes to lines 70 and 126). A-AN was translated 'there will be':

209. *In the rope basket, blood there will be. In the rope basket, prey there will be.*

210. *In the rope basket, precious metal there will be. In the rope basket, lapis lazuli there will be.*

211. *In the rope basket, yarn there will be. In the rope basket, linen there will be.*

The six-fold repetition of 'basket' in *The Story of Sukurru* comes from MAL. That word also closely follows on from TUK A AN here (notes to line 61 here below), leading me to consider that both texts are based in the same original story of musical gifts carried by Orpheus, referring to celestial measurement and to frequencies. TUK is repeated on line 66.

At the time of translating (2016), the three baskets were matched to the images on Pillar 43 where they were carved above a depiction of the three channels of the Milky Way. *The Story of Sukurru* is incomplete, certain passages broken, and in need of an overhaul to include the newly discovered themes of astronomy, measurement, music and bees.

<u>Line 61</u>

The gods in amicable rivalry vied with one another in offering gifts. But you, Delian Apollon, you said the following 'Phoibos (Phoebus), you must try your skilful art [music] which will surpass the masterpieces of Hephaistos (Hephaestus).' (Callimachus, Iambi Fragment 202, trans. Trypanis)

NI, 'oil', 'thick', 'beautiful' and 'good' applied here in the context of EŠ₂, cord of the lyre. EŠ₂ is another of the six-fold repeated words across lines 209, 210 and 211 of *The Story of Sukurru*. Also MAL given twice here (notes to line 60).

At the time, I took EŠ₂ to be the weave of the baskets and the cord used in a musical ritual to pull the gifts offered to the matriarchal goddess up to the top of the stone pillar. That meaning can be extended to the measure of the strings of the musical instrument (Orpheus, Pythagoras) and to the measure of the rope wound around the axle shaft of the mill in the theme of precession (notes to line 54). Further to those concepts, it became the cord stretched around and defining the limits of the cartouche carrying the pharaoh's 'throne name' in Ancient Egypt. The cord is the measure and limit of their reign (see below).

Six-word phrase given twice (line 17). MU, 'name' and 'year', 'music' and 'movement' (notes to line 10). Indicator of time on the *Sumerian King List* where MU with BI, inverted in this line, signal the total number of years of each period on the *King List*. In that context, BI indicates that the additions have been made, allowing the addition of words such as 'total', 'all' or 'entirety' to its various meanings. Source of 'binary' through Latin. The Egyptian equivalents of the MU BI pair are the bee and sedge hieroglyphs (illustrating line 61).

The Behemoth, its name derived from BI with HI (the veil) and MU, is an obscure astronomical reference which, in the overall context, appears to tie Taurus to Pisces – not the only strange creature in this text (line 74 and notes to line 79).

PISAN, another transliteration of the word for 'basket', derives from three words found opposite MAL in the lexical entries:

PI is the musical 'pitch' while SA is the string of the archer's bow and of the musical instrument – and part of the original Greek name of Osiris (notes to lines 56 and 57). Those three words together translate:

(the basket is equal to) the pitch of the celestial string (net, trap, matrix)

Taking MU UN followed by the double MAL as lunar houses (notes to line 17), a further link is made to the origins of Pythagoras' music of the spheres, all of which sourced from Ancient Egypt according to the record of his life (p.37).

<u>Line 62</u>

First of two lines incorporating three GIZ denoting Giza. GIZ here is both the wood of the Sagittarian archer's bow and element of the harp (notes to line 63). Third ZAG of six (Lines 43, 52, 62, 75, 108, 129), 'mark', 'boundary', 'shoulder', 'knot', 'to tie'. Between two 'beams', ZAG SAL, the shoulder bow. Also the cave where the cries of newborn Zeus are muffled by the noise of the Kouretes (notes to lines 7, 43 and 124). Here sandwiched between the beams of the Great Pyramid, the four words refer to its innermost sanctuary. ZAG SAL appear together on the last line of several Mesopotamian texts.

ZAG is also given as 'to compete', perhaps indicating a musical contest between the two harps apparent in line 63.

The presence of the lyre is confirmed by pictographic BALAG: given as 'large drum or harp' and source of 'balalaika'. Shown with just three strings but nevertheless... The lexical entries break it down to BA with LAG/ŠID, 'below to count' or possibly 'less counting below'. ŠID is the 'lofty administrator' on line 103 of *The Story of Sukurru*, giving instructions to Noah there. Also one source of 'sidereal' (notes to line 125).

<u>Line 63</u>

Second of two lines incorporating three GIZ.

The duplication of three on earth with three in the sky is the encoded message in this six-fold repetition of GIZ: Alnitak, three belt stars of Orion above and the three pyramids of Giza below.

(line) 63 / 3 = 21   21 / 3 = 7

A division of the line number here by 3 leads to number 21. Line 21 comprises 9 words. A further division by 3 gives number 9.

According to the ETCSL composite version, there are seven lines in this text which comprise fourteen words (6, 41, 63, 66, 79, 98 and 101). Commonly collocated words (NI.UD and A.AN) are counted as one. The long acrostic beginning on line 106 comprises fourteen lines, all of which indicating that the number 14 was also deliberately encoded.

But when Isis had gone to see her son Horus (who was at nurse in the city Buto), and had put the coffer away, Typhon being out a hunting moonlight came upon it, and recognizing the corpse, tore it into fourteen pieces, and scattered them abroad. (Plutarch, On Isis and Osiris, Bk XVIII)

63 / 7 = 9 (Thoth)

HAR/HUR/MUR, the mill and partial epithet of the Great Sphinx (p.65, notes to lines 74 and 121), appears 7 times in this text (lines 15, 38, 40, 63 twice, 74 and 121).

The mill on Earth and the mill in the sky, both linked to the notion of a seven-stringed harp, leading to both the seven Pleiades as musicians (lines 67 and 125), to the constellation of Lyra and pole star Vega (p.40).

GIZ HAR HAR GIZ
MURMUR

Two GIZ, 'beam', surround two HAR, 'mill': Two mill shafts facing each other (two pole stars along the rim of the north pole) and, at the same time, two harps where GIZ serves as either the two sides or the crossbeam of the instrument (*Hamlet's Mill*[2], Appendix 10, p.369). That interpretation is confirmed by the following SA, the string. Never forgetting that GIZ is also the bow of the Sagittarian archer.

Two musicians facing off in a contest or, alternatively, joining together to create a great harmony involving two octaves. The celestial mill is controlled by music as attested by all three transliterations – HAR, HUR, MUR - all resulting from lexical entries found opposite the original word. The following are all derived from a hitherto unknown source:

Harp: *Old Norse harpa, Dutch harp, Old High German harpfa, German Harfe "harp" of uncertain origin. Late Latin harpa,*

Harmony: *Greek harmonia "agreement, concord of sounds,"*

Murmur: *Latin murmur (n.) "a hum, muttering, rushing,"*

SA, the strings of the lyre and element of the Greco-Egyptian epithet Osiris (notes to line 56), here with NE, the fire, gives more information on the trap set by Seth in the Egyptian myth.

The 'fiery strings' (14 strings of the two lyres) and/or 'trap of fire' follow GIZ, the beam inside which Osiris is trapped before floating down a mighty river to become a roof beam in the palace of the king at Byblos. Also the firestick in which the fire of the sun will be trapped by Greek Prometheus. And the entire scene set to the music of Orpheus, son of Apollo, who also floated down a river as nothing more than a skull (p.41).

Second use of GIZ, 'beam', with MI, 'black' and 'night' (notes to line 53) transliterated JESSU/JISSU. This from *Lost Stones*, p.176:

JISSU is found on numerous tablets beginning in the ED IIIa period, ca.2600–2500 BC, age attributed to The Story of Sukurru. Line 247 of that text refers to the fate of the young son who has been carried off to the nest of the Bird of Knowledge. It begins with GEŠ-MI, awkwardly translated at the time to: Under the shady tree stump…

URU collocated with GAL is given as 'underworld'. URU is associated with Orion by Assyriologists through URU-AN-NA.

Erebus and Eurydice are other names associated with URU/ERE/ERI. Erebus, the underworld where Eurydice, wife of Orpheus, has disappeared:

Then from the deepest deeps of Erebus,
Wrung by his minstrelsy, the hollow shades
Came trooping, ghostly semblances of forms
(Virgil, *Georgics*, Bk.4)

TUM used twice encircles GIZ MI URU, indicating Osiris trapped inside the beam (descent of Greek Orpheus into the underworld). Given meanings of TUM include 'middle', 'cross-beam', 'inherit' and, as part of a phrase, 'belt' or 'weir'. My suggestion is that the tips of the three Giza pyramids relate to the belt stars (see line 12), while the bulk of the Great Pyramid equates to the celestial figure's lower body, pictographic TUM – source of both tumulus and a tomb. Also the sound of the drum.

To retrieve his love from the underworld, Orpheus must interrogate an old man called Proteus, a seer. Not an easy task. His mother advises:

> *Him, son, you must first clap in shackles, so that the whole cause of malaise he may unriddle and rally your fortunes (…) For suddenly he'll be a bristled boar, a deadly tigress, a scaly dragon, a tawny-necked lioness, or blast out the piercing hiss of flame and thus slip out from his bonds, or melt into mere water and spill away (…) but when no design wins deliverance, defeated he returns to himself, and speaking at last with the mouth of a man…(Virgil, Georgics, Bk.4)*

Line 64

> *Atlas the baleful; he knows the depths of all the seas, and he, no other, guards the tall pillars that keep the sky and earth apart.* (Homer, Odyssey 1. 52 ff, trans. Shewring)

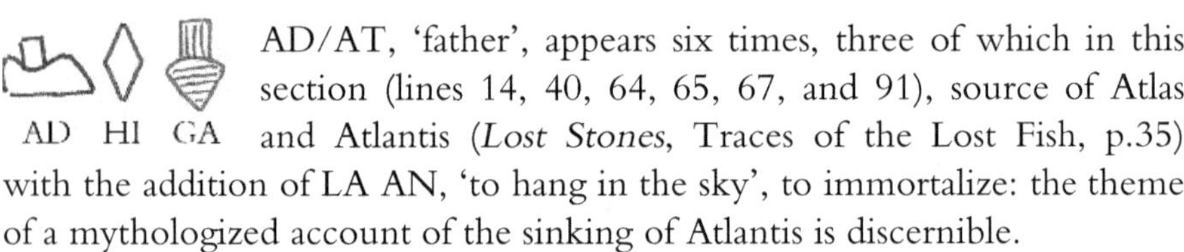

AD/AT, 'father', appears six times, three of which in this section (lines 14, 40, 64, 65, 67, and 91), source of Atlas and Atlantis (*Lost Stones*, Traces of the Lost Fish, p.35) with the addition of LA AN, 'to hang in the sky', to immortalize: the theme of a mythologized account of the sinking of Atlantis is discernible.

HI with AD give the source name of the Hyades, asterism next to the Pleiades above the cow, GA. Also quoted in the notes to line 40:

> *Atlas, the Endurer, the father of the Hyades and Pleiades, so skilled in knowledge of the skies that he was shown as their supporter;* (Star Names [6], p.19)

Second mention of the 'word of the guide', source of Greek kanon (line 16), confirms the interchangeability between NUN, the guide and whale thanks to HA, the fish, found after AD on the next line (65).

BUR₂, given as 'snake' 'light' and 'to release' amongst others, followed by RI, 'bird', suggesting a description of the flying serpent or dragon on which the hero will descend, accompanied by the musical offering. Pictographic BUR₂ is an enigmatic combination of BUR, 'bowl', and downward arrow. In one version of the text, it's replaced by repetition of KA NUN.

<u>Line 65</u>

Nothing proves that Plato's far later mention of Atlantis is either myth or uniquely astronomical. The fact that the origin of the name appears in this section – the pyramids of Giza and Ancient Egyptian figures – confirms that Atlantis stands at the beginning of the counting of time. The meaning of this line and its presence alongside NI-IB, the dark cloud (of Nibru) does nothing to detract from the story of a real and catastrophic sinking.

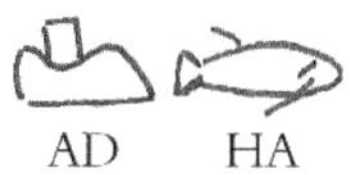

Second AD in this section, this time with HA, 'fish', partial source of Hades (notes to line 67) and probably Arabic hadwa, another link to music in this section (see below). This also has the merit of connecting the story of Atlantis to the region of the Pleiades and Hyades:

> (Capella) *and the synonymous Al Hadi of the Pleiades, as, on the parallel of Arabia, it rose with that cluster. Wetzstein, the biblical critic often quoted by Delitzsch, explains this last term as " the singer riding before the procession, who cheers the camels by the sound of the hadwa, and thereby urges them on," the Pleiades here being regarded as a troop of camels. (Star Names [6], p.87)*

NI, 'oil' and 'thick', with IB, given meaning 'oval' to which I add 'cloud' and 'ark according to context. 'Oil on the wing' and 'thick cloud'. (Also on lines 82 and 116.) Source of:

- Nephilim, the biblical Watchers,

- Niflheim, Old Norse 'Home of Mist'.

- Latin nebula, 'mist' and source of 'nebulous', also Old High German nebul meaning 'fog'.

- 'Neb' or 'nib', the beak of the bird and tip of the stylus.

- Nibiru, name given by Zechariah Sitchin, but more likely originally sourced from academia's EN KI KID. (See notes to lines 96 and 104.)

<u>Line 66</u>

In the beams of Giza all the measurements are found. One of 7 lines comprising 14 words, linking to the Osiris myth and the division of his body (notes to line 63). 'Ocean floor' results from the context. Source of algae through Latin alga: 'seaweed'. The image is from a copy of an unreferenced clay tablet.

BA, between NI₂, the 'soul' and MU, the 'movement of time' and 'music', is used as 'less' and 'below': giving 'lesser souls', 'soulless', 'without music', 'land below', 'less on the stones'. TUK, 'to play', confirms the continuation of the musical theme as Atlantis sinks. Is the line number 66 relevant to that theme of descent into the underworld? It appears so.

NI₂ BA MU UN NA TUK

TUK, following NA, the 'stone', carries the stone-moving music of Orpheus through to the following line and to the Pleiades, also musicians.

<u>Line 67</u>

NAR, also LUL or LIB, pictogram of a fox head, with given meanings 'fox', 'false', 'musician', is used twice (line 125). Another aspect of Greek Orpheus, associated with the number seven through the strings to his lyre but also the number of stars of the Pleiades, their name sourced from the pitch of his music: PI EL (notes to line 56).

NAR 7

Third AD in this section (lines 14, 40, 64, 65, 67, and 91) follows the seven musicians. In the context of Greek mythology, it's Atlas descending into the underworld for the purpose of supporting the planet on his shoulders. According to that legend, Atlas was the father of the Pleiades and either condemned to hold up the heavens or appointed guardian of the 'pillars'.

If this is understood as a reference to the pillars marking the two ends of the Milky Way (p.11), then Atlas, as father of the Pleiades, might be Taurus at its northern gate. However, there is another set of celestial pillars that fit the context: known as the Golden Gate of the Ecliptic, the two pillars being the Pleiades and the Hyades through which all the planets pass at some point.

First of four IM MI, 'black clay' or 'spirit of the night', source of 'imme' a swarm of bees through Proto-Germanic. Here with IB, 'oval' and 'wing' given in *The Story of Sukurru* as 'ark'.

IM MI IB

<u>Lines 68-69</u>

Although an old constellation, Cetus is by no means of special interest, except as possessing the south pole of the Milky Way and the Wonderful Star, the variable Mira (Star Names [6], p.162)

GA, 'milk' and 'white', with AN, 'sky', are the two components of GAN, the 'womb' and 'crucible (line 67). With KA as 'mouth', a reference to both the south pole of the Milky Way and the constellation of Cetus, the whale, as confirmed by BAL-E-NE, source of 'baleen', also in this line (*Lost Stones*, Great Fish in the Sea, p.185). Repetition of KA, the mouth, as first word over the two lines 68-69 indicates an acrostic, perhaps the passage of the lord between them and into the mouth, an obvious allusion to Jonah. Unfortunately, this is the line with a short breakage – two words missing.

ŠU, 'hand' and 'show' with NU, 'not': 'to not show' or 'show the knot'. NU is source of Greek noos, 'mind' and 'thought', and relating to intelligence. Together source of Greek nosos, disease, and of the 'nosoi', plagues that escaped from Greek Pandora's jar.

> *"Truly blooming health (hygeia) does not rest content within its due bounds; for disease (nosos) ever presses close against it, its neighbour with a common wall. So human fortune, when holding onward in straight course strikes upon a hidden reef." [N.B. Hygeia and Nosos are scarcely personified in this passage.]* (Aeschylus, Agamemnon 1001 ff, ca. 5th B.C. trans. Weir Smyth)

That quote is reminiscent of another ancient story, that of the mythological sea creature called the Aspidochelone (quote under lines 68-69). A remote island on which sailors landed in good faith – not seeing any problem - but which turned out to be a huge fish, presumably a whale, which then rolled over and sank, taking everyone down with it (notes to line 79).

BAL, given as 'spin', is source of the weaver's spindle (GIZ BAL in the acrostic, line 227 of *The Story of Sukurru*). BAL with E, 'levee', 'high', and NE, 'fire' or 'again' together give the source of 'baleen', the spinning whale:

> *Not only do I take responsibility for the baleen whale but will add other unorthodox meanings into the mix for good measure:*
>
> → *BAL as the source of 'wall'.*
>
> → *KA-BAL: the words on the wall.*
>
> → *BAL and EN as direct source of Greek palin, first word of 'palindrome', meaning 'back' and 'again', and given as 'from PIE root'.*
>
> (*Lost Stones*, p.228)

(Also see notes to line 73.)

<u>Line 70</u>

I baptize you with water for repentance, but after me will come One more powerful than I, whose sandals I am not worthy to carry. He will baptize you with the Holy Spirit and with fire. (Matthew 3:11)

LUH AN PAP ŠIg   NE

Pictogram assimilating lyre and quiver. Mesopotamian musicians are shown with quiver. (Also on line 18.) LUH, given as 'to clean', 'wash' and 'to be frightened' here in the context of baptism. Source of 'loosen' as in 'to loose an arrow' with connotation of purging in an initiation rite. LUH is linked to weeping at the pain of separation. Potential source of Latin luo: 'I suffer'. Luha has the meaning 'tears' in Cebuana, a language of the Philippines.

PAP, given as 'to be estranged', one source of both 'bap-tism' and Babylon, and also 'pap' the nipple from which the newborn will be weaned (*Before Babel*, p.4-5). PAP is collocated with ZU/SU, 'knowledge' and 'to sink', on numerous tablets. In early versions it's placed above the tip of the triangle. ŠIg, the striated eye, with NE, 'red', 'red-eyed', is indicative of weeping. NE gives the 'fire' of the biblical verse here above (also see notes to lines 18 and 43).

<u>Festival of the Crossing</u>

A time of renewal through cleansing, which became the ritual of baptism in 'living waters' found in various religions. The line number fits with the Egyptian 70-day mummification and purification rituals, in turn linked to the 'ablutions' of the land due to the rising and temporarily red waters of the Nile (as mentioned by Robert Bauval in *The Egypt Code*, p.139 [29]).

An important addition to this line after LUH AN PAP.ŠIg and before NE appears in the Ashmolean transcript, bringing confirmation of the 'Apkallu' aka Oannes, the fish-god, as central to the ritual of baptism (notes to line 48) while also linking to Egyptian Nu/Nun as source of the flood waters:

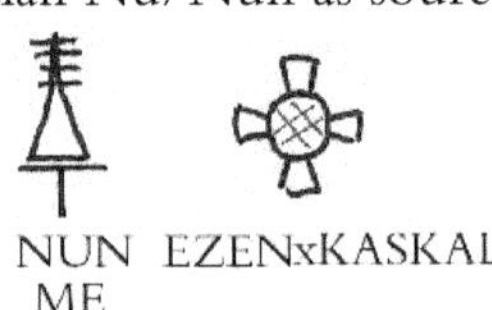
NUN EZENxKASKAL
ME

EZEN is given as 'song' and 'festival' with KASKAL, the 'crossroads' at its centre. In this text it links to Sirius (line 126). In *Before Babel*, EZEN is analysed as partial source of the name Hermes and of Greek piezein:

The suggestion of electricity generated by some form of resonance and pressure is the direction in which the crystal of Hermes continues to turn. And if we are being energetically nudged, then it surely couldn't be for the sake of a tiny diamond in a Swiss watch or a piece of quartz for some small gadget. It must be a stone of much greater force, of a far-reaching effect. If used to create useful energy here on Earth in times so ancient that we have lost the knowledge of them, what other evidence might there be? (Before Babel The Crystal Tongue, 2019, p.234-235)

EZEN with KAS/KASKAL is transliterated as Ubara in the *Sumerian King List* (line 32) where it is taken to be an epithet of the last king before the great flood. (Also see EZEN in the notes to line 126 here.)

Third and final appearance of KULLA (lines 14, 20 and 70), the foundation peg(s) on which the story of the skies is written, visually an undulating path, river or wall pierced by pairs of nails, equivalent to the shifting pole shafts and their crowning stars in this context.

Jonah will be restored to health at the heart of the whale by Greek Hygeia (line 71) before rebirth (line 73). The questions that remain are: How many whales were there in the ancient sky? Apart from the constellation of Ketus/Cetus, is there a veiled whale at the heart of the north pole?

Line 71

Hemithea, Hygeia, Hekate

And most important of all, when the Persians were the dominant power in Asia and were plundering all the temples of the Greeks, the precinct of Hemithea was the sole shrine on which they did not lay hands, and the robbers who were pillaging everything they met left this shrine alone entirely unplundered, and this they did despite the fact that it was unwalled and the pillaging of it would have entailed no danger. And the reason which men advance for its continued development is the benefactions which the goddess confers upon all mankind alike; for she appears in visible shape in their sleep to those who are in suffering and gives them healing, and many who are in the grip of diseases for which no remedy is known are restored to health; furthermore, to women who are suffering in childbirth the goddess gives relief from the agony and perils of travail. Consequently, since many have been saved in these ways from the most ancient times, the sacred precinct is filled with votive offerings, nor are these protected by guards or by a strong wall, but by the habitual reverence of the people." (Diodorus Siculus, Library of History 5. 62.1, trans. Oldfather)

Second and final use of the six-word phrase (notes to line 18). HI/HE, 'veil', with ME, 'spirit, are source of Greek 'hemi-' and Hemithea (see quote here above). HI with GE gave Greek Hygeia becoming 'hygiene', the healing goddess found here with SAL, her 'chamber' or 'cave' and who became Roman Salus. Note the hemispherical shape of the wings and the three arrows (copied from the Adda seal, *Lost Stones*, p.21). The phrase follows mention of the 'nosoi', the hidden diseases released when Pandora's jar is opened (notes to line 68).

In Egyptian imagery, the goddess Nut points the ankh at the lips of the dead king. In Greek myth, Hekate, triple goddess of boundaries, shows the way.

SAL HI GE EŠ   IM   ME
three branches

HE–ME
Mehi

GE EŠ
Giza

GI with EŠ, 'three branches', become GIZ, the 'beam' and 'tree'. In this context, 'three arrows' or stars vying for central position at the north pole? With the 'indestructible' Kochab, four (or three) candidates in this text:

- Kochab in Ursa Minor (notes to line 32-33, and 81),

- Thuban in Draco (notes to line 41),

- Polaris (Kiblah) in Ursa Minor, also given as Kochab (notes to line 24),

- Vega in Lyra (notes to line 22).

<u>Line 72</u>

(line) 54 ← (-18) (line) 72 (+18) → (line) 108

The Teacher sought to find delightful sayings and write words of truth accurately. The words of the wise are like goads...(...) like firmly embedded nails. The sayings are given by one Shepherd. (Ecclesiastes 12:10-11)

KAK is the thorn or nail of truth dropped onto the heads of humankind by the Mother Goddess who is Egyptian Ma'at. Source of words such as 'cactus' and 'acacia', both hallucinogenic (line 92). The concluding section of *The Story of Sukurru* also brings the theme of nails and words of truth to the fore.

Apparent on the Ashmolean prism, the ten words of line 72 are separated into two identical five-word phrases, the third and central word being KAK, 'thorn', 'nail', 'keystone', followed by A, the 'flow' signalling the culmination of a star or planet (notes to line 52). Placed in third position on the third line of the third face of the Ashmolean prism, KAK is part of that tablet's hidden message (notes to line 108):

Measured at sunrise or sunset on the two equinoxes and two solstices, the sun is perceived to have moved approximately one degree against the backdrop of the constellations.

It's interesting to consider MU-UN, given here on either side of the central gap, as source of English 'moon', which would imply that it was involved in this measurement. The method of calculation might have involved marking the relative position of the new moon (at the moment in its cycle when it is unilluminated, on the opposite side of earth from the sun) rather than staring directly at the rising sun. My knowledge of astronomical calculations is too limited to speculate further. Otherwise, MU UN translate to 'age of the land' and, through Latin mundus, to 'world'. Mundus is thought to be linked to Greek kosmos, the orderly arrangement of the universe (notes to line 84).

Line 73

Sothic Cycle

The preceding line 72, taken in the context of precession and measurement of time, represents the pause after baptism and before rebirth. Line 73 is understood as the beginning of the next 72 years of the sun's backward movement in the context of the Great Year. But it also reflects the annual heliacal rising of the star Sirius which occurs after approximately 70 days of invisibility and began the Ancient Egyptian New Year (see p.52).

The rising of the bright star shifts forward by one day every four years in relation to the sun. Thus the return of the Egyptian New Year at its original calendar date occurs only once every 1,460 years:

$$365 \times 4 = 1460 \quad \text{or} \quad 73 \times 20 = 1460 + 1$$

Two comb-like structures discovered in the 1980s along the west side of Khafre's pyramid at Giza are comprised of a line of 73 short walls followed by one standing alone, a single tooth. Adjacent to them was another line of 20 short walls - according to the archaeological reconstructed image. Special thanks to Graham Chase who remarked that this was a Sothic calendar on Graham Hancock's website in January 2024. Without it, I would have missed the reference. Line 73 confirms that his observation is correct.

It also appears that ancient references to the Sothic cycle were made in the number of crenelations that once existed in the west perimeter wall of the Pyramid of Djoser (*The Egypt Code*, p.74 [29]) and in the number of stars on the Senenmut Calendar, both resulting in a total of 1,461.

Sirius would have been seen rising above the horizon for the first time after a long absence ca.8300 BC (p.49-50). The complexity of the astronomical calculations and implications of the long cycle and far-flung movements of Sirius stretch the subject beyond the scope of this analysis:

In this connection it is interesting to note Al-Sufi's statement concerning the Arab name for Sirius, "Al-abur." According to this noted astronomer Sirius was so-called because it had passed across the Milky Way into the southern region of the sky. It is a remarkable fact that the proper motion of Sirius would have carried it across the Milky Way from the eastern to the western border in 60,000 years. Possibly the Arabian story may be based on a tradition of Sirius having been seen on the opposite side of the Milky Way by the men of the Stone Age. (Olcott William, Star Lore of all Ages, p.105)[18]

IM MA ANU IL₂

IM MA appear together on 12 lines (lines 8, 17, 19, 20, 34, 37, 73, 90, 93, 97, 106 and 122), twice on lines 19, 20 and 93, giving 15 appearances in all. Their importance is demonstrated by the positioning to signal the magic square of Daedalus (lines 35-37) where AN takes central position.

IM MA AN appear together three times (lines 73, 106 and 122).

IL₂ appears four times (lines 27, 30, 73 and 76) in two contexts: passage through the false door and here as the newborn soul. With IL₂ given as 'raise' and 'carry', to fully demonstrate the exactitude of the source name Immanuel, AN is shown with another of its transliterated forms: ANU, partial source of Egyptian Anubis, another name for Sirius.

Biblical Immanuel is the new born, the disappearing and rising fish of NUN KI (*Lost Stones*, p.35). The three words IM MA ANU, in the dual context of the biblical virgin birth and the Egyptian New Year heralded by the heliacal rising of Sirius translate:

'clay of truth (Ma'at) of the sky'.

At the same time, there appear to be a number of confusing but real connections between GALAM/SUKUD, the rising Mesopotamian fish-god, and the rising of the star Sirius.

LA, pictogram of a cord hanging down, with given meanings 'to weigh', 'hang', 'suspend' amongst others, before BA, 'to diminish', 'reduce', 'withdraw'. Rotate them to discover another reference to the spinning whale (BAL E NE in notes to line 69). The lexical entries give:

The theme of the newly rising fish is confirmed through repetition of HA, 'fish', over three lines 78, 79 and 80 – culminating in a threefold rising on line 80.

If it were not for the reference to Sirius, the implication would be that this line refers to Pisces rising at the spring equinox and that the astronomer-scribe who wrote the lines down some time between 1900 and 1600 BC was referencing a period either in the past or in the future, i.e. from approximately 25800 BC to 23640 BC and again in our time:

Pisces rising at spring equinox

End	(2,160 x 11)	Start	Pisces	End
X		X	X	X
23640 BC		120 BC		2040
	(1600 BC)			

<u>Line 74</u>

Following the 72-year shift, this section – which comprises a detailed account of astronomical movements – becomes increasingly difficult to translate. It involves a multi-facetted creature on line 79 linked to the biblical behemoth and other hybrid beasts of mythology. I have attempted to identify the most likely references in context but, as the notes to line 73 show, probably not got to the bottom of it.

Line 74 appears to refer to the constellations of Sagittarius and Pisces. When Pisces rises at the vernal equinox, Sagittarius rises at the winter solstice. They are tied one to the other, moving forward in lock step, onward to the next of their four stations (p.11).   But that is not the only astronomical reference here.

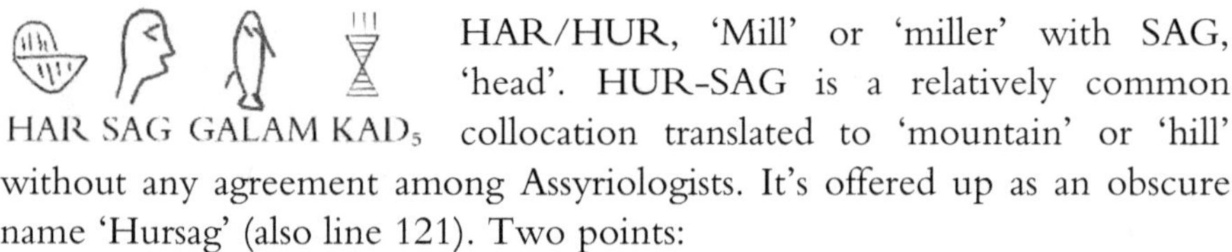

HAR SAG GALAM KAD₅

HAR/HUR, 'Mill' or 'miller' with SAG, 'head'. HUR-SAG is a relatively common collocation translated to 'mountain' or 'hill' without any agreement among Assyriologists. It's offered up as an obscure name 'Hursag' (also line 121). Two points:

- HAR is the harp or lyre of Orpheus, where SAG is his 'skull' (line 26). Potentially a double reference whereby Vega/Lyra temporarily leads the dance at the north pole while the constellation of Sagittarius (referenced as SAG on line 26) is the permanent guardian at the southern pole of the galactic plain. But Dog-Head (Sirius) is also a candidate here.

- HUR as the Great Sphinx (Hor-em-Akhet) and its twin, the celestial lion, where SAG, 'head', is the sickle asterism, head of Leo with the star Regulus at its base. Seen at Dendera looking backwards from the Sagittarian centaur's head.

(Regulus) *So, too, it was the leader of the Four Royal Stars of the ancient Persian monarchy, the Four Guardians of Heaven (Star Names* [6]*, p.256)*

When Leo rises at the spring equinox, it will be half a Great Year before Pisces takes on the same role. In that way, the two constellations are constantly separated by about 12,960 years, whether rising with the sun at the spring equinox or at the three other markers of time (p.11).

Confirmation of the reference to the rising constellation of Pisces at the spring equinox in this section of text comes in the form of collocated GALAM, pictogram of the rising fish (notes to line 52) associated with KAD$_5$, with given meanings 'to tie' and 'tuft'. KAD$_6$, a close match, is also transliterated ZIB, with the meanings 'tie' and 'mark' (also see Zep Tepi):

> (Pisces) *Zib, of the later Graeco-Babylonian astronomy ; although this last word may mean " Boundary " as being at the end of the zodiac. (…) Al Biruni asserted that " the name of the sign in all languages signifies only one fish,"* (Star Names [6], p.337–338)

Flowing between the two A, with SI given as the verb 'to place'. SI is also identified as the 'announcing' horn. Is it the horn of Taurus, the constellation lying at the northern gate of the galactic plain and in opposition to Sagittarius at its southern gate? Or another reference to sound and to Vega on the horn of the lyre? E BA AN as source of 'evangel', announcement of good news, helps confirm the overall context.

Line 75

ZAG, mark on the shoulder of GA, the cow, referring to the Pleiades (notes to line 52). Again, potential reference through GA, the milk, to the Milky Way and Taurus at its northern gate. Second use of A NI (notes to line 6), the animation, 'coming to life' as the celestial elements begin their new cycles.

GIZ GI, 'branch of the tree', 'wooden rod' or 'shaft of Giza'. In context, the lowering branch of the tree and also the prod used to move the cow (see line 12).

First of five appearances of KU (lines 89, 101, 106, 108) with given meanings 'hole', 'seat' and 'seize' and important element of the acrostic over lines 106 to 108. These are the holes (navels) into which the shafts separating earth from sky are to be inserted.

<u>Line 76</u>

GIZ SAR

Collocated GIZ, 'beam', with SAR as 'garden' are always translated to 'orchard' which fits with the context of Eden. However, SAR has another apparently unrelated given meaning: 'to write' and is part of DUB SAR, given as 'scribe'. The underlying meaning here is that the scribe and the writing are in the beam (of Giza). This line of text brings the story of Adam and Eve firmly back to its Meso-Egyptian origin in astronomy.

(Corona Australis) *some considered it the early Bunch of Arrows radiating from the hand of the Archer, often imagined as a wheel* (*Star Names* [6], p.173)

(Corona Borealis) *when the Sun was in Taurus the Crown was specially noticeable in the midnight sky* (*Star Names* [6], p.175)

GURUN IL$_2$ LA

GURUN is given as 'fruit', an elusive pictogram reconstructed here according to the explanation in the Manuel d'Epigraphie Akkadienne (Geuthner Manuals) which mentions it as a circle of four BAD (notes to line 55). The transliteration derives from KUR-RU-UN found opposite the symbol, potentially translating to the 'rotation of the hills of the land'. I have added 'wheel' and 'rotation' to the dictionary meanings of RU ('to fall'). GURUN is one of two sources of the word 'crown'. Shown here before IL$_2$, 'raise', and LA, 'hang', it's the hanging fruit in the garden of Eden (line 98). It's also the hero on a journey to become king.

But which of the two celestial crowns? Is it in the north or in the south? The reference to the hero bringing down the cow's shoulder with his prod on line 75 is highly reminiscent of the Greek story of Theseus killing the minotaur. He then uses the light of Corona Borealis to escape the labyrinth.

<u>Line 77</u>

HU E ZUM

HU, 'bird' and 'to fly', is one element of transliterated HUR, the mill (*Lost Stones*, p.91), partial source of Egyptian Horus, and a word which also applies to the Great Sphinx through its ancient name, Hor-em-Akhet. HU is also seen perched above the false door of UR$_3$ (lines 28 and 29).

Also source of the pre-Islamic Arabian god Hubal. BAL, to 'turn' is replaced here by ZUM, 'revolving'. (See *Hamlet's Mill* [2], p.221.)

ZUM, 'to revolve,' takes the appearance of SAL, the 'chamber', with two sets of parallel striations below, indicating ropes. The transliteration derives from ZU, 'knowledge' with UM, 'cord'. Pictographic UM is a striated version of DUB, the 'tablet' and 'scribe'. Together they provide:

ZUM   ZU UM

Knowledge of the umbilical cord (and navel).

Third use of BI MU UN MAL MAL where BI MU together indicate the end of a series of kingships on the *Sumerian King List* (lines 17, 61 and 77).

<u>Line 78</u>

Four times E, with the meanings 'levee' and 'raise' perhaps to indicate four key positions, four levees, the movements of the four constellations in lockstep (p.11). From Pisces to Aquarius? The milk on line 76 followed by the honey on this line create a dilemma between fish:

> (Piscis Austrinus) *This idea of the Fish drinking the Stream is an ancient one, and may have given rise to the title Piscis aquosus, found with Ovid and in the 4th Georgic, which has commonly been referred to this constellation; Vergil mentioning it in his directions as to the time for gathering the honey harvest.* (Star Names[6], p.344)

SUHUR/UBI$_2$, given as 'tuft' or 'carp' appears with HA, 'fish'. According to the above quote, this appears to be a reference to Piscis Austrinus and, more precisely, to its main star Fomalhaut which lies at the mouth of the fish. The pictogram varies and can appear as one double-headed vertical fish. Potentially synonymous of GALAM/UBI who is Oannes (notes to lines 9, 28, 52 and 74).

> (Piscis Austrinus and Fomalhaut) *In early legend our australis was the parent of the zodiacal two, (…) Fomalhaut, from the Arabic Fum al Hut, the Fish's Mouth, has long been the common name for this star, (…) No other star seems to have had so varied an orthography. (…) Flammarion says that it was Hastorang in Persia 3000 b. c, when near the winter solstice, and a Royal Star, one of the four Guardians of Heaven, sentinels watching over other stars; while about 500 b. c. it was the object of sunrise worship in the temple of Demeter at Eleusis; and still later on, with astrologers, portended eminence, fortune, and power.* (Star Names[6], p.344–346)

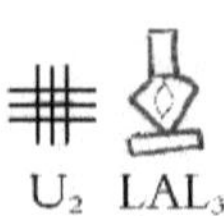

U$_2$, the 'pipes' or 'channels', with LAL$_3$, 'honey', in context refer to the 'Stream' flowing from Aquarius into the mouth of Piscis Austrinus.

Line 79

Bahamut, Behemoth, Aspidochelone

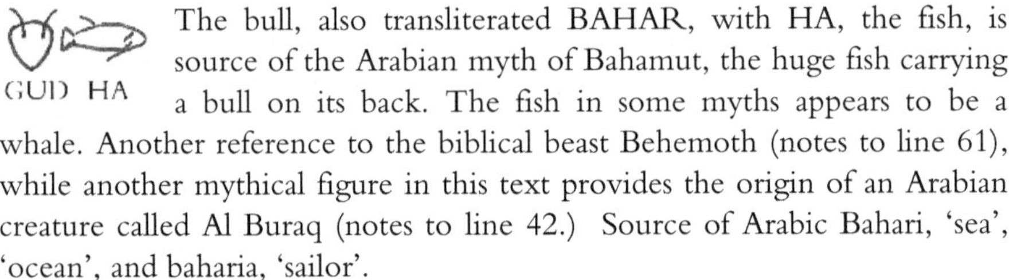

The bull, also transliterated BAHAR, with HA, the fish, is source of the Arabian myth of Bahamut, the huge fish carrying a bull on its back. The fish in some myths appears to be a whale. Another reference to the biblical beast Behemoth (notes to line 61), while another mythical figure in this text provides the origin of an Arabian creature called Al Buraq (notes to line 42.) Source of Arabic Bahari, 'sea', 'ocean', and baharia, 'sailor'.

Another related mythological sea creature is the Aspidochelone (lines 68-69).

TUR has given meanings 'small', 'child' and 'sagacity'. Translated here to 'turtle' entirely according to context along with the presence of the tortoise-shell lyre elsewhere in this text. This is the mythological turtle that supports the world on its back; in this case the bull and the fish. It's also the moving Moon Turtle of the Cherokee Indians (p.46-48).

Latin torquere 'to twist, turn, wind, wring, distort' (Etymonline)

GUD, the bull, with HA, the fish of Pisces (plural indicated by TUR TUR), and TUR TUR, the turtle of Lyra but also potentially, the turning and twisting 'children' of the bull, i.e. the Taurids, meteor stream in the constellation of Taurus (notes to line 93).

There is another link to the world turtle and to the lyre in KUN, given as 'tail' and 'canal outlet' and to which I add 'weir'. This is the twisting tail of the Moon Turtle covering the sun (p.46-48) Ancient Greek kunkhe has the meanings 'shell' and 'mussel' while the Egyptian god Khunsu is generally said to be linked to the moon.

MU-UN-NA, the heavy world (see line 66) but also the full moon eclipsing the sun.

SUD has given meanings to include 'distant' and 'sink', to which I have added 'south', French 'sud'. The original pictographic word takes the form of the head of a horned snake with one or more horizontal striations. It might well be the source of Greek Sothis, epithet of Sirius (notes to line 17).

The line is complex with too many astronomical references to fully develop its meaning. It contains a bull (GUD), a fish (HA), a tortoise or turtle (TUR TUR) and tail. Does it also have a rising snake-head (SUD)?

Line 80

80 / 12 (words) = 6.666666666666667 (.6 x 14 pieces of Osiris)

25,920 / 80 = 324

324 / 9 (Thoth) = 36

This was now the third time that Jesus appeared to the disciples after He was raised from the dead. (John 21:14)

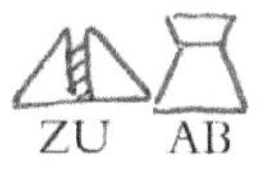

ZI/ZE, 'to rise' and 'life', takes the form of GI/GE, the reed, with accompanying short vertical striations. Repeated three times, it is interpreted here as 'rising three times' but also matches GE-EŠ (notes to lines 18 and 71), the three branches of the tree, taking the story back once again to GIZ and to Giza. ZE is source of 'zenith'.

Given together at the end of line 80, NA, 'stone' and 'heavy', appears three times between lines 79 and 80. Zi appears four times. They translate to 'raising of the stone', 'the rising stone', 'the raised stone'; theme continued on line 81. (Also see Ziz in the notes to line 55.)

(Also see Dog-head (Sirius) as Anubis preventing new life from rising again on line 71 of *The Story of Sukurru*.)

Line 81

ZU AB, the 'father to know' but also the 'sinking of the father' or 'sinking into the sea' where ZU/SU takes its given meanings 'sink' and 'flesh'. The link to Greek Sophia is made through 'sinking into flesh' (*Lost Stones*, p.177-178).

Apart from this being the name of the circumpolar star in Ursa Minor, Kochab, also written Kakabel or Kokabiel, was fourth of the twenty Watcher angels according to the Book of Enoch and commanded an army of 365,000 spirits. As a fallen angel, he fits rather well with the pyramidion absent from the Great Pyramid. Found at last in situ?

The Benben Stone

ŠI, 'eye' with E_2, 'temple', transliterated together as U_6, are invariably translated to 'ziggurat' in conventional translations (*Lost Stones*, p.115). 'Eye of the temple' is a straightforward translation referring to both the Egyptian benben stone, topmost point of the pyramid, and to the Ancient Egyptian 'indestructible' circumpolar stars through ZU/KUŠ AB, first two words of this line identified as Kochab (notes to line 33).

Another transliteration of the two words is LIBIR/LIBER resulting from the lexical entry:

LI   BI   ER   =   ŠI   E₂
LIBER

'Altar of the erring', 'Altar of the bier', 'altar of the brew', 'altar of the erring bee'. LI/ARA is an element of the name Kitara (p.75-77, line 117), pictogram of an incense burner with rising smoke (with or without the addition of 'seeds' above).

BI ER, the 'erring bee' but also the king 'on his bier', astronomical reference to Ursa Major (lines 17, 39 and 97). On line 17, the dead king is given as rising and followed by a reference to Sirius through UB (origin of 'up' and 'obelisk', notes to line 17).

I posit that the three-word phrase giving phonetic LIBER and found opposite the 'eye of the temple' is source of both 'liberate' and 'levitate', applying to both the rising king and to the raising of the sacred Egyptian benben stone or capstone of the pyramids:

> Latin liber "free, unrestricted"
>
> Latin levis "light" in weight, (Etymonline)

MA, 'land' and 'truth', with DU, 'carry', 'establish', contents of the basket carried by the Mesopotamian fish god Oannes, is repeated five times (lines 19, 20, 52, 81 and 127).

DU, 'foot' and 'carry', as the last word signals a two-line acrostic (notes to line 82).

<u>Line 82</u>

First of the four-line riddle beginning MU (notes to line 85).

Second line of the two-line acrostic formed by the final DU (see below).

HUL₂ LA

Given as 'joyful' and 'uplift', HUL$_2$ is also collocated with LA on line 241 of *The Story of Sukurru* and twice in a proverb which incorporates PI, the 'pitch' of the music. My translation there gave:

When the pitch is joyful, the sky is full of joy.

Line 82 continues the description of the ritual involving the raising of the benben stone and further links it to the ancient Greek concept of installing mythological figures as stars or constellations.

Two DU together are given as 'sailor'. A double version appears in the text and image of the ouroboros (line 10) Here the feet are linked to earth by MA, 'land', and to sky by IB as 'wing'. IB was translated to 'ark' in *The Story of Sukurru* (line 111). Also the winged sandals of Greek Hermes.

81. MA DU

82. IB DU

The now extinct dodo is mentioned in the context of stones in *The Story of Sukurru* (line 66) and compared to the image of the big-footed bird with its stone at Göbekli Tepe. I wrote in the notes:

The origin of 'dodo' is unknown, first attested in Portuguese as discovered and eaten by Portuguese sailors.

"About 1638... (...) The keeper called it a Dodo, and ... (...) there lay a heap of large pebblestones, whereof he gave it many in our sight, some as big as nutmegs. Observed in London by Sir Hamon l'Estrange. (source Wikipedia)

In 2016 from an incomplete text and with the information in hand which at that time did not include astronomical references:

65-66. A soft regal whisper from (behind) the façade, he who the wooden spindle created without any knots: "Look not! For the leader in water a lofty destiny shared with the lofty dodo, flight of the noble (lord)." (tears from the heart of the reed façade), "And both from their homeland stones estranged."

Line 83

The title stems from a Jewish tale of David digging the temple foundations and causing a flood by lifting out a stone (*Hamlet's Mill²*, p.220). Potentially, the name given as Eben Shetiyyah leads back to Sirius through ŠI TI (notes to line 113). DIM₂, given as 'create', is repeated on line 84.

First of three consecutive lines incorporating MU UN (notes to line 85).

MU UN DA — DA has the meaning 'by the side of' and 'river bank'. Possible translations include 'next to the moon'. DA alone might be understood as a renowned arm next to a river (line 112), particularly as 'a great river' begins the next line 84. Origin of Greek daimon, a spirit let loose onto the world:

Demon c. 1200, "an evil spirit, malignant supernatural being, an incubus, a devil," from Latin daemon "spirit," from Greek daimōn "deity, divine power; lesser god; guiding spirit, tutelary deity" (sometimes including souls of the dead); "one's genius, lot, or fortune;" from PIE (Etymonline)

Source of Arabic Sidr Al Muntaha, a lote tree at the boundary of the seventh heaven, analogous to the lotus tree of Greek myth (milk of fools on line 90):

16. But they paid no heed, so We let loose on them a flood from the dam and replaced their two gardens with others that yielded bitter fruit, tamarisk bushes, and a few lote trees. (Quran 34:16, Trans. Abdul Haleem)

Line 84

Second of three consecutive lines incorporating MU UN (notes to line 85).

ID₂ MAH DIM₂ — ID₂ MAH, 'great river' associated with both the Milky Way and the river Nile (notes to line 55). Boötes, ox foreleg ploughing at the centre of the Dendera Zodiac, is the 'creator' of a hole through which the waters of a great river pour (notes to lines 15 and 59), perhaps more precisely the star Arcturus.

MU UN DU — With dictionary-given meanings, we find 'the age of the land to establish'. Source of Latin mundus which, according to etymologists, is of unknown origin but has a connection to Greek kosmos meaning 'orderly arrangement'. MU UN is identified as source of 'moon' (notably in the notes to line 79 in the context of the Moon Turtle).

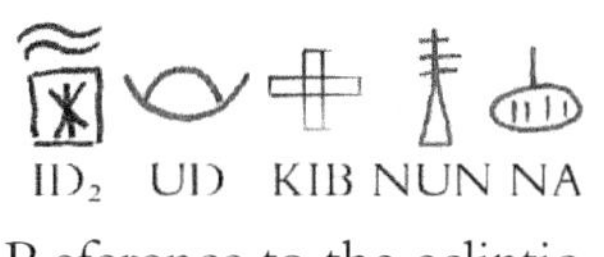

'To establish' but also 'to carry' with RI, 'to fly' and 'to gather'. DU and RI are elements of the word 'Eridu', one of the transliterations used for NUN (*Lost Stones*, p.206-207) the guide, which is found on the next line in the name of the Euphrates.

Line 85

Second of two lines beginning 'river'. Second use of the words translating to 'Euphrates' (notes to line 24) with the addition of NA, 'stone'. Reference to the ecliptic.

URU, pictogram of the step-pyramid and associated with Orion with MIN, 'two', at its centre transliterated GIZGAL and commonly collocated with LU, 'light' (lunar). GIZ with GAL translate to 'great beam' with the addition of MIN also reading 'two great beams or pillars', potentially the two central pillars in the stone circles of Göbekli Tepe. GIZGAL is found opposite UD, 'sun', in the lexical lists.

SAG, 'head', with striations, given as 'troubled'. SAG is the skull of line 26, reference to Sagittarius. The damaged (faceless) stone head illustrating this line was found at Nevali Çori in Turkey.

'Arm rising to the sky' and 'Dan' of Scorpio.
Preceded by UN which takes the pictographic form of the standard or 'banner of Dan' (Danaus, p.35–36).

Given the full name of the river Euphrates on this line, it links back to the section from lines 24 to 26.

Further analysis according to the lexical entries (*Lost Stones*, p.67 and 208) gives DA-AN as the breakdown of DAN/KAL and brings confirmation of the reference to the moon in this line:

The repeated use of ID-KAL-TUK in The Story of Sukurru leads to the understanding that KAL was regularly 'called upon' in situations requiring a strong arm – or a wing. (...)

Sumerian KAL is source of Greek kallein and Latin calare which gave us 'to call' and of Old Norse kalla also meaning 'to summon, to name, to call by name'. Collocated with ID which is 'time' (...)

KAL is also the ultimate source of 'calendar' through Latin kalendae which was the first day of the lunar month in Roman times, a date on which priests climbed a mount and called out to the population to

The arm of (pointing to) the river in the sky.

Fourth of four consecutive lines in which MU signals an encoded message:

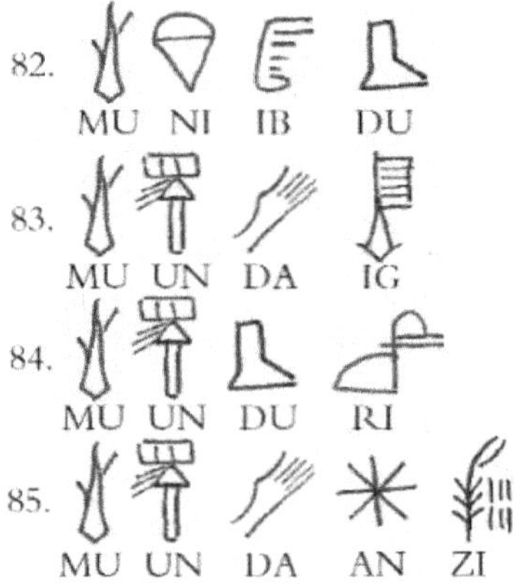

MU is also transliterated MEHIDA while UN takes the form of a standard giving the three 'banners of Dan':

> *Mehida: a word given in a Hebrew dictionary of biblical terms as 'riddle' and 'sharpness of wit'; a major key to something...but to what?* (Lost Stones, p.284)

Read vertically:

- IB DA DU DA: the two riverbanks with the foot of the bird (DU RI) between them, with IB also translating 'ark carried by the bird'. Also the two arms of MU (ME-HI-DA), Mehi of the Sphinx, carrying the collected (DU RI) information.

- (DU) DU IG RI AN: With the addition of DU from line 81, IG, 'door' and 'guard', RI, the bird with the given meaning 'dividing line':

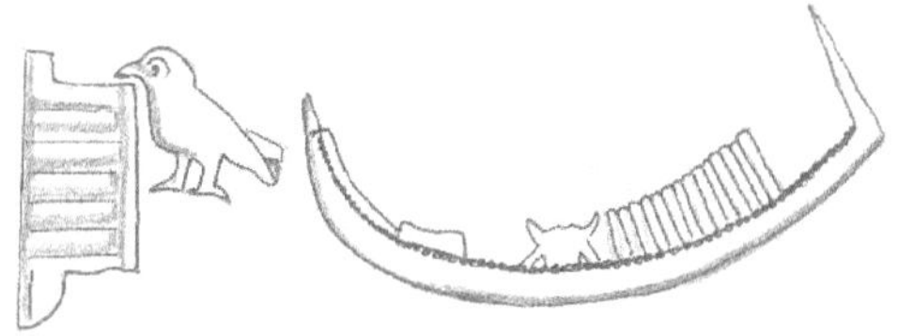

The guardian of the door to the sky. (Narmer palette)

<u>Line 86</u>

> (Draco) *Vergil had Maximus Anguia, 'which, after the manner of a river, glides away with tortuous windings, around and through, between the Bears' (Star Names [6], p.204)*

GI MUŠ — MUŠ with given meaning 'snake' appears twice, confirming the link to Dan as a serpent (see quote in notes to line 85) and a source of Musa (*Lost Stones*, The Serpent and the Staff, p.138).

After GI, rod and snake (see bible verse below line 86), two snakes join as one - the snakes of the *Emerald Tablet* (line 41), one with GE, 'Earth' and one with AN, 'sky', snakes of above and below. Winding around the rod or branch, symbol of Asclepius, Greek god of healing, who is said to be linked to the ancient zodiacal constellation of Ophiuchus, the serpent-bearer.

A NI — Given together seven times in all (lines 6, 75, 86 twice, 87, 88 and 105) of which four on these three consecutive lines, translates to 'flow' with 'oil' or 'thick' but also a general meaning of fertility and abundance (first syllable of the rivers Nile and Niger), and gives the source of Latin animus, meaning 'life' and 'breath' (notes to line 6). It is likely that the waving line of A also signals 'snake' and that the waving lines ending in snake heads at Göbekli Tepe indicate the original animistic mindset of its people.

One version of line 86 replaces AN MUŠ, the snake in the sky, with IM DU DU, 'spirits of sailors' given in brackets in the translation or alternatively 'in clay (two feet of the dodo) established' where the double DU indicates the plural (see the acrostic over lines 81 and 82).

Bearing in mind that snakes and rivers, both earthly and celestial, were synonymous (*Lost Stones*, p.140), certain verses of Revelation 12:3-4 (notes to line 41) are relevant, and a huge red dragon striking one third of the stars from the sky might lead to a red river (line 91).

<u>Line 87</u>

GIZ followed by a combination of BI with another smaller GIZ attached to it. BI–GIZ are transliterated GISAL and given as 'oar' or 'rudder'. The transcript of the Ashmolean prism confirms that this is the correct wording; an important point in that some of the earliest words transliterated as GISAL have a different appearance.

BI as 'total' surrounded by the two beams and followed by A NI (notes to line 86) give:

'all of the beams set in motion'.

Thus the meaning can be applied indifferently to the beams of a celestial ship and to the beams of the Great Pyramid in the context of measurement and resonance. BI, the hallucinogenic brew, is also transliterated PI_2 and, in this context, synonymous of PI, the musical pitch created by the sound of the bees (another use of BI) between the beams.

GI as 'reed' with TUR, given as 'small' and 'child'. In *Before Babel*, I likened the pictogram, which has varying forms, to the mother's breasts and the subject of weaning. However, in the analysis of the Sator riddle (and in reference to both the Giza plateau and Atlantis), I wrote:

SA with TUR, the string of the musical instrument and the youth, calls to mind the story of Orpheus, the bard who charms wild animals and birds with his music, whose head ends up hanging from his own cord around the neck of Athena. See line 36 of The Story of Sukurru. See pages 277 to 278. In The Story of Sukurru, TUR MU is (partially) translated to 'young Mu' on line 34. One solution might have been to translate the two symbols to 'the renowned youth'. Given the references to ballads, chords, and hanging from a cord on the next few lines, it surely links to the myth of Orpheus. But it's not easy to disentangle the threads from the chords, remembering that this text precedes every other piece of writing that we possess. (Before Babel, p.261)

Here, in the context of astronomy (for the most part left out of that first translation) and reference to some strange creature, GI becomes the 'reeds' of Hermes, where the double TUR indicates a plural (see p.268). (Also see TUR MU in the notes to line 123). With repetition of A NI from line 86, the mill shaft terminating in the pole star Vega/Lyra is set in motion.

Line 88

*And I saw in those days how long cords were given to those angels,
and they took to themselves wings and flew, and they went towards
the north. And I asked the angel, saying unto him: 'Why have those
(angels) taken these cords and gone off?' And he said unto me: 'They
have gone to measure.'* (Book of Enoch)

AN EN KI HU SI A NI — Transliterated as U_5, HU, the 'bird', with SI, the 'horn' have given meanings 'to ride' and 'to gain control' among others. In the company of the lord and translated as 'beak of the bird', a reference to Cygnus, also closely linked to Orpheus and the constellation of Lyra (line 87). It lies in the Milky Way with its beak pointing to the dark rift at its centre.

MU GAN IG SUD GA — Repetition of MU GAN IG (line 5), GAN identified as the Milky Way and IG, its gate. Line 50, in which Noah's ark and the constellation of Argo Navis are identified, has BI GAN IG SUD GA, an interesting variation (notes to line 50). (See MU with BI as 'total years' in notes to line 61.)

Line 89

Orderly I stopp'd their ears; and they as fair did ply
My feet and hands with cords and to the mast
With other halsets made me soundly fast
(Odyssey, Bk XII, trans. Chapman)

Not only the ship of Odysseus but also the ferry boat of Greek Charon (line 113).

GIZ MA₂ — Only two uses of MA_2, the 'boat', in this text despite the overall theme of travelling (see line 113). In this position, GIZ would be understood as silent prefix meaning 'wooden', a 'wooden boat'. However it's also a 'beam', the mast of the boat, or a 'shaft' and can be opposed to the last word on this line, KU, which translates to 'seize', 'foundation' and 'hole' (see the riddle of lines 106 to 108). This is the scene of Odysseus tied to the mast of his ship to better resist the call of the sirens. (*The Story of Sukurru*, line 124. *Before Babel*, p.216. *Lost Stones*, p.210, p.212.)

NI₂ BI NAM

Appearing twice in this line, NI$_2$, the 'soul', with BI as 'all' but equally the 'brew' carried in the boat and led by NAM, bird of destiny. This is the boat of Greek Charon who ferries the dead to Hades (line 113).

NAM GAB ES₂

In this instance where the 'spreading of the rope' around Odysseus and the (musical) 'chord' join together in the context of snakes coming to life (line 86), they represent the great coiling and uncoiling winged dragon-snake generally known as Sumerian Tiamat. Through the elongated body of Egyptian Hathor, the Holy Cow, the boats of stars and souls sail, from birth to death and back again.

Two NAM, 'birds of fate' are the Greek Sirens, their songs luring sailors to their deaths. Lines 27 to 28 of *The Story of Sukurru* have them in the context of a three-tiered pyramid:

> *NAM – The thick cloud over the land to measure.*
>
> *NAM – His name in words of clay to know.*
>
> *NAM – His name to spread on high.*

Between the beam, the stretching of the cord and KU with its given meaning of 'foundation', an encoded reference to Ancient Egyptian rituals and architecture. The shaft is inserted into the hole – as are the unsecured stone pillars at Göbekli Tepe.

<u>Line 90</u>

(line) 90 / 9 (Thoth) = 10 (ouroboros)

There are nine words (TE.A is transliterated KAR) in line 90, nine being the line number containing mention of Thoth. The resulting line 10 is the ouroboros. Hermes/Thoth is again identified with the circling snake.

GA LIL₂

KID, here transliterated LIL$_2$, the 'ghostly fool on his mat', with GA, 'milk', becomes the 'milk of fools', that of the hallucinogenic Egyptian blue lily and source of the name of the plant.

After the boat and birds of fate on line 89, the theme of attaching Homer's Argonauts to their ship continues with the story of the lotus eaters. Lily and lotus are different plants but the origin of both is here:

the Lotus-eaters, who did them no hurt, but gave them to eat of the lotus, which was so delicious that those who ate of it left off caring about home, and did not even want to go back and say what had happened to them, but were for staying and munching lotus with the Lotus-eaters without thinking further of their return; nevertheless, though they wept bitterly I forced them back to the ships and made them fast under the benches. (Oddysey, Bk IX, trans. S. Butler)

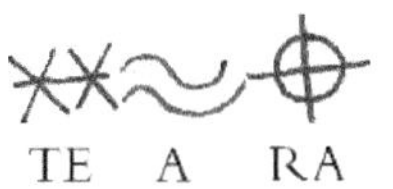

The theme of the dragon-snake/basilisk continues. TE-A, transliterated KAR/KARA, has given meanings 'harbour', 'to flee', 'to take away' and 'to save' amongst others. Pictographic TE comprises two crosses joined by a horizontal line, providing a sense of moving between two places, with A indicating a passage across water.

TE as 'tether' (see Prometheus on line 33) with A as 'flow' and RA as 'churn', this is the winding movement of a water snake (see TE as 'tether' on line 98), but also the journey of the sun and ship of a lord sailing across the sea to its harbour; Odysseus homeward bound.

Source of Greek 'tiara' which is (as always) from an unknown source. (See the three-tiered crown on line 109.) A turban might be said to resemble a coiled snake. But does a turban lead to a tiara? There is an unfinished kudurru stone in the Louvre Museum. It shows two snakes, one coiled around the bottom of the stone and the other around the top. Eight archer-musicians playing long-necked string instruments and carrying quivers circle around its four sides. Horizontal and vertical markers had been set out between its four pillars for the purpose of inscribing the text. I have to wonder if it was going to be *The Path to Sky-End*. Other boundary stones also have a large snake curled around their summits.

Line 91

Then Death and Hades were thrown into the lake of fire. This is the second death—the lake of fire. And if anyone was found whose name was not written in the Book of Life, he was thrown into the lake of fire. (Revelation 20:14-15)

ID₂, the 'river', associated here with NE, the 'fire' and 'red' (notes to line 13). NE/BIL is one of the key words in the sixteen-line acrostic (see lines 110 to 113) where it has connotations of renewal (see the red brew on line 110). The waters of the river Nile became red at the time of flooding, a phenomenon visually linked to the heliacal rising of Sirius by the Egyptians (See *The Egypt Code*[29], p.139). In the Egyptian *Book of the Dead* the lake of fire is surrounded and guarded by four baboons:

Symbols U.KA, the 'covered mouth', are given together as 'skull'. Here we have the hitherto unknown source of the three seated monkeys who hear no evil, see no evil, speak no evil. The two words are also given as phonetic ELE in the later Akkadian versions. I wonder if the source of the secretive Greek Eleusinian (p.169) mystery school is to be found in them. (Lost Stones, p.32)

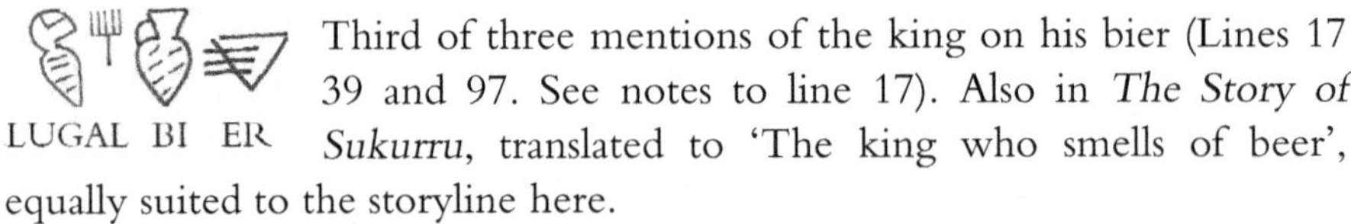

Third of three mentions of the king on his bier (Lines 17 39 and 97. See notes to line 17). Also in *The Story of Sukurru*, translated to 'The king who smells of beer', equally suited to the storyline here.

LUGAL BI ER

IM MI together appear on lines 67, 91, 95, 108 and 109. In this ominous setting and with given meanings, they read 'spirit of darkness' or 'black clay' as opposed to IM-MA, the 'clay of truth' which is immaculate. Black clay less so. They can also read 'night wind' which, with IB as 'cloud', announces stormy weather (notes to line 109). Here surrounded by AD, the 'seal', and whirling reeds.

IM   MI   IB

Line 92

This piping sound of the actual queen to which the young queens respond ' in a voice sounding hoarse from the recesses of their prison' is constantly heard just before swarming, which is also a period of great agitation in the hive, (Virgil, Georgics, Bk.4, notes T.E. Page)

Threefold repetition of KA (also on line 14), voices of at least three bees. 'Kak kak' is one of the sounds called 'piping". Origin of the European tradition of 'telling the bees' of important events. Apollo, musician and father of Orpheus, received the gift of prophecy from three bee-maidens.

KA BI

Very little is known about the Ancient Greek Kabeiri:

and so he (Zeus) instructed him in the initiatory rites of the Mysteries [of the Kabeiroi (Cabeiri) of Samothrake], which had existed on the island since ancient times but was at that time, so to speak, put in his hands; it is not lawful, however, for any but the initiated to hear about the Mysteries. (…) but the fame has travelled wide of how these gods [the Kabeiroi] appear to mankind and bring unexpected aid to those initiates of their who call upon them in the midst of perils.(….) and since they were wizards (gonta), they practised charms and initiatory rites and mysteries, (Diodorus Siculus, *Library of History*, 5, sourced from Theoi.com)

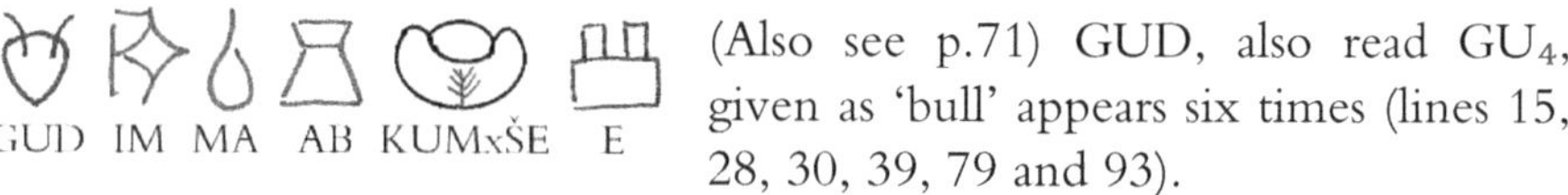

Given as 'calf', AMAR is the central word used for the name of the so-called god Marduk. Source of the biblical golden calf. AMAR breaks down to A MAR giving 'flow of bitterness' (*Lost Stones*, p.63 and 163):

As Moses approached the camp and saw the calf and the dancing, he burned with anger and threw the tablets out of his hands, shattering them at the base of the mountain. Then he took the calf they had made, burned it in the fire, ground it to powder, and scattered the powder over the face of the water. (Exodus 32:19-20)

The source story that became the biblical account of Moses and the burning bush are found here and provide the only reasonable explanation for the curious actions of the angry prophet. That account is also better explained by the comet appearing on the following line 93; the strange idea of grinding the calf into powder corresponding to the darkly humorous mixing of mortar there.

<u>Line 93</u>

(Also see p.71) GUD, also read GU₄, given as 'bull' appears six times (lines 15, 28, 30, 39, 79 and 93).

On line 15 with DIM₂, the ox foreleg, Boötes in the region of the north pole. On line 28 with AN-NA, 'above and below', where it might be a reference to Taurus as guardian of the northern gate of the galactic plain, this last also Egyptian Hathor, the celestial cow.

On line 30 with SI, the horn, and subsequently on line 39 GUD appears to refer to Taurus. However, it's possible that there is an underlying reference to Vega in Lyra on line 30. On line 79 with 'HA' followed closely by 'TUR-TUR', giving the source name of Egyptian Hathor. Other mentions are of GA, the 'milk cow' or GAN, the Milky Way. On line 93, considering the presence of the seed-crusher, GUD refers to Taurus.

The combination of KUM with ŠE, transliterated GAZ, has the given meanings 'kill', 'crush' and 'mortar' (p.61). This is one source of 'comet' through the Greek word which apparently stems from 'long-haired', describing the tail of the comet:

Latin cometa, from Greek (aster) kometes, literally "long-haired (star)," from komē "hair of the head" which is of unknown origin. (Etymonline)

Castration of the bull and the scattering of its seeds is the analogy for the astronomical event that created the Taurid meteor stream in the constellation of Taurus. That memory, also detectable in *The Story Of Sukurru*, was transformed into the far better known and much later tale of biblical Moses who, in a fit of anger, sets about breaking up the golden calf and scattering its ashes (notes to line 92).

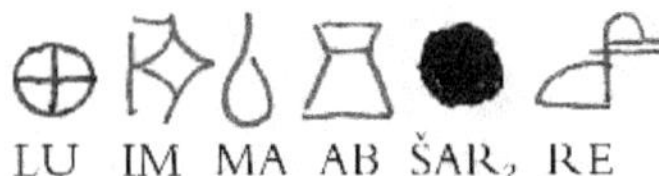

IM MA AB, 'clay', 'spirit' or 'wind' of 'land and 'sea', and of 'mother and father', appear twice here, four times in all (lines 17, 20 and 93). On line 17, the phrase follows mention of Sirius (UB). On line 20, it's associated with the suffering of Greek Deukalion.

LU given as 'sheep' to which I add 'light' and 'lunar', the pictographic form of a cross inside a circle close to that of RA, the 'churning'. ŠAR₂ (p.61) also has the dictionary-given meaning 3,600. Associated here with RE, 'collect'. Read vertically:

Total obliteration of the levee (dam or seawall). E with RI give the source name of the river Eridanus (notes to lines 30, 36 and 113) connected in Greek mythology to the fall of Phaeton. URU has the given meaning 'city'.

<u>Line 94</u>

ZU, also transliterated SU, is given 26 times of which 13 in collocation with AB. Here translated 'knowledge' and followed by ID, with given meanings 'arm', 'wing', 'strength' and 'time', it is the locked and guarded Pyramid of Knowledge of Time (*Lost Stones*, p.65). The reference is most obviously to the Great Pyramid.

The six-word phrase giving 'not open hang' and 'place to be cordoned off', is repeated on line 95. Between the two a hitherto unimagined theme (notes to line 95).

6th and 7th use of IG, the gate, corresponding to the seven gates of the *Book of the Dead*. The 6th was called 'Raging of Voice'.

DI, 'division', with 'IM', 'clay', together become DIM, with given meaning 'pole'. The pyramid holds the word of the divisions − alluding back to the 3,600-degree circle on the preceding line − of time and space recorded in the clay.

Line 95

The Brazen Bull

AB$_2$ with ŠA$_3$, 'cow' and 'inner', given as 'drum' a meaning which might well result from its use here. (AB$_2$ figures among the carvings at Göbekli Tepe and similar symbols given as axe-heads were found at Stonehenge.) AB$_2$ is mentioned in relation to Sirius (p.52). Three-word phrase UD KA BAR, 'sun' or rather in this case, 'heat of the sun' with 'voice' and 'distant', given four times and transliterated ZABAR (lines 95, 99, 111, 112), has the given meaning 'bronze'. Following the 'innards' of the cow and accompanied by a distant voice, this is by far the most ancient mention of the brazen bull; torture used on Saint Antipas (p.14).

Then there is the story of otherworldly instructions given to Greek Aristaeus who is weeping for the loss of his bees. Here, according to Virgil, the swarm is regenerated through the death of the bull:

> *Meantime the moisture, warming in the softened bones, ferments, and creatures of wondrous wise to view, footless at first, soon with buzzing wings as well, swarm together, and more and more essay the light air, until, like a shower pouring from summer clouds, they burst forth . . .* (Virgil, *Georgics*, Bk.4. 281−558, trans. Fairclough)

The method of summoning a new colony of bees can also be applied to the carcasses of lions or tigers. See the case of Samson (p.18). The theme here leads not only to the Great Pyramid but also to the side panel of pillar 43 at Göbekli Tepe where the feline and the insect are found.

'Place of the rope to the bee', or even 'place of the native brew'. Used twice over line 94 and 95, the three-word phrase encloses the foolish lord inside the brazen bull. This also corresponds to the two ropes on either side of the weighing scales which lie in the constellation of Libra. And the chords of Lyra are never far away.

Line 96

Up to this point, the cataclysmic events take the form of a warning. In a more earthly context, we might imagine that the hero of the story is currently hanging onto a rope against a cliff face and about to stretch out his arm in order to smoke out the bees and to steal their honeycomb.

Always transliterated and translated as 'nibru'. For example, the academic translation of this line of text begins:

In the shrine of Nibru

When the same words appear in a different order, written EN KI KID, they are generally translated to the name 'Enki'.

EN KID KI is source of Nibiru made famous by Zechariah Sitchin, and which he claimed to be the name of a twelfth planet.

'Nibru' derives from NI IB with RU appearing opposite EN KID KI in the lexical lists. There is a serious link to be made between the lord who is EN and NI IB RU but not that they are interchangeable and meaningless. In this text on lines 65 and 82, NI-IB are translated to 'thick cloud'. They might equally translate to 'oil on the wing', the melting wax of the wings of Greek Phaeton, cause of his death. I also give NI-IB as source of 'nib', the beak of a bird, perhaps an ibis (notes to line 116).

(See notes to line 104 for the correct and monosyllabic wordplay there between EN KI KID and EN KID KI.)

AŠ, given as 'blow', 'strike', 'single', 'unique', is also transliterated DIL, source of the dill stalk, the firestick, used by Prometheus to gather the fire. *The Story of Sukurru* gives AŠ four times in the context of the crushing and slaughtering of humankind (lines 69 and 70), once again demonstrating that this story dates back to at least 2500 BC. Probable source of the biblical Asherah pole:

When he makes all the altar stones like crushed bits of chalk, no Asherah poles or incense altars will remain standing. (Isaiah 27:9)

Asherah was also the name of a Canaanite goddess. My suggestion is that her name was derived from the feminine aspect of the celestial mill, the pole being the axle shaft and ithyphallic element. It may well be that the biblical account here above involved the elimination of the extremely ancient practice of goddess worship in the region of modern-day Syria, the original meaning of which had no doubt already been lost.

AŠ/DIL with MU UN gives the origin of Old Norse mundil, the handle of the movable millstone (*Hamlet's Mill²*, p.139). (Also see 'daemon' in the notes to line 112.) It is possible that MU–UN–DU in this context became Ancient Egyptian Montu, an early figure connected to destruction and to the force of raging bulls.

Line 97

NA, the stone, sits between the two AB, the 'sea'. The striations inside the first AB (indicated by 'g' in transliterations) show the water at a tilt.

Taking the next word E, 'levee', into account, a stone dam has been placed across a water channel, creating a build-up of water; a levee designed for water management. But in the context of celestial events, this would be a fitting description of the effect of a comet or meteor strike (line 93), causing an imbalance of monumental proportions and resulting in devastating floods.

That three-word phrase in its original pictographic form is as good as it gets in terms of confirming that, where possible, translation of this language must include study of the original pictograms and their collocations (also see line 8). Another excellent example is EN KID KI on line 104. These examples also tend to indicate that certain lines of this text – if not all - were originally devised in the pre-cuneiform era of the 4ᵗʰ millennium BC.

Illustrated here by the dancing trio at Nevali Çori, DA AN, the 'arm in the sky', is given three times (lines 36, 85 and 97), confirming the connection to 'divine Danaus' and from there to Egypt (p.35). The two arms (plural reinforced here by repetition of KU₄) as banks of a river connect to the side panel of Pillar 43 where they relate to the tiger, the river

Tigris, to celestial Eridanus and the constellation of Scorpio (notes to line 85). The seeds are also understood as those of Danaus.

KU$_4$ with the given meaning 'to enter' derives from a combination of EŠ$_2$, 'rope', with ŠE, 'seed'. Unable to find a version earlier than the Early Dynastic archaeological period (ED IIIa, ca. 2600-2500 BC) already an abstract form, the pictogram is a reconstruction showing it as the combination would have appeared a few hundred years earlier. The same collocated words and theme of 'entering two by two' had been written in the ED IIIa period (2600-2500 BC):

> 95. *That the place they enter side by side if they agree…(The Story of Sukurru*, line 95)

That line provides further evidence that sections, if not the entirety, of this text already existed some one thousand years before the Old Babylonian period of 1900-1600 BC. In *The Story of Sukurru*, the context was Noah's ark. Here, the suggestion is that they also connect to the Taurids (line 93), through ŠE, the seeds of the bull.

Repetition of IM MA DA here leads back to the Magic Square of Daedalos analysed in the notes to line 36 and to Deukalion (see DU KA)

> *[Deukalion (Deucalion) speaks aloud, after the Great Deluge has wiped out all of mankind :]* 'O for my father's [Prometheus'] *magic to restore mankind again and in the moulded clay breathe life and so repopulate the world!*' (Ovid, *Metamorphoses* 1. 363, trans. X)

Line 97 can be linked to the myth of the 'tilting of the table' by Zeus which takes place on the Mountain Lykaios and causes the Flood of Deukalion. According to Pindar, this is also the place of Pan's birth, Pan is assimilated to Sirius and the table is 'the earth-plane through the ecliptic' according to the authors of *Hamlet's Mill*[2] (p.178-179). It all fits quite neatly as it should. This is by far the oldest version of events.

Line 98

DIN/DEN, given as 'beer', has the added dictionary-given meaning of 'vine' when it follows GIZ. Source of both 'vine' and 'wine' through Latin vinum and vinea. Also source of Greek dendron, 'tree'. See 'rhododendron', source of hallucinogenic honey (notes to line 38). In Arabic and Malay, 'din' has the meaning 'religion'. With E, the levee, DIN, here is the source of biblical Eden.

'High and low to join', reference to an earthly and celestial snake. The constellation of Draco as we know it is confined to the region of the North Pole. Draco was also Greek Ophis, a name that might correspond to an alternative transliteration of GALAM, the rising fish, as UBI. Whatever the original form of the Mesopotamian basilisk, here it is an analogy for one or more vines wound around the tree of life in the biblical garden: perhaps a direct reference to the ayahuasca vine (line 110). Perhaps also Ophiuchus, identified with Asclepius and healing, or his snake Serpens (also Ophis). This is the unseen force of the *Emerald Tablet* (mentioned on line 41), a joining of the snake(s) above with its earthly – and perhaps subterranean – twin:

It ascends from the earth to the heaven and again it descends to the earth and receives the force of things superior and inferior.

Ancient Greek baitulos, 'a meteoric stone', gave Latin baetylus, a stone shaped like a beehive, while Greek Phaeton takes his name from phaein "to shine, gleam."

Line 99

He who has an ear, let him hear what the Spirit says to the churches. To the one who overcomes, I will grant the right to eat from the tree of life in the Paradise of God. (Revelation 2:7)

Repetition of DIN from the preceding line. Considering the context of the garden of Eden, this is a very 'great tree' and 'great vine'.

Followed by the phrase UD KA BAR (also ZABAR) which is repeated four times in this text (lines 95, 99, 111 and 112) with the given meanings 'metal bowl' and 'bronze', a large copper bowl is added in for good measure.

The Temple of Dendera takes its Greek name Tentyris from DIN/TIN with TIR, a word stemming from TI, the 'arrow', with ER. Tir is the Persian name for Sirius. DEN TIR KI appear together a number of times in the lexical lists, KI indicating that it is a place name.

Given as 'to pour', the obvious conclusion in this context is that the combination of UMUM, the 'smith' and 'source of knowledge' with KASKAL, the 'crossroads' and the 'brew', is a reference to the constellation of Aquarius.

<u>Line 100</u>

AŠ₂, with given meanings 'curse' and 'wish', and AŠ, meaning 'unique' and 'blow' or 'strike' (notes to line 96)), are not found together by chance, the make-up of the brew being the key to its effectiveness.

The direct connection between line 100 and the following mysterious verse from Revelation extends to the verse number of 10 x 10:

> *So I took the small scroll from the angel's hand and ate it; and it was as sweet as honey in my mouth, but when I had eaten it, my stomach turned bitter.* (Revelation 10:10)

In more than one bible verse, honey is synonymous of the word of God. 'Beer of (wishing or) cursing to be', the four words together are transliterated to ULUŠIN for the simple reason that they appear opposite the following in the lexical lists. My translation gives:

'*In the stream of light (lucida) to see.*'

(Also see notes to line 47.)

'Vin' of Ashvin was sourced from DIN, the vine (see lines 98 and 99) giving the epithet 'unique vine' or 'the uniting brew'. The Hindu Ashvins were twin gods of healing, associated with honey and Soma and also with Ushas, goddess of dawn.

<u>Line 101</u>

DUG, meaning 'pot', the unstable vessel with the brew placed into the slot (KU) dug (KAK) in the hill (KUR), seemingly straightforward and logical in context. Is DUG also the origin of 'dog'? KUR, three hills and a dog? (notes to line 7).

BI, the two 'brews' of the rivals, surround HI HI, two 'mixtures' with GA and GAB. BI HI is the 'mixture of the bee' and source of Greek Hebe who mixes the wine for the gods. Opposed to the bee is HI GA, the 'mix of the cow', also 'veil' and source of Greek Hekate, goddess of boundaries. GAB, the musical gap, with given meanings 'release' and 'spread' applies to the releasing and mixing of the two brews but also to the separation of the two channels of the Milky Way.

DI, 'compare', 'compete', 'to be equal', 'judgement' and 'rivals', is source of 'divide', 'divinity'. Here the duo give the source of Greek didymos, 'twofold' and 'twins'. This is where 'doubting Thomas' gets his epithet:

> *Now Thomas called Didymus, one of the Twelve, was not with the disciples when Jesus came. So the other disciples told him, "We have seen the Lord!" But he replied, "Unless I see the nail marks in His hands, and put my finger where the nails have been, and put my hand into His side, I will never believe."… (John 20:24-25)*

The Dioskouroi, Castor and Pollux, the two brightest stars in the constellation of Gemini, were the twin sons of Zeus (notes to line 119). The constellation of Gemini lies on one side of the northern gate of the galactic plain with Taurus on the other (p.11). Or twin dogs?

Line 102

> *When the flight of a swarm is imminent, a monotonous and quite peculiar sound made by all the bees is heard for several days, and for two or three days in advance a few bees are seen flying round the hive; it has never as yet been ascertained, owing to the difficulty of the observation, whether or no the king is among these. (Aristotle, The Nature of Animals, Part 40)*

Two KA, the voices, the words and the mouths surround the beer and the honey. A judgement is being made. Two KA with BI as 'bee' and LAL$_3$ as 'honey become 'voices of the honeybees' and give the source of the extremely obscure Greek Kabeiri (notes to line 92).

> *The ithyphallic images of Hermes [the Hermai]; the production of these came from the Pelasgians [of Thessalia (Thessaly)], from whom the Athenians were the first Greeks to take it, and then handed it on to others . . . Whoever has been initiated into the rites of the Kabeiroi (Cabeiri), which the Samothrakians learned from the Pelasgians and now practice, understands what my meaning is. (Herodotus, Histories, Bk 2, 51, trans. Godley)*

HUM, also transliterated LUM, with a variety of given meanings to include 'to be tufted', 'to twist', 'to be replete' gives the source of both 'hum' and 'loom'. MA has the given meanings 'land' and 'fig'. HUM with MA is the sound of of the Great Weaver's loom in the sky, yet another direct reference to the music of the spheres. Everything is linked by that thread or chord, returning ultimately to Egypt and to the Goddess of Truth, Ma'at.

It's also the hum of the bees preparing to take flight, an indication that either the Pleiades or Praesepe in Cancer (notes to line 92) are being referenced here.

Bees in the context of the Pleiades:

> *They retire for the winter at the setting of the Vergiliæ (Pleiades), and remain shut up till after the rising of that constellation, and not till only the beginning of spring, as some authors have stated;* (Pliny, Natural History, Bk XI:5)

Line 103

The pictograms on this line are particularly revealing. GAB as 'pause', 'spread' and finally 'release' begins and ends the line while A, the 'flow' – in this context, it's the brew – sits in the middle. In their choice of positioning, the scribe demonstrated the all-encompassing nature of the action.

Three words combined into one: the 'divider' (see line 43) of 'water' but, in astronomical and musical terms, of the 'flow'. Reference to a tsunami-like event is confirmed on line 141 of *The Story of Sukurru* where MUŠ₃.A.DI is repeated twice, and the line begins:

A-RA-ZU is given as 'supplication' in dictionaries. With the biblical account in mind, my translation:

> *That the midst of water Ra know…*

The translation of RA to 'churn' gives 'the churning waters to know'.

The Mirror

But in that Mirror if with purged eyes
Thy Shadow Thou for Shadow recognise,
Then shalt Thou back into thy Centre fall
A conscious Ray of that eternal All.
(…)
Come you lost Atoms to your Centre draw,
And be the Eternal Mirror that you saw:
Rays that have wander'd into Darkness wide
Return, and back into your Sun subside.
(Conference of the Birds, Attar, Trans. Fitzgerald)

After a journey fraught with difficulties, the few remaining birds discover that the ruler they have been seeking, the Simorgh, lies within themselves. (Tajidar on lines 3, 115 and 124.)

Culmination of the Churning of the Milk Ocean. Two EN, 'foolish lord' come face to face with the ancestor AB (confirming that modern-day Enki and Enlil do not exist). The line reads inwards from both sides, beginning with the two AN; 'in the middle of the sky':

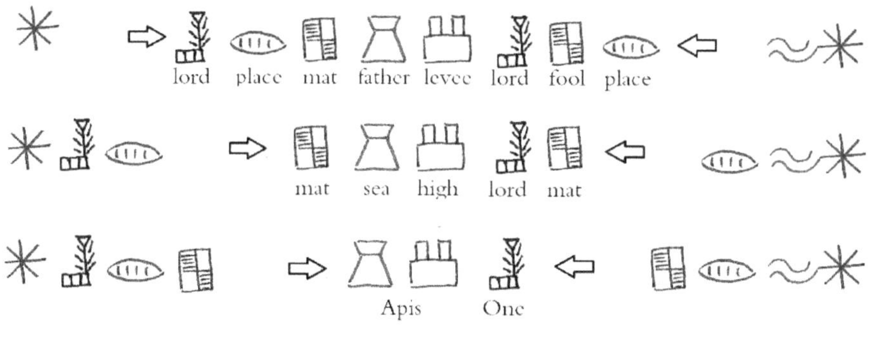

AB E: source of Latin apex, apices: 'peak, point, top, summit, crown'.

Latin apeirona, unlimited (*Hamlet's Mill²*, p.133)

Latin apiarium "bee-house, beehive," from apis "bee," a mystery word unrelated to any similar words in other Indo-European languages. (Etymonline)

Now Apis is the god whom the Greeks call Epaphus. (Herodotus, Bk.3:27).

AB E EN: Danish Aben, 'monkey' or 'ape' from Old Norse api, 'fool'.

Double A is repeated on line 129. The two streams flowing from the shoulders of the father figure in numerous images. Here also as A NI, source of 'animate', bringing to life (notes to line 6).

KID with RA, 'the churning mat', 'mat of Ra'. Following the reference to the shoulder of the father figure, KID becomes Cedalion, the guide, on the shoulder of blinded Orion (p.13). In consequence, Orion becomes AB, the Mesopotamian father figure.

KID RA, where RA is the 'beat' of the music, give one source of kithara, the other being KID LI (line 117):

> Greek *kithara* "cithara," *a triangular seven-stringed musical instrument related to the lyre,* (Etymonline)

In consequence, Orion either morphs into Orpheus playing the lyre of Lyra or carries them on his shoulder. It would seem that father and son are, if not one and the same, then closely connected. Did they both originate at the altar of the Empire of the Sun, also known as Kitara? (p.75-77)

RA, the sun, and MU UN, the moon, around GAR, the measuring. Following on from KID RA as reference to the string instrument, RA with GAR give 'the measure of the beat', that of the music of Orpheus moving stones (Also *The Story of Sukurru*, line 37).

GAR is given twice, once in a grouping with KA, transliterated together as GU_7, with given meaning 'to consume'. Thus GAR, the measurement along with the notion of consuming, surrounds MU UN, source of 'world' and our word 'moon' – a reference to the waxing and waning of the moon but probably also to the eclipses of the sun when the moon crosses its path. MU UN retains the notions of 'age of the land' and the meaning 'world' that became Latin mundus.

The positioning of this line, three lines prior to line 108, serves as introduction to the acrostic beginning on line 106 and to the encoded message therein.

<u>Line 106</u>

First line of the three-word acrostic signalled by the last word: KU

First line of the four-line acrostic signalled by the first word: AN.

Here begins a fourteen-line acrostic (lines 106-119), the first word of the first four lines (106-109) being AN, eight-pointed pictogram, 'sky' and all things 'above', 'celestial'.

AN   NE   TA   AN   NA
4   4   2   4   2

The next four (lines 110-113) end in NE/BIL, 'fire of the phoenix'.

The 9th and 10th (lines 114-115) end in TA, 'question' and 'death'.

The final four (lines 116-119) begin again with AN.

The final two lines (118-119) begin with AN and end with NA, giving AN NA: 'above and below'.

The 14-line riddle in its entirety begins AN and ends in NA:

As above, so below.

It is possible that the unexplained name for the Mesopotamian fish-god, Annedotus, given by Berossus was sourced from AN with NE (beginning and end of the first eight lines 106-113).

KI   MAH   Kimah, the 'Great Place' in Hebrew and Al Thurayya in Arabic (notes to line 120) were names given to the Pleiades (line 56):

The patriarch Job is thought to refer to them twice in his word Kimah, a Cluster, or Heap, which the Hebrew herdsman-prophet Amos, probably contemporary with Hesiod, also used; (Star Names [6], p.393)

This coincides with the biblical Kimah and the Arabic word for them - Al Thurayya (Star Names [6], p.395)

<u>Line 107</u>

Second of the four-line acrostic signalled by the first word: AN.

Second of the three-line acrostic signalled by the last word: UŠ

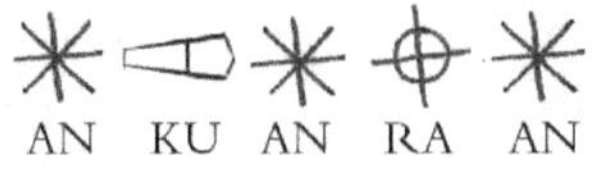

AN KU, 'hole in the sky', last two words of line 106 with the first three words of line 107, give three times AN (together read as MUL, meaning 'stars' and 'constellations', also on line 41 in the context of the Emerald Tablet) signifies the crossing of the skies with RA, the sun.

RA AN, 'churn of the skies', is source of Ran, Norse goddess of the sea who carries a net in which to catch and to drown sailors (also *The Story of Sukurru*, line 153). Probable source of the word 'rain' associated with the Pleiades and the rainy season they announce. The Norse myth links to Osiris through his name: UŠ with SA, the 'net' (line 56), the net of men.

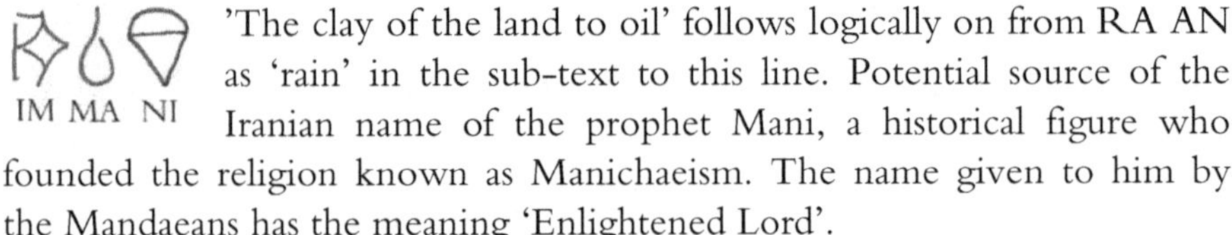

'The clay of the land to oil' follows logically on from RA AN as 'rain' in the sub-text to this line. Potential source of the Iranian name of the prophet Mani, a historical figure who founded the religion known as Manichaeism. The name given to him by the Mandaeans has the meaning 'Enlightened Lord'.

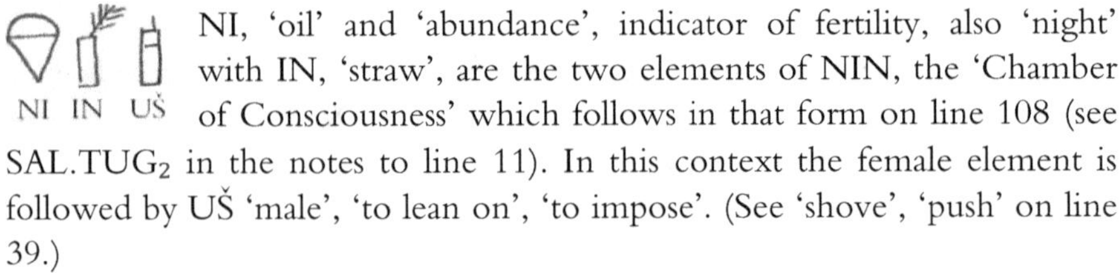

NI, 'oil' and 'abundance', indicator of fertility, also 'night' with IN, 'straw', are the two elements of NIN, the 'Chamber of Consciousness' which follows in that form on line 108 (see SAL.TUG₂ in the notes to line 11). In this context the female element is followed by UŠ 'male', 'to lean on', 'to impose'. (See 'shove', 'push' on line 39.)

<u>Line 108</u>

Third of the four-line acrostic signalled by the first word, AN.

Third of the three-line acrostic signalled by the last word, KU.

Following the female and male elements on line 107, SAL with TUG₂ transliterated NIN (notes to line 11), becomes the place of birth: 'In the celestial Chamber of Consciousness to be born'.

TU, enigmatic pictogram of what appears to be an arrow piercing the yolk of an egg, is given twice in this text; at the very beginning (line 2) and here near the end. In some versions of the name Ubara Dudu, last king before the flood on the *King List*, DU DU, the 'feet' are replaced by TU TU (*Lost Stones*, p.262-263).

KU UŠ KU

Cusco is named through KU UŠ KU, which results from a combination of the last words across those three lines 106, 107 and 108. In the Quecha language, Cusco has the meaning 'navel' and line 108 can be understood as the navel or centre point of this text (p.47-49).

The three lines together appear to indicate a moment when the Pleiades would somehow be connected to the Great Rift of the Galactic Plain as seen from the ancient site of Machu Picchu, the mountain peak above Cusco in Peru.

Riddles of the Numbers

36 + 36 = 72   72 + 36 = 108

Distance between Earth and moon: 108 times the diameter of the moon.

Diameter of the sun: 108 times the diameter of Earth.

Another link between two precession numbers, the musical interval:

108 / 72 = 3 / 2   (Perfect fifth, notes to line 11)

Line 72 marks the number of years giving one degree of the sun's precession which takes the form of a gap at its centre between the two repeated five-word phrases. It reads:

72. *"From one age of the world to another to flow,*

carved on two keystones in the water below."

On the Ashmolean transcript, the space is visible, presumably correctly copied from the cuneiform as the words appeared there:

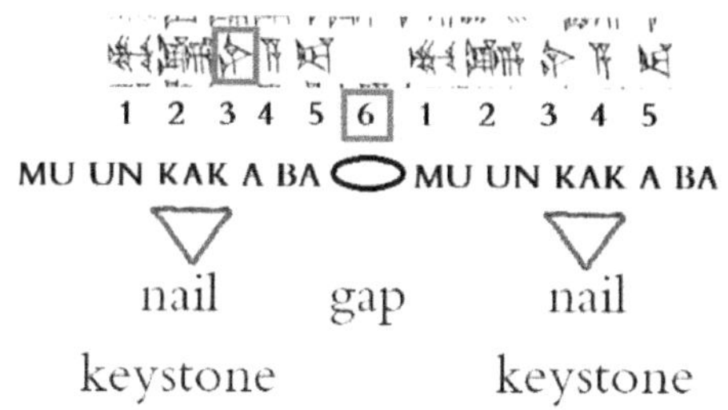

- 243 -

Bringing together the two nails with the gap of line 72 and the KU UŠ KU (navel) of lines 106-108, perhaps a visual rendering of the message behind those three lines:

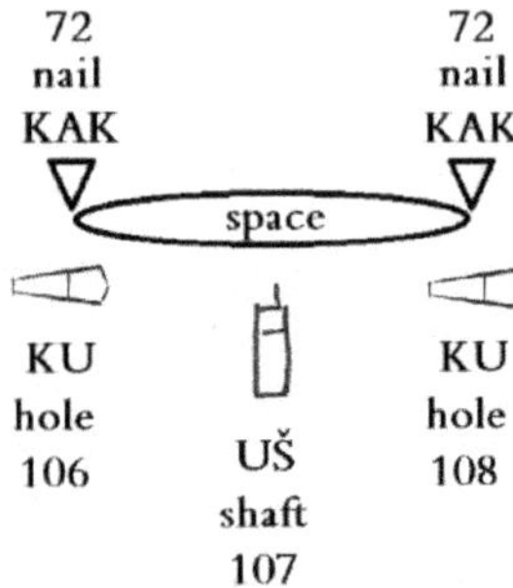

The Ashmolean Prism (CDLI ref. P386427)

Using the transcript and moving in an anti-clockwise direction (with the sun) four times around the sides of the prism, beginning on the fourth face:

- Line 108 appears on the 9th line of the 4th face of the Ashmolean prism where ZAG, the 'mark', is the 4th word.

- Line 72 appears on the 3rd line of the 3rd face where KAK, the 'nail' is the 3rd word.

- Line 36 appears on the 2nd line of the 2nd face where either BI, the 'total' or ZU, the 'knowledge' is the 2nd word (See below and the notes to line 22 for the reference to Zep Tepi).

- Line 1 appears on the 1st line on the 1st face where either A, the 'water' or UD, the 'sun', is the first word. (See below and the notes to line 9.)

One reading of the encoded four-word message (with inclusion of the Ashmolean prism words in brackets) and associated number gives:

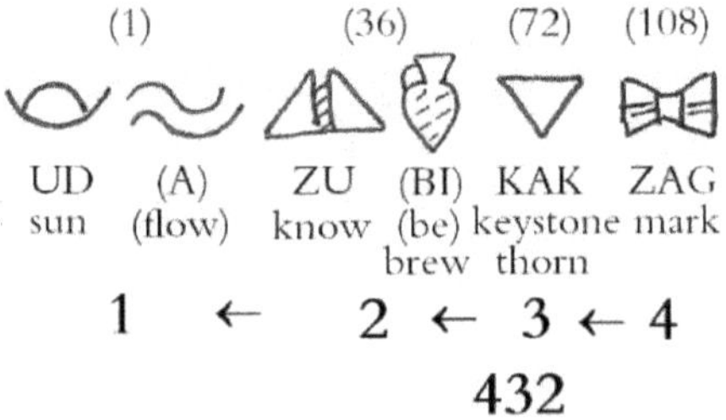

Knowledge of the (flow of the) sun is marked
on the keystone of the pyramid.

(honey and acacia brew)

There are a few variations between the wording of the transcript taken from the Ashmolean prism and the composite version, of which:

- A (Ashmolean) replaces UD on line 1.

- BI (Ashmolean) replaces ZU on line 36.

 ZAG, 'to mark', 'equal', 'boundary' and 'shoulder', designation of the Pleiades on the shoulder of Taurus. The 129 lines of this (composite version) text end with ZAG in 6th position: 129.6.

 KAK, nail of the builder, 'keystone', 'foundation peg' 'culmination', source of 'cactus' and 'acacia'.

ZU/SU, 'knowledge of the pyramid'. SU as source of Greek Sophia (*Lost Stones*, p.178) to which I add the apparently synonymous BI (Ashmolean prism) giving SU-BI. This is the Queen Bee who knows the recipe of the brew:

Greek Sophia: 'skill, knowledge of, acquaintance with; sound judgment, practical wisdom; cunning, shrewdness; philosophy,' 'wisdom personified.' (Etymonline)

Finally, A and UD are found together in the name Thoth which comes at the end of line 9 - not a coincidence. His epithet is also a reference to the

TA UD DU A

flow of the sun. A, last word on line 9 circles back and, in the case of the Ashmolean prism, connects to the A, water of the flood, in the first word of line 1. In the composite version, A connects with UD, the 'sun'.

4+3+2 = 9 (Thoth and the Carriage of the Sun)

The transcript is misleading in that it counts the longer single lines as two; a problem not encountered in the composite version. For that reason, the line numbers don't correspond to the total 129 of the original text. However, the original layout of the lines over those four faces was carefully planned in order for line 108 to occupy the 9th line, number of Thoth, on the 4th face (see the notes to line 9):

432 / 4 (faces) = 108 (9th line on the 4th face)

A combination of the line number (108) with the position of ZAG, the 'mark' as the fourth word, and the number of words in the line (10) gives:

108 (line) x 4 (Mark) x 10 (words) = 4,320

The four-sided prism is pierced through with a hole into which a shaft was once inserted, reminiscent of the rotating pole stars and their imaginary shafts separating the above from below. In terms of the precession of the equinoxes linked with the base number of the Mesopotamian counting system:

$$25,920 \ / \ 432 = 60$$

The central gap on line 72 can be understood as the 6th space on that line:

$$432 \ / \ 72 = 6$$

Inasmuch as this text is referencing knowledge contained in the monuments of the Giza plateau and their relation to the sky, I suggest that 432 is of particular importance in that regard (see Graham Hancock's comments on p.54). I was also intrigued by Robert Bauval's theory concerning Zep Tepi, the 'First Time', which involved the calculation of a 43°20 angle between the stars of Orion's Belt and the meridian mirrored by the same angle of 43°20 between the two largest pyramids of Giza and the meridian (*The Egypt Code* [29], p.148).

<u>Line 109</u>

Fourth of the four-line acrostic beginning with AN. The quote beneath this line links into the theme of regeneration of bees out of the ox, bull, lion or tiger skin (see p.26).

> *For oft 'twixt king and king with uproar dire*
> *Fierce feud arises, and at once from far*
> *You may discern what passion sways the mob,*
> *And how their hearts are throbbing for the strife;*
> *Hark! the hoarse brazen note that warriors know*
> *Chides on the loiterers, and the ear may catch*
> *A sound that mocks the war-trump's broken blasts;*
> *Then in hot haste they muster, then flash wings,*
> *Sharpen their pointed beaks and knit their thews,*
> *And round the king, even to his royal tent,*
> *Throng rallying, and with shouts defy the foe.*
> (Virgil, *Georgics*, Bk.4)

(Middle English 'thews' means 'muscular strength'.)

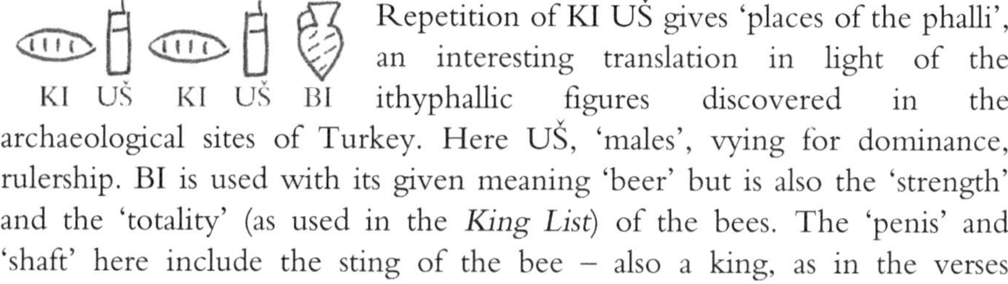

Repetition of KI UŠ gives 'places of the phalli', an interesting translation in light of the ithyphallic figures discovered in the archaeological sites of Turkey. Here UŠ, 'males', vying for dominance, rulership. BI is used with its given meaning 'beer' but is also the 'strength' and the 'totality' (as used in the *King List*) of the bees. The 'penis' and 'shaft' here include the sting of the bee – also a king, as in the verses borrowed from Virgil's text above (translator not named).

The shafts of this line are to be placed in their astronomical context. They follow on from the planting of the mill shaft, its two ends apparently separating the place where the counting of the Great Year begins (Pleiades) from the Great Rift at the southern gate of the Milky Way (between lines 106 and 108). At the same time, the mill shaft is responsible for holding the entire mechanism in place (see Plato's text on the Spindle of Necessity). Do the shafts inside the Great Pyramid have a similar function or did they once symbolically allow the regenerated bees to escape its skin?

Osiris and the Stone Phalli

But Isis tracked down the murder of her husband, and after slaying the Titanes and fashioning the several pieces of his body into the shape of a human figure, she gave them to the priests with orders that they pay Osiris the honours of a god, but since the only member she was unable to recover was the organ of sex she commanded them to pay to it the honours of a god and set it up in their temples in an erect position. (Diodorus Siculus, Library of History 4. 6. 1, Trans. Oldfather).

UŠ, first symbol of Osiris, with A give 'urinate' (notes to line 39). A notably masculine manner of marking one's territory and affirming leadership whether man or other animal is the pissing match. Portrayed on the recently uncovered portion of wall at Sayburç in south western Turkey and dated to around 9000 BC, the figure illustrating line 109 faces forward holding his phallus, unphased by the fierce predators on either side; leader of the pack. How high and how hard did those waters need to fly? (Notes to line 111. *The Story of Sukurru*, line 32.) Predecessor of a plethora of similar scenes where the figure is more simply holding back the animals on either side.

Looking much further back to the Upper Paleolithic era (ca.50,000 to 12,000 years ago), a small ithyphallic man taunts the huge bull of Taurus in the caves of Lascaux, France. Was he taking aim at the bees of the Pleiades above or endeavouring to release them from the ox hide?

Illustrating line 2, the female figure scratched into stone at Göbekli Tepe ca.9600 BC shows the two shafts of the celestial mill pointing to the vulva, the strange form of the head indicating the celestial context.

ŠI, 'eye', is given on the Ashmolean script but left out in the composite version. ŠI with IM become ŠIM, the 'brewer'. IM with MI, second mention of the Great Rift but also referring to the swarm of bees.

Fourfold repetition of IM over four lines, twice as IM MA, (immanent: see notes to lines 7-8) and twice as IM MI.

Latin imminentem (nominative imminens) "overhanging; impending," present participle of imminere "to overhang, lean towards," hence "be near to," also "threaten, menace, impend, be at hand, be about to happen,"

Latin immensus: immeasurable, boundless, endless, vast, immense (Etymonline)

KU, 'hole', with RU, 'to fall' and NE, 'fire', read 'into the fiery hole to fall', the earliest reference to what became the biblical hell and Hades. With RU as 'wheel' and source of 'rotate', the 'hole in the rotation', it might indicate a reference to the Great Rift in the galactic plain and the end of time.

'Three crowns', where KU RU NE give the source of Greek korone meaning 'anything curved', 'a kind of crown' and source of the far later three-tiered papal crown or tiara. (See the tiara on line 90.) Also source of Greek khronos: time' and Greek Kronos, Father of Time, the phrase translating to 'three times of fire'.

NE SIN connects to the following line 110 where NE is written three times. Note that KU appears as the last word on lines 106 and 108 where it figures in the three-word acrostic (notes to line 108). Here on line 109 (of both the composite transliteration on ePSD and that of the Ashmolean prism) the word is given as DUR2, visually close and having similar given meanings. However, the transcript of the Ashmolean prism confirms that it is KU. The same error is made in the riddle of the *Sumerian King List* (see p.55).

Line 110

First of four lines ending in NE, the fire, and threefold repetition of the word on this line (see line 109). Focus on the theme of renewal by fire.

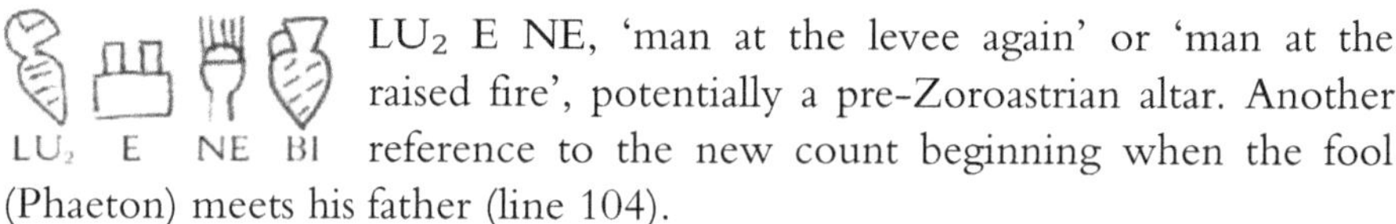

LU₂ E NE, 'man at the levee again' or 'man at the raised fire', potentially a pre-Zoroastrian altar. Another reference to the new count beginning when the fool (Phaeton) meets his father (line 104).

E with NE, interchangeable with EN E, 'raised lord', take centre stage at the heart of 'Tenet' in the context of the Sator Square (*Before Babel*, 2019, p.242).

NE with BI, 'new' and 'bee', given twice, the regeneration of bees.

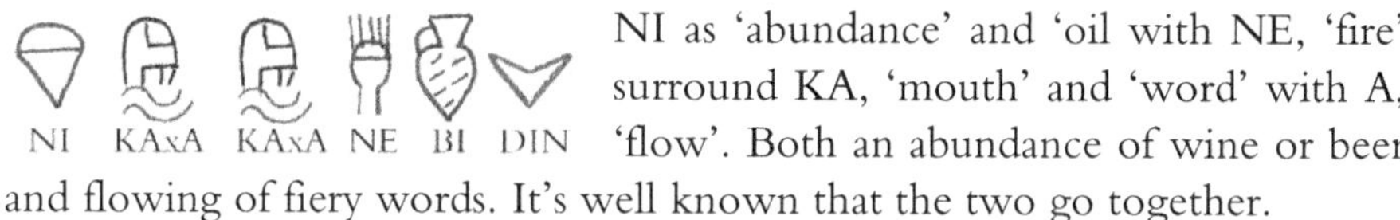

NI as 'abundance' and 'oil with NE, 'fire' surround KA, 'mouth' and 'word' with A, 'flow'. Both an abundance of wine or beer and flowing of fiery words. It's well known that the two go together.

BI DIN, 'bee of the vine', 'brew of the vine' preceded by NE as 'red'. DIN as source of 'wine'. Also potentially the South American ayahuasca brew. (DIN in notes to line 99.) Together read as KURUN, another source of the 'crown' (notes to line 109) from KU RU with UN, 'land' giving the 'hole in the rotation of the land' or 'seat of the wheel of the land':

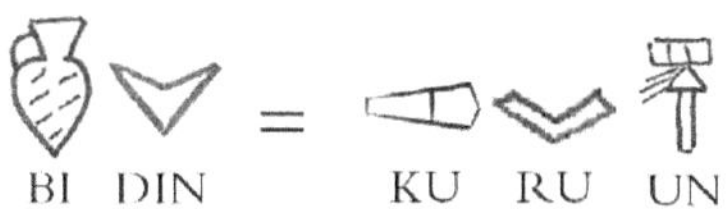

HI with GE are source of Greek Hygeia, whose brew is health-giving (also on lines 18 and 71). Two unorthodox translations of HI are 'veil' and 'here' with both HI-GA and HI-GE as source of Latin hic also meaning 'here'.

GE, as rod, with NE, fire, become the 'rod of fire', the torch of Greek Hekate also present in this text (HI GA on lines 122 and 126). One source of Greek *genea* meaning 'generation' and first two syllables of 'genesis', the other being GE with EN, the 'lord' (*Lost Stones*, p.77).

<u>Line 111</u>

(Betelgeuse on the shoulder of Orion) *The title Mirzam, from Al Murzam, the Roarer, or perhaps the Announcer, originally used for y (Bellatrix), also is applied to this as heralding the rising of its companion* (Star Names [6], p.311)

Appears four times (lines 95, 99, 111 and 112). Given meanings 'bronze' and 'metal bowl', the breakdown to 'sun', 'mouth' or 'voice' with BAR as 'outside', the wild or wilderness. Here in context before the MIR of Mirzam, the 'roaring voice of the sun'.

MIR has dictionary-given meanings 'herald', 'angry' and 'mythical snake'. The message is written in both metal (ZABAR) and clay (IM) on two blocks (KILI). Pictographic KILI is variable, sometimes square or slightly more rectangular, others circular, also transliterated LAGAB. With HAL, 'divide', it's ENGUR (notes to lines 34–35).

MIR with SI on line 32 of *The Story of Sukurru* was translated 'herald horn'. Like a number of others in that text, the line is incomplete but the overall context identified as the source story of Moses on the mountain – with some confusion between the subjects of circumcision and the stone tablets. Nevertheless, it links extraordinarily well into the theme of the pissing contest perceived here on line 109:

32. *A fiery ark out to fly … strong and high…? The virile herald horn on Sina the stones of wisdom in the sky…*

<u>Wisdom of the Phoenix</u>

RE, 'to gather' and 'fly', pictogram of a bird, followed by E, the 'levee', and NE, the fire; 'bird of fire' and renewal, the Phoenix.

NE is also read BIL/PIL/PEL, becoming the 'vel' or 'veil' of the Latin word 'revel-ation' and French 'reveil', the 'awakening':

Latin revelare "reveal, uncover, disclose," literally "unveil," from re-"back, again," here probably indicating "opposite of" or transition to an opposite state (see re-) + velare "to cover, veil," from velum "a veil" from PIE root. (Etymonline)

The lexical entries give NE opposite both PE-IL and BI-IL:

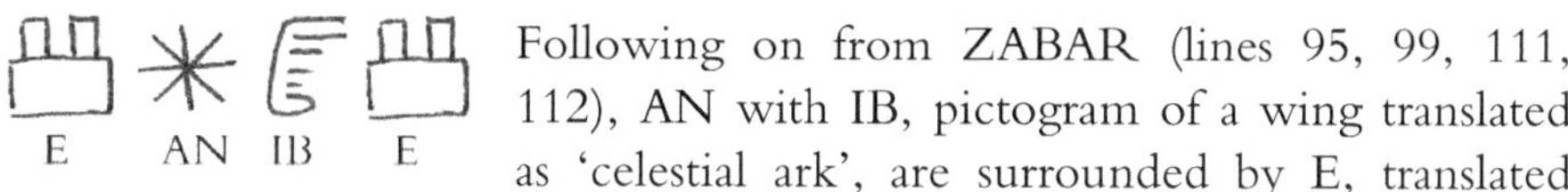

Alternatively, BI before IL gives 'the brew to raise', the rising brew (fermentation). IL is given as 'to be high' (shown here as IL$_2$, 'raise') and is linked to 'song'.

PE-IL is source of Pleiades and Greek pelagos, the 'sea'. From there, it links to the original Greek words in the account of the lost city of Atlantis told by Plato. The city of Heliopolis in Egypt is the source of that knowledge.

<u>Line 112</u>

Hold fast to what you have, so that no one will take your crown. The one who overcomes I will make a pillar in the temple of My God, and he will never again leave it. Upon him I will write the name of My God, and the name of the city of My God. (Revelation 3:11-12)

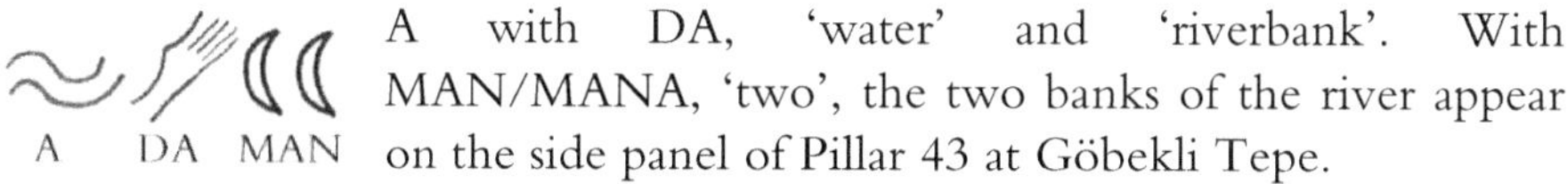

Following on from ZABAR (lines 95, 99, 111, 112), AN with IB, pictogram of a wing translated as 'celestial ark', are surrounded by E, translated here to 'rises', is found four times on line 78 where it appears to indicate the changing positions of the constellations. Pictographic E might be understood as two pillars, two markers, mountain peaks or architectural features between which the sun is seen to rise. The Egyptian illustration with this line shows the arms to be those of Nut, Egyptian goddess of the sky.

A with DA, 'water' and 'riverbank'. With MAN/MANA, 'two', the two banks of the river appear on the side panel of Pillar 43 at Göbekli Tepe.

- Greek adamantos: adamantine, of the hardest material.
- Proto-Polynesian mana: some form of 'spiritual power', perhaps from a more ancient 'force of nature'.
- Latin manus: 'hand'.
- Hebrew 'Adam'.

DI/DE as 'division' but also 'judgement' with NE/BIL, giving 'divided by fire' and 'judgement by fire'. Direct source of 'devil' (through Old English) no doubt linked to the DI of Greek diabolus and to dæmon, the demon, this last from DA with MU-UN (notes to line 83).

MU UN DI BIL

Line 113

"after Phaeton died, Cycnus dived repeatedly into the river Eridanus attempting to retrieve Phaeton's body. The gods turned him into a swan".

TI, 'arrow', with ŠI, 'eye', became Hindu Tishiya and Zoroastrian Tishtrya, alternative names for Sirius. Sirius is found by following a line to the southwest of the three stars of Orion's Belt. Somewhere along the way there lurks an archer taking aim. Still used as a protective symbol on boats, the eye is generally named as that of Egyptian Horus.

TI ŠI

(Sirius) *The later Persian and Pahlavi have Tir, the Arrow.* (*Star Names* [6], p.122)

Second mention of the ferry boat of Greek Charon (line 89). TE is striated here, the single horizontal line between the two crosses replaced by $EŠ_2$, the rope that pulls the bark of Hades from one side of the river to the other.

MA₂ TEg

Here in context, KUK, also the 'cog-boat', is source of Greek cycnus, the swan. Confirmation comes with RI/RE, 'to fly' and partial source of the bird of Revelation (see below). With BA, source of 'bari', the 'heavy' in 'barytone' through Greek,

KUK IM BA BA RI

The constellation of Cygnus situated along the galactic plain is associated with Apollo/Orpheus, the nearby constellation of Lyra and ancient pole star Vega (notes to line 22). The swan diving to retrieve the body of Phaeton in that Greek myth is comparable to Orpheus descending into the underworld to retrieve his wife Eurydice. Both refer to death and regeneration, to music and musicians (*Lost Stones*, p.211).

Second ending in RE-E-NE (notes to line 111), the 'revelation', here linked to the constellation of Cygnus.

RE E NE

E, the 'levee', appears over 30 times in this text. As versions differ slightly, the exact number is not evident but it is above average compared to the other words here.

<u>Lines 114–115</u>

Both lines end in TA, sandwiched between the two four-line acrostics from 110 to 113 and 116-119. TA is mentioned three times here, translating to 'question'. First syllable of Tautu from TA-UT (see Thoth on line 9). Tat, disciple of Thoth. TA with E_2, also BIT, gave Arabic thabit, 'enduring'.

GIR$_3$ appears four times (lines 34, 96, 102 and 115). Tajidar, the wise bird of Attar's poem, takes its name partially from DAR (see lines 3 and 124) and, for the rest, from these two words which together translate 'the path of death' or 'the path of questioning' (*Lost Stones*, p.57, p.218). Confirmation of that reference is found in the following line 116.

The context is spiritual journeying and involves the hallucinogenic brew, the 'milk'. TA with HI, the veil, at its centre becomes transliterated LAL$_3$, the honey (lines 38, 78, 102 and 103. See notes to line 38.) Another translated form gives 'Question the (prophetic) cow'.

BI A, 'flowing brew', became Bia, Greek goddess of mighty force and compulsion. With her siblings, Nike, Zelos and Kratos, a guardian of the citadel of Zeus.

<u>Line 116</u>

First line of the second series of four with AN as the first word.

Continuation of the word play on the name AN EN KI KID as demonstrated on line 104. Here the sky and earth surround two EN KID, with possible translations 'ghostly lords', 'foolish lords' or 'lords on their mats'. Followed by HUL$_2$, given as 'joyful', the meeting is amiable.

> *'O Birds, by what Authority divine*
> *I speak you know by His authentic Sign,*
> *And Name, emblazon'd on my Breast and Bill:*
> *Whose Counsel I assist at, and fulfil:*
> *At His Behest I measured as he plann'd*
> *The Spaces of the Air and Sea and Land; (…)*

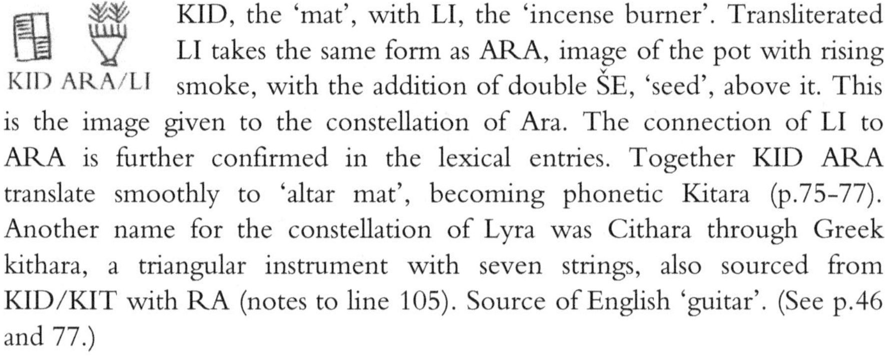

MU, 'Name', NI, 'oil' or 'thick', IB, 'wing' and DU, 'carry'. Translating to 'the name on the nib carried' (notes to line 65). A neb, through Old Norse, is the beak or bill of a bird.

NI–IB together give the source of Latin nebula, the mist or cloud, providing more evidence of a direct link to the *Conference of the Birds* a few lines after the above quote:

> *The Blast that bore Sulayman's Throne: and led*
>
> *The Cloud of Birds that canopied his Head;*
>
> (*Conference of the Birds*, Attar, lines 47-48, Trans. FitzGerald)

Appearing together four times (lines 65, 67, 82 and 116) IB, the wing, with DU, as 'foot', might also indicate the winged sandal of Hermes.

Line 117

KID, the 'mat', with LI, the 'incense burner'. Transliterated LI takes the same form as ARA, image of the pot with rising smoke, with the addition of double ŠE, 'seed', above it. This is the image given to the constellation of Ara. The connection of LI to ARA is further confirmed in the lexical entries. Together KID ARA translate smoothly to 'altar mat', becoming phonetic Kitara (p.75-77). Another name for the constellation of Lyra was Cithara through Greek kithara, a triangular instrument with seven strings, also sourced from KID/KIT with RA (notes to line 105). Source of English 'guitar'. (See p.46 and 77.)

> *another of the names for our Ara, a reduplication of the zodiacal Altar, was Pharus, or Pharos, the Great Lamp, or Lighthouse, of Alexandria, one of the seven wonders of the world. This Lamp also has been found shown on boundary stones as held in the Scorpion's claws,* (Star Names[6], p.274)

> *On this altar the gods are thought to have first made offerings and formed an alliance when they were about to oppose the Titanes (Titans). The Cyclopes made it. From this observance men established the custom that when they plan to do something, they make sacrifices before beginning the undertaking.* (Pseudo-Hyginus, Astronomica 2. 39, Theoi.com)

First of two mentions of the 'Anunna gods' in this text and both in this section, the second on line 119. Their presence lends weight to the theory of an ancient people linked to Kitara on the African continent resulting from analysis of the words in this section of the text (see Egyptian khet on p.77).

AN A NUN NA

Analysed in *Lost Stones of the Anunnaki*, this is not a meaningless four-syllable name. Does it involve a connection between earth and sky? Here and taken in context, the words translate to 'onto the stone guide' where NUN, always the central word in this phrase, breaks down to NU-UN, 'the knot of the land', 'not of the land' and 'otherworldly guide'.

'Renowned voice and word' and/or 'to tell the name and age'. Source of Arabic and Swahili 'kamus' meaning 'dictionary' and 'ocean'. 'Kamus' has been said to derive in some unexplained manner from Ancient Greek okeanos, the ocean, but clearly there is no phonetic similarity. The 'dictionary' and 'ocean' come directly from the account of the celestial ocean in words on stone, its dictionary. Further to that, KA MU appear with UŠ in the lexical lists opposite GUD, the 'bull', the reasoning behind one of its transliterated forms: KAMUŠ

KA MU

KA MU UŠ = GUD/KAMUŠ

KA-MUS, 'the word or mouth of the snake', are also found together in the lexical lists. Is this the snake that swallowed the sun?

<u>Line 118</u>

13th line of the 14-line acrostic.

1st of two lines ending EN ZA NA.

> *the Galaxy was long known as Eridanus, the Stream of Ocean. Indeed during all historic time it has been thought of as the River of Heaven.* (Star Names [6], p.474)

GAL, also symbol of kingship in LUGAL. Given twice after 'celestial' and in the same line as the words for 'sailor', probably indicates two or more galley ships (see line 12) and/or is a reference to the total extent of the galactic plain, a belt across the sky from north to south. GAL with LA 'hanging', as source of 'galaxy'.

AN GAL GAL LA

GE EN, 'Rod or staff of the lord', partial source of 'genesis' and 'generate', an alternative to GE NE (notes to line 110, *Lost Stones*, p.77). 'Rod of fire', firestick of Prometheus.

Two NA (lines 118 and 119) become the two stone tablets.

ZA, generally a pictogram of discs or beads threaded together, perhaps a sistrum, having the meaning 'sound' and 'four', is also given as the transliteration of another very different pictographic form:

A striated form of NI, 'abundance', 'oil', perhaps indicating a full vessel. At its centre, the number 4. Above it, three strokes.

Two ZA (lines 118 and 119) become 'zaza', source of a pejorative name used for the Dimli, a group of people in eastern Turkey. Zaza is pejoratively derived from a word meaning 'stutterer'.

Line 119

> *...the first day of the lunar month in Roman times, a date on which priests climbed a mount and called out to the population to announce the new moon. Both the Greek and the Roman calendars based their months on the phases of the moon. (Lost Stones, p.67)*

Fourteenth and final line of the acrostic that began on line 106. Last of four lines beginning AN and second mention of Anunnaki (notes to line 117).

Second of two lines ending EN ZA NA (notes to line 118).

UB, 'angle', with ŠU, 'hand', 'to show': The angles are shown. UB is source of 'obelisk' and a reference to Sirius (notes to line 17). ŠU UB became ŠUB, also transliterated RU, 'fall' and 'rotate', possible source of Egyptian goddess Sopdet associated with Sothis and Sirius. KA, 'word', with ŠU, 'show', are given as 'dedication'.

Three times NA, the stone, on this line, referring to both URU, the step pyramid linked to Orion, and KA, the words inscribed.

URU is also associated with the heavenly river Eridanus (*Lost Stones*, p.207). Here with BAR, 'elsewhere', 'outside', pictogram of the shepherd's crook, at its centre, it has the given meaning 'assembly'. Here below analysis of the words linked to URUxBAR (transliterated to UNKIN or UKKIN) through the lexical tablets:

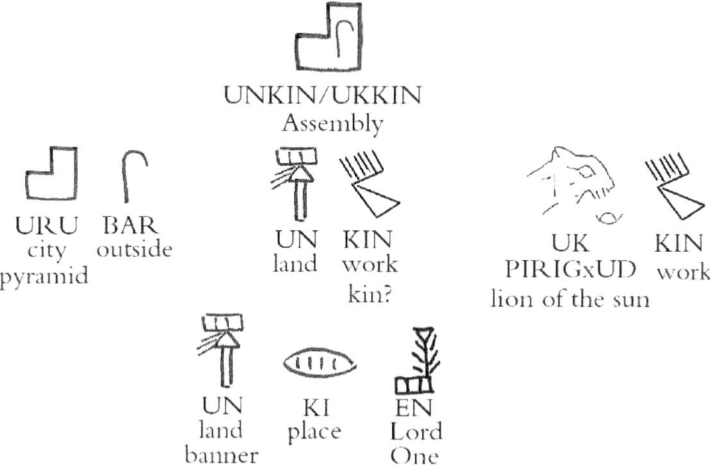

URU has the given meaning 'city' to which I add 'step pyramid' (*Lost Stones*, p.207) and BAR as 'stranger' (notes to line 48), both of which justified through their pictograms and to some extent their dictionary-given meanings – plus the context in which they are found.

BAR is also given as 'fleece', that of the sheep and the cover of the shepherd represented by his crook. Also see its use on lines 47 and 48 where it is linked to the Mesopotamian Apkallu. From there to the biblical notion of the shepherd and his sheep, the twelve disciples of Christ.

BAR might also indicate the outer snow-white limestone covering of URU, both pyramid and constellation of Orion (notes to line 63).

Bearing in mind KID-ARA, the altar mat on line 117 and the implication of an otherworldly connection in the African myth of Kitara, this line of text does nothing to dispel the notion of an otherworldly association, a 'corporation' of 'gods' (p.75-77, notes to line 117).

KIN is given as 'work' and 'reap', to which 'kin' would be a reasonable addition thanks to both the sound and the overall dictionary-given meaning 'assembly' of UNKIN. Thus, UN KIN might also translate 'land of kinship' or 'standard/banner of the kin', linking back to the tribe of Danaus (p.35).

Either the horns of Taurus where MU UN translate 'age of the land' or a crescent moon. Taurus and Gemini form the two pillars of the southern gate of the galactic plain. SI also translates 'announce' after KA, 'word' (see quote from *Lost Stones* above).

Second appearance of DI-DI, the twins, potentially Castor and Pollux of Gemini. Source of Greek didymus, 'twin'. Doubting Thomas or Simon? (Notes to line 101.)

<u>Line 120</u>

The heliacal rising of Sirius fell at the beginning of the Egyptian calendar month (of 30 days) every 120 years – referenced in the line number and in its wording.

TUR with given meanings 'to be small' and 'child', appears before MU in *The Story of Sukurru* in connection with Ubara Tutu, the last king before the flood. It was left untranslated. 'Renowned youth' fits the bill (*Lost Stones*, p.182). Here TUR MU is found just once in the text, in this concluding section.

TUR derives from TU UR, which translates to 'birth of the dog', also linking to the double TU of Ubara Tutu, the sailor.:

TUR TUR is source of the turtle or tortoise, whose shell serves as a calendar for the moon and as the lyre of Orpheus (notes to line 79), a youthful musician. Orpheus tells the story on the tortoise–shell lyre

MU, the 'ages' surround E₂, the 'temple' and, with the addition of UN, it offers a glimpse of the renowned Temple of the Moon said to have once existed in Harran. The words translate to 'Temple of the Ages of the Land'. MU MU, the 'months' or 'years', together give the source of Greek Momus, god of mockery and complaint, already discovered bitterly complaining on a clay tablet in *The Story of Sukurru* (line 168). In the notes there:

Perhaps also the origin of the Hopi myth of Momu, a bee spirit.

<u>Line 121</u>

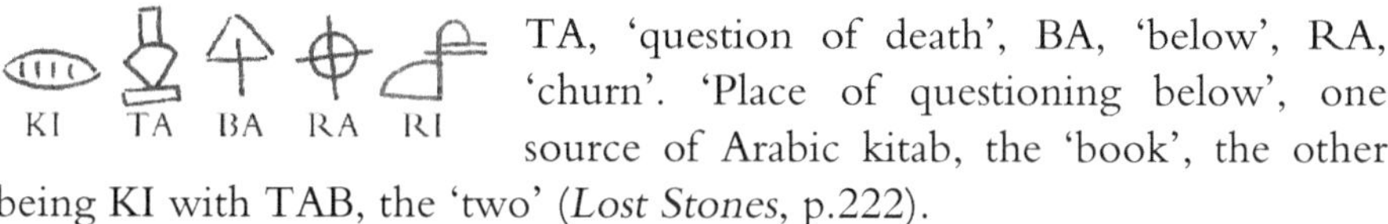

NUN KI are given together nine times (lines 13, 46, 49, 53, 73, 90, 121, 123 and 128) demonstrating the importance of the name. Also on lines 2, 3 and 5 of the *Sumerian King List* where it's transliterated 'eridug ki', the first city. Analysis shows it to be an element of 'Anunnaki' and synonymous of 'flowing and disappearing fish' (*Lost Stones,* p.35):

HUR SAG appears twice (lines 74 and 121). On line 74, they precede GALAM, the Great Fish.

Enclosed between two KI to clearly indicate that the three words are to be read as situated in one place, HUR with SAG refer to the Great Sphinx with human head. Followed by DIM$_2$ which is the foreleg of the ox turning the mill (Boôtes) at the North Pole.

TA, 'question of death', BA, 'below', RA, 'churn'. 'Place of questioning below', one source of Arabic kitab, the 'book', the other being KI with TAB, the 'two' (*Lost Stones,* p.222).

TA-BA-RA links back to line 1 with references to kings, basilisks, frogs and toads. Source of 'tobacco':

1580s, from Spanish tabaco (Etymonline)

Batara, the medicine man, conducts the Tobacco Ceremony and presides over distribution of the South-American ayahuasca brew. (See notes to line 110 along with the connection to Peru on lines 106-108.) Another ceremony is that of bufo, the hallucinogenic toad; its venom is burnt into the skin.

There is no certainty as to the etymology of 'tobacco' from 'tabac', no more than anyone knows where the Greeks got their word 'batrakhos' to describe the toad. Or the origin of the Malaysian batara shaman for that matter (notes to line 1).

The Book of Above and Below is preserved below ground, hidden from view as is Pan (*Hamlet's Mill²,* p.286-287, notes to line 126).

After NUN KI beginning line 121, KI in first place here, and NUN KI KI beginning line 123, a pattern emerges.

Reading vertically the first three words, NUN KI NUN indicates that the KI of line 122 is placed between two 'guides'. To its right, HI is the 'heavenly veil' (line 64) leading to the 'womb' of the Milky Way.

GA, 'milk', is followed by collocated A AN, separately 'water' and 'sky', together 'to be'. Thee three elements constitute transliterated GAN, pictogram of a crucible, with the dictionary-given meaning 'child-bearing'. This is the circling cow known as Hathor in Egyptian mythology; the galactic plain, giving birth to the entirety of the solar system.

IM MA is understood in all cases as 'clay of truth', the truth of the guide (see KA NUN in the notes to lines 16). MA AN, 'land' and 'sky', are elements of MAN/TAB meaning 'two' and source of 'man'. Third and final example of IM MA AN:

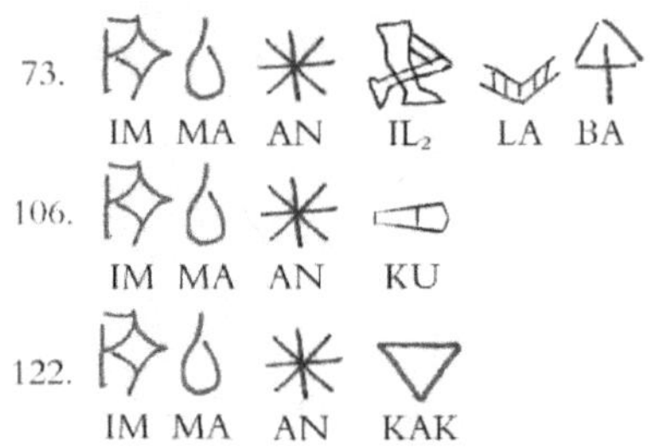

Image of the celestial womb from Göbekli Tepe, ca.9600 BC.

The most obvious comparison is to the biblical story of animals entering two by two into the ark. That notion is also present in *The Story of Sukurru* (line 95). However, the phrase also appears on line 97 and the context there goes beyond a purely mythical account which might be compared to other later, similar stories, the wobble being that of Earth on its axis. (See p.35 for 'divine Danaus'.) In this concluding section of text which takes the form of a number of practical points - the creation of temples and meeting places - it would be reasonable to see the architect-astronomer-scribe burying a warning for future generations.

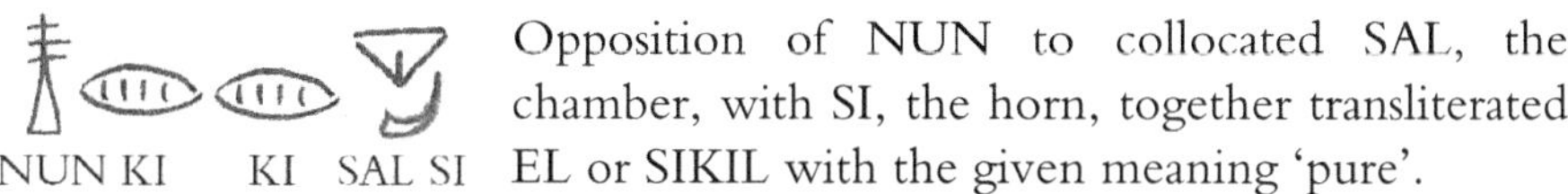

Opposition of NUN to collocated SAL, the chamber, with SI, the horn, together transliterated EL or SIKIL with the given meaning 'pure'.

NUN KI — KI SAL SI

SI has the given meaning 'remember' and, taking the horn to also be a musical instrument whether part of the lyre's frame or in its own right, I have added 'announce'.

SAL SI is found on lines 33 and 44 where the combination follows ZU AB, Kochab, two lines apparently referring to two places.

<u>54 Keys</u>

KI, usually translated to 'place' and used by academia as silent suffix in city names, is given 54 times in the composite text (the Ashmolean transcript is partially damaged and the second KI UŠ of line 109 was erased on that tablet). I have added the meaning 'key' which takes on extra significance if the reference to the precession number 54 was intentional.

Here a unique collocation of two KI on line 123:

121. NUN KI

122. KI

123. NUN KI — KI SAL SI

The 'key' is placed between two 'guides' or, alternatively, at the heart of the whale, an obscure reference to Jonah who disappears into the fish, and to Mesopotamian Oannes, also in the habit of disappearing at night according to the account attributed to Berossus.

To the lower right is EL, the 'chamber or cave of the pure horn'. Preceded by KI, together found opposite KIL/KILI, the 'block' (notes to line 111):

KI EL = KIL

KIL is the most important and ubiquitous of generic place names left to us from extreme antiquity, and still in existence across a wide swathe of languages. Through Middle Dutch, we find kill as water channel. In the ancient Norse language, kell is a spring. The Celts take their name from this symbol and it is particularly widespread in Irish place names. (…)

KEL would also be acceptable as the kil- origin of Latin cella, 'chamber' or 'cellar', celare, 'concealed' and 'kept secret', and, interestingly, cellere, 'to raise'. (…)

There is an important lexical entry that tends to confirm the concept of KIL as a place of burial rituals and enlightenment. (…)

A keel is a manmade stone formation having a wedge-shape or ridge and found at ancient pagan sites. Kil means 'wedge' in Scandinavian languages too. (*Before Babel*, p.85-97)

LU₂, 'man', NU, 'not', KU₄, 'to enter', DA, 'side' or 'riverbank'. Found on the same line, the two KI, 'places', are linked to the two KU₄, 'enter', which appear twice in this text (line 97).

DA AN, 'arm in the sky' links to Scorpio. Reading the two phrases together, there are two arms, the riverbanks surrounding 'man'. The fall of Greek Phaeton into the river Eridanus is the most obvious myth where LU₂ NU, 'that man not…' is understood as a warning.

Either that or the negative indicates that these are not the seed-ropes of man…

Or the two arms are those of men praying to the sky. DA AN appears in line 188 of *The Story of Sukurru*, translated somewhat awkwardly for the purpose of fully matching word to word, and without integrating the now obvious astronomical themes:

For man his life to extend anew, that man on the Sabbath his arm its prayers to the sky he multiply.

Finally, it is possible that the men will not enter side by side because the two places in question refer to different time periods and to forewarnings about cyclical events.

Read vertically, AN with NU give 'knot of the year' and 'ring', that of the ouroboros (line 10). The four KU_4 as 'seed-ropes' remain obscure but, in the context of a catastrophe, can be linked to line 93 and the threat of raining down 'seeds', apparently from the region of Taurus. The Taurid stream emanates from below the Pleiades in the region of Aldebaran on the horn of Taurus. But nevertheless, there is a slight possibility of a link:

Miss Clerke where, alluding to recent photographs of the cluster (Pleiades) *by the Messrs. Henry of Paris, she says :*

"The most curious of these was the threading together of stars by filmy processes. In one case seven aligned stars appeared strung on a nebulous filament "like beads on a rosary." The "rows of stars," so often noticed in the sky, may therefore be concluded to have more than an imaginary existence." (Star Names[6], *p.395)*

Line 124

First of two lines with E_2, 'temple', as first word.

E_2, 'temple', with KUK GA, 'circle of milk'. KUK has the given meaning 'metal' and with GA as 'white' becomes 'silver'; 'a silver temple'. E_2 KUK GA is repeated four times (lines 11, 61, 124 and 128). With the addition of KAK A, five-word phrase given twice (lines 124 and 128).

KAK, 'thorn' and 'keystone', with A, 'flow' and 'water', is given five times (lines 52, 72 x 2, 124 and 128). KAK-A, 'a nail in the flow' signals the culmination of a star or planet (line 52). The two words also form part of the 'pause' on line 72 and encoded message linked to 432 (notes to line 108).

Last of six ZA KUR NA (lines 6, 11, 21, 29, 37 and 124). Translating to 'sound in the stone hills', following on from the cave and pure horn on line 123, and here surrounded by two A, 'water', KUR is source of the noisy Greek Kouretes and Korybantes who protected Zeus as a baby:

"O secret chamber the Kouretes (Curetes) knew! O holy cavern in the Kretan (Cretan) glade where Zeus was cradled, where for our delight the triple-crested Korybantes (Corybantes) drew tight the round drum-skin, till its wild beat made rapturous rhythm to the breathing sweetness of Phrygian flutes! Then divine Rhea found the drum could give her Bacchic airs completeness." (Euripides, Bacchae 120 ff, trans. Vellacott, Theoi.com)

Circling back to RI/RE A, 'Rhea' on line 1, this connects to the theme of birth, the waters of the goddess breaking, causing a great flood over the earth.

Line 125

Second reference to LUL/NAR/LIB (line 67), the seven musical foxes are identified here as the Pleiades thanks to the indication of the two horns of Taurus and to their role in setting the wheels of the Great Year in motion.

Both the Pleiades and Lyra/Vega, are linked to the number 7 and to music. Sirius, the dog star, is Orpheus (notes to line 17).

Are the following lines describing the fate of Orpheus as the analogy of a star that drifts from its original position, either Sirius in relation to the sun (notes to line 73) or Vega/Lyra to the north pole?:

Rent from the marble neck, his drifting head,

The death-chilled tongue found yet a voice to cry

Positioned between two E, 'levee' and the lifting, SI, 'horn', 'to place' and 'to remember', with DI given as 'to tie', 'to compare' and 'to equal', the 'divine horn' and 'divisions announced'.

SI-DI give the source of Latin sidereus:

"starry, astral, of the constellations," from sidus (genitive sideris) "star, group of stars, constellation," which is of uncertain origin, perhaps from PIE root... (Etymonline)

Line 126

Transliterations of pictographic EZEN include ŠIR₃, HER/HIR, KIRIS, KIRID with given meanings 'sing', 'festival', 'squeeze', and 'bind'. ŠIR₃ is just one of the many words pertaining to the star Sirius (notes to line 17). KIRIS is source of the Roman goddess Ceres who is linked to the Greek goddess Demeter. Also linked to the god Pan (*Hamlet's Mill²*, p.286-287). Source of Greek syrinx, a shepherd's pipe made from hollow reeds. Transliterated HER/HIR is partial source of the name Hermes (*Before Babel*, p.197). Also see the notes to line 70.

EZEN appears in *The Story of Sukurru* (line 208) in the section of the three offering baskets corresponding to the three baskets riding the waves of the galactic plain on Pillar 43 at Göbekli Tepe. EZEN x KASKAL, 'crossroads' and first king of the *Sumerian King List* (notes to line 70).

KUK, the circling cog-boat (see p.41) here becomes the circle of the dog Sirius, the Sothic cycle (notes to line 17 and 73).

 E₂, 'temple', with KI, 'place', 'key temple', all those temples that can be shown to follow the movements of Sirius.

In statuary Hekate was often depicted in triple form as a goddess of crossroads.

The concluding lines of *The Path to Sky-End* are stylistically close to those of *The Story of Sukurru*, bearing in mind that most of the now obvious astronomical references in that translation went unnoticed in 2017. According to my understanding at that time, there was mention of construction with or without nails and line 272 reads:

272. Measure the heart with water and the truth of Ma's word with beer.

Line 127

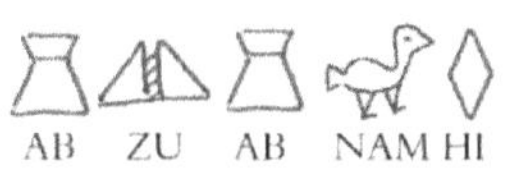 ZU, 'knowledge' of the pyramid between two AB, 'seas' and 'sailors'. NAM, the bird of destiny, with HI indicates purpose: the 'mixing' and/or the piercing of a magic veil.

 HI with ME surround AN EN KI KID, the four-word phrase given fourteen times in that order and spread quite evenly through the text (lines 4, 16, 25, 38, 41, 58, 66, 68, 73, 93, 98, 104, 120 and 127). Here the lord is found enclosed within the two parts of what I suggest is the visual equivalent of the Egyptian ankh, the 'veil of the magician'.

ME, 'magic', with GALAM, 'fish', linked to the Meso- of Mesopotamia and 'in-between' (notes to lines 48 and 52). Repetition of the five-word phrase (line 52).

Illustration from the earliest known representation of the Feathered Serpent (La Venta in Mexico). The figure carries the well-attested bag linking him to the Mesopotamian fish-god and is transported by the ouroboros snake (line 10). Same figure riding on fish or snake in different cultures (Oannes, Al Khidr, *Lost Stones*, p.189).

<u>Line 128</u>

NUN KI, first city of the *King List*, is given nine times (lines 13, 46, 49, 53, 73, 90, 121, 123 and 128). First combination with E₂ KUK GA, 'temple of the circle of milk', or 'the cog-boat circling on the milk', that of the foaming Milk Ocean, thoroughly churned.

The three-word phrase also appears twice on line 72. KAK A signals the culmination of the Pleiades on line 52. KAK, the keystone, peg, thorn or nail, is given 11 times in all. It also translates to 'a nail in the flow' with A BA as 'less water' or 'waterless' which might indicate the end of a flood rather than its continuation. Richard Allen cites a Korean myth concerning the Milky Way:

> *Nor must I forget to mention that the trouble in the royal household originated from the Prince's unfortunate investment of the paternal sapekes in a very promising scheme to tap the Milky Way and divert the fluid to nourish distant stars. (Star Names[6], p.58)*

The final A BA, indicating the flowing water, connect to the two A of the final line 129.

<u>Line 129</u>

$$25{,}920 \, / \, 1{,}296 = 20$$

A begins lines 1 and 129 in the composite version. On line 1 of the Ashmolean prism, A is replaced by UD, the 'sun'. A also ends line 9 (notes to line 108).

'Water' and 'flow' point to the well-attested image of the father figure who, in some cases, displays rising fish in the streams (Piscis Austrinus on line 9) flowing from both shoulders. These are the two rivers Euphrates and Tigris flowing down from the Taurus mountain range. The constellation of Taurus in 10500 BC rose behind them and was defeated by the sun at the winter solstice. Their waters are sourced from the great river Eridanus in the sky.

Double A is transliterated as AYA. Is this the 'aya' of ayahuasca? Perhaps it is and the 'hu' is the HU of the great Egypto–Mesopotamian bird Horus, of the equally great Sphinx, Hor-em-Akhet (p.65) and even of melodious Homer (line 102).

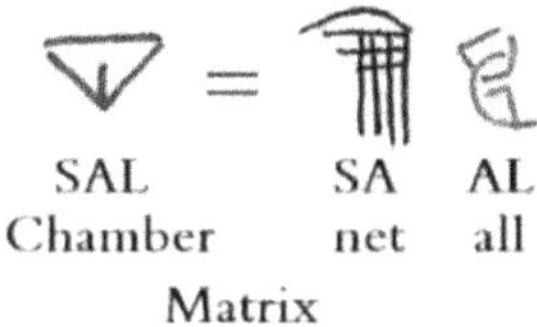 ZAG, 6th word, encodes the precession number 1,296 (notes to line 108). Given as 'to praise' and 'lyre', ZAG breaks down to ZA with AK, 'sound to make' (notes to line 43). Here it sits on the shoulder of the ancestral figure, marking the cave and the place of the rising or sinking sun.

In the context of mountains as sources of spring water, the Zagros mountains also fit the bill here, particularly since the discovery of a cave at Shanidar containing Neolithic remains. Also see Greek Zagreus, a 'god of the Orphic mysteries'.

SAL, the matriarchal chamber; source of Latin salvus, 'safe', 'salvation' and Latin salire, 'to spring forth', 'to flow down'.

Cairn of Gavrinis

The Neolithic stone mound of Gavrinis on the Atlantic coast of France, just a short distance from the better known Carnac alignment, is not only aligned to the rising sun at the winter solstice. It also takes into account the southerly maximum moonrise, the width of its entrance and passage adjusted to receive both. Apparently, their lights meet at the 7th stone in the passageway: a quartz stone. All the others are granite.

On the wall of its innermost chamber, a ledge with three compartments is carved out of the rock, perhaps to signify the three lunar phases or simply to safely place a light of some sort. The roof of the chamber was made out of a broken piece of a larger slab recuperated from an even earlier monument. Archaeologists, having taken the stones of Gavrinis apart to better study the site, discovered part of a whale carved on its uppermost face.

The cave of Shanidar in the Zagros mountains and the cairn of Gavrinis on the Atlantic coast: two Great Chambers of Consciousness from deep antiquity, wombs of regeneration, of sun and moon and humankind.

<u>The Number of Thoth-Hermes</u>

On the Ashmolean prism there are four additional words and two numbers inscribed below line 129. They appear on the transcript (copy of the original words) but are left out of the academic transliteration and translation:

KILI KILI MIN TUG₂ ŠI ILIMMU
block circle 2   cover eye   9
                           hidden
                           forethought   **Thoth**

'Cover' and 'forethought' are both dictionary-given meanings of TUG₂ and possibly originate in the story of the tortoise-shell lyre of Hermes (p.45). Was the ox hide covering the shell linked to the story of the bee-generating bull?

The message seems relatively clear. Preserved for future generations, two blocks, covered and hidden from view, contain the secret knowledge of Thoth (see Berossus on p.160). Never forgetting that ŠI, the Mesopotamian eye, is that of Sirius, the all-seeing eye on the celestial ferry boat (line 113).

As a swift thought darts through the heart of a man when thronging cares haunt him, or as bright glances flash from the eye, so glorious Hermes planned both thought and deed at once. He cut stalks of reed to measure and fixed them, fastening their ends across the back and through the shell of the tortoise, and then stretched ox hide all over it by his skill. (Hymn 4 to Hermes, 25, 44-55, Trans. Evelyn-White)

He already knows the various meanings of TUG₂, but which one to choose here? They have their avowed origin in the textile mill. The sign could be 'garment' or the verb 'to clothe', but equally it might be 'hearing' and 'ear' from the renowned rhythmic songs of the mill workers as they tug at the wool to clean and soften it. Other less evident notions of 'attention', 'awareness', 'forethought,' and 'planning' may also be expressed through this symbol; the consciousness of being clothed, the awareness of being. Thus, according to context, an apparently simple sign goes far beyond the confines of any textile mill. Most of the meanings are still in use in his time, and the milling songs continue. Little is ever truly lost; only faded and misunderstood. (*The Story of Sukurru*, introduction to the translation, 2017)

Bibliography and References

The Ashmolean prism of Enki's Journey to Nibru/Nippur and transcript (see 'line art') appear on the CDLI website under reference P368427.

Transliterations and given meanings are traceable via the electronic Pennsylvania Sumerian Dictionary (ePSD).

Pictograms are visible online thanks to the Cuneiform Digital Library Initiative (CDLI) now managed by Oxford University. (Advanced search, enter transliteration and Uruk IV to Uruk III periods.)

[1] *Enki's Journey to Nibru* (renamed *The Path to Sky-End*), Old Babylonian period ca.1900–1600 BC, composite transliteration and academic translation online at the Electronic Text Corpus of Sumerian Literature (ETCSL), reference 1.1.4.

[2] Giorgio De Santillana & Hertha Von Dechend, *Hamlet's Mill*, David R. Godine, Boston, 1977.

[3] Marija Gimbutas, *The Language of the Goddess*, Thames & Hudson, 1989.

[4] *The Instructions of Shuruppak* (renamed *The Story of Sukurru*), Early Dynastic III period ca.2600–2500 BC, composite transliteration and academic translation online at the Electronic Text Corpus of Sumerian Literature (ETCSL), reference 5.6.1.

[5] Graham Hancock, *Magicians of the Gods*, Hodder & Stoughton Ltd., London, paperback edition 2016.

[6] Richard H. Allen, *Star-Names and their Meanings*, G.E. Stechert, 1899.

[7] Prism containing a version of *Enki's Journey to Nibru*, Ashmolean Museum, (CDLI ref. P368427).

[8] Graham Hancock, *Magicians of the Gods*, p.316 (ref.[5]).

[9] Paul D. Burley, https://grahamhancock.com/burleyp1/ 2013

[10] Andrew Collins and Rodney Hale, *Göbekli Tepe's Pillar 43: An Astronomical Interpretation*, www.andrewcollins.com.

[11] Graham Hancock, *Magicians of the Gods*, p.429 (ref.[5]).

[12] Robert Bauval and Adrian Gilbert, *The Orion Mystery*, William Heinemann Ltd., 1996.

[13] Graham Hancock, *Magicians of the Gods*, p.296 (ref.[5]), citing Selim Hassan, *Excavations at Giza*, Vol. VI, Part I, Government Press, Cairo, 1946.

[14] *Sumerian King List*, composite transliteration and academic translation, online at the Electronic Text Corpus of Sumerian Literature (ETCSL), reference 2.1.1.

[15] Fresco in the Monastery of Rousanou, Thessaly, Greece.

Bull of Phalaris: Diodorus Siculus, *Bibliotheca Historica*, 13.90.4-7.

[16] E. A. Wallis-Budge, *The Book of the Dead*, Hymn to Ra, notes p.78, Kegan Paul, Trench, Trübner & Co. Ltd., 1909.

[17] See the constellation of Canis Major in *Urania's Mirror*, 1824.

[18] Contacts between French ethnographers Marcel Griaule and Germaine Dieterlen and the African Dogon tribe led to the heavily disputed claim that they possessed ancestral knowledge of the existence of Sirius B.

[19] Al Biruni, *The Book of Instruction in the Elements of the Art of Astrology*, 1029 AD, p.163-164, Trans. R. Ramsey Wright.

Olcott William, *Star Lore of all Ages*, p.105.

[20] Graham Hancock, *Magicians of the Gods*, p.355 (ref.[5]). Also see *Hamlet's Mill*, The Twilight of the Gods, p.162.

[21] Garcilaso de la Vega, *The Royal Commentaries of the Inca*, 1539-1616, The Orion Press, 1961 (cited in *Magicians of the Gods*, p.379, ref.[5])

[22] Article on Graham Hancock's website, The Trouble with Gilgamesh: https://grahamhancock.com/dainesm10/

[23] Kitâb sirr al-Halîka, *Book of the Secret of Creation*, 9th century AD.

[24] Robert Steel and Dorothea W. Singer, *The Emerald Tablet, Journal of the Royal Society of Medicine*, 1927.

[25] Harold Scheub, *A Dictionary of African Mythology*, Oxford University Press, 2000.

[26] http://blog.swaliafrica.com/cwezi-cult-of-africa-humans-extra-terrestrials-or-demi-gods/

[27] Peter Robertshaw, Dept. of Anthropology, California State University: Nyame Akuma, No. 48 December 1997, Archaeological Research in Bunyoro-Kitara: Preliminary Results.

[28] Joshua Mukama Rwakamani, The Cwezi/Kitara and the remnants of their ancient empire. (https://kaxsite.wordpress.com/2021/08/17/the-cwezi-and-the-remnants-of-their-ancient-empire/)

[29] Robert Bauval, *The Egypt Code*, Arrow House Books, 2006.

Index

Abraham 156

Acacia 189-190, 209, 244-245

Achilles 179

Adda Seal 137, 208

Al Buraq 178, 216

Al Hadi 203

Al Safinah 34, 35, 187

Algol 171

Allegro John M. 191

Allen Richard H. 3, 271

Alnitak 62-63, 191, 199

Amanita 174

Ananke 138

Anen 44

Angkor Wat 39, 47

Ani (Temple of) 137

Antipas 42, 43, 231

Anunnaki 16, 20, 35, 75, 76, 150, 256, 259

Apis (Epaphus) 239

Apkallu 35, 185, 206, 257

Apollo (Hermes, Phoebus) 41, 45, 46, 48, 50, 77, 139, 142, 153, 174, 182, 183, 197, 201, 228, 252

Aquarius 10-13, 155, 215, 216, 235

Aquila 146

Ara 75, 77, 146, 254

Arcturus 143, 220

Argo Navis 33-35, 144, 187, 225

Argonauts 34, 35, 185, 226

Aries 11, 184-186

Aristaeus 231

Artemis 165

Ascella (Axilla) 196

Asclepius (see Ophiuchus)

Asherah pole 232, 233

Ashmolean Museum 3

Ashvin 236

Aspidochelone 205, 216

Assyria 134

Astarte (Ashtar) 181

Athena 183, 186, 224

Atlantis 59, 65, 67, 148, 176, 202-204, 224, 251

Atlas 175, 176, 202, 204

Ayahuasca 235, 249, 259, 266

Aztec 188

Babylon 36, 154, 206

Bahamut 216

Basileus 134, 177

Basilisk 134, 136, 176, 177, 227, 235, 259

Batara 134, 259

Beehive 24-26, 37, 38, 140, 141, 167, 235, 239

Behemoth 198, 212, 216

Belus 35, 36, 171

Benben 218, 219

Berossus 16, 160, 241, 261

Betelgeuse (Mirzan) 250

Bia 253

Bigo 76, 77, 149

Book of the Dead 29, 44, 135, 178, 187, 228, 231

Boötes 149, 220, 229

Brazen Bull 42, 149, 231, 232

Buddhism 155, 165

Buranun (see Sippar)

Cabeiri (Kabeiri) 228, 229, 237

Calliope (Kalliope) 173

Cancer 11, 24-26, 140, 167, 192, 238

Canis Major & Minor 49, 51, 52

Canopus 34, 52, 167, 187

Capella 203

Carnac 267

Caspian tiger 19

Castor & Pollux (see Dioskouroi)

Cedalion (Kedalion) 43, 240

Cetus (Ketus) 204, 205, 207

Chaldeans 20, 36, 74

Charon 225, 226, 252

Cherokee 46, 47, 216

Chronos (Kronos) 140, 145, 155, 156, 199, 248

Comet 71, 72, 229, 230, 233

Corcog (Manannan) 37

Corona Australis & Borealis 214

Corvus 139

Cusco 57-59, 148, 243

Cwezi (Chwezi) 75-77

Cygnus 10, 141, 146, 158, 161, 162, 164, 166, 177, 225, 252

Dagon 142

Danaus (Dan) 35, 36, 48, 171, 173, 177, 221, 233, 234, 260

Deborah 135

Dendera 32, 52, 136, 148, 149, 165, 184, 212, 220, 235

Deucalion 155, 173, 234, 239

Didymus 237, 258

Dioskouroi 237

Dodo 9, 144, 219, 223

Dodona 30, 144

Dogon 51

Draco 136, 166, 176, 177, 208, 223, 235

Drum 39, 40, 156, 171, 194, 199, 201, 231, 263

El 169

Eleusis 215, 228

Emerald Tablet 69, 70, 136, 142, 144, 176, 177, 223, 235, 242

Engonasis (Hercules) 43

Enki 7, 41-43, 80, 136, 232, 239

Enlil 7, 80, 136, 239

Enoch 4, 5, 42, 217, 225

Erebus 201

Eridanus 18, 20, 166, 171-173, 230, 234, 252, 255, 257, 262, 266

Ermine 141, 142, 180, 183

Ethiopia 75,181

Euphrates 16-19, 33, 36, 156, 160, 161, 187, 221, 266

Eurydice 41, 201, 252

Fish god (Oannes) 142, 165, 189, 206, 215, 218, 261, 266

Fomalhaut 142, 215

Galactic Plain (Milky Way) 12, 15-17, 23, 34, 39, 52, 158, 162, 163, 165, 173, 187, 192, 194, 196, 197, 204, 205, 210, 213, 220, 225, 229, 237, 247, 260, 266

Gallina (see Cygnus)

Gavrinis (cave of) 8, 268

Gemini 11, 12, 51, 237, 258

Gilgamesh 61

Giza plateau 2, 23-25, 54, 61-63, 144, 147, 154, 156, 163, 170, 174, 180, 190, 191, 193, 195, 196, 199, 201, 203, 210, 213, 214, 217, 224, 268

Göbekli Tepe 4, 8, 13, 15, 16, 19, 21, 23-26, 33, 40, 49, 50, 52, 67, 68, 77, 134, 141, 142, 144, 147, 159, 162, 171, 180, 187, 195, 219, 221, 223, 226, 231, 232, 248, 251, 260, 265

Golden Gate 204

Gordian knot 170

Gorgon 170, 171, 173, 193

Great Pyramid 8, 26, 32, 54, 57, 63, 138, 154, 169, 171, 177, 180, 183, 186, 190, 195, 199, 201, 218, 224, 231, 232

Great Rift 12, 15, 162, 243, 247, 248

Great Year 10, 23, 189, 209, 213, 247, 248, 264

Gulgul drums 171

Hades 201, 203, 226, 227, 248, 252

Harp 45, 46, 67, 174, 175, 199, 200, 212

Harran 2, 4, 20, 24, 35, 36, 49, 63, 65, 149, 174, 187, 258

Hathor 80, 226, 229, 260

Hebe 152, 174, 236

Hekate (Hecate) 207, 208, 237, 249, 265

Heliopolis 251

Helios 139, 158, 162

Hemitheia 154, 207, 208

Hephaistos 198

Hera 136, 143

Herakles (Heracles) 139, 151, 162

Hercules (Engonasis) 43

Hermes 3, 24, 30, 45, 46, 48, 61, 69, 70, 77, 142, 152, 176, 195, 197, 206, 207, 219, 224, 226, 237, 253, 254, 264, 268

Homer 18, 136, 142, 147, 163, 202, 226, 257, 267

Hopi 154, 258

Hor-em-Akhet (see Great Sphinx)

Horus 135, 151, 200, 214, 252, 267

Horae 143

Hydra 43, 139

Hygeia 154, 205, 207, 208, 249

Icarus 17, 18

Idris 4

Igbo 137

Immanuel 52, 164, 167, 184, 211

Indus Valley 38

Ixion 143

Jason 33, 34, 185

Jesus 217, 237

John the Baptist 4, 180

Jonah 4, 42, 150, 165, 205, 207, 261

Kali 173, 183

Kalliope (see Calliope)

Karahan Tepe 4, 159

Karnak 8, 156

Khafre 210

Khufu 156, 180, 185, 186

Khunsu 216

Kimah (see Pleiades) 179, 188, 194, 195, 241

King List 27, 31, 53-55, 58, 66, 157, 160, 165, 168, 198, 207, 215, 243, 247, 249, 259, 265, 266

King's Chamber 169

Kitara (also Kithara) 44, 46, 75-77, 166, 218, 240, 254, 255, 257

Kochab 63, 66, 169, 177, 182, 194, 208, 217, 218, 261

Kore 37

Korybantes (Kouretes) 263

Kültepe 34

Lake of Fire 227, 228

Leo 11, 23-26, 63, 66, 67, 140, 167, 172, 186, 212, 213

Leviathan 193

Libra 11, 232

Lilith 44

Lotus (Eaters) 44, 220, 226, 227

Lucifer 184

Lunar mansions 153, 164

Luxor 156, 157

Lyra 10, 45, 46, 146, 161, 162, 164, 166, 172, 182, 200, 208, 212, 216, 224, 225, 229, 232, 240, 252, 254, 264

Ma'at 4, 29, 63, 141, 189, 209, 211, 238

Mahabharata 178, 195

Manannan (see Corcog)

Marduk 177, 229

Marsyus 46

Matrix 194, 199, 267

Mayan Calendar 12, 13, 23

Medusa 171, 178, 183

Milky Way (see Galactic Plain)

Mimir 41

Minoan 18, 49, 138, 188

Mirzan (see Betelgeuse)

Moon Turtle (see Turtle)

Momus 258

Moses 44, 48, 140, 192, 223, 229, 230, 250

Mount Meru 47, 191

Muses 163, 173

Narmer Palette 51, 166, 192, 223

Nephilim 203

Nevali Çori 48, 172, 221

Nibru (Nippur) 203, 232

Niger 137, 223

Nile 23, 44, 49, 134, 137, 148, 156, 190, 192, 195, 196, 206, 220, 223, 228

Noah 33-35, 39, 46, 138, 141, 150, 161, 187, 199, 225, 234

Nut 208, 251

Oannes (Fishgod)

Odysseus 4, 33, 225-227

Olympus 152

Ophiuchus 223, 235

Orion 23, 43, 46, 50, 52, 62, 63, 135, 137, 139, 144-147, 165, 166, 174, 184, 191, 193, 194, 199, 201, 221, 240, 250, 252, 257

Orpheus 40, 41, 45, 48, 50, 51, 67, 77, 138, 139, 153, 158, 161-164, 166, 172-175, 182, 190, 192, 194, 196-198, 201, 202, 204, 212, 224, 225, 228, 240, 252, 258, 264

Osiris 34, 41-43, 45, 63, 174, 182, 185, 186, 193, 194, 197, 199-201, 203, 217, 242, 247

Ouroboros 21, 68, 143, 154, 219, 226, 246, 263, 266

Pallas (see Athena)

Pandora 205, 208

Pegasus 46, 178, 183

Persephone 37

Perseus 178, 183

Phaeton 9, 17, 18, 136, 155, 159, 163, 166, 230, 235, 249, 252, 262

Phoebus (see Apollo)

Phoenix 80, 137, 173, 241, 250

Pi 156

Pillar 43 (Göbekli Tepe) 15-17, 19-21, 23, 67, 147, 162, 171, 195, 197, 232, 233, 251, 265

Pisces 10, 11, 150, 153, 165, 189, 198, 211-213, 215, 216

Piscis Austrinus 142, 150, 153, 165, 189, 215, 216, 266

Pleiades 11, 25, 26, 46, 140, 164, 175, 179, 188-190, 194, 195, 200, 202-204, 213, 238, 241-243, 245, 247, 248, 251, 263, 264, 266

Polaris 10, 63, 160, 169, 177, 208

Praesepe (Beehive Cluster)24, 26, 140, 167, 238

Prometheus 4, 137, 157, 168, 169, 171, 182, 201, 227, 232, 234, 256

Pythagoras 5, 26, 39, 40, 145, 157, 191, 197-199

Qurna 48, 156, 157

Ra 30, 48, 133, 156, 238

Ragnarok 181

Ran 242

Regulus 65, 66, 212

Rhea 133, 155, 263, 264

Sabian 20, 24, 34, 35, 63, 187

Sagittarius 10-12, 16, 17, 160-163, 171, 178, 183, 186, 196, 200, 212, 213, 221

Samson 23, 231

Sator Square 42, 152, 157, 224, 249

Sayburç 167, 247

Scorpio 10-12, 15-17, 19, 36, 115, 141, 161, 162, 177, 221, 234, 254, 262

Shanidar (cave of) 27

Sheba 57, 137, 146

Sidr Al Muntaha 220

Simorgh 79, 80, 135, 239

Sippar (Buranun) 16, 160, 161

Sirens 225, 226

Sirius 12, 49-53, 67, 135, 138, 139, 150-152, 155, 156, 161, 163-165, 167, 184, 187, 190, 191, 206, 209-212, 217, 218, 228, 230, 231, 234, 235, 252, 256, 258, 264, 265, 268

Siwa 158, 183

Solomon 137, 146

Sophia 217, 246

Sothic cycle 49, 51, 52, 151, 170, 184, 209, 210, 265

Sphinx 2, 23, 24, 50, 62, 63, 65-68, 139, 143, 144, 150, 164, 167, 169, 172, 175-177, 190, 193,

195, 196, 200, 212, 214, 222, 259, 267

Tajidar 79, 80, 136, 239, 253

Tara 133

Tartarus 133, 136, 137, 189

Taurids 72, 216, 230, 234, 263

Taurus 10, 11, 12, 21, 24-26, 52, 72, 140, 159, 164, 165, 167, 189, 198, 204, 213, 214, 216, 229, 230, 237, 245, 248, 258, 263, 264, 266

Tekmor 159

Thebes 135, 156, 157

Thoth 3, 5, 24, 61, 70, 80, 84, 133, 136, 142, 159, 176, 189, 200, 217, 226, 245, 253, 268

Thuban 63, 136, 176, 177, 208

Tiamat 226

Tigris 16, 19, 20, 21, 34, 68, 147, 156, 159, 161, 187, 195, 234, 266

Tishiya (Tishtrya, Sirius) 152, 252

Titans 136, 247, 254

Turtle (tortoise) 45-48, 77, 153, 216, 217, 220, 258, 268

Typhon 200

Ubara Dudu 53, 152, 207, 242, 258

Uganda 75, 76

Ursa Major 31, 133, 135, 150, 218

Ursa Minor 143, 153, 156, 177, 208, 217

Ushas 236

Vega 10, 45, 46, 158, 162, 164, 182, 183, 196, 200, 208, 212, 213, 224, 229, 252, 264

Venus 181

Virgo 11, 181

Warau 143

Warka Vase 138, 141

Whale 9, 41-43, 52, 134, 142, 150, 158, 165, 190, 202, 205, 207, 211, 216, 261, 267

Whale Valley (Egypt) 190

World Turtle (see tortoise)

Zagreus 267

Zagros 267

Zazakis 193

Zep Tepi 213, 244

Zeus 17, 18, 47, 140, 143, 145, 153, 159, 175, 186, 187, 196, 199, 228, 234, 237, 253, 263

Zib (see Zep Tepi)

Ziggurat 168, 170, 218

Zimbir (see Sippar)

Ziz 193, 217

Zodiac 213, 215, 223, 254

Also by Madeleine Daines:

The Story of Sukurru (2017)

(Retranslation of a literary text ca.2600–2500 BC,
aka *The Instructions of Shuruppak*.)

Before Babel The Crystal Tongue (2019)

(Study of the monosyllabic and pictographic origins of the cuneiform script
and its role as the foundation of many later words in other languages.)

Lost Stones of the Anunnaki
and the mind–altering journey to find them (2021)

(Study of the Mesopotamian origins and meanings of names
found in various ancient myths and biblical texts.)

www.ingramcontent.com/pod-product-compliance
Lightning Source LLC
LaVergne TN
LVHW050854200726
843508LV00011B/2020

ADVERTENCIA DEL AUTOR

Todas las fórmulas, recetas y prácticas que se mencionan en este libro sobre el mundo de los curanderos se presentan únicamente con fines históricos y meramente informativos.

Muchas de estas prácticas y liturgias que se citan pueden ser muy peligrosas para las personas, ineficaces ante una enfermedad o no estar respaldadas por evidencia científica. No se recomienda bajo ningún concepto ni se debe intentar reproducir ninguna de las recetas, tratamientos o rituales descritos en las páginas de este libro que tienes abierto en tus manos.

Se insta a todos, en su conjunto, que busquen siempre el consejo y la supervisión de los profesionales médicos capacitados para cualquier problema de salud.

El autor y el editor no se responsabilizan por cualquier daño o consecuencia adversa resultante de la aplicación de alguna práctica que cita en la información contenida en este libro.

Tampoco pretendo hacer una guía de salud natural ni sustituir a ningún facultativo ni tampoco buscar enfrentamientos directos. Mi objetivo es recuperar estas prácticas olvidadas, sus procesos, testimonios, sus anécdotas, supersticiones y remedios que se aplicaban, más allá de que sean efectivas o no.

Por respeto, he preservado el anonimato de los testimonios de esta obra, ya que los ofrecen personas de edad muy avanzada. Pese a ello, conservo grabadas las conversaciones como memoria y prueba.

Gracias por vuestra comprensión.

«Sanad enfermos, limpiad leprosos,
resucitad muertos, echad fuera demonios,
de gracia recibisteis, dad de gracia».

Mateo 10:8

AGRADECIMIENTOS

Sin duda, el primer agradecimiento es para las personas mayores de mi localidad, Alfafar, y sus áreas cercanas: Massanassa, Albal, Catarroja, Alginet, Algemesí, Guadassuar, Ontinyent, Sedaví o el valenciano barrio de Natzaret, entre otras, como también para muchos contactos de Almansa, de Villena y de la mágica comarca del Maestrazgo de Castellón. Sin darnos cuenta, ellos conservan tantas historias que nos darían para un serial acerca de las prácticas de curanderismo, con sus milagros, curiosidades y experiencias personales, incluso muchos de ellos son familiares de curanderos y han llegado a ejercer durante un tiempo. Gracias por vuestros testimonios, ayuda y recuerdos ancestrales.

Al Dr. Miguel Ángel Pertierra, persona que admiro por su labor, sencillez, profesionalidad y ese granito de arena que me aporta con su prólogo. Es conocedor de este fenómeno, sabe de qué trata en estas páginas, con los aciertos y errores de estos variopintos personajes que nos ha inspirado a ambos en muchos trabajos y divulgaciones. Gracias de todo corazón, doctor.

A Palmira, pues sin su amor diario y paciencia no hubiera sido posible esta obra.

PRÓLOGO

La lucha contra la enfermedad y frente a la muerte ha sido un nexo de unión entre todas las culturas, las cuales lo han manifestado de una forma muy similar y hasta peculiar a lo largo del espacio y el tiempo.

Muchos piensan que el fenómeno del curanderismo es algo que se remonta a unos tiempos relativamente cercanos, donde una persona a la que se atribuía el poder de sanación realizaba estas prácticas al margen de la medicina convencional. Pero el curandero, con distintas acepciones y consideraciones, ha existido desde tiempos ancestrales y, de hecho, en la cueva de Es Càrritx en Menorca, por ejemplo, ya hace miles de años se usaba la belladona, ya que se han encontrado restos de la misma, o en la Cueva de Los Murciélagos (Zuheros, Córdoba), en la cual se han hallado restos de manzanilla, adormidera o aquilea, que incluso hoy en día tienen usos medicinales.

En este libro os vais a encontrar un viaje desde estos tiempos ancestrales hasta hoy, donde los curanderos, no exentos de polémica, siguen practicando de una forma o de otra más o menos honesta su actividad.

Como médico, muchos de los remedios que han usado y usan los curanderos, tienen una base científica beneficiosa para el ser humano. De hecho, la manzanilla, anteriormente mencionada, se sabe que tiene propiedades digestivas importantes, al igual que otras plantas sirven para paliar otras acepciones.

De hecho, en la Edad Media, sobre todo en la Europa occidental, eran mucho más eficaces los curanderos/as o los remedios de los hechiceros/as o brujos/as que los de la llamada «medicina oficial», donde más que curar podían acabar contigo, mediante sangrías, purgas u otras técnicas que producían un cataclismo en la salud del paciente. El saber popular de muchos curanderos proviene de la cultura popular; de hecho, recuerdo como mi abuela, cuando sufríamos de pequeños un «empacho», nos trataba con friegas de aceite de oliva en el vientre, lo cual hacía que se distendiese la musculatura intestinal y así nos mejoraba los dolores tan incómodos de nuestro sistema digestivo.

Me llama la atención porque, leyendo las páginas de este magnífico libro, he encontrado un remedio que ya un rehabilitador me realizaba hace más de cincuenta años, tras una fractura en el pie, y que son las friegas de alcohol de romero, muy populares en las tierras andaluzas que tan bien conozco y que todavía hoy en día son usadas en muchas patologías osteomusculares.

Tratamientos prescritos por médicos rehabilitadores para el síndrome de distrofia regional compleja (SDRC) que en los miembros se conoce como enfermedad de Südeck, consistente en una alteración del sistema nervioso simpático, que se puede producir, por ejemplo, después de una inmovilización, escayolado o vendaje del miembro afecto, entre otras causas. Puede incluir el introducir el miembro afecto en agua caliente con sal y posteriormente en fría y viceversa para mejorar el cuadro. Esto, que seguro alguno de los lectores lo habrá hecho por causa de esta patología, lo realizaban algunos curanderos ya hace cientos de años. Tendréis ocasión de conocer este tipo de tratamiento y otros al uso con más extensión en este interesantísimo libro.

Por desgracia también existe el «lado oscuro» de estas prácticas, puesto que personas que se aprovechan del mal y de la desesperación del enfermo, para depauperarlos o, en el peor de los casos, causarles graves daños o incluso la muerte, por inducir a que dejen tratamientos alopáticos que estaban intentando mejorar al paciente.

En más de una ocasión me han entregado en la calle de alguna populosa ciudad octavillas de «maestro» tal o cual que cura cualquier tipo de males físicos o anímicos con éxito garantizado, según ponía en el papel, y que son charlatanes que lo único que van a hacer es estafar a personas desesperadas.

Un punto, para mí muy grave, son aquellas personas que dicen curar enfermedades graves con tal o cual remedio, como nos indica el autor de este libro, habiendo un individuo que decía que con aromaterapia se podía curar un proceso muy serio, o los que denuestan prácticas como el *reiki*, siendo unos desahogados que se autonombran «maestros», uno de los cuales conocí en una charla donde aseguraba que curaba con esta práctica cualquier tipo de cáncer. Fue entonces cuando levanté la mano y le dije que, literalmente, estaba diciendo una barbaridad, respondiendo concretamente que «no éramos *reiki*» e inmediatamente unos «señores» muy altos, musculados y con cara de pocos amigos nos invitaron a salir del recinto donde se realizaba la charla.

En otra ocasión, durante una investigación sobre el curanderismo, me encontré a un supuesto curandero que, tras «comprar» sus poderes (sí, el lector ha leído correctamente: «comprar» a un aparente vidente-sanador, que tiene montado un buen «chiringuito»), te hacían firmar un documento que decía que si te curas es por el poder del sanador y, si no, porque tú no quieres; y, claro, que solo cobra la voluntad, en aquel tiempo, en los inicios del milenio nos indicaron que «la voluntad mínima eran cincuenta euros». Seguro que os vais a sorprender en este libro sobre técnicas y prácticas de supuesta sanación, en muchos casos basadas en la tradición. Lo curioso, es que bastantes funcionan, aunque, hoy en día, hayan sido desplazadas por técnicas más modernas de la «medicina oficial». De hecho, todavía en muchas casas, reconozco que incluida la mía, todos esos remedios que he tenido la ocasión de conocer de personas (llamados «santos» en algunos lugares; en otros, «curanderos»; y, en otros, «estudiosos en conocimientos ancestrales», o bien, simplemente, «ancianos») siguen siendo utilizados. A mí mismo me ha proporcionado una perspectiva de que existen muchas formas y remedios alternativos para sanar.

Por supuesto, el origen de toda la farmacopea actual son los remedios naturales, que han sido y siguen siendo utilizados por muchas personas, y que en algunos casos sirven para mejorar algunas patologías, aunque dejo claro que no son para nada la panacea, como los embaucadores intentan vender, pero que están ahí y que algunos de ellos vais a poder conocerlos o reconocerlos en estas páginas.

Solo os diría, para finalizar, que os cuidaseis de los charlatanes, timadores y estafadores sin escrúpulos y que disfrutéis, como lo he hecho yo, de las páginas de este magnífico libro escrito por Ángel Beitia.

Dr. Miguel Ángel Pertierra
Doctor en otorrinolaringología y experto en hipnosis clínica.
Colaborador en «Cuarto Milenio».

INTRODUCCIÓN

Mencionar la palabra «curandero» supone, en la mente de la mayoría de las personas hasta una edad promedio entre los cuarenta y los cuarenta y cinco años, un salto en el tiempo a tratamientos arcaicos, a prácticas obsoletas de medicina, a unas habitaciones oscuras en viviendas, a direcciones casi clandestinas rodeadas de parafernalia extraña de imágenes de santos, velas e inciensos, incluso a estafas médicas.

Por el contrario, aquellas personas que superaban esa edad, es totalmente diferente a los conceptos de las últimas generaciones, algunos guardan buenos recuerdos, otros albergan diversas decepciones, pero creen que aquellos personajes tenían algo especial, eran primordiales en el día a día de una pequeña localidad o comarca donde brillaba la ausencia de servicios decentes en la rama de la sanidad y bienestar.

El curanderismo ha sobrevivido a través de los siglos, a través de caminos velados, por sendas subterráneas, buscando la discreción, y destacaba esta dedicación cuando resurgían diversos conflictos sociales, guerras, plagas, epidemias y crisis económicas.

Este mundo está todavía muy vivo en la memoria de nuestros mayores, muchos de los cuales depositaron en algún instante de su vida su fe y esperanzas en sanar de alguna dolencia que ellos mismos, incluso sus padres, sufrieron en el pasado, al no tener los recursos médicos necesarios al alcance de sus manos. Bien por temas de distancias y aislamiento rural, bien por motivos económicos, bien por los daños colaterales que supuso la guerra civil, ocasionando un desastre social o porque no había más remedio que aceptar con resignación la situación que les tocó vivir sin ningún avance de medicina ni cercanía hospitalaria o posta sanitaria, era aceptar los supuestos prodigios de las personas con esos dones mágicos junto a sus ceremonias de esa «folkmedicina» ancestral de remedios naturales.

Ya no estamos en esa España oscura y rural que se aferraban a las creencias y tradiciones, de ello no hay duda, pero quedan vestigios, herencias y recuerdos de estas habilidades que denominamos como «medicina popular o curanderismo».

Mi objetivo, al ser un tema de índole antropológica y basado en la «folkmedicina», es recoger la mejor información posible y analizar estos procedimientos buscando los últimos movimientos del curanderismo de las últimas décadas. Para entender mejor los comienzos de la práctica del curanderismo, debemos ubicarnos en sus primeros pasos, en sus primeras influencias y su impacto en la evolución social.

Sus orígenes se pueden apreciar en los albores de la humanidad cuando, en su lucha diaria por sobrevivir en un mundo hostil e inseguro, descubrieron que el poder de la sanación residía en su intuición y no solo en la naturaleza y el conocimiento profundo de las plantas, sino también en la conexión espiritual con el universo cuando alzaban la mirada al cielo de ese asombroso firmamento cubierto de estrellas que en sus creencias consideraban como la morada de sus antepasados, de sus dioses o seres mágicos.

Y esos primeros personajes que surgen como la «célula inicial» de la evolución del curanderismo, que llega hasta la figura del médico moderno del siglo XXI, emergen en la historia como tejedores de esta conexión entre lo terrenal y lo divino: los llamados «chamanes» o «hechiceros».

Con sus ceremonias en éxtasis y sus visiones inducidas por plantas sagradas que fueron conociendo y dominando, los chamanes no solo curaban enfermedades físicas, sino que también guiaban a sus comunidades en la búsqueda de respuestas a los enigmas más profundos de la existencia y que todos los que formaban ese clan o tribu respetaban sus decisiones.

Sin embargo, el curanderismo no se limita a una sola cultura o geografía. Desde las estepas más profundas de la lejana Siberia hasta las selvas más inaccesibles de las regiones amazónicas y desde las rocosas montañas de los Andes hasta el mágico y ancestral continente africano, las diversas tradiciones basadas en la curación de la humanidad reflejan la diversidad que existe en todo el mundo en su constante búsqueda de la sanación y la conexión espiritual.

A lo largo de los siglos, y hasta la actualidad, el curanderismo se ha enfrentado a la persecución y el olvido, pero su llama nunca se ha extinguido por completo, continúa viva en la memoria de muchas personas, con sus recuerdos, sus éxitos y sus fracasos. Su camino ha sido una carrera de constantes obstáculos, incluso durante la época de la posguerra española la Iglesia católica ya los tenía señalados y buscaban contrarrestar la influencia que ejercían los curanderos en el mundo rural, puesto que también afectaba a la religiosidad, pues aplicaban unas prácticas de fe cristiana que no estaban acordes a las normas eclesiásticas, como esas extrañas bendiciones que realizaban, plegarias, un exceso de devoción antinatural, rezadoras que aseguraban tener poderes divinos y que sanaban numerosas perturbaciones irreales… Todo esto en su conjunto lo denominan «religiosidad popular».

Estamos, en la actualidad, en una extraña encrucijada entre la ciencia y la espiritualidad, donde el curanderismo sigue siendo un faro de esperanza y sanación para aquellos que buscan respuestas más allá de lo convencional, pero es complicado dar con esos portadores de este curioso poder de sanación.

Vivimos en una época marcada por las prisas, el estrés diario, las presiones externas (emocionales, económicas o de cualquier índole) y es, curiosamente, donde la figura del terapeuta psicológico junto con las actividades relacionadas con el curanderismo resurgen.

Presenciamos unos tiempos que los avances científicos intentan arrinconar y dejar en desuso estas creencias y prácticas, por arcaicas y remedios caducos. Pero esto surge porque el misterio y la magia aún circulan, afortunadamente, por las venas de la humanidad, recordando esos momentos en que confiábamos y cedíamos nuestra fe al curandero o una sanadora local, dado que las sanaciones van más allá de la piel, de los huesos o de nuestros órganos: las profundidades del alma y del espíritu.

Desde tiempos remotos, las clases populares han adoptado unos sistemas defensivos muy particulares, desde métodos de protección y la presencia de la figura del curandero rural a través de sugerentes ritos que actúan en unos procesos de receptividad humana.

La medicina popular y sus prácticas basadas en el curanderismo no pueden, en términos generales, compararse con la medicina científica, no tiene nada que ver, pues hay que interpretarla y entender que es un mundo con un enfoque totalmente diferente, porque los principios en los que se basa la mayor parte del mundo del curanderismo tienen un predominante basado en las características mágicas, las creencias locales y la realización de rituales.

De hecho, las prácticas de curanderismo y de la medicina popular suelen señalar el origen de la mayoría de las enfermedades a factores externos como el conocido «mal de ojo», maleficios e incluso la temida intervención del demonio, que puede actuar a través de posesiones o incubar posibles enfermedades.

Añado también algo curioso que se conoce en algunas zonas de la Península como «susto», un momento en nuestra vida que puede dejar «al aire» nuestras defensas físicas y espirituales, causando un notable desorden en el equilibrio de la persona afectada, cuya sanación suele recurrirse a diferentes ritos de índole religiosa a través de las manos y conocimientos de los curanderos.

Estas intervenciones y diversos rituales desencadenan en el ser humano unos procesos psicosomáticos. Además, tras analizar mis comparaciones, notas, lecturas, estudio y experiencias de pacientes que han utilizado estas prácticas en las consultas a diferentes curanderos, es imprescindible no subestimar la posible influencia, tanto en el diagnóstico como en la terapia, de los eventuales fenómenos de sensitividad liberados por el curandero quien, a menudo —aun de manera inconsciente—, muestra una serie de habilidades psíquicas y de pranoterapia. Esto último es una práctica terapéutica que se basa en el manejo y canalización de la energía vital para promover la salud y el bienestar de la persona.

El término *prana* proviene del sánscrito, y se refiere a la fuerza vital y universal que está presente en todo ser vivo del planeta. Según esta creencia, cuando el flujo de *prana* se siente bloqueado, obstaculizado o desequilibrado, pueden surgir diversos problemas de salud física, emocionales e incluso espirituales.

No podemos evadir la constante utilización, por parte de la mayoría de los curanderos, de una medicina basada en el uso y estudio de las virtudes plantas, cuya eficacia está siendo redescubierta en la actualidad. Muchas de esas virtudes, en diferentes plantas, ayudan a mejorar el estado de salud, incluso en algunos casos, sanar definitivamente de una dolencia o un padecimiento para intentar olvidar remedios artificiales que, seguramente, ayudan a mucho, pero dañan otros órganos con efectos secundarios o, lamentablemente, no consiguen los objetivos marcados. Un dilema que hoy, en nuestra actualidad, siguen intentando minimizar. Insisto en un detalle: no es mi objetivo restarle méritos a la moderna medicina de nuestro tiempo. Son dos conceptos que han tenido diferentes caminos.

Pero ¿cuándo surgen los ritos y técnicas mágicas que aplicaban los curanderos o sanadoras, y que incluso hoy en día se siguen practicando en algunos sitios, aunque sea en la clandestinidad?

Es difícil dar un momento exacto. Con seguridad, en los primeros pasos de la humanidad ya se sabía algún recurso para calmar alguna dolencia y buscaban en la naturaleza, por su propia intuición como parte del reino animal, buscar y elegir ciertas plantas para mejorar su indisposición.

Tenemos una sencilla prueba y muestra de ejemplo en aquellos hogares donde tenemos algún perro o gato: ¿cuántas veces hemos visto a nuestro querido compañero peludo estar comiendo césped como si estuviera pastando y sin tener referencia ni obligarlo a ello?

Sabemos que lo engullen como un purgante, pero ¿quién le enseña ese remedio? Ahí existe una relación intuitiva con la naturaleza y los beneficios que puede aportar al organismo.

Como he citado en unas líneas anteriores, con la aparición de los primeros clanes humanos es cuando surge la figura del chamán o hechicero en las antiguas sociedades tribales y cazadoras-recolectoras. Los chamanes surgieron como figuras clave en el desarrollo de la humanidad, cuyo origen se encuentra entre las conexiones con lo sobrenatural y las experiencias visionarias.

Estas experiencias son, a menudo, desencadenadas por el riguroso ayuno al que se someten, la ingestión de plantas psicoactivas o la exposición constante a unas condiciones extremas que pueden ser basadas en el dolor, el aislamiento o condiciones meteorológicas adversas que les proporcionaban un acceso a un conocimiento espiritual profundo y una conexión con las dimensiones invisibles. Estas habilidades conferían a los chamanes un estatus especial en la comunidad, dando lugar al desarrollo gradual de tradiciones y prácticas chamánicas transmitidas de generación en generación.

El chamán se distingue por sus habilidades para llevar a cabo una amplia gama de diversos rituales. Estos rituales van desde ceremonias destinadas a rendir homenaje a diversas deidades hasta los ritos que acompañan los momentos más trascendentales del ser humano, como nacimientos y muertes.

1.Los chamanes fueron y siguen siendo grandes referentes en curanderismo en Sudamérica. Imagen: Jad Sanhaji.

El chamán iba trazando los senderos hacia el más allá, hacia ese reino invisible, al cual solo ellos tienen acceso y pueden establecer conexión con los espíritus o ancestros. Y eso ya era mucho poder para respetarles dentro de su comunidad.

Además de su papel en las ceremonias rituales, el chamán desempeñaba la función de ser el sanador, empleando una gran variedad de métodos que abarcaban desde el uso de las hierbas medicinales y su experimentación con ellas hasta rituales de purificación del espíritu y otras prácticas psíquicas que no estaban al alcance de cualquiera de su tribu. Estos métodos estaban dirigidos a tratar tanto las dolencias físicas como las mentales, demostrando así sus profundos conocimientos de la conexión entre el cuerpo y la vinculación con la naturaleza y el espíritu.

En resumen, el chamán primitivo se erige como el principal sanador en su comunidad. Sus dotes de curación eran vistas como una gracia otorgada por los espíritus o los dioses, según sus creencias locales. Con el devenir del tiempo, estos conocimientos y prácticas fueron legados a otros miembros de su misma comunidad, bien a través de sus enseñanzas o adquiriendo experiencias propias y compartidas con el chamán, dando origen a los primeros pasos de los futuros curanderos o sanadores tradicionales. A partir de sus rituales, plegarias y creencias, ha ido floreciendo una amplia variedad de prácticas mágicas que están destinadas a la curación o, al menos, a mitigar el sufrimiento del ser humano.

Estas costumbres terapéuticas de los chamanes o hechiceros han ido evolucionando, superando etapas en todos los ámbitos geográficos.

Sin embargo, en Europa algo es diferente: con la llegada de la época que controlaba el cristianismo, muchas costumbres terapéuticas antiguas eran consideradas paganas en numerosas ocasiones, incluso vinculadas con la brujería, se han ido forzosamente modificando sus métodos, sus gestos, palabras, superponiendo nombres cristianos y rituales a lo largo del tiempo. De hecho, los curanderos rurales utilizan un gesto y al mismo tiempo invocan a los santos católicos: utilizan la señal de la cruz. La señal de la cruz es, en efecto, una característica constante de su intervención terapéutica que aún sigue vigente en algunas zonas geográficas más aisladas de los núcleos urbanos. Y es una herencia del pasado para huir de las vigilancias más radicales de la historia: la Inquisición.

En un mundo y en una época que ha estado marcada por la incertidumbre, el miedo y la persecución, los curanderos (junto con las sanadoras, parteras, yerberos, hueseros, rezanderos, saludadores, sangradores…) se convirtieron en guardianes de la salud y el bienestar, bajo la amenaza constante de la Inquisición y otras instituciones que cuestionaban sus prácticas y creencias, puesto que estaban fuera de sus dogmas de fe. En este contexto de desafíos y adversidades, el curanderismo encontró diversas formas ingeniosas de preservar sus tradiciones, adaptándose a las circunstancias cambiantes mientras continuaban aportando alivio y dosis de esperanza a aquellos que buscaban su ayuda.

Y esas ayudas, esperanzas, remedios e incluso decepciones han llegado hasta nuestros días.

Posiblemente, el cenit de los curanderos en España sea el periodo de la posguerra. La extrema pobreza de muchas regiones, el aislamiento urbano generalizado, la ausencia de avances sociosanitarios y los escasos recursos por falta de médicos tras la guerra, junto con la fuerte devoción por el catolicismo (sobre todo, las supersticiones y los pocos medios de comunicación con columnas describiendo en sus páginas hechos y acontecimientos milagrosos de dudosa credibilidad en nuestro tiempo), han dado un retrato de las cualidades y normas que debe adquirir y poseer una persona que se dedicada a sanar, tanto en hombres como en mujeres. Por supuesto, no era estudiar nociones de medicina natural que, en términos generales, muy pocos estudiaban, sino tener la «gracia» o señales divinas.

Hoy pocas personas ejercen el curanderismo popular, ya solo quedan recuerdos, iconografías descoloridas, portentos milagrosos, recuerdos de unas manos arrugadas con la carga divina que tocaban sus cuerpos, el folclore de una España extraña, mística y mágica a la vez.

Su figura como sanador popular en el presente siglo XXI lo afrontan con incertidumbre. No se ven acabados, sino que deben asumir unos cambios y evolucionar en sus creencias, cambiar su atractivo sin perder los dogmas de fe en la sanación ni sus tradiciones, que han pasado de generación en generación. Saben que es complicado en la actualidad ganarse la confianza, a veces es más sencillo acudir a ellos que complicarse el tiempo en las esperas de los ambulatorios u hospitales cuando la situación no reviste gravedad, incluso para ayudarte espiritualmente, según parece, no hará falta recurrir al cotidiano antidepresivo Orfidal ni al Prozac. Ni tampoco a rituales de alta magia esotérica. Basta con escucharlos y dejar que emitan su magia.

I. DE LOS RECUERDOS

En mi baúl de memoria infantil, mientras me documentaba, estudiaba y recopilaba información de este mágico mundo de los curanderos ibéricos, especialmente los más locales de mi zona, arribaron unos recuerdos, como una desgastada fotografía en blanco y negro, de aquellos tiempos de la década de 1970, cuando comenzaban a soplar ciertos aires de libertad, pero que jamás se perdieron las tradiciones que aún perduraban en esa época llegadas desde lo más profundo de la España rural.

Familias enteras emigraron desde unas localidades casi inaccesibles en aquellos instantes, en busca de un futuro mejor en las grandes urbes que iban creciendo por aquel tiempo por su diversidad de servicios, ofertas de trabajo, de los nuevos barrios obreros y modernidad: Madrid, Valencia, Barcelona, Málaga..., así como las poblaciones que rodeaban a estos grandes núcleos también se vieron favorecidas con un notable aumento de población y actividad. Es patente que se buscaba la supervivencia, el futuro de su numerosa prole (entonces se tenían más hijos que hoy en día), mejorar sus estudios, o no tenían la confianza y economía suficiente para emigrar a Alemania, Suiza o Francia, donde se podía ganar más salario. O, simplemente, huir de un entorno rural

al que no llegaban las mejoras prometidas que, por aquel
entonces, se ansiaban: óptimas carreteras de acceso, canali-
zaciones de agua, electricidad, escuelas o medios de transporte, entre otros servicios.

En esos traslados no olvidaron añadir en sus maletas sus
viejas costumbres: sus recetas de cocina; sus enormes ollas
de porcelana esmaltada para cocinar sus suculentos pucheros; su costurero, con el que nos reparaban nuestras madres
cualquier incidencia en nuestras indumentarias; sus objetos
de pertenencia sentimental que heredaron de los abuelos; la
reducida caja de herramientas de nuestros padres, que ayudaría a salir de algunos apuros en algunas reparaciones en el
hogar; sábanas; mantas; repertorios de tazas y, por supuesto,
sus remedios de botica para calmar dolores e incluso sanarse:
Agua del Carmen, mercromina, manzanilla, sales de Epsom,
aceite de hígado de bacalao o ungüentos naturales de diversos componentes atávicos.

*2. Sales de Epsom, cuya base de sulfato de magnesio se utilizaba
en baños para mejorar dolencias musculares y articulares.
Museo de Etnología de Peñarroja. Imagen: A. Beitia.*

Esto último es una fabulosa herencia ancestral, que ha pasado de generación en generación, como una llama que arde dentro con la sabiduría de quienes les sanaron con anterioridad.

No todos los que se desplazaron a otras tierras conocían estas técnicas o fórmulas magistrales, pero sabían quiénes las portaban o ejercían en sus proximidades.

Por esas causas recordé unas escenas de infancia, de cómo me llevaron a una desconocida sanadora de una localidad vecina para quitarme unas molestias estomacales, que no eran más que una típica mala digestión, después de todo. Aquel personaje femenino solo me roció unas gotas de aceite (desconozco qué tipo de óleo, supongo que de oliva virgen) sobre mi vientre para darme un masaje en mi abdomen.

Recuerdo que, previamente, aquella mujer, ataviada con riguroso luto y una enorme cruz colgando sobre su pecho, miró un gran cuaderno que depositó sobre una pequeña mesa redonda, con esos manteles de ganchillo casero multicolor. Debía de ser añejo el cuaderno, pues contenía una páginas amarillentas bastante gastadas en la que aparecían algunas fotografías de color pajizo que servían de separador, así como notas, imágenes sagradas y algún que otro garabato. No sé si estaba consultando el remedio a mi molestia, estudiando algún dato útil para otro paciente o repasando la lista de citas del día, pues había una larga cola en la calle, cuyo riguroso orden nosotros nos saltamos. Ignoro la causa, posiblemente ya estaba concertada previamente o eran conocidos de mis padres que nos hacían un favor.

Sin más, las molestias remitieron, el pago fue una pequeña bota de buen vino, para su esposo, y una ristra de chorizos «de pueblo», como suele decirse en ese argot rural entre los que se conocen. Eso sí, no me quitó el miedo inicial al entrar en su cuarto, era algo abrumador en mi ignorante e infantil mente de un niño: estampas de santos, calendarios ambarinos con diversas vírgenes como reclamo, fotografías en un extraño color sepia, que eran un pequeño lujo por entonces, ya que pocos disponían de cámaras fotográficas. Era más cercano a un cementerio que otra cosa, por la cantidad flores y alguna extraña corona, que seguramente habría sustraído de algún camposanto, sospecho. Todo parecía servir para inhibir al que accediera a su casa. Por entonces, yo debía de tener poco más de cinco años, demasiada sugestión y pavor para asimilar aquella escena imborrable en mi memoria.

3. Agua del Carmen, recurso habitual de hace décadas y muy valorado por los curanderos.

Años después, mi padre sufrió un doloroso esguince en su pie derecho mientras ejercía su trabajo de transporte y mudanza de muebles. Las bajas laborales, por entonces, eran complicadas, pues se perdía mucho salario, había que luchar día a día y no podía permitirse el lujo de perder días, ya que nuestra familia la formábamos siete personas en aquel momento. No tuvo más remedio que acudir con una notable cojera y dolor a un conocido «reponedor o componedor de huesos» de mi barrio popularmente como el tío Paco, «el huevero». Prácticamente estaba al lado de mi casa, y de su patio colindante recuerdo que salía y entraba un cierto trajín de personas.

El tío Paco era un personaje ya adulto, orondo, vestía una típica camiseta interior blanca de tirantes, tan ajustada que hacía destacar su voluminoso vientre, con sus gruesas gafas de pasta, sin titulaciones ni estudios (que yo sepa), que se dedicó muchos años de juventud a ser un masajista de equipos de fútbol que se arrastraban por aquellos campos pedregosos y de barro, donde jugaban con balones duros como piedras. Aquellos partidos eran una batalla contra las lesiones, de tratar quemaduras en la piel por las caídas y arrastrarse sobre aquella tierra polvorienta y áspera como un papel de lija de la máxima dureza, de calmar dedos de los pies doloridos por el uso de botas de balompié muy incómodas, duras y rígidas.

En su habitación, en este caso más amable respecto a mi otro recuerdo, solo embriagado por ese extraño y clásico olor de linimento barato, se sentó en una pequeña silla de esas que se denominan «de abuela», de asiento de paja y recia madera. Le hizo meter el pie en un barreño de agua fría tras descargar una cubitera de plástico que guardaba en el reducido congelador de su nevera; luego a otro recipiente caliente, que calentó en una enorme olla de porcelana de color rojo esmaltado, de aquellas en las que nuestras madres o abuelas removían aquellos sabrosos pucheros. Repitió el sanador la operación unas cuantas veces, en un extraño vaivén de ese dolorido pie que soportaba los cambios de temperatura del frío al calor que aplicaba el tío Paco.

Tras secarlo escrupulosamente, vertió un generoso chorro de alcohol farmacéutico y comenzó a realizarle un rumboso masaje en su maltrecho e inflamado tobillo durante un largo tiempo. Lo rodeó con una típica venda de fino hilo que anudó al final y la sesión finalizó sin más preámbulos. Al día siguiente, la cojera, el dolor, la inflamación y la incomodidad desaparecieron como por arte de magia. Ya no cojeaba absolutamente nada y aseguraba mi padre que dicho dolor e inflamación remitió por completo, y lo pudimos comprobar tras quitarse la venda al día siguiente, pues no se parecía en nada aquel tobillo maltrecho e hinchado como un globo que pude ver con mis propios ojos. Lo elogiaban en nuestra casa, valoraban sus dones de sanador de lesiones y roturas de huesos. Ahí despertó un curioso interés en mi mente de niño que me acercaba imparablemente a la adolescencia y comenzaba a interesarme por el mundo del misterio, de lo inexplicado e insólito, puesto que comenzaba a curiosear algunas revistas que llegaban casualmente a mis manos llamadas *Karma-7* o fascículos coleccionables de *Lo inexplicado*, incluso algunos números perdidos de *Historia y vida* e incluso algún episodio de nuestro añorado Dr. Jiménez del Oso, que aparecía por televisión en aquellos programas llamados *Más allá* y *La puerta del misterio*.

Siempre me preguntaba de niño si aquellos personajes que sanaban tenían poderes sobrenaturales, si conocían todas las panaceas, hasta la de la inmortalidad, si eran capaces de entablar conversaciones con Dios o con los diversos santos o santas, dado que, cuando accedes a su consulta, es todo un repertorio de estampas de san Pancracio, de diferentes vírgenes del Carmen, de santas vestidas de monja, de diversas imágenes de san Miguel derrotando a la simbología del mal, de ese sugestivo Jesús del Sagrado Corazón de vivos colores o rostros de Jesús sufriendo con esa corona de espinas sangrante en su frente…, todo ello aderezado como lo haría un buen chef, en una extraña mescolanza de fotografías personales que te llevan a tiempos insólitos, a rostros marcados por duras arrugas, a unas manos fibrosas, a las mujeres con delantales negros y polvorientos junto a los ojos del hambre y el sufrimiento que plasman sus retratos.

Es la magia de los curanderos, de los sanadores. También de numerosas mujeres que sabían moverse en estos complejos campos de la herboristería y la etnobotánica, además de guardar los secretos de oraciones y diversos ritos. Pero ¿qué hay de cierto en ello? ¿Hasta dónde llegaban? ¿Cómo se aprendía? ¿Cuál era el límite ético de esta dedicación? ¿Sanaban de verdad?

Todas estas dudas han sobrevolado hasta nuestro tiempo. Y creo que es un buen momento para hacerles un repaso a estos últimos personajes que ejercen o ejercían esta profesión de forma casi clandestina; para estudiar sus estructuras, sus funciones e incluso sus códigos y paradigmas. Ya no quedan apenas vestigios de ese oscuro pasado de ritos de sanación con sus aciertos y errores. Y, por supuesto, con los charlatanes y los que ejercían con buena destreza y respeto.

Unos eran componedores de huesos; otros, masajistas. Existían las mujeres que aplicaban el rito del «enfit» o empacho. Otros variopintos personajes aseguraban curar enfermedades como un cáncer, diversas úlceras, diabetes o infecciones de piel, entre otras dolencias. Algunos se dedicaban a extraer solo las muelas. Y había mujeres que aceptaban asistir como parteras. Existían otros enfoques dedicados a influencias de hechizos como el «mal de ojo».

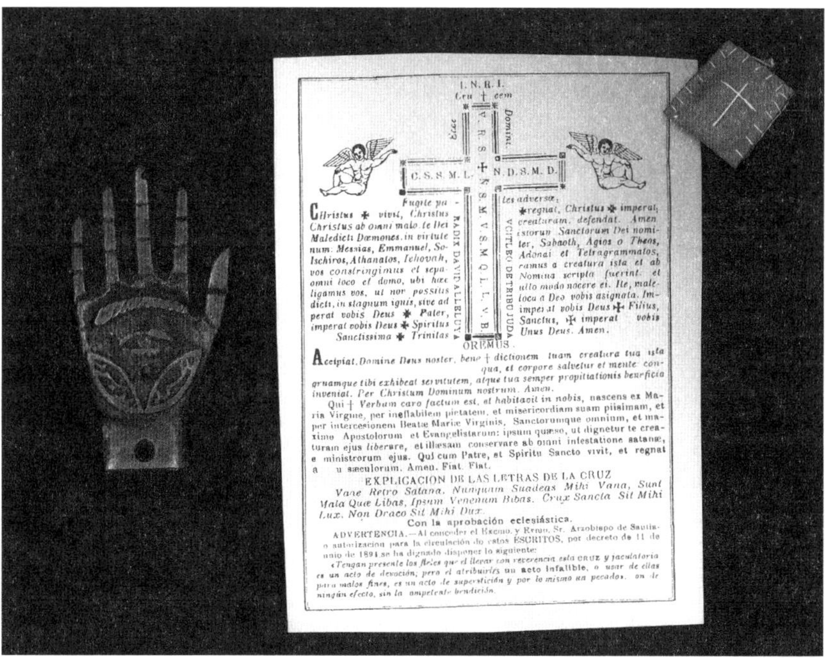

4. Amuletos contra el «mal de ojo». Museo vasco
de la historia de la ciencia y medicina.

Curiosamente, sus descendientes han sido de los primeros en ejercer como modernos fisioterapeutas, naturópatas e incluso sanadores espirituales en nuestra época moderna. Han tenido que adaptarse a los nuevos tiempos, a la persecución por intrusismo médico, y buscar estudios que pudieran avalar de alguna forma sus conocimientos. Parece que todo está unido de alguna forma, con la sensación de estar caminando por los mismos senderos que fusionan la sabiduría ancestral, los secretos de la naturaleza y el poder espiritual.

De ahí que rebuscara en mi memoria la escena más antigua que pudiera retener sobre un sanador, oficio que está ya obsoleto, arrinconado por la evolución de la medicina y la presión de las autoridades por ser titulados para ejercer junto con los ritmos e intensidad del proceso de medicalización moderna se vieron obligados a una decadencia y una casi desaparición. Sin embargo, aún resisten unos escasos personajes que se aferran a las prácticas más ancestrales y todavía muchos pacientes confían su salud a la esperanza de un milagro.

Pero ¿sanaban todo tipo de enfermedades y problemas de las articulaciones o musculares? ¿Cómo se alcanzaba ese privilegio de ser curandero?

No puedo tampoco olvidarme de algunos de los remedios caseros que empleaban mis padres cuando enfermaba de algo cotidiano como un leve proceso febril, que aplicaban paños húmedos de agua fría y vinagre en mis sienes, acompañado de una tableta del popular analgésico Okal. Si la cosa no mejoraba en uno o dos días, no había más remedio que pedir ayuda al médico, de forma presencial en el punto de atención, pues no había tanto teléfono, y que tardaba lo suyo en atenderte (y eso si llegaba a hacerlo), o lograr una cita en los servicios locales del consultorio de la Seguridad Social, que después se hacía eterna. Ignoro de dónde surgió el siguiente remedio, pero recuerdo a mi padre y a mi abuelo materno tomarse una copa de brandi con miel para combatir la tos, cuando ambos proceden de culturas totalmente diferentes, ya que mi padre es de origen vasco y mi abuelo materno es andaluz, como mi madre. Seguramente, era una aplicación que aprendieron de otros, y estos de algún «charlatán» sanador de su región, pues es así como van surgiendo algunas recetas caseras que mejoramos con la experiencia y conocimientos. Lo único útil que observamos para combatir la tos es el uso de la miel, la razón del brandi la ignoro, aunque posiblemente sea por el calor que aporta durante las épocas frías, ya que es más frecuente este síntoma durante los periodos invernales, o por su efecto sedante causado por el alcohol.

5. Recurso muy habitual de automedicación:
Analgésico Okal. Imagen: A. Beitia.

La presencia de curanderos en los pueblos del interior de España ha sido fundamental para el bienestar de esa comunidad, cuyas tradiciones se iban fusionando con la evolución de aquellas décadas de 1960 y 1970, de cuyos cambios pude ser testigo, tanto los tradicionales como los ancestrales y los científicos.

El curandero representaba un vínculo vital con el pasado. Entre los callejones de piedra, en cortijos aislados y en las plazas polvorientas de esas localidades, la gente acudía a él en busca de alivio para sus dolencias, confiando en sus conocimientos transmitidos de generación en generación. Sus manos, ágiles y sabias, aplicaban ungüentos y hierbas curativas, mientras sus palabras resonaban con el eco de tiempos pasados, con oraciones que daban extrañas sensaciones que erizaban el vello de nuestra piel, asegurando la mayoría que su virtud procede de otros mundos mágicos, celestiales o divinos.

II. ¿QUÉ ES UN CURANDERO?

Según el diccionario de la RAE, es una persona que, sin ser médico, ejerce prácticas curativas o rituales. Su etimología proviene del latín *curare* (curar), al que le añadimos el sufijo *-dero*, indicando una actividad relacionada con la sanación o curación.

Sin embargo, se debería ajustar algo mejor su descripción, puesto que está algo vacía, ya que el curanderismo es un ejercicio de ciertas capacidades que, por otras vías totalmente diferentes a las que acepta la sociedad médica de índole oficial, aplican esas virtudes a la curación del paciente o, en su defecto, pueden aliviar distintas enfermedades o las diversas dolencias que puede cargar el afectado.

Puedo considerarlo como un sistema de sanación ancestral, basado en la conexión y conocimiento probado con la naturaleza, de la mente y del espíritu cuyos conocimientos, en su mayoría, se han transmitido a través de generaciones familiares.

Evidentemente, está la opción de ser curandero a través de adquirir un don que brota en un momento determinado de su vida causado por una experiencia cercana a la muerte o por una manifestación mística, es decir, una aparición divina o de sus ancestros.

Respecto al intrusismo, es un debate de leyes. Es cierto que algunos recurrían a fórmulas absurdas, peligrosas e inútiles, poniendo, a menudo, en cierto riesgo al paciente. Otros se aprovechaban de la ingenuidad del paciente para hacer caja con masajes y bendiciones irracionales. Sin embargo, sí que hay sanadores y curanderos que, sin tener una carrera o reconocimiento oficial, poseen unos conocimientos muy válidos en nuestra actualidad, sapiencias que han aprendido con la práctica, la observación de sus atenciones a sus clientes o pacientes y el análisis autodidacta. Especialmente, saben los beneficios que ofrece la herboristería. Pero esto no significa que sustituyan al facultativo académico, ni mucho menos.

¿Qué causas inducen a las personas a convertirse en curanderos o curanderas?

La respuesta es casi unánime: que se aferran a una manifestación espiritual, es decir, a un mandamiento divino.

Da igual el origen de su habilidad o quién se lo ordena. El resto cree, por tradición familiar, que deberían seguir ayudando a los demás.

Sin duda, la pregunta más valiosa de este universo mágico basado en la «folkmedicina» y sus rituales es constante: ¿sanan los curanderos?

Definitivamente, no puedo afirmarlo con una respuesta concreta, pues todo depende de la situación, del paciente y de otros factores. Desde mi punto de vista, se queda en el aire la respuesta, no puedo inclinarme ante un positivismo o un negacionismo. Ambas respuestas son correctas, ya que existen diversos casos a tratar y genera un intenso debate en todos los sentidos. Es cierto que existieron y existen una mayoría de casos que son un auténtico fraude, de parafernalia sugestiva, cuyos tratamientos de nada sirven ante una enfermedad o problema emocional, salvo unos minutos de relax del paciente durante su consulta. Incluso algunos casos en estos últimos tiempos han terminado en los juzgados.

Sin embargo, también hay que mencionar diversos hechos que han facilitado una evidente mejoría, incluida la sanación por completo de su enfermedad, según los testimonios de quienes acudieron a visitar un sanador, a los cuales aplicamos el beneficio de la duda, aunque se carezca de un informe médico fiable de su historial o un seguimiento posterior. El número de beneficiados aumenta cuando se trata de lesiones y molestias musculares como desgarros, sobrecarga o esguinces. Sin embargo, bajo mi punto de vista, no puedo agrupar este tipo de sanadores en el grupo de curanderismos, ya que no es una enfermedad en sí. Los veo como personas con unos conocimientos fisioterapéuticos que están alejados del concepto de la enfermedad, y la mayoría de ellos no tratan ningún tipo de padecimientos crónicos o enfermedades, ya que no están a su alcance ni tienen ese «don» para curar.

Podemos observar que los curanderos, cada uno a su estilo, transfieren diversas energías que canalizan y liberan un mecanismo psicosomático que puede ser capaz de aliviar diversas dolencias incluso de sanar. Sin embargo, no todos pueden hacerlo, solo un bajo porcentaje de personas logran alcanzar esa cualidad de la sanación. El problema surge cuando se trata de buscar una evidencia médica que confirme esta sanación y sea aceptado por toda la comunidad médico-científica que el curandero ha sanado, aportando datos contrastados de una determinada enfermedad y su evolución. Ahí radica la mayoría de los problemas para confirmar la sanación o las virtudes de un sanador o curandero.

O quizá estemos confundidos y sean tan solo casos de sanación espontánea. Esto último es un estudio curioso y fascinante, ya que existen evidencias documentadas en hospitales que han remitido un cáncer o infecciones peligrosas. Posiblemente, sea debido a la reacción del sistema inmunológico del paciente o la apoptosis, un proceso de muerte celular, donde las células dañadas, infectadas o que ya no son necesarias en el organismo son eliminadas por el cuerpo sin causar inflamación ni dañar los tejidos circundantes, aunque esto último es bastante raro. En términos generales, se estima que puede rondar, según reportes, a 1 caso de cada 100 000 personas.

Aunque la fe de muchos pacientes les hace creer que ha sido por una mediación divina, lo que se denomina como un milagro médico. O bien podía ser el estado hipnótico que ha sido sometido el paciente a manos del curandero, según sus teorías, el cuerpo puede responder de manera más efectiva ante una enfermedad o dolencia.

Por ello es importante buscar una respuesta coherente ante todas las posibles sanaciones realizadas por los curanderos basándonos en cómo han logrado ese paso y el porqué de esa sanación.

A menudo ha sucedido que muchas personas ya estaban curadas o en el proceso final de su curación que, ante su impaciencia, acuden a los curanderos por probar unas alternativas totalmente diferentes a las convencionales. Tal y como se aprecia, existen muchas respuestas ante las posibles sanaciones, incluso es probable que solo sean enfermedades psicológicas, es decir, solo existen en la mente del paciente y realmente no tiene nada, son las denominadas «personas hipocondríacas». Pero no es menester quitar mérito en algunos casos que sí han podido realizar diversos curanderos con métodos naturales y efectivos.

¿Cómo alcanzan ese éxito o popularidad en su zona?

Observando diversos casos acontecidos en varias zonas de la geografía española, las aportaciones de hemeroteca de antaño, revistas, libros de diversos profesionales médicos, varios encuentros con antiguos pacientes, curanderos retirados… parece que nos indican que el éxito o el fiasco como figura sanadora radica en la colaboración que obtiene de los pacientes tratados.

El éxito se obtiene a menudo por la propia seguridad del paciente, su disposición a colaborar, su confianza y fe en sus manos, hace que obtenga un resultado óptimo en su tratamiento. Sin embargo, la ausencia de fe en el curandero o un ambiente de escepticismo y suspicacia hacen enrarecerse la determinación en sanar su problema de salud o dolencia.

El factor psicológico influye mucho en el resultado final, además de conseguir la confianza del paciente, en las zonas rurales más aisladas geográficamente marca también su folclore local para creer en las sanaciones milagrosas, causado por las numerosas apariciones marianas, leyendas de almas en pena, espectros por sus lares, presencia de brujas y hasta las presencias de seres mágicos como duendes. Todo en su conjunto ha aportado su granito de arena a la fe, ya que los curanderos de su comarca eran los mediadores o recursos frente a los fenómenos extraños, ya que aportaban los amuletos y diversas protecciones, detalles que con el paso del tiempo han reforzado la figura del curandero como personaje primordial

¿Cómo se gana la confianza del paciente y desprende esa buena voluntad de que va a curarle?

La pregunta correcta, previamente, es por qué acuden a un curandero. ¿Qué está pasando con los profesionales de la salud para que aumenten (al menos en estos últimos años) las consultas a los curanderos?

Personalmente, una de las causas principales se debe a un fracaso en la atención por parte del facultativo titulado (médico de cabecera, hospital…), no por desconocimiento de la enfermedad e ignorar el tratamiento adecuado, sino que se debe a la ausencia de empatía y nulo interés que se interesan y preocupan por su paciente que entra a consulta. Solo somos parte de su labor, sin más, no les preocupa nada nuestro futuro bienestar una vez que abandonemos su consulta. ¿Cuántas veces hemos acudido a nuestro médico de consultorio local y nos ha despachado en un suspiro?

Esto hace que, a menudo, en nuestra maravillosa mente actúe de forma diferente, vilipendiamos la atención del facultativo, pese a darle una acertada receta farmacéutica que hará remitir su dolencia. La mayoría de los pacientes piensan que solo somos un número. No hay cercanía humana. Eso es justo lo contrario, en muchos aspectos, de lo que encontraremos con un curandero: el factor humano, la empatía, el interés por el paciente por detalles ajenos a su dolencia.

Existen casos que también hacen dar un extraño giro en las consultas médico-hospitalarias y desanima al paciente:

«no tiene cura», «está complicado» o «va a peor», por poner unas expresiones de ejemplo. Esto hace que miremos con desesperanza la posible mejoría, que afecte a nuestro ánimo psicológico o, como puede ocurrir a menudo, no estemos conformes con la observación del facultativo y opten en la búsqueda de otra opinión médica o fuera de la ciencia: el milagro, la fe, la última esperanza que se aferran y en la que no tienen nada que perder.

Los curanderos saben manejar los tiempos de la naturaleza psicológica, saben el punto ideal donde atrapar al paciente, saben escuchar al paciente, se suman a sus preocupaciones diarias, de su familia, de su trabajo y hasta de sus aficiones literarias, gastronómicas o deportivas, si fuera preciso. Sobre todo saben comprender su enfermedad, le abren las puertas a la esperanza, exponiendo sus virtudes, estimulando los sentimientos del paciente.

Una de las virtudes de las que también se hacen valer para sumar adeptos o pacientes es su perspectiva por su enfoque integral, abordando el bienestar emocional, mental y espiritual.

Con ello deseo explicar que no solo tratan las enfermedades cotidianas o padecimientos, también se aproximan a las desestabilidades y enajenaciones que afectan a la persona, pues consideran que su malestar es el resultado de un desequilibrio espiritual, magnético o energético incluso ligado a creencias que arrastran desde tiempos ancestrales basados en la hechicería, como el mal de ojo, chakras mal alineados, envidias, el «susto» (se refiere a una impresión o susto que se cree puede causar enfermedad), el mal de amores o supuestas posesiones, entre otros asuntos mágicos o esotéricos, y ahí el curandero suele ofrecerse como un intermediario entre lo terrenal y lo espiritual, cuyo trabajo consiste en ejercer de buscador de seres superiores, entidades de la naturaleza e incluso de los seres fallecidos del paciente o del propio curandero, cuyo objetivo no es más que buscar un consejo al problema presentado por el interesado.

¿Qué perfil tiene un curandero?

Sus prácticas, manuales de aplicación, ritos, oraciones y recetas magistrales son otras historias que abordaremos más adelante en este libro, pero hay algo que tienen en común la mayoría de los curanderos (tanto en hombres como en mujeres): proceden de entornos rurales y aislados geográficamente. Sí que se observa que hay más presencia femenina en las regiones de Galicia, Andalucía y la zona del País Vasco. Muy pocos, por no decir nadie, tenían una educación escolar básica. Esto no significa que tuvieran desconocimiento de la escritura y no supieran leer, aunque sea a niveles ínfimos. Este último punto en cuanto a lo educativo lo asumo durante un periodo que abarca desde 1900 a 1970: su educación fue adquirida a través de sus familiares, mediante la observación, son autodidactas y, por supuesto, la práctica paulatina.

Son buenos conocedores de su hábitat, conocen bien las virtudes de las plantas, gracias a los aprendizajes y conocimientos de su entorno natural incluso. Pese a su escaso nivel pedagógico, algunos sabían leer, especialmente las mujeres, lo cual les aportó unos complementos extras para sus prácticas de herboristerías y la aplicación de recetas.

Uno de esos libros que han recurrido algunos curanderos y sanadoras que tenían la virtud de saber leer era *Dioscórides*, traducido por Andrés Laguna, que recopiló esos conocimientos de las plantas medicinales. También disponían de algunos libros de interés religioso basados en la vida de los santos que incluían episodios de sanaciones y sus plegarias para poder invocarlos y solicitar su mediación con su noble objetivo de curar, que fueron un modo de inspiración a la hora de dirigir sus ensalmos.

Otro ejemplar que muchos han consultado es un clásico y recurrido grimorio: *El libro de San Cipriano*, ya que sus páginas contienen diversas oraciones, conjuros y remedios para ciertas enfermedades, especialmente cuando nos acercamos a ese mundo esotérico y espiritual denominado «mal de ojo». Aunque no todos estaban en posesión de estos ejemplares, poseer estos manuales era un privilegio en sus tiempos.

Realmente, sus libros oficiales eran las notas que guardaban de sus ancestros, anotaciones en cuartillas sueltas o personajes que les enseñaron el arte del curanderismo.

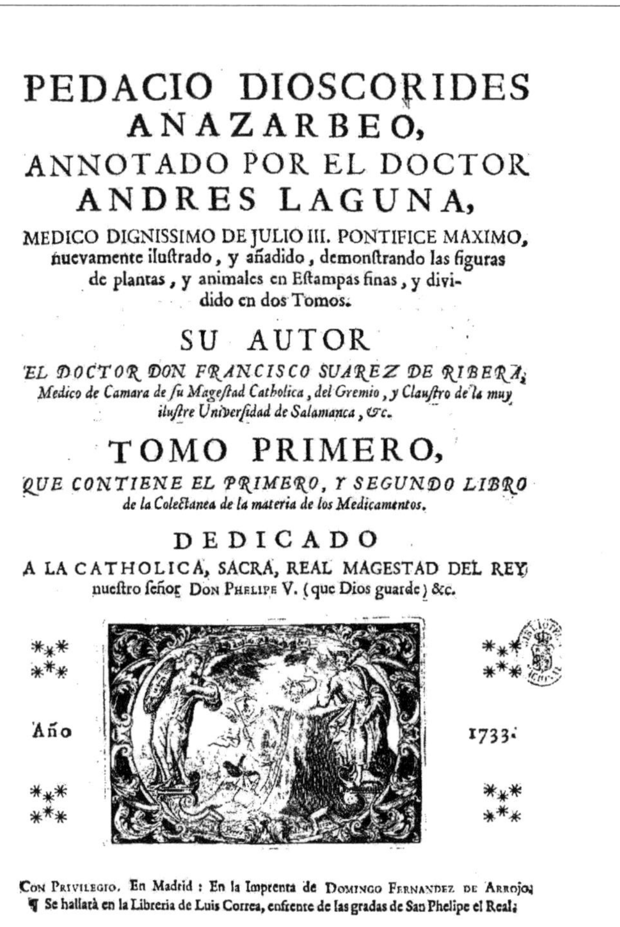

PEDACIO DIOSCORIDES
ANAZARBEO,
ANNOTADO POR EL DOCTOR
ANDRES LAGUNA,
MEDICO DIGNISSIMO DE JULIO III. PONTIFICE MAXIMO, ñuevamente iluftrado, y añadido, demonftrando las figuras de plantas, y animales en Eftampas finas, y dividido en dos Tomos.

SU AUTOR
EL DOCTOR DON FRANCISCO SUAREZ DE RIBERA, Medico de Camara de fu Mageftad Catholica, del Gremio, y Clauftro de la muy iluftre Univerfidad de Salamanca, &c.

TOMO PRIMERO,
QUE CONTIENE EL PRIMERO, Y SEGUNDO LIBRO de la Coleétanea de la materia de los Medicamentos.

DEDICADO
A LA CATHOLICA, SACRA, REAL MAGESTAD DEL REY nueftro feñor Don Phelipe V. (que Dios guarde) &c.

Año   1733.

Con Privilegio. En Madrid : En la Imprenta de Domingo Fernandez de Arrojo, ¶ Se hallatà en la Libreria de Luis Correa, enfrente de las gradas de San Phelipe el Real.

6. Dioscórides, un manual de importancia para el curanderismo rural.

La facilidad para generar empatía, saber escuchar al prójimo, sentir los problemas de su comunidad como algo propio…, también forma parte de ese perfil general de un sanador. Todo esto es primordial para su puesta en escena, le facilita ganarse un respeto dentro su entorno y una notable popularidad, evidentemente, siempre que su labor no se desvíe o se produzca una tragedia, bien por mala praxis o por desvaríos, estados de histeria, consumo de psicotrópicos o estados de esquizofrenia.

Por último, algo evidente es el aumento en los últimos años de consultas de sanadores y diferentes curanderas por parte de la inmigración procedente desde las regiones subsaharianas y de Sudamérica, donde existe una cultura muy amplia de acudir a un curandero local de sus tierras.

Esto no es nuevo, sino una herencia de su pasado tradicional de antes de la llegada de los europeos y su influencia. Este movimiento migratorio de personas ha propiciado la llegada de otros conocimientos curativos desde diferentes regiones, al igual que sus creencias religiosas, suministraron un desarrollo propio y casi exclusivo en el continente americano.

Respecto al origen africano, sus tradiciones y prácticas de curanderismo se han integrado paulatinamente en Europa, especialmente en Francia e Inglaterra, donde los curanderos de origen africano ofrecen terapias rituales a las personas de esta diáspora basándose en las costumbres de sus países de origen, donde el uso de diferentes plantas, masajes, cantos y otros rituales forman parte de su universo mágico de la sanación y prosperidad, incluidas las ceremonias de invocación, aunque muchos de ellos están más cerca de la manipulación mental y la difusión del miedo a través de los cultos vudú o yoruba de origen africano. De hecho, utilizan este recurso para amedrentar a sus pacientes a cargo de *nganga*, el sanador espiritual, indicando que ocurrirá una desgracia al paciente o sus allegados si no siguen sus pautas. Es una forma de retener al cliente y seguir ganado beneficios a costa de muchas ignorancias y desconocimientos culturales.

Creer o no creer en sus poderes mágicos es un dogma de fe, sea cual sea su origen.

III. ¿CUÁNDO Y COMO SURGE LA PRÁCTICA DEL CURANDERISMO?

La práctica ancestral del curanderismo está arraigada en todas las tradiciones culturales y espirituales de cualquier ámbito geográfico. Por ello, es muy difícil determinar en qué momento surge o el origen exacto y su antigüedad. Se cree que su base parte de las más profundas raíces de la prehistoria y la evolución del ser humano.

7. Ilustración de un chamán en Siberia (s. XVII).
Imagen: Wikipedia, Nicolaes Witsen.

Muchos expertos en el estudio de los orígenes de la medicina, del desarrollo humano y de la antropología citan la figura del chamán como la base del nacimiento de este oficio, posiblemente para superar la muerte primero y sanarse en los momentos necesarios, junto a la exégesis de la naturaleza y hasta la interpretación de los sueños. Aunque no es la única propuesta, pues el curanderismo es mucho más diverso que la propuesta chamánica, pese a ello, ha sido una figura clave para el desarrollo de las prácticas de sanación.

Asumieron que existían motivos suficientes para que a estos personajes de antaño se les atribuyesen unos poderes mágicos inimaginables o el «don» de sanar. La humanidad siempre ha confiado en los poderes prodigiosos de forma inconsciente, sobre todo si alguien en su tribu o su colectivo disponía de una persona adecuada para ser ese mediador entre lo físico y lo espiritual.

Los chamanes eran figuras importantes en muchas sociedades antiguas o en sus clanes y se creía que tenían la capacidad de comunicarse con el mundo espiritual para curar enfermedades, resolver problemas sociales que pudieran surgir y, sobre todo, poder guiar a sus comunidades a través de sus ritos, visiones, sueños o prácticas de índole mágica.

Tras ellos, a través de los siglos y las civilizaciones, surgen otras figuras como los *swnw* (puede traducirse como «el que cuida del enfermo» y se pronuncia, aproximadamente, como «sunu») del antiguo Egipto, que practicaban una mezcla de medicina y magia.

En la zona de la región de Mesopotamia los médicos eran conocidos como *asû* y se encargaban de las enfermedades físicas usando diversas plantas botánicas y otros tratamientos, mientras que sus compañeros llamados *âšipu* trataban las diferentes enfermedades espirituales mediante unos rituales y misteriosos conjuros, lo que puedo describir en una palabra más acorde a la mayoría: «exorcistas», aplicando rituales de purificación con agua, objetos simbólicos, invocaciones a los dioses Ea o Marduk, incluso a través de un rito llamado «transferencia», que consiste en traspasar el mal del paciente a un animal (ave, cabra…) y después sacrificar ese animal infectado lejos del lugar. Este rito ha perdurado en el mundo del curanderismo a través de diversas adaptaciones, incluso en España o Italia, se ha utilizado este recurso por algunos curanderos para expulsar algunos maleficios transfiriendo ese mal a un objeto, para purificarlo después en agua bendita o bien destruirlo.

Llegarían posteriormente los populares druidas, que combinaban una maravillosa mezcla del conocimiento de la naturaleza y prácticas espirituales, sumando a ello unos elementos primordiales como amuletos, utilizar los ciclos estacionales y la astrología, invocaciones de deidades e incluso encantamientos. Todo ello conjugado a menudo para las sanaciones de su clan.

Uno de los conjuntos de anotaciones más antiguos que se conocen sobre medicina y sanaciones se remonta a unos 4700 años atrás (2697-2597 a. C.): el texto chino de *Huangdi Neijing,* que se basaba en la teoría del ying y el yang, además de conocer la circulación de la sangre antes que el científico William Harvey (1578-1657) —por lo visto, en Europa fuimos con bastante atraso en muchas facetas—. En sus anotaciones citan que tomaba el «pulso», que usaban drogas vegetales y que practicaban la acupuntura. Un texto que rechaza la participación de fuerzas maléficas en la enfermedad, señalando al estilo de vida, la edad y la alimentación como las causas de los problemas de salud. Esto último es muy actual en nuestro tiempo, pues muchas personas siguen comiendo mal y teniendo malos hábitos.

En los antiguos valles de la India, donde la naturaleza y la espiritualidad confluyen, existía una floreciente cultura de sanación. Además, ayudó a su desarrollo pertenecer a una de las regiones que habitualmente intercambiaban diversos objetos y conocimientos, gracias a la Ruta de la Seda, como también la filosofía y la espiritualidad. Además, se vio forzada crear dos tipos de medicina tradicional: la *unani,* exclusivamente para musulmanes, y la ayurvédica, para los hindúes de tradición védica.

8. William Harvey, en una de sus disecciones.

Posiblemente, durante el dominio del Imperio romano es cuando las prácticas de curanderismo más se extienden en nuestra geografía. El curanderismo en el Imperio romano era extremadamente diverso y sincretista, incorporando influencias y creencias de las tradiciones médicas griegas, egipcias, celtas y de otras culturas que el Imperio había conquistado o con las que había comerciado. Especialmente se alimentaron mucho de las tradiciones y de la medicina mágico-religiosa de la civilización griega.

Es importante examinar los antecedentes históricos durante la época romana y las raíces de estas prácticas en las culturas antiguas. Las tradiciones curativas que eventualmente se fusionarían en el curanderismo romano tienen muchas bases en sus orígenes de las prácticas chamánicas de las culturas prehistóricas, donde los chamanes eran figuras importantes que, como he citado en líneas anteriores, se creía tenían la capacidad de comunicarse con el mundo espiritual para curar enfermedades y problemas sociales.

Los curanderos romanos empleaban una variedad de métodos para tratar las enfermedades, que incluían el uso de hierbas medicinales, amuletos, rituales religiosos, oraciones, invocaciones de deidades, encantamientos y a veces incluso prácticas mágicas basadas en símbolos, incluso en auspicios, examinando el hígado y otras vísceras de un animal sacrificado para tomar una decisión o un augurio acerca de la enfermedad que cargaba el paciente.

Muchos aspectos del curanderismo romano estaban entrelazados con la religión. Los curanderos frecuentemente invocaban a los dioses, especialmente a Asclepio, el dios griego de la medicina, y a Esculapio, su contraparte romana, en busca de la sanación. Los templos de Asclepio, conocidos como *Asclepieions*, eran centros de curación donde los enfermos que acudían buscaban el tratamiento y la curación mediante sueños reveladores y rituales de purificación. Las consultas a los oráculos para interpretar los sueños eran importantes para entender sus enfermedades y poder actuar antes de que la situación pudiera empeorar.

Estos templos estaban gestionados por los llamados *aitromantes (yatromantes),* que eran unos médicos-videntes. Aunque su mayor virtud parece que estaba en la interpretación de los sueños. Se creía que la curación podía ocurrir a través de sueños reveladores, rituales de purificación y la intercesión directa de los dioses. Además de Asclepio, otros dioses y diosas también eran invocados por los curanderos según las necesidades específicas del paciente y la naturaleza de la enfermedad.

A pesar de ello, no estaban exentos de numerosos problemas, ya que las autoridades a menudo les perseguían bajo la acusación de realizar magia ilegal o de estafar a numerosos enfermos con medicaciones ineficaces, llegando a ocasionar la intoxicación grave y la posterior muerte del paciente. Se vieron presionados bajo una creciente vigilancia de los cargos romanos, incluso de aquellos que ya comenzaban una medicina más oficial e institucionalizada que provocó que muchos de ellos tuvieran que esconderse u ocultar sus prácticas sanadoras, gestos que no les impedía recibir visitas de pacientes que aún creían en las tradiciones medicinales y en la intervención espiritual. Posiblemente estemos ante los primeros curanderos clandestinos.

A pesar de las regulaciones y ciertos hostigamientos, el curanderismo romano dejó un legado duradero que continuó influyendo en la medicina y la cultura de las Europas medieval y moderna. Muchas de las prácticas y creencias asociadas con el curanderismo persistieron a lo largo de los siglos, adaptándose y evolucionando con el tiempo. Incluso en la actualidad, hay comunidades y regiones donde el curanderismo sigue siendo una forma importante de tratamiento y curación, especialmente en áreas rurales y entre poblaciones marginadas. Además, no podemos olvidar que el curanderismo romano contribuyó al desarrollo de la medicina empírica, al explorar nuevas formas de tratamiento y entender la relación entre la mente, el cuerpo y el espíritu.

Algo importante que se adapta bien en las prácticas de sanación durante el Imperio romano es la sanación por la palabra: los ensalmos.

Estos implican la curación o sanación a través de oraciones, remedios empíricos o fórmulas mágicas, si bien no es exclusiva del Imperio romano, pues es cierto que los griegos también tenían una larga tradición de prácticas mágicas y místicas, incluido el uso de encantamientos para la curación. Esta práctica también estaba presente en varias otras culturas que formaban parte del Imperio romano. Estos ensalmos podían ser recitados durante rituales religiosos, durante la administración de remedios o como parte de prácticas de purificación y protección. La creencia en el poder de las palabras para influir en la salud y el bienestar era común en muchas culturas de la Antigüedad, incluida la romana.

No olvidemos que en el contexto del Imperio romano hubo una sincretización de prácticas mágicas y religiosas entre las diversas culturas y regiones que componían el Imperio. Esto significaba que las prácticas de curación por la palabra o los cantos, incluso acompañados de melodías, podían haber sido compartidas, adaptadas y adoptadas por diferentes grupos étnicos y culturales dentro del Imperio, incluidos los griegos, los romanos y otras poblaciones, que ha llegado hasta nuestros días: los curanderos emplean oraciones y rezos a diversos personajes del santoral cristiano para sanar o influir en el proceso de sanación.

Esta evolución de las prácticas mágicas de sanación se detiene en esta época, durante el dominio de Al-Ándalus, época que también nos dejó otras costumbres y hábitos que aún perduran en las prácticas del curanderismo ibérico.

Desde el siglo VIII hasta el siglo XV, el curanderismo que aportó la cultura de Al-Ándalus fue una práctica multifacética que combinaba elementos de la medicina tradicional islámica, la magia, las técnicas de herbolaria y, por supuesto, la religión. La convivencia islámica durante algunas épocas con los cristianos y los judíos también ayudó e influyó significativamente en el desarrollo de las prácticas de curanderismo.

Esos añadidos que aportó el mundo islámico, a parte de su medicina, había que sumar los conocimientos de anatomía, la fisiología, la farmacopea y la astrología.

La astrología desempeñaba un papel importante en el diagnóstico y tratamiento de enfermedades, ya que se creía que los movimientos de los astros influían en la salud y el bienestar de las personas. Y esto también se sigue practicando hasta cierto punto, pues muchos sanadores de la actualidad creen en la influencia de los astros durante los procesos de la sanación y la responsabilidad de contraer problemas de salud.

Como sucede con las prácticas del Imperio romano y otras culturas anteriores al islam, también formaba parte de su manual de curanderismo la curación por ensalmos o por la palabra. Los curanderos a menudo invocaban a Alá y recitaban pasajes del Corán como parte de sus rituales de curación. Se creía que la fe y la devoción religiosa eran componentes importantes para la recuperación del vigor, salud y bienestar, y los enfermos eran alentados a poner su confianza en la voluntad de Alá para su curación. Tradiciones que aún resisten en la actualidad, la invocación. Quizá lo más importante es la implantación de sus prácticas en las zonas rurales y las clases más bajas, ya que la costumbre de ellos no distinguía de clases sociales y eran accesibles, además de ser más supersticiosas.

Ya en la Edad Media, fue un periodo de numerosos cambios políticos y culturales que, evidentemente, también afectó al desarrollo de la práctica del curanderismo en general. En esta época no fue nada fácil adaptarse a los cambios.

A medida que la Iglesia consolidaba su poder en Europa durante la Alta Edad Media, aumentaba al mismo tiempo la influencia de la religión en la práctica médica en todos los ámbitos. La Iglesia desconfiaba del curanderismo y lo consideraba una forma de herejía o brujería. Sin las quejas de los médicos y los primeros practicantes de cirugía, es muy posible que la Inquisición nunca hubiera perseguido estas prácticas, ya que tenían una obsesión por la confiscación de propiedades y bienes de los condenados, pero los curanderos en general eran pobres, muy pocos tenían una gran potestad de adquisición, era una economía de subsistencia.

La temida Inquisición, establecida en el siglo XII para erradicar la herejía religiosa, también tenía en su objetivo perseguir a los curanderos y sanadores locales, acusándolos de prácticas mágicas o demoníacas, especialmente al género femenino, ya que ellas contribuían a la elaboración de fórmulas de medicina natural, ejercían de comadronas y, evidentemente, calmaban diferentes dolencias. Este periodo de estigmatización del curanderismo contribuyó a una mayor marginalización de estas prácticas y al fortalecimiento del poder de la medicina oficial respaldada por la Iglesia. Pero no siempre ha sido objetivo del Tribunal perseguir el curanderismo. Por ejemplo, durante la segunda década del siglo XVIII el Tribunal de la Inquisición de Valencia mantuvo resuelta la persecución a los judíos, una situación que le permitió después poder prestar toda su atención y perseguir otros asuntos de interés como la hechicería y las prácticas ajenas a la fe de la Iglesia, como el curanderismo popular. Hasta el momento, estas personas apenas tuvieron incidencias o problemas con las autoridades. La Inquisición conocía quién practicaba el curanderismo y quiénes tenían más fama popular en Valencia, así como el tipo de habilidades que realizaban, de manera que fue muy fácil recurrir a ellas cuando hubo ausencia de otras ocupaciones para aplicar sus leyes de fe. Durante ese férreo control que ejercían, muchas personas que eran poseedoras de algunas facultades paranormales, como la videncia, tener instintos adivinos…, acabaron en la hoguera o castigados duramente, que luego la Iglesia ganó un aliado que sería fundamental para su persecución: la clase médica, que comenzaba sus primeros pasos y su formación en las primeras universidades.

Posiblemente, de este férreo control surja una actividad que se desarrolló especialmente durante los siglos XVI-XVIII, que era el «charlatanismo». Era una forma de vender sus panaceas en las plazas públicas, montando un espectáculo, donde daban fe de sus éxitos empleando falsos testimonios que se hacían pasar por personas curadas, con sus extraordinarios ungüentos, remedios de ingredientes estrambóticos y otros potingues extraños… Todo ello rodeado de parafernalia festiva, con música, juegos, bailes… Las autoridades operaban con relativa impunidad ante los charlatanes, salvo que existieran asuntos religiosos o señales de brujería en sus remedios.

A menudo y en diversos casos, la práctica del curanderismo era una forma de medicina espiritual, una alternativa que entraba en clara competencia con la religión, no solo la cristiana, y este motivo facilitó el aumento de la desconfianza y, por supuesto, la condena por parte de la Iglesia, que observaba claramente una seria amenaza a su control, especialmente en lo que respecta a la espiritualidad, porque para ellos todo estaba en manos de Dios. Sin embargo, el curandero sabía que no era así, sus conocimientos y virtudes con el contacto con la naturaleza facilitaba la mejoría y sanación de muchas enfermedades.

9. Charlatán, de Gerard Dou (1652).

Y así ha estado durante muchos años, clandestina y ocultada a los ojos de las temidas autoridades hasta la disolución de estos tribunales tan crueles e inhumanos, estaban forzados a realizar sus destrezas y habilidades en clandestinidad.

Sus prácticas se iban inspirando en las actuaciones de la naturaleza, de las experiencias con otros pacientes y de las herencias de culturas que han aportado a lo largo de los siglos.

Explorar los orígenes del curanderismo en el mundo rural de España de los principios del siglo xx nos lleva a un contexto donde la medicina académica era, a menudo, inaccesible para la mayoría de las personas, especialmente las que vivían en zonas más remotas geográficamente y desfavorecidas a nivel económico. Ser curandero era una alternativa asequible en términos generales por costo y proximidad, cuyas prácticas entre estas comunidades agrícolas y campesinas (en general) facilitó una curiosa evolución que entrelazaba las culturas y tradiciones locales.

En este entorno, los curanderos eran como una figura clave en el cuidado de la salud y el bienestar del área que habitaba, además de ser vistos como personajes con ciertas habilidades mágicas. Arraigados a las creencias locales, muchos de ellos heredaban sus conocimientos de generaciones anteriores, aunque también comenzaban a surgir otros curanderos, hechiceras, brujas… que adquirieron su experiencia y conocimientos a través de formación informal o tras una revelación mística.

A causa de ese temor heredado por el pasado de persecución inquisitorial, sus prácticas se han modificado y sus ritos también. Por esta causa, el curanderismo está estrechamente ligado a la religión católica, y muchos curanderos combinaban sus prácticas curativas con elementos de la fe cristiana. Las oraciones, invocaciones a santos y rituales religiosos eran comunes en las prácticas curanderas, y el paciente cree que la intervención divina juega un papel crucial en el proceso de curación, no el curandero, puesto que solo era una cortina de humo para ocultar su herejía.

Pero también es cierto que los curanderos de esa oscura España rural han abusado de sus privilegios en la comunidad para conseguir ganancias extras mediante rituales y recetas de efecto placebo, incluso basadas en el fraude o engaño premeditado, motivo que facilitó también a contribuir que aumentase la percepción sobre este oficio como negativo o pagano por parte de las autoridades eclesiásticas.

A pesar de todos los obstáculos y el arraigo en su ámbito cultural, esta práctica ha sido en numerosas ocasiones muy marginada por la medicina más común.

Pero se observa un curioso dato al alza: en los últimos años, he notado un aumento e interés por el estudio de las prácticas de curanderismo antiguas por parte de la medicina académica, ya que pueden verla como un accesorio más para mejorar el bienestar humano.

10. El hombre hechizado, de Francisco de Goya.

IV. LOS NEXOS DEL CURANDERISMO Y LA BRUJERÍA

El curanderismo y la brujería son, actualmente, experiencias y hábitos totalmente distintos. Sin embargo, han estado a lo largo de nuestra historia muy unidos y vinculados en la apreciación de la cultura popular y la condena por parte de las autoridades tanto religiosas, en su mayoría, como civiles. El curanderismo y el mundo de la brujería han viajado a la par, junto a la religión, al universo de la magia, y no existía una clara distinción durante la Edad Media entre la brujería y el curanderismo.

Comparten muchas similitudes y enfoques parecidos, pero existen unas pequeñas diferencias de una habilidad y la otra que, entre ambas praxis, diferencian sus contextos culturales y percepciones sociales. No olvidemos que se ha estigmatizado la figura femenina, siendo centro de cualquier acusación si era vista realizando alguna recolecta de plantas medicinales, hacer pócimas o brebajes. Las mujeres eran percibidas como una amenaza por la Iglesia por sus conocimientos y autonomía, lo cual contribuyó a que se las acusara más fácilmente de ser «brujas», una etiqueta que, en muchos casos, la aplicaron como una herramienta de control social para restringir el poder y la independencia de las mujeres. Los hombres, en cambio, se beneficiaron de los sesgos de género y del hecho de que sus prácticas eran vistas como un aporte de ayuda a la medicina y no una amenaza al orden establecido.

Analizando lo que pueden compartir entre el mundo de la brujería y el curanderismo, hay evidencias que no podemos pasar por alto, especialmente cuando involucran las prácticas espirituales y diversos rituales en sus métodos de curación.

En estos ritos coincide el uso de diversas plantas medicinales, oraciones de todo tipo (tanto religiosas como algunas de otra índole de fe) e incluso las invocaciones a las fuerzas espirituales de la naturaleza y la manipulación de las denominadas energías humanas, vitales o bioenergéticas, en las cuales pueden ser conducidas y se necesitan para solucionar esos desequilibrios magnéticos.

Lo más común entre ambas prácticas en la fuerte conexión con la naturaleza botánica incluso estaban sus hogares muy próximos a fuentes manantiales, bosques, entornos que actualmente llamamos «lugares de poder», ya que utilizaban ingredientes naturales de sus hábitats para sus diferentes fórmulas magistrales y algunos ritos. Ambas tradiciones valoran positivamente las propiedades medicinales y mágicas del amplio catálogo de la variedad de plantas, también un profundo uso y conocimiento de los minerales.

Aunque el curandero también ha tenido que adaptarse y buscar otras soluciones, crear nuevas recetas debido a los escasos recursos a su disposición, pues muchas plantas no crecen en ciertas zonas o eran complejas de conseguir. Muchos en la actualidad no salen al campo a buscar hierbas medicinales, ofrecen numerosos productos envasados (naturales o no) y esto hará que, posiblemente, la figura del curandero tradicional, aquel que buscaba lo mejor en el campo o bosques próximos, sin importar la estación del año y buscando posteriormente la bendición de su recolección con agua bendita o dejando su recolecta bajo protección de una imagen taumatúrgica o recibir una sencilla consagración por las manos del párroco local, sea una imagen que muy pronto desaparezca para siempre si no se eleva espiritualmente y se vincula con la naturaleza ancestral los actuales o los venideros interesados en el curanderismo.

Aquellos que buscaban nuevas plantas medicinales o simplemente recolectar las que necesitaban, se recogían a menudo en los días marcados por el calendario cristiano que estén relacionados con la sanación: san Blas, san Juan, san Roque, san Judas Tadeo… y aquellos manojos de plantas recolectadas se llevaban después a la iglesia local para que el párroco pudiera bendecirlos, gesto que, supuestamente, concedería un plus de carga positiva y efectividad en su uso junto con la aprobación de la iglesia, al tiempo que se le reconoce el poder de las plantas como un poder divino. En su conjunto, era un acervo de conocimientos de botánica transmitidos oralmente de generación en generación junto con sus tradiciones y devociones.

Por supuesto, comparten una dura realidad histórica: la estigmatización y la persecución. Ambas fueron duramente castigadas y calificadas como prácticas heréticas o supersticiosas. Precisamente en este momento histórico es cuando comienza a distanciarse una práctica de otra, influida por el poder religioso, el social y, poco después, el científico.

Y de esto existe un amplio conjunto de archivos y juicios de la Inquisición y la Justicia Civil a lo largo de varios siglos, aunque el mundo de la brujería fue más hostigado y castigado por ello. No solo fueron marcados para aplicar su acoso en toda Europa, pues en el continente americano es muy abundante la información acerca de procesos inquisitoriales y diversas denuncias tras la llegada de los europeos.

Una muestra son las inculpaciones en los territorios coloniales de ultramar desde 1569, cuando, en el virreinato del Perú y México, la Inquisición se instauró con sus tribunales, que se basaban en la recurrida acusación de actos de brujería, algo que siempre han negado los indígenas locales, ya que ellos se basaban en sus ancestrales tradiciones de medicina específica de su entorno o, en algún caso extremo, recurrir a algún tipo de ritual para detener los maleficios. Siempre negaron los indígenas ante los tribunales religiosos que volasen en escobas, invocasen las fuerzas del mal o usasen otros medios como las narraciones fantasiosas de brujería que procedían del viejo continente. Siempre se han considerado curanderos, que nunca han tenido inclinaciones por ser brujos o brujas locales y, evidentemente, no forman parte ni actúan como el folclore europeo de la brujería. En esos remedios suelen utilizar como sanadores ajo, tabaco, albahaca, ruda o congona, entre otras plantas, dependiendo de la zona.

Sin embargo, durante los procesos aceptaron los cargos de invocar al demonio sin saber quién era realmente, admitieron acudir a diferentes cerros sagrados como el Chimborazo (Parque Natural Henri Pittier, en Venezuela) o Samborondón (Ecuador) para invocar a diversas fuerzas maléficas tras estar sometidos a terribles interrogatorios que incluían la tortura, confesaron bajo ese brutal martirio con tal de parar el dolor más inhumano conocido.

Desde el nacimiento de los tribunales inquisitorios, el curanderismo está centrado en sanar un problema de salud y encontrar el bienestar de las personas que acuden en su auxilio o consulta. Buscan mitigar el dolor, los diferentes problemas que exponen de salud en su consulta y también aportan sugerencias espirituales al interesado.

El curanderismo, tras la imposición inquisitorial, excluye la práctica de brujería, aunque tienen la capacidad para usarla, ya que usan las mismas recetas de sanación en muchos casos, según mis consultas y análisis de diversos trabajos de antropología. Tienen prohibido ejercerla, pues de emplearse perderían sus virtudes benignas para sanar, ya que el objetivo de la brujería, en numerosas ocasiones y en esa visión de sus conceptos mágicos, tiene un aura oscura, donde la diferencia se establecía en la intención percibida y en el juicio de la sociedad.

Para protegerse de la persecución, los que decidieron diferenciarse de las prácticas alejadas de la ética cristiana no dudaron en señalar y acusar a los que seguían ejerciendo prácticas ancestrales con tal de ganarse los posibles clientes y, de paso, las «simpatías» de los jueces de zona. Insisten los curanderos en que no son brujos ni practican actos de magia ni nunca invocaban al diablo, sino que sus invocaciones eran a Dios y a la Santísima Trinidad, al menos en la vertiente europea. Sin embargo, en el continente americano cambian un poco algunos conceptos de invocación, ya que incluyen referencias a las fuerzas de naturaleza e incluso a ese sincretismo que se ha fraguado con la llegada de las creencias africanas al continente americano en el siglo XVI a través de la trata de esclavos, dando lugar a prácticas de sanación basadas en la religión yoruba, vudú, umbanda o candomblé junto con las creencias de los bantús, que con ellos también viajaban los denominados *ngangas*, figuras clave en las comunidades bantús que ejercían de curanderos y chamanes. Ellos buscaban alternativas botánicas en el continente americano para sustituir sus remedios originales de África.

Ellos eran como intermediarios entre los humanos y el mundo espiritual que desempeñaban un papel importante en la curación, la protección contra los malos espíritus y la adivinación. Su presencia fue primordial, puesto que dejó una herencia de prácticas muy llamativas aplicadas a la salud popular de estas comunidades de origen africano.

11. Los cultos de origen afroamericano han sido y son recursos en la actualidad para protegerse en salud y del mal de ojo. Imagen: A. Beitia.

No era lo habitual en la trata humana, pues a menudo solían sustituirlos otros esclavos que tenían algún que otro conocimiento, en un momento crucial de su historia, no por la esclavitud, sino por la presencia de enfermedades que nunca habían tenido y las nuevas condiciones climáticas a las que se enfrentaban tras ser forzados a abandonar sus orígenes.

La disparidad del curanderismo con la brujería contiene otros objetivos más amplios, incluyendo la sanación y manipulación de energías. Debemos incluir una sublime diferencia en sus ritos: el uso frecuente de la adivinación, los hechizos y la elaboración de amuletos para proteger el hogar o la salud, además de realizar rituales estacionales o ciclos lunares.

Históricamente, el ámbito del curanderismo ha tenido un concepto mucho más amable y axiomático en las culturas del mundo más rural, donde su presencia era respetada. En contraste con la brujería, la percepción dentro de la sociedad era más nefasta. Generaba temor y desconfianza, y siempre la vinculaban con el mundo de la magia negra o aplicar sus poderes adquiridos por fuerzas malignas para fines de mala fe, a destruir hogares y cosechas e incluso a propagar la enfermedad, aunque todo este conjunto de acusaciones ha sido más difundido por las autoridades religiosas para crear un aura de malicia ante la sociedad y alejarse de estas prácticas, lo que generó un ambiente de desconfianza y colgó al mundo de la brujería el sambenito de ser culpable de todos los males que pudiera acontecer en su día a día. En esta persecución buscaban controlar a la figura femenina y su autonomía, buscar chivos expiatorios para los males sociales y, sobre todo, eliminar tradiciones paganas y la sabiduría popular.

No era así la figura de la bruja, esta palabra tan humillante en muchos sentidos, y su vínculo iba más allá de una simple acusación de realizar magia, pues empezó a utilizarse para describir a mujeres (y a veces hombres, aunque en menor medida) que practicaban la magia negra o hacían pactos con el diablo.

No es menester olvidar que la brujería ha sido condenada a causa de sus prácticas, que las involucraban con el diablo y la aplicación de maleficios. Todo lo contrario al curanderismo, pues, aunque existen algunos casos de vínculos con el mal, no ha sido tan estrechamente relacionado con el mundo sombrío y maligno que la imaginación popular atribuye a la brujería. Quizá la rebeldía de aquellas personas, que practicaban la brujería basada en la sanación y que ayuda a la salud, se negaba a sincretizar con la creencia cristiana sus ritos de sanación ancestrales, y tal vez ahí esté la clave de su demonización. En este grupo es donde surge la desconfianza de una sociedad cegada y manipulada por la Iglesia. Esto también era un factor del que se aprovecharon las primeras academias médicas para poner veto a esos hábitos que no podían controlar, sobre todo influían a los altos cargos de los diversos feudos, ya que eran ellos quien ejercían de médicos y la medicina académica solo estaba al alcance de las clases económicamente más pudientes.

Para los tribunales de la Inquisición, en términos generales dentro del mundo del curanderismo, hechicería o brujería, serán siempre suspicaces de herejías aquellos que realizasen ritos oscuros, sortilegios, auspicios…, si para ello recurrían al uso de elementos sagrados como el agua bendita, hostias consagradas y santos óleos o no mostraban respeto alguno por los sacramentos, ya que no estaban autorizados para su uso.

Un vínculo que se atribuyen a estas prácticas de brujería eran las parteras, que, al margen de su amplio conocimiento del parto y del cuerpo femenino, tenían una notable agudeza para usar la botánica en su uso medicinal, un motivo que las parteras eran respetadas en sus comunidades. Eran, además, las primeras protectoras contra el llamado «mal de ojo», ya que al venir al mundo ese retoño, le aplicaban aceite en la frente, haciendo una cruz o un símbolo protector mientras recitaban una oración, usaban algunas plantas protectoras como romero, ruda… o bien le ataban un hilo de color rojo para protegerlo de las envidias. Otra muestra más curiosa es el uso de la saliva: solía escupirse sus propias manos la partera antes de tocar al recién nacido o bien le solía soltar un escupitajo a su pequeño cuerpo para protegerlos de cualquier maleficio. Ambas prácticas eran para protegerlo de cualquier energía nociva, influencia maligna o «mal de ojo».

El hecho de escupir tiene connotaciones purificadoras y protectoras, ya que es una forma de expulsar algo negativo, y aplicarlo a los recién nacidos ejercería como un escudo protector ante cualquier maleficio o intento de hechizos. Por poner un ejemplo, en la actualidad, por algunas zonas rurales de Grecia, el sur de Italia e incluso la costa turca se hace un gesto de imitar escupir simbólicamente tres veces como acto de protección contra el mal fario o envidias al nacer un bebé.

Sin embargo, estos conocimientos eran un arma de doble filo, pues también las hacían sospechosas a los ojos de las autoridades eclesiásticas y civiles. Además, ejercían normalmente alejadas de la vista y control de los hombres. Estaban basculando entre el curanderismo y la brujería, sin olvidar que podían ejercer como la conexión en esos momentos críticos de la muerte con su presencia, apaciguando al moribundo o simplemente estando presentes para vigilar, como cuidadoras paliativas y oradoras por su alma. Esta relación de vida-muerte (partera y matrona de la muerte) les ha concedido un estatus místico, que por un lado agradecen su buena labor humanitaria atendiendo a moribundos o personas con procesos dolorosos terribles, pero por otro lado puede señalarlas como máximas responsables de la muerte de neonatos.

La sociedad de aquel tiempo estaba arraigada en la imaginación popular con una connotación negativa y dañina. A menudo los curanderos y, especialmente, las parteras han sido consideradas como brujas malvadas y con un historial espeluznante, a las que se culpa de cualquier mal.

*12. Las matronas también cumplieron facetas de
curanderismo y fueron perseguidas por la Inquisición.
Imagen: Eucharius Rösslin, Thomas Raynalde (1545).*

Esto era a causa de la terrible e inhumana publicación del
Malleus Maleficarum, escrito por Heinrich Kramer y James
Sprenger en 1487, que señala a las parteras de usos maléficos de sus conocimientos y habilidades para matar a los
recién nacidos o dedicar algunos de ellos al diablo. Aunque
realmente uno de sus más duros perseguidores era Nicolau
Aymerich, que publicó el *Directorium Inquisitorum* y fue el verdadero precursor del *Malleus Maleficarum*. En dicha obra de
Nicolau, ya se describen numerosas prácticas de brujería,
cultos, conjuros y otras consideradas pecaminosas y de ser
unas herejías que merecen el máximo castigo.

El acceso al mundo de la obstetricia por parte de la medicina académica era el último refugio al que se aferraban las
mujeres curanderas. Esta práctica estaba solo en sus manos,

pues conocían bien el cuerpo femenino, sus ritmos y los procesos de gestación y parto. Sin embargo, se lo «expropiaron», añadiendo un cartel de nefastas personas en sus labores médicas durante el parto como el uso ilegal de hierbas, marginando su figura por género. Esta actitud ayudó a crear en sus regiones una red casi clandestina de mujeres parteras para recurrir a ellas, no solo por salud, que también, sino porque albergaban muchas sapiencias y conocían bien la botánica de la medicina popular. Por temor a las autoridades, se recurre a otro tipo de parteras, que pueden ser una vecina (por tener algo de experiencia propia), enfermeras monásticas, algún clérigo con conocimientos medicinales… O bien pueden dar luz a solas, lo cual aumentaba en términos generales el riesgo durante un parto.

Sanar y ayudar al prójimo estaba vetado para ellas, por eso supuso un serio problema la aplicación de esta normativa impuesta por la Inquisición en los pequeños núcleos poblacionales, al no disponer de una persona que se dedicase a la asistencia médica. Consideraban que sus prácticas estaban auspiciadas por el diablo, así que, si las curas de estas sanadoras daban resultado, constituía una obstrucción a las normas de la divinidad de la Iglesia e imponían su dictamen de que fue la mano del mismo demonio quien había ejercido la virtud de curar e intervenir, no las fuerzas celestiales. Incluso si recurrían a amuletos para ayudar durante la gestación y el posparto, por ejemplo, recomendaban muchas curanderas/parteras el uso de una piedra llamada «limonita», conocida popularmente en algunos sitios como «piedra aquilina». Este mineral se ataba en el brazo derecho de la mujer embarazada y prevenía partos prematuros, y después de dar luz se pone esa piedra en el muslo derecho de la mujer, ya que la ayudaría a proteger al recién nacido de diversas enfermedades de neonatos y las posibles influencias negativas.

Esto era evidente para la Iglesia, son recursos paganos y de intrusismo que solo sus médicos y sus religiosos tenían ese poder de ser mediadores a través de Dios, no en las manos de una vulgar mujer que se dedicaba, a menudo, a tareas de campo o cuidar la familia, incluso de hombres cuyas virtudes también eran el campo, la herrería y la ganadería, por citar unos ejemplos.

Sin embargo, estos códigos suponían un problema, ya que la Iglesia tenía una doble vara de medir y juzgar, así que solo afectaba en los niveles más bajos y en la pobreza. Los reyes, burgueses de alta subsistencia, diversas autoridades de notable poder… permitían que pudieran asistirlos esas mujeres con conocimientos de salud si sus médicos no daban con la solución a sus males, actitud que la Iglesia miraba al otro lado, incluso de ayudar o encargarse de los nacimientos de su matrimonio.

Estas mujeres, con sus profundos conocimientos de curanderismo, fueron vilipendiadas y despojadas de muchos conocimientos, aunque estos se transmitían oralmente y pudo mantenerse un gran legado tradicional. Estas prácticas basadas en la salud han ido superando etapas, rebeliones frente a ese poder de atribuirse los conocimientos de la medicina por parte de las autoridades y vetando todo conocimiento ancestral que fuera impropio de las leyes eclesiásticas. Tan vetadas estaban estas habilidades que los remedios académicos no daban resultado y temían usar las recetas de las llamadas «brujas», que estaba penadas. Por ello surgen unos remedios absurdos como la sangría, el uso de sanguijuelas, rezar a Dios y utilizar elementos imposibles y fantasiosos, incluso en prácticas que se remontan a Hipócrates y que luego replanteaba Galeno, estudios que se basan en la teoría de los cuatro humores: sangre, flema, bilis negra y bilis amarilla, algo bastante alejado de nuestra actualidad de salud.

Precisamente esa publicación editada por los inquisidores alemanes sirvió de base para sus leyes, facilitó la separación y un cierto distanciamiento del curanderismo con los métodos de brujería que, hasta ese momento, puedo sugerir que estaban casi de la mano ambas prácticas, pues era difícil distinguir una habilidad de otra. Además, era una forma de señalar a unos grupos o personas individuales y facilitaba el señalamiento por la sociedad y, con seguridad, un juicio en los tribunales de la Santa Fe inspirados en este tipo de manuales contra hechicerías, brujerías y herejías.

La brujería, como práctica mágica o ritualista que tiene gran parte del colectivo humano en la actualidad, no existía, y las personas acusadas de brujería eran en su mayoría víctimas de una paranoia colectiva, misoginia y conflictos sociales. Tampoco existía una diferenciación de sexo, ni aspectos físicos de las personas que utilizaban la brujería.

Hoy puedo citar que la brujería es una práctica que se basa en el respeto a la naturaleza y la conexión espiritual, que debería estar alejada de todo tipo de magia llamada «magia negra o demoníaca», no tiene nada que ver, está más cerca de un curanderismo espiritual que físico. Lamentablemente, estos personajes que se dedicaban al curanderismo que estaba vetado por la Inquisición, las mal llamadas «brujas», las mujeres parteras, los pobres y los analfabetos, no nos ha dejado apenas testimonios escritos de sus remedios, por ese miedo a las instituciones eclesiásticas, así que casi todo aquello de lo que se dispone nos ha llegado a través de la tradición oral y las experiencias vividas.

Contra esas maldades que iban de boca en boca desde épocas oscuras sobre las brujas no existía otro remedio para combatirlas que usar la magia o las virtudes que aportaba la religión. Esa maldad tan recurrida era el llamado «mal de ojo», y para ello se apelaba a la ayuda del poder divino contra un maleficio que tiene un origen que no es material, sino que proviene de fuerzas o entidades no físicas, incluso sobrenaturales. Por eso se considera como una enfermedad del «alma», y esos médicos que podían hacer frente a esa maldad brujeril eran los religiosos o, evidentemente, los curanderos, que estaban más próximos a la fe y conocían bien las artimañas y sus antídotos.

Esta conclusión no es generalizada, pues en muchas localidades rurales del interior ven el mal de ojo como un enigma sin resolver, ya que nadie causa el mal por hacer daño, sino de forma involuntaria. Por ejemplo, una mujer que menstrua en Viernes Santo puede «aojar» sin querer. Otra forma de temer el maleficio es cuando llega un forastero a su aldea, bien puede ser un sencillo caminante que pasa por allí o un simple trabajador que viene de lejos para hacer alguna reparación. Sus dos ojos pueden venir cargados de energía nociva que transportan desde otros lares y «contagiarla» a otras personas.

Protegerse del mal de ojo requiere un estudio profundo de esta superstición, analizando sus orígenes y vínculos con la hechicería, brujería… La atribución del mal de ojo puede ser una forma habitual de acusar a alguien de tener malas intenciones o de practicar brujería, lo cual puede tener consecuencias sociales significativas, especialmente en comunidades donde la brujería es temida o condenada según normas inquisitoriales.

El curanderismo ha hecho gala de saber hacer frente y sentir si una persona estaba «hechizada», utilizando variedades técnicas para tratar este mal que siempre ha estado supeditado a otro mal: la envidia.

Para ello recurren a menudo a exorcismos, inspirados en oraciones del libro Enchiridion leonis papae, el libro del papa León III publicado en Roma en 1660, del que fueron llegando diversas copias hasta nuestra época. En ese curioso libro se pueden encontrar exorcismos contra mordeduras de animales venenosos, la tristeza, lombrices… y, por supuesto, el mal de ojo o aojamiento.

Es llamativo el ritual que incluye contra lombrices, pues se lo relaciona por su aspecto con la serpiente, siempre vista como el mal dentro de la Iglesia, a las que un curandero puede solucionar las molestias, y se dictamina un exorcismo para eliminarlas:

En el nombre de Jesús Nazareno, vosotras,
lombrices, convertidas en agua, marchéis de este cuerpo.
Por la señal de la Santa Cruz, hazte sana, criatura
de Dios, de toda enfermedad, y estos gusanos mueran al ins-
tante, y enseguida, arrojados fuera, salgan de tu cuerpo.

Tras la oración, se bendice por tres veces el cuerpo del afectado. Si no se recurriese a esta práctica de índole de fe religiosa, siempre quedará la tradición del uso de amuletos. Frente al mal de ojo, era tradicional protegerse de diversas formas, y tenemos buena prueba de ello en nuestra rica herencia cultural y ancestral en toda España. Quizá la más popular era la higa junto a las campanillas para ahuyentar el mal en los niños.

Indagar y tocar el mundo del curanderismo sin acceder al extraño poder del aojamiento es tarea complicada, pues todos los sanadores tienen su remedio para saber si estás bajo la influencia, y su reparación. A ello hay que añadir la dificultad en dar con sus oraciones, dado el hermetismo en que se mueve esta maldición. El mal de ojo, temido por muchos, encuentra su contraparte en los rituales y remedios de los curanderos, cuya destreza a menudo bordea lo que algunos consideran brujería, posiblemente esté muy unido a la brujería por una sencilla causa: las rezadoras.

Para combatir el mal, siempre se recurre a una mujer, que está más preparada para esto que un hombre, y puede ser una curandera o lo citado anteriormente: una rezadora. Tras sus ritos de limpieza, asume un riesgo posterior, el cansancio, los mareos, angustias… Esto ocurre porque, según tradiciones, el mal entra a la rezadora por desafiar a los poderes del maligno.

En resumen, puedo decir que las relaciones entre la brujería y el curanderismo son un fenómeno cultural complejo, y el mal de ojo es un término muy utilizado por los curanderos para describir un problema espiritual e incluso de salud, una práctica que tiene, según las creencias, la capacidad de dañar con una mirada envidiosa o malévola. Disponemos de numerosos recursos en medios de prensa con noticias de sociedad, donde surgen a menudo mujeres que se dedican a este menester de aplicar remedios de sanación, como este ejemplo de una curandera de la Alpujarra granadina, Ana Manuela Rodríguez, a sus 77 años en el momento de la noticia:

El mal de ojo lo puede echar una persona de forma intencionada o voluntaria. Cuando es intencionada es por envidias, malas energías, etcétera. También curo sosteniendo en mis manos una fotografía de la persona que precise que la sane. El mal de ojo lo hacen hombres y mujeres. Aquí se lo han hecho a unas personas para ver si se las cargaban pero no se las han cargado porque las curé yo. Yo tengo más de 500 fotografías de gente de muchos lugares. Y cuando algunas de ellas me llana para que la sane y atienda, busco su foto y al verla y tocarla desaparece el mal. Yo soy muy católica. Mis santos son lo primero que tengo. Por ejemplo, a la entrada de mi casa tengo instalada una hornacina de madera de mi propiedad con la imagen de la Virgen Milagrosa. En mi vivienda tengo muchos santos para que me protejan y porque los quiero mucho. Todas las noches, antes de acostarme rezo mucho.

Ideal (15/11/2021).

Los sanadores son a menudo vistos como intermediarios entre los reinos físico y espiritual, y utilizan una amplia gama de técnicas antiguas para diagnosticar y tratar el mal de ojo.

La brujería y el curanderismo tienen un vínculo muy aferrado en el control del mal de ojo, que revela una compleja interacción entre la superstición, la fe y el deseo humano de comprender y manejar lo desconocido. Los sanadores siguen siendo símbolos prominentes que transmiten esperanza y protección contra las fuerzas invisibles e inescrutables, y lo seguimos haciendo, aunque no estemos recurriendo a ellos. Es tan frágil la línea que divide estas prácticas que, como se ha observado en este capítulo, numerosos curanderos se han visto rodeados de acusaciones de brujería y hechicería, especialmente en aquellos tiempos de intolerancia o superstición.

Ofrecían protecciones contra embrujos, aplicaban purificaciones o sanaciones que solo estaban en manos de Dios y eran vistos como empleados del diablo, capaces de utilizar los mismos poderes maléficos que pretendían combatir. La hechicería, más que una práctica del mal en sí, era entendida en el acervo popular como el uso de conocimientos ocultos y perversos para alterar el curso natural de las cosas, ya fuera para bien o para mal. Por ello, el curandero y el hechicero compartían a menudo el mismo espacio ambiguo en la mentalidad popular.

V. LA DIVERSIDAD CULTURAL Y SUS PRÁCTICAS DEL CURANDERISMO EN OTRAS CREENCIAS

Sería importante hacer una pequeña comparativa de tradiciones entre diversas etnias o regiones del mundo en el aspecto del mundo del curanderismo, pues creo que es importante para tener unos conceptos. No trato de hacer una tesis histórica de la medicina ni extraer una conclusión definitiva, ya que el mundo de los curanderos abarca un enorme espacio de estudio antropológico, pero merecía que dedicara unas líneas para observar ciertos detalles que unen a estos oficios del curanderismo, al menos en las facetas primordiales de sus objetivos y la tarea.

Aunque mantienen muchos elementos en común, si comparamos un curandero de formación cristiana y culturalmente educado en el mismo entorno con otro de diferentes creencias religiosas, existen unas disparidades que conviene destacar.

Por ejemplo, el curanderismo judío está vinculado a la tradición religiosa y espiritual de su dogma. Eso sí, se ha centrado siempre primordialmente en la curación de enfermedades y la búsqueda del bienestar de las personas. A este tipo de curanderismo no vinculado a la ciencia médica se lo conoce como *Refuah Shelemah,* que es la oración que dentro del judaísmo se realiza rogando al Todopoderoso por la completa recuperación de alguna persona que está gravemente enferma.

Los curanderos judíos basan toda práctica en los textos sagrados como la Torá o el Talmud, además de la inevitable tradición oral que va traspasando a lo largo de las generaciones.

No solo citan partes de sus textos sacros, a veces recurren a recitar ciertos pasajes de la Biblia cristiana o algunas plegarias para conseguir invocar la ayuda divina durante el proceso de curación. Entre esas jaculatorias está la oración de intercesión o la oración de fe.

Al igual que otras formas de sanación mística, necesita el uso de hierbas medicinales para poder gestionar la enfermedad que, precisamente, citan en la Torá. A los curanderos judíos se loes conoce como *Baal Shem,* y son muy respetados dentro de la comunidad por su gran habilidad de sanar, aliviar el sufrimiento de los pacientes e incluso hacer milagros. Muchos de ellos lo hacían gracias al conocimiento del nombre de Dios, llegando a tener mucha fama de ser unos excelentes exorcistas durante los siglos XVI-XVII en gran parte de Europa. Por supuesto, la Cábala también forma parte de sus estudios y aplicaciones para poder sanar. Esto es algo casi desconocido, donde creen que el equilibrio de los diez *sefirot* puede traer la sanación. No lo tuvieron sencillo durante el medievo debido a la presión del Tribunal de la Santa Fe, y por ello solamente actuaban con los suyos, con gentiles de confianza y en máxima clandestinidad.

Mencionar el *Tetragrámaton*[1] para aplicarlo en sanaciones es extraño, pues se usaba en causas de fuerza mayor y, aun

---

1 Término que se refiere a las cuatro letras hebreas הוהי (YHWH), que componen el nombre sagrado de Dios en la tradición judía. Su significado exacto es complejo y ha sido interpretado de diversas maneras en el pensamiento místico y teológico judío.

así, temían usarlo, ya que era un elemento sagrado y solo se recomendaba mencionarlo en el interior del Templo de Jerusalén. Su uso era muy restringido y causaba temor.

Ocultos también y solo con los de su etnia eran los de la comunidad gitana. El curanderismo gitano sigue las mismas pautas de cualquier otro sanador tradicional: va de generación en generación y, sobre todo, dentro del ámbito femenino, pues las mujeres eran mayoría en estas prácticas con sus características distintivas.

Ellas tenían un profundo conocimiento de las plantas medicinales, usaban indistintamente la oración cristiana como a su santa propia de la etnia gitana: Sara la Kali. Entre otras características, en sus formas de curanderismo estaban el canto (sanación por la palabra), las danzas, el uso de amuletos contra el mal y la protección de salud, incluso consultar las estrellas y las cartas del tarot o los naipes españoles con un único fin de saber qué tipo de enfermedad estaba instalada en el paciente, ya que puede ser también causada por un hechizo.

Donde se ha observado una enorme amalgama de diferentes prácticas ha sido en el curanderismo africano. Su sincretismo ha dado lugar a una variedad única, pues se fusionaron sus propias creencias basadas en la naturaleza y religión con las costumbres musulmanas, las cristianas y ciertas dosis del mundo judío.

Pero, como todas las pericias de curación, no difieren en exceso de sus objetivos: sanación y reestablecer el equilibrio físico y espiritual. El sanador africano ha dedicado mucho tiempo a la observación de la naturaleza y reconocer diversas utilidades de las plantas que pueden aportar un uso medicinal.

En términos generales, se cree que los antepasados tienen un papel muy importante durante el proceso de sanación y la protección de su tribu o comunidad. Para ello, los curanderos actúan de intermediarios entre el mundo de los vivos y de los espíritus de los antepasados del enfermo, para encontrar la ayuda y la orientación para proceder a mejorar su salud. Contactar con ese mundo del «más allá» es muy habitual en todos los tipos de curanderismo, y para ello recurren a la meditación, al uso de la videncia o a diversos rituales para facilitar ese vínculo de conexión con los espíritus o divinidades, algo muy presente en los últimos curanderos de España del último tercio del siglo xx.

Sus rituales de invocación para sanar también forman parte de su mundo. Los curanderos africanos pueden utilizar símbolos de índole sagrada o amuletos que se cree que tienen poderes protectores o curativos. Estos pueden incluir objetos naturales como piedras, huesos, plumas o conchas, así como objetos fabricados como colgantes, brazaletes o bolsas medicinales. Si observan, son prácticamente las bases y elementos de la religión *yoruba*, los *afa* o los *bantú*, por poner unas creencias como ejemplo.

La adivinación era también parte habitual de los sanadores africanos, que, en términos generales, es una práctica muy común entre ellos. Se basaban en la lectura de huesos, lanzamiento de caracoles, conchas de cauri… e incluso en observar ciertos patrones de la naturaleza como sonidos, la lluvia o la percepción de alguna presencia animal.

Como sucede en todos los ámbitos geográficos, el curandero es una figura respetada en su entorno, ya que eran los únicos que podían ser capaces de aportar alivio durante los procesos de enfermedad y abordar asuntos espirituales.

Los conceptos no cambian si saltamos al continente americano. Por ejemplo, los indios de Norteamérica y su sistema de sanación. Ellos han desarrollado prácticas de curanderismo únicas y diversas que han desempeñado un papel fundamental en el cuidado de su tribu.

Sus objetivos son los mismos que los de cualquier otro sanador. Sin embargo, ellos se basan más en la conexión profunda del mundo espiritual con la naturaleza. Sus curanderos, normalmente, son personas ancianas y muy veneradas, que tienen una gama de recursos que van desde la botánica hasta los ritos ceremoniales basados en danzas, cantos (de nuevo, la sanación por la palabra), la adivinación, el contacto y la comunicación con los antepasados… Además, son excelentes «onironautas», pues la interpretación de los sueños es una parte muy importante para diagnosticar su enfermedad y recibir el tratamiento adecuado.

Tampoco estuvieron exentos de problemas. A lo largo de su historia, la colonización hizo mella en su desarrollo y cultura, así que perdieron sus tierras, recursos y sus herencias ancestrales. El curanderismo en las tribus de los indios de Norteamérica era fundamental para mantener un equilibrio espiritual en tiempos de adversidad, a menudo se vieron desprotegidos de aquellas enfermedades que su chamán lograba contener con sus remedios y, en muchas ocasiones, no supieron cómo sustituirlos.

España, como bien sabemos, ha sido hogar de múltiples culturas a lo largo de su historia y cada una ha dejado su huella en interesantes herencias de sanaciones ancestrales, desde los íberos, los romanos o los visigodos hasta principios del siglo xx, cuando ya la medicina científica comenzaba a despuntar en todo el país. Este periodo fue testigo de numerosos avances en áreas como la bacteriología, la cirugía, la farmacología y la salud pública, donde comienzan a surgir numerosos hospitales y centros sanitarios. Se realizaron importantes descubrimientos en el campo de las enfermedades infecciosas y se desarrollaron vacunas y tratamientos más efectivos. Esta época ya suponía ver el final de un conjunto de prácticas que iban quedando obsoletas dentro del mundo del curanderismo.

¿Cómo surge el interés por el curanderismo en España?

Posiblemente, la figura del curandero tradicional que conocemos comienza en el siglo xiii. Hasta esa fecha, existía un nivel de estudios y prácticas de medicina al más alto nivel, pues Córdoba, Toledo y Sevilla, entre otras, eran centros de estudio, de intercambio cultural y científico. Se habían traducido numerosos escritos médicos del griego, persa, árabe, hebreo…, y esos médicos que enseñaban o ejercían eran musulmanes.

Tras la denominada Reconquista, era evidente que el cristianismo tenía la ventaja de mandar y organizar. Los médicos cristianos estaban menos formados en general en comparación con los que iban saliendo de aquellas academias en las que llegaron a enseñar, por ejemplo, los médicos y filósofos musulmanes como Ibn Sina (Avicena) o Ibn Rushd (Averroes), y consideraron que estos médicos de fe musulmana eran una competencia y se aplicaron en considerar, difundir y propagar en todos los sentidos que sus prácticas eran paganas, que estaban rodeadas del ocultismo, aunque más bien era por su filosofía y fe, dado que fueron la base de muchos estudios de medicina como Tomás Aquino.

Con ello, y con la ayuda de la justicia civil y eclesiástica primero y después de 1478 con la terrible Inquisición, las medidas no tardaron en imponerse a la fe musulmana y judía, que afectó a muchos médicos y limitó el intercambio y desarrollo del conocimiento médico, por lo que se vieron obligados a ejercer en clandestinidad, y se comenzó a vetar y prohibir numerosas prácticas médicas de moriscos y judíos. Incluso se revisaban los textos médicos que se estudiaban en las academias para depurar lo que se observaba contrario a la fe cristiana, por lo que ejercieron un control estricto de las publicaciones médicas como el *Canon de Avicena*.

No conformes con esto, también amenazaban a los que recurrían a ellos bajo pena de excomunión si se hacía alguna consulta o buscaban remedio a un médico no cristiano, incluso aunque fuera converso o «marrano» (judío convertido al cristianismo), podía tener muchas consecuencias. Tiempos complicados, que durante mucho tiempo eran tolerados y se pasaron las más duras restricciones para ejercer.

Estos vetos facilitaron que, con la picaresca española, ingeniasen formas de consultar a estos sanadores, lo que hace surgir, posiblemente, las primeras consultas clandestinas a los curanderos.

No es una propuesta muy académica, pero sí que fue una de las formas que más empujó al nacimiento de la figura del curandero o curandera que ejercía en lo más recóndito de un bosque o a escondidas en su hogar en horas intempestivas.

Curiosamente, el cristianismo surge como la religión de la salvación, en un sentido integral. Desde sus orígenes, está vinculado a las numerosas curaciones de Jesús de Nazaret.

Su figura es importante, ya que es la referencia y ejemplo de extraordinario curandero: sanó a leprosos y paralíticos, los ciegos volvieron a ver, los sordomudos recuperaron sus funciones de voz y oído, expulsó demonios a través de su exorcismo de manos y hasta resucitó a los muertos. Tantas virtudes mágicas que finalmente entró en conflicto con la autoridad religiosa de su tiempo, que fue acusado de realizar actos de magia aportados por Belcebú (Marcos, cap. 3, 22).

De esas luchas contra los curanderos, hechiceras, comadronas, etc. existen varios documentos históricos que no dejan duda del odio generalizado que desprendía la Iglesia católica hacia este mundo que buscaba el bienestar y la reducción del dolor. Por ejemplo, desde 1413 en Valencia estaba prohibido y condenada la práctica del curanderismo como cita en el *Manual dels Consells*[2], que ya penalizaban desde 1413 las consultas para mejorar la salud incluso a adivinos, sortilegios y demás conjuradores:

> [...] los honorables justiciers, jurats prohomens e Consell han stablit e ordenat e manan publicar e esser observat que alguna persona de qual sevolo ley, estament e condico sia no gos o presumesca recorrer e anar a devins o devines, encantadors, sortilers, o conjuradors o a altres de mal saber o art reservada per saber e demanar Consell e ajuda de coses perdues o amagades ni per altra raó o specie de divinacions o encantacions, encara que fos per recaptar salut o medesina a qualque persona o per qualsevol altra cobrada causa o rao, no ser alguna manera gos e presumesca invocar dimonis de fer rotlles o altres sortilegis e divinacions, encantacions o conjuracions o altra cosa que toque art de nigromancia o invocació de dimonis [...].

Pero ¿qué es lo que relaciona la medicina con la brujería? En la cultura popular de siglos anteriores, las enfermedades no tenían un origen científico, sino que se pensaba que eran las intervenciones de la mano del diablo en la vida de las personas. Por ejemplo, si se sentía excesivamente cansado o con un malestar general, no era por una mala alimentación o falta de ella, sueño irregular o exponerse al frío o incluso una carente higiene, sino porque ha agraviado a algún demonio o es víctima de una maldición (por ejemplo, mal de ojo) solicitada o provocada por algún enemigo personal.

Por tanto, si la enfermedad tiene su origen en el mundo oculto, es precisamente recurriendo a los elementos del mundo oculto como se puede curar.

De hecho, muchos curanderos practicaban exorcismos para curar una enfermedad. Sin embargo, existe el exorcismo oficial y el no autorizado. El primero lo practicaban los sacerdotes autorizados a ello, empleando el manual correspondiente, usando agua bendita, sal y la citación de oraciones en latín. Aquí el sacerdote asume la función de médico, pues pregunta dónde está el dolor o los síntomas, para poder recomendar después del rito los fármacos que figuran en las listas oficiales de los tribunales.

Por el contrario, el exorcismo no autorizado por la Iglesia (por tanto, es un rito mágico, herético y perseguido por la Inquisición), es practicado por los curanderos (tanto hombres como mujeres) e incluso algunos frailes y sacerdotes pero sin la autorización correspondiente.

Los remedios, recetas y tratamientos que pudieron recomendar no están reconocidos, sino que pertenecían a una sabiduría ancestral, ligada a la naturaleza y los secretos.

Esto último respecto a exorcismos, recurrir a sanadores y sus fórmulas magistrales no es casual, en tierras levantinas el gran santo valenciano Vicente Ferrer (1350-1419), antes de la creación oficial del Santo Oficio, ya condenaba y animaba a castigar a aquellos que recurrían a prácticas de curanderismo o hechiceras.

Para san Vicente, la iglesia se hace meritoria de los sucesos de curación de la ciudad. Si se curaba algún afortunado por medios aplicados de la hechicería, curanderismo y brujería, es decir, con los productos de herboristería y otros ungüentos naturales, había sido obra e intermediación de la mano de Dios, no de los sanadores, brujas o remedios. Por el contrario, si no se curaba el enfermo con los remedios de las curanderas o similares, Dios mostraba la ira divina por el engaño y el recurrir a los personajes vetados para sanar y no sanarán por castigo divino.

13. Escena de la Inquisición. Brujas en la hoguera en Derenburg (Sajonia-Anhalt, Alemania) en 1555.

En su obstinación, era la providencia quien decidía el destino de las personas. Si las oraciones realizadas tampoco surtían efecto, era mejor que esa persona muriese, en especial si era niño, puesto que, de lo contrario, estaría viviendo de conjuros y serían finalmente carne de horca o de hoguera por usar semejantes pócimas o rituales alejados de los dogmas de fe, o serían *morts de mala mort* (*Sermones de san Vicente Ferrer*, 1414-1415), lo que equivale a ganarse el infierno y la condena eterna, pues vivían de forma «artificial» en el mundo terrenal.

En resumen, puedo decir que era mejor que muriese el enfermo o cruzar los dedos para que las plegarias u oraciones cristianas pudieran surtir algún efecto si no deseaban verse en problemas con el tribunal de la Santa Fe. Además, se podía producir un efecto dominó en todo su entorno familiar que también podía tener consecuencias por ello, un tremendo riesgo cuando una persona del entorno familiar se ponía enferma.

Estos motivos fueron más que suficientes para difundir cierto temor ante las prácticas mágicas de sanación y fomentó la clandestinidad y el éxodo de los grandes núcleos urbanos para asentarse en zonas rurales, lejos de las miradas eclesiásticas, con una ventaja respecto a las ciudades: no había médicos ni nada parecido en la mayoría de las localidades rústicas, todo estaba más retrasado y mantenían algunos pueblos ciertas costumbres ancestrales. Pocos podían permitirse el lujo de pagarse un médico autorizado o al menos licenciado. Si la ciencia no había llegado a ese punto geográfico aislado, el enfermo se podía sentir imposibilitado y tan desesperado que daba con sus huesos en la tumba, y el curandero o la sanadora local eran su única esperanza de luchar contra el mal.

Y esto ha sido una constante, una evolución dentro del mundo rural, prácticas que han ido de generación en generación. O bien a través del aprendizaje de las tradiciones o costumbres locales y llega hasta bien entrada la década de 1980. Aun así, continúa siendo un fenómeno sociológico que aún resiste en ciertas localidades, aunque ya casi imperceptible y de casos aislados.

VI. EN LA SALA DE ESPERA

Mi objetivo en esta obra es recordar las prácticas de este oficio que está obsoleto en términos generales, pero no está exento de numerosos enigmas y extrañezas que giran en torno a los personajes que hacen de su «don» una esperanza para aquellos que buscaban (y algunos siguen buscando en la actualidad) mejorar o curar su enfermedad, especialmente esas décadas que ya estaban dando sus últimas manifestaciones, como sanador, curalotodo, curandero, yerbero o ensalmador. Esos tiempos que manejo son los años 1960 a 1980, un lapso de dos décadas que es más que suficiente para pensar, percibir y analizar cómo era este mundo y los cambios que han ido modificando su imagen ante la sociedad.

Los curanderos pretenden llegar donde el médico habitual no consigue esa deseada mejoría, y ellos, con sus virtudes, su mística, sus dones adquiridos por la experiencia y la gracia divina, nos ofrecen un atisbo de esperanza a nuestra calidad de vida. Es una salida a nuestra desesperación. Si miramos nuestras fechas de actualidad, existe un cierto aumento de consultas a curanderos, alentado por la llegada de la inmigración sudamericana y africana. Estas personas tienen un punto más de fe en las manos de los curanderos que los occidentales, incluso en posibles maldiciones. Hay numerosos reportes de miedo de ciertas mujeres de origen africano que, engañadas, ejercen la prostitución con el temor de que un maleficio alcance a su familia si denuncian o no cumplen su labor. Incluso las personas de origen del continente americano también tienen sus temores por las aplicaciones de santería yoruba y sus vertientes como el vudú, pues tanto la una como la otra están basadas en el control de paciente con la consigna del miedo.

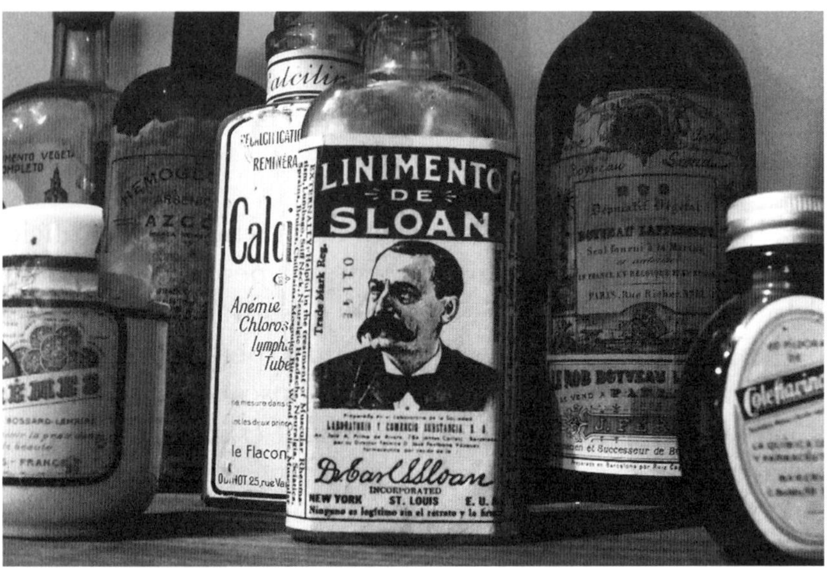

14. Recursos de antaño que eran habituales en la botica del curandero. Museo Etnológico Peñarroja. Imagen: A. Beitia.

En épocas pasadas, los más pudientes podían recibir la asistencia médica como asistencia privada y exclusiva, los que se movían entre la clase media basculaban entre una asistencia domiciliaria si tenían la suerte de encontrar algo de tiempo libre el médico o, junto a la clase denominada «baja», acudir a consulta pública que podía no existir en su localidad o estaría saturada y, en última instancia, las circunstancias sociales, geográficas e incluso folclóricas deciden acudir a un curandero a cambio de la voluntad. Algunos citan que, si se negaban a la voluntad, ellos podían perder sus poderes curativos o bien (como método de presión) el paciente podía no sentir síntomas de mejoría.

Optamos, en nuestra imaginación, por lo último: una visita al curandero. Imaginemos un viaje al pasado, a unas décadas atrás, en un pueblo casi aislado y con las comunicaciones complejas de su tiempo y arraigado en sus tradiciones. Lo visitamos en su humilde casa. Normalmente, casi todos los vecinos saben cuál es el domicilio donde está establecido uno de los más notables habitantes de la localidad, dado que la figura del sanador es notoria. Deseo la sanación de un malestar generalizado en mi cuerpo, ignoro la causa de esta enfermedad que me abruma, me agota y me impide mi labor cotidiana, no sé qué enfermedad padezco o si tengo un trastorno psicosomático.

Acudo a esa consulta por su popularidad local, por la recomendación de muchos lugareños, por la eficacia difundida y el tratamiento prescrito y, sobre todo, porque no hay servicio médico que pueda acercarme al instante o pueda atenderme en mi domicilio.

15. Las creencias en prácticas ancestrales de dudosa eficacia, siguen presentes en nuestra actualidad.

No es solo por esas referencias que acuden a un curandero, sino también porque, habitualmente, no hay una tarifa de consultas. No se paga la consulta, sino que se basa en algo que está al alcance económico de la mayoría, son bastante baratos, aceptan la limosna, la voluntad o un simple trueque de algo necesario para vivir (comida, ultramarinos…). Es algo primordial para mantener su fama: la accesibilidad a los niveles de pobreza, motivo de que muchas recetas que dispensan los sanadores son de ingredientes relativamente pobres o de fácil adquisición y van dirigidas a estos en términos generales. Pese a recibir unas dádivas humildes, muchos de ellos llegaron a hacerse con una buena cuenta de fondos, incluso adquirieron varias casas en la localidad donde ejercen y otras ciudades cercanas. Era una inversión de futuro. Son numerosas las visitas que recibe diariamente, desde los interesados locales hasta personas que proceden de otras localidades y provincias próximas siendo alentados por el boca a boca.

Otras anotaciones que debo destacar son los problemas e inconvenientes que sufren para obtener una ayuda digna de los centros de salud locales o próximos, debido a su larga lista de espera, diferentes turnos y que, fuera del servicio sanitario estatal, el médico titulado es caro en su servicio privado. Recurrir al curandero o personaje con los dones adecuados para curar es una salida a la angustia, a los afligidos por huir del dolor, e incluso salvar su vida, que está ya en la cuenta atrás, dado que el dictamen médico oficial nada puede hacer y el paciente no pierde absolutamente nada por utilizar esta opción, por muy peculiar o atípica que sea. Además, los tratamientos de los curanderos o sanadoras están basados en remedios muy poco traumáticos, no son agresivos ni realizan maniobras dolorosas para el paciente, aceptan una apuesta basada en la curiosidad, pero también en el anhelo de mejorar.

Un motivo que insisto y hacen acudir al curandero, al margen de la fe, son las relaciones humanas entre el médico y paciente: existe una distancia, un muro que no atraviesa el médico y hace imposible un contacto más personalizado, salvo a nivel privado, pero hay que pagar un alto precio por su consulta y el término medio del paciente no está dispuesto a ello, pues la economía familiar o personal no puede permitirse ese privilegio. La sencillez de su lenguaje y, a veces, el hecho de que recurren a refranes populares hacen que el paciente se sienta con tranquilidad y confianza frente al curandero.

En esta época actual, sigue existiendo en las instituciones sanitarias oficiales una alta tendencia deshumanizada. No me refiero a malos tratos, sino a estar excesivamente basada en el mercantilismo, y eso hace que en muchas atenciones se queden desvinculados los pacientes de su objetivo: sanar y paliar el dolor.

Acuden a la consulta del curandero en compañía de un familiar o alguien de su confianza, rara vez acuden solos a la consulta. Si está algo alejada su dirección, a veces suelen quedar entre otros vecinos y trasladarse juntos en un vehículo, ya que no había tanta facilidad de servicios públicos de transporte, salvo en las grandes ciudades, así que se llegaban a desplazar en taxis hasta el domicilio de un prestigioso curandero, sin que importara la larga cola que pudiera existir en el exterior de personas que acudían a su consulta. Y procedían de diversas zonas los interesados, lo que demuestra un misterioso dominio: sin el uso de medios digitales, noticieros o plataformas, existía un extraño poder de convocatoria que llega hasta los lugares más insospechados.

La consulta se hace en cualquier día y hora, sin importar la edad del paciente o su sexo. Sin embargo, en ciertas regiones como Levante o zonas de Murcia, Albacete o Teruel, es importante elegir un día de la semana que no tenga la letra R. Es decir, los mejores días para sanarse son lunes, jueves, sábado y domingo. El resto no son recomendables. Se ignora la causa de este motivo, traté de averiguar algo más referente a la molestia de la letra R y su influencia para obstaculizar una posible curación, pues podía ser algo relacionado con alguna superstición antigua, influencia de numerología, astral o un simple capricho de un curandero que se extendió esa moda supersticiosa, pero, por el momento, no hay una fuente fiable. Solo me surge la idea de que los fines de semana son los días libres en general, y eso hace que acudan más visitas, teniendo un curioso «efecto llamada», similar a los centros comerciales de nuestro tiempo.

Esos problemas que lleva el paciente a casa del curandero son de varias índoles, desde unas tradiciones socioculturales como tener sueños extraños, que están asustados, que creen que son víctimas del mal de ojo o un hechizo de embrujamiento e incluso un escaso interés en la comida hasta el malestar causado por enfermedades cotidianas como una indigestión, resfriados, algún problema de visión, dolores de espalda, infecciones cutáneas o simples lesiones musculares o esguinces. Raro es el paciente que tenga un cáncer, hepatitis o tuberculosis, por citar algunos males peligrosos.

Es frecuente que muchas enfermedades estén relacionadas con el entorno socioeconómico del área en la que vive el paciente: viviendas inadecuadas, falta de higiene, aguas poco salubres…, destacando la desnutrición que facilita que el sistema inmunitario esté por debajo de los niveles recomendados, lo que aumenta las infecciones y diversas enfermedades como diarreas, neumonías, fiebre tifoidea, tuberculosis…, que eran problemas sanitarios muy frecuentes en la España de hace unas décadas y que asolaban los espacios rurales.

Antes debemos estar en la sala de espera. Aunque varía dependiendo del entorno geográfico y cultural, en términos generales estaba dentro de la propia casa del curandero o en una pequeña casa adyacente. Estar dentro de esa habitación sobrecoge, causa un conjunto extraño de sensaciones que abarcan desde el respeto hasta el temor, el desconocimiento y el sentirse cohibido ante la sugerente decoración que nos presenta, cargada de decenas de imágenes de santos, velas y objetos de índole religiosa, como rosarios, imágenes del sagrado corazón de Jesús, misales, ramos de flores, estatuillas de vírgenes y cruces que causan una singular reacción al verlas. Un extraño ambiente que se acerca más a un lugar de exvotos de santuario o capilla de una ermita que a la consulta de un sanador. Curiosamente, a la mayoría de los curanderos no les agrada la imagen de la cruz con Jesús crucificado, ya que representa el dolor y la muerte, prefieren otra imagen más amable con un simbolismo basado en el amor, compasión y sanación: la imagen del sagrado corazón de Jesús, una estampa que refuerza el papel del curandero, e incluso de la Virgen de los Dolores, esa imagen envuelta en su manto negro que soportaba un corazón herido por siete espadas, los siete dolores que ha soportado en su vida, lo cual le confiere ese estatus de patrona del sufrimiento y del dolor.

16. Los hogares y salas de atención de un curandero son auténticos altares sugestivos. Imagen: Archivo UAM.

La presencia de cirios encendidos refuerza el ambiente y es una forma habitual de invocar a fuerzas divinas aportando luz, pues recordemos que el lugar de trabajo del curandero no era neutral, sino un espacio sacralizado que necesitaba para crear una atmósfera especial.

Con mucha frecuencia existe un catálogo de aromas: desde los naturales florales que cuidaban en macetas propias hasta clásicos olores de incienso y de sándalo. Las esencias olorosas de aceites también podían sentirse en las salas de espera, como el eucalipto, el romero o la lavanda.

Este conjunto de efluvios, más la provocativa decoración religiosa de la sala, ayudaba mucho a relajarse en ella, a confiar y tener fe en las habilidades misteriosas del hombre o mujer que ejercía la profesión, sobre todo recibir una carga de fe. El paciente podía llegar a percibir que existía una conexión psíquica con la divinidad.

La sala de espera de un curandero era un lugar preferente para el sanador, donde los pacientes y sus acompañantes podían interactuar y conversar entre sí intercambiando sus historias personales y sus dolencias, así como compartir diversas experiencias personales, opiniones o simplemente interesarse por su procedencia, creando un ambiente amable. También había un ayudante del curandero entre ellos, para facilitar la conversación y elogiar las virtudes mágicas del sanador para que confiasen en él o ella.

Esto es importante porque aquí comienza la «redacción» de la ficha del visitante primerizo, recabando información. Aunque la presencia de este «falso paciente» no está muy documentada, podía ser una de las tácticas que haya utilizado en algún momento un curandero. Y esto es un detalle importante para su prestigio y difundir su conjetura como sanador. La comunicación en la antesala entre los pacientes presentes para consultar al curandero es clave. A menudo coinciden en las citas, llegando a crear un vínculo de amistad entre ellos, que refuerza la confianza en el curandero; y, por ende, difunden buena publicidad de sus virtudes.

La espera a su llamada para atenderlos suele ser larga, ya que al curandero le gusta hacer esperar, y para ello en general escucha al paciente atentamente, sin realizar interrupción alguna durante su conversación. Son buenos psicólogos, saben el punto débil de los sentimientos del paciente. No solo tratan los problemas físicos, sino que también se acercan a los aspectos emocionales, y necesitan crear un vínculo de confianza.

Como dice el popular refrán, «cada maestrillo tiene su librillo». Y en esta faceta lo tiene aún más. Es complicado basarse en un único manual de trabajo, ya que todo ha sido aprendido a través de experiencia, de la observación de la naturaleza, por los intercambios entre otros practicantes del arte mágico de la sanación, por la lectura de diversos libros y publicaciones y, por último, adquieren muchos de esos dones de curar por la mediación divina.

Prácticamente la mayoría de los curanderos suelen tomar de la mano a los dolientes o enfermos, para poder poner las suyas encima y sentir ese primer contacto. En este gesto crea una conexión inmediata con el paciente, añadiendo un conjunto de oraciones incoherentes y difíciles de escuchar o entender, como si estuviera haciendo una primera llamada a sus mediaciones divinas, mientras el paciente siente una reducción del estrés y una sensación de apoyo ante su enfermedad.

Por esa última causa, gracias a algunos testimonios que pude consultar de pacientes que acudieron, muchos de ellos me aportaron una referencia curiosa, como un pacto, como una condición *sine qua non*, es que para atenderlos deben realizar un conjuro, siempre que sea la primera vez que acuden: su renuncia al diablo o satanás, y realizar unas oraciones de protección a diversos santos, a Dios o a la Santísima Trinidad y con las palmas abiertas hacia arriba. Una breve ceremonia ritual con un sentido religioso y mágico. Tras el cristiano conjuro, el paciente pasa a sus consultas con el curandero. Y esto es otra historia: sus prácticas, tratamientos y rituales.

En nuestros días, las consultas han cambiado por completo, las salas se han transformado en auténticas clínicas, deslumbrantes, sin parafernalia religiosa. Incluso ofrecen productos que no son elaborados por ellos, sino que proceden de laboratorios, e incluso presumen de extraños títulos que ignoramos si son oficiales o un certificado de estudios, sin más.

17. Diversas protecciones de un curandero. Imagen: A. Beitia.

Una vez dentro, comienza la aventura de confiar en sus manos, en sus dones, virtudes y «gracia», incluso en los remedios caseros que puede recomendarle. Tras abandonar el domicilio del curandero, dejará el paciente una dádiva generosa. Pocos poseen una tarifa fija de consultas, pues no ven ético cobrar al paciente, ya que consideran sus acciones como un servicio a la comunidad y sienten que cobrar por sus servicios sería profanar ese don que la divinidad les ha otorgado, facilitando que no exista ninguna clase social ni exclusiones por motivos económicos. De saltarse este código, según algunos curanderos consultados, podían perder su «don» o «gracia».

VII. VIRTUDES Y HABILIDADES DEL CURANDERO

Convertirse en curandero, al margen de ser una vocación, es una tarea mágica, arrastrada por las tradiciones ancestrales y supersticiones que aún perduran en nuestros tiempos. Deberíamos separar en tres grupos los curanderos según el origen de sus dones.

En un primer grupo estarían los señalados por diferentes signos físicos, fechas de nacimiento o coincidencias astrológicas. El siguiente grupo sería algo más natural, por tradición familiar, que van heredando esos conocimientos (la mayoría lo hereda de sus abuelas), o bien ser identificado por otro curandero por percepción, clarividencia o perspicacia. Y, por último, el tercer grupo serían los sanadores por designio divino, el don recibido por Dios, la Virgen o los fallecidos, donde mantener el contacto con ellos es fundamental.

¿Por qué se emprende un camino para convertirse en curandero tras esos puntos?

Al margen de las herencias familiares y los conocimientos que van pasando de generación en generación para proveer el bien a las personas, existe una razón realmente misteriosa en sus historiales y motivos: el mandato divino, aunque también está, en muchos casos, el interés económico.

Una de las grandes excelencias del curandero o curandera es la virtud de la «gracia».

¿A que denominamos gracia?

La mayoría de los curanderos afirman que esa gracia que poseen se la entregó Dios en un momento determinado de su vida, siendo ellos y las mujeres unos meros intermediarios entre esa divinidad y el paciente, señalando a Dios o la Virgen que han sido los que han sanado a ese individuo que confiaba en sus habilidades y portentos y con quien nunca han dejado de estar en conexión.

Desde mi opinión, no es lo que se denomina el supuesto «don» recibido por la divinidad, sino que poseen un conjunto de habilidades que van desde el conocimiento de las plantas hasta la habilidad de diagnosticar enfermedades y el dominio de diversas técnicas de sanación. Por supuesto que también debo añadir esa gracia que conocemos como el «don» divino, aunque esto deja una bruma de misterio que difícilmente podemos disipar.

Comparando con otras regiones europeas y culturalmente unidas, como Francia o Italia, el asunto de este privilegio divino es menos común, pues solo se da en España, salvo en algunos casos puntuales, puesto que están más vinculados a tradiciones técnicas locales. Posiblemente se deba a la rigidez de la Iglesia ante supuestos casos de gracia divina, mientras en España se toleraban algo mejor las prácticas populares.

¿Cómo se consigue lo último?

Aquí es más complejo, ya que científicamente no hay evidencia. Todo se basa en la experiencia personal vivida en un momento determinado e imprevisto, que va desde estar muerto y tener unas vivencias extracorpóreas, visiones de luces desconocidas y hierofanías que destacan la manifestación de la Virgen, entre otras revelaciones. A menudo suele acompañarse de un mensaje auditivo, que les sugiere un camino como sanador, como persona que busca el bien dentro su comunidad, teniendo como ejemplo la figura religiosa de Jesús. En este punto me surge una duda respecto a esa actividad de hierofanía, la manifestación de lo divino: ¿por qué tantos casos de apariciones y mensajes de la divinidad a ellos?

Una de las causas es su fuerte vínculo religioso, ya que pueden interpretar sus experiencias personales como mensajes divinos. Sin embargo, también es posible que su constante actividad entre plegarias, oraciones y usos de plantas enteógenas puede inducir al curandero a estados alterados de conciencia, donde puede ser testigo de visiones y experiencias místicas. Carl Jung ya sugirió que las manifestaciones sagradas son parte del inconsciente colectivo y pueden manifestarse a través de sueños o visiones (ver sugerencia de bibliografía).

Aunque la transformación en curandero tras una experiencia de una manifestación sagrada es compleja, se debe a situaciones traumáticas y procesos de enfermedad muy graves. O bien pueden estar aprovechándose de la fe de las personas que viven en su entorno, que saben actuar con empatía y apoyo emocional y cuyas visiones, entonces, podemos considerar como un fraude, ya que no aportan suficiente información con un mínimo de rigor, a base de relatos inconsistentes y ambiguos. Podía ser que dichas manifestaciones, sin tener como objetivo el fraude o el engaño, sean para reforzar su figura y conceptos como curandero. A pesar de ello, estas manifestaciones pueden ser vistas, por parte de los sanadores, como una señal de bendición a la que se aferran, que es lo que manejamos en estas líneas como la «gracia».

Es posible que relatar que es testigo de una aparición mariana o de cualquier otra índole sea como una «autenticación» de su validez como curandero, lo cual le supone conseguir un estatus dentro de su comunidad, dado que la cultura religiosa del lugar sigue vigente y anclada en esa España oscura y rural, a lo que sumo un «efecto contagio»: si un curandero ha sido testigo de una manifestación religiosa, seguirá como un efecto dominó en varios más.

Es posible que también ha sido motivado por una tradición nacional de la España católica, las apariciones de la virgen en diversos puntos de la geografía, desde la aparición primigenia de la Virgen del Pilar en Zaragoza hasta la Virgen de la Cabeza en Jaén, sin olvidarnos otras hierofanías menos conocidas como la Virgen de Cortes (Albacete) o del Remedio (Utiel), son más de 4000 recintos de apariciones que están dedicados a la Virgen. Todos los curanderos podían estar influenciados por estas causas. Sin duda, España es una nación con fuerte arraigo católico, donde la fe, junto con las prácticas y tradiciones religiosas, ha sido parte integral de la vida cotidiana.

Observando algunos datos diversos y fuentes de hemeroteca que citaban noticias de curanderos y mujeres sanadoras durante la época que abarca desde 1930 hasta 1970, parece que es más frecuente la «gracia divina» en mujeres mayores de 50 años. Posiblemente, sean ellas las que más fe religiosa depositan. La causa era el sistema patriarcal que dominaba ese tiempo, y asumía un rol de ser la educadora en casa a nivel religioso, sobre todo ante las escasas oportunidades laborales incluso en la sociedad, encontraron un refugio en la iglesia controlada por el nacionalcatolicismo.

Entre esas creencias místicas, para adquirir esa gracia de ser curandero, estaba haber nacido durante una fecha y circunstancias determinadas durante el parto. Esto no es una herencia del cristianismo, puesto que en España es primordial nacer en uno de los días sagrados de la Semana Santa, especialmente un Jueves o Viernes Santo, o bien el Día de Navidad, aunque ciertas zonas pueden darse en festividad de un santoral determinado, como por ejemplo san Lorenzo.

Los nacidos en el Día de san Lorenzo tienen la *gracia* de sanar quemaduras, pues recordemos que este santo fue martirizado en una parrilla, de ahí su representación iconográfica. Sin embargo, a menudo esas quemaduras las sanan con la saliva propia del curandero.

El uso de la baba humana no es exclusivo de los curanderos, sino que, desde tiempos del medievo, la aplicaban en diversos remedios los conocidos «saludadores», que aseguraban con sus dones sanar la enfermedad de la rabia, la sarna y diversas heridas, tanto del ganado como en el ser humano, aunque estos personajes están rodeados de una llamativa extática mucho más amplia y simbólica.

No es exclusivo de España venir al mundo en una fecha mística. En la Europa oriental es necesario haber nacido durante una fase lunar específica o en días festivos. En Rumanía, la Noche de San Andrés es conocida por las creencias en magia y protección contra los espíritus malignos, una herencia ancestral de los dacios que se ha añadido al calendario cristiano. Se cree que aquellos nacidos en esa noche tienen habilidades especiales para protegerse y curar. O una fecha clásica en términos generales en varias regiones: la Noche de San Juan, el 24 de junio.

En Hungría podía ser una persona con virtudes especiales, entre los que se encuentra la sanación si viene al mundo el día 13 de diciembre, santa Lucía. Este último lugar está bastante relacionado con unas creencias basadas en brujería. Según la tradición popular húngara, en este día aparecen brujas y otras personas de fuerzas mágicas, de quienes la gente debe esconderse. En este día se les frota la cabeza a los animales con ajo y se dibuja una cruz a las puertas de los gallineros o corrales. Habitualmente, se come pan con ajo, para disipar los malos espíritus con el olor, o se rocía la casa con tabaco mientras esconden sus escobas, para que las brujas no puedan robárselas o volar en ellas.

En la India se defiende a menudo que nacer durante una alineación de estrellas o planetas aporta la virtud de ser sanador. Mientras, en el área de Sudamérica es similar a la cultura española respecto a fechas, y su motivo es evidente: la colonización española con la influencia de la Iglesia católica y las costumbres tradicionales españolas.

La causa de ser importante por haber nacido durante la Semana Santa se cree que se debe a una conexión divina, y lo ven como una responsabilidad que debería asumir por el bien de la comunidad o el área en la que vive.

En resumen, podemos señalar que al nacer en una determinada fecha es posible que se obtenga un don especial para sanar algunas dolencias según el santoral del día, como hemos visto en unas referencias. Otros ejemplos locales son nacer en los días de santa Lucía, para curar los ojos, o de santa Apolonia, en este caso para sanar los dientes y las muelas.

18. Postal colección de Charles Géniaux Rebouteux.
Sanadoras de la Bretaña francesa.

Dentro de un conjunto de señales físicas, aseguran que si se tiene en la mano una cruz (+) o bajo la lengua, también es indicio de poseer virtudes sanadoras. Igualmente, es señal de un porvenir de curandero si el bebé antes de nacer llora en el vientre de su madre. Según las tradiciones sobre este episodio, la madre no puede contar este detalle hasta que dé luz a su retoño, pues si lo hiciera perdería la gracia y, con ello, sus posibles atributos mágicos. El origen de esta creencia es complejo, no es posible encontrar una base sólida para este mito. Aunque, según parece y aporta la tradición, la cruz en la boca es una virtud del poder de la palabra, lo cual podía tener virtudes sanadoras a través de oraciones, mientras que, en la mano, quizá lo podemos imaginar: el poder está en la imposición de manos, que están bendecidas por un poder celestial.

Siguiendo los dogmas de los neonatos, la videncia es parte de las características de numerosos curanderos. En la región de Galicia, cuna de muchas leyendas y gran folclore antropológico, poseen esas virtudes de clarividencia y, al mismo tiempo, de curar diversas enfermedades, aquellas personas que, cuando las fueron a bautizar en su correspondiente iglesia parroquial, el sacerdote que oficia el rito del bautismo confunde los óleos de unción, se le pone el óleo de extremaunción en vez del aceite consagrado para el bautismo. A causa de ese error humano, les facilita un peculiar «don» de anunciar la fecha aproximada de defunción de cualquier persona.

Venir al mundo dentro de la bolsa amniótica, conocido generalmente como «nacer con el manto» o «velado» (según regiones, reciben otras denominaciones como «zurrón» o «venir vestido») también es conocido como un signo de estar protegido por la divinidad, lo cual le confiere un poder de conexión espiritual. Se ignora el motivo de esta creencia, pero es posible que sea a causa de relatos mitológicos o leyendas ancestrales. Además, está citada en muchas culturas como la asiática o la africana. Posiblemente, por ser tan excepcional nacer con «zurrón», es la causa de considerar este elemento, puesto que, según datos que pude observar en la actualidad, se calcula que nace 1 persona en la bolsa amniótica por cada 80 000 nacimientos.

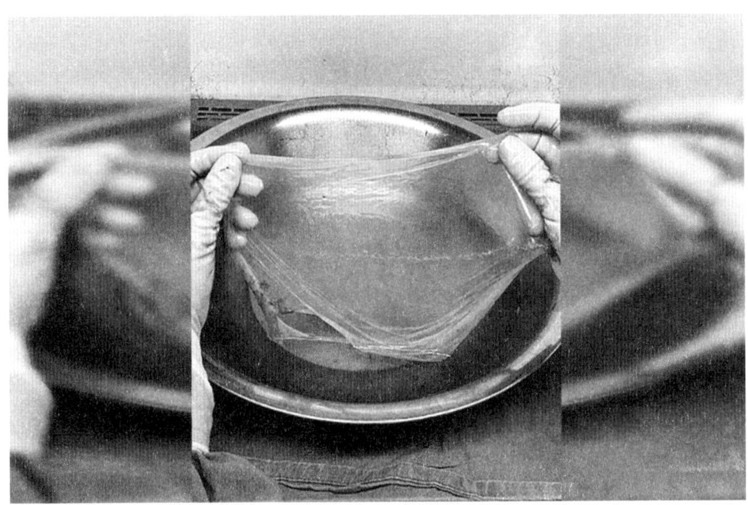

19. *Membrana amniótica, cuya leyenda asegura que aporta virtudes mágicas y sanadoras.*

Os puedo citar una línea de una popular novela de Charles Dickens publicada entre 1849 y 1850 (por entregas primero, luego llegó el libro) titulada *David Copperfield*, que incluye el mágico «velado»: «Nací envuelto en una membrana que trató de venderse, anunciándola en la prensa, por el modesto precio de quince guineas…».

Napoleón Bonaparte, según leyendas, se cita que nació con una membrana amniótica, y eso en Córcega, lo mismo que en muchos lugares, es interpretado como un signo de buena suerte. Personajes con buena estrella como Einstein o Freud también se cree que nacieron velados. Tan mágico han considerado venir al mundo protegido por ese manto que muchos de estos curanderos y sanadoras lo han conservado como un talismán, incluso diversas regiones del mundo lo conservan como un elemento sagrado.

En la cultura céltica ya citan varias tradiciones que traen suerte y pueden tener habilidades únicas, no solo de sanar. Incluso entre las etnias gitanas, ya se considera una virtud mágica, especialmente eran dotados para visualizar el futuro, que muchas mujeres que usan los naipes españoles de su etnia, aseguran que vinieron al mundo en ese mágico manto y le confirieron esas características de ser buenas visionarias.

Hoy en día, nacer con membrana se antoja complicado, pues en la actualidad, si no se rompe espontáneamente, durante el parto los facultativos que intervienen en ello la rompen para que el neonato pueda respirar.

Según pude recoger en diversos aportes y testimonios, cuando ven que se nace con el *zurrón* que aporta esas virtudes mágicas, antes de romperlo se citan unas oraciones y plegarias, además de hacerle el signo de la cruz al cuerpo. Otros añaden que podían colocarle en la mano un objeto al recién nacido, tras salir de esa membrana, un objeto que se relacione con una enfermedad para que sea un curandero con virtudes contra este mal. Por ejemplo, podían darle un trozo de carbón como símbolo del fuego y tener virtudes contra el llamado «fuego de san Antonio» (ergotismo, cornezuelo…) o ponerle una pequeña medalla con la representación de algún santo o santa, como santa Lucía (para que pueda sanar de la vista en el futuro), por citar unos ejemplos clásicos, sin olvidar otros detalles para alejar cualquier malignidad que pudiera afectarle, como son los sonajeros o diversos escapularios.

La membrana no se descartaba, se conservaba. Incluso hoy en día se sigue conservado para fines médicos en los hospitales, ya que pueden ayudar a regenerar células madre o ayudar en la oftalmología, entre otros beneficios.

Cuidar de la membrana con la que se vino al mundo era, antaño, muy importante, ya que conserva numerosas virtudes mágicas y curativas. Al retoño se lo bautizaba junto con la membrana y, para reforzar su poder mágico, a menudo solían hacerse misas sobre ella. O bien, para padres más audaces, eran capaces de esconderla bajo pedestales de figuras santas de las iglesias o ermitas durante tres noches seguidas o durante días sagrados del calendario cristiano, pues estaban convencidos de las capacidades de su nuevo miembro familiar. Incluso podía alcanzar cotas de santidad, que eso era mucho decir en las pasadas décadas. Era tan importante venir al mundo con ese velo que algunos deseaban obtenerlo para su propia protección, pues tenerlo a su lado era un talismán para protegerse contra el enemigo incluso en conflictos bélicos. O los abogados, que la usaban como amuleto de buena estrella para sus trabajos judiciales.

A veces la genética o los caprichos de la naturaleza se nace con ciertos detalles físicos que saltan a la vista, como tener seis dedos, aseguran ciertas zonas que tienen cualidades para mejorar la salud de los que acuden a ellos para una imposición de manos, los consideran afortunados. En estos tiempos, toda superstición ya se ha modificado por completo, pero antaño era algo prodigioso tener esta malformación genética llamada «polidactilia». Hubo una época en que casi todos los habitantes de un pueblo (Cervera de Buitrago, Madrid) tenían seis dedos, de ello se encargó un desaparecido periódico en dejar un curioso reportaje (*La*

Estampa, 1929), aunque estos no tenían ningún poder curativo, según la reseña, incluso se llegaron a vincular ciertas visitas de objetos volantes no identificados (ovnis) durante la década de 1970 a esa localidad. Ese fenómeno físico que destacaban los lugareños se debe, posiblemente, a los matrimonios consanguíneos y la endogamia.

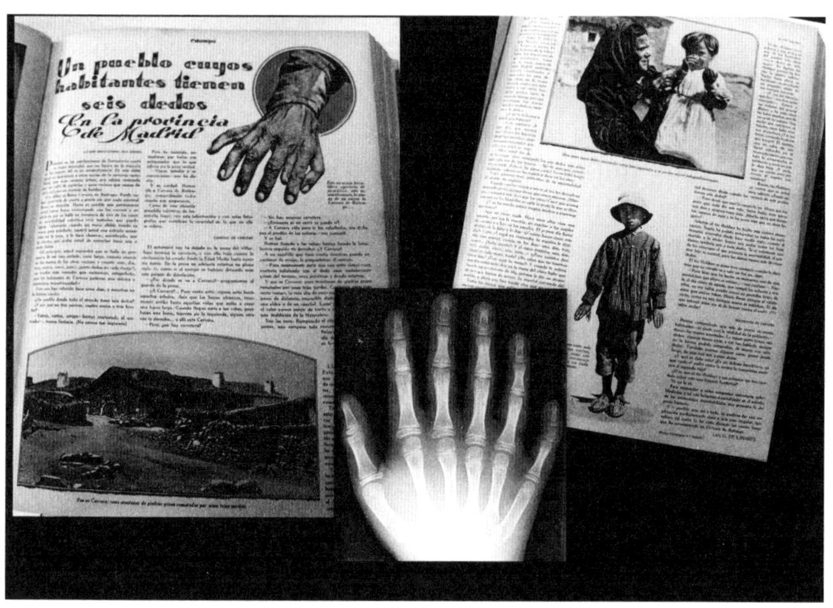

20. *Se cree que poseer seis dedos puede ser un vínculo mágico con el curanderismo. La Estampa. Montaje: A. Beitia.*

Ser el séptimo hijo (sin mediar hembra entre ellos o viceversa) también tiene esa connotación mágica de tener atributos de curandero, visionario, profeta u otras cualidades místicas. La elección del siete es compleja, pero se cree que procede de la tradición bíblica de crear el mundo en seis y el séptimo descansó, lo cual simboliza un número de la perfección o quizá sea por el número de días de la semana. Además, podían referirse al número de cuerpos celestes que se conocían hasta el siglo XVII. No solo podían ser curanderos, algunas culturas de Sudamérica aportan que era una señal algo maléfica, ser un futuro *lobishome,* es decir, un hombre lobo (o bien, en el caso femenino, una bruja). Aunque podían ver algunas virtudes interesantes, puesto que también podía verle con cierto poder de curación, ya que lo veían con posibilidades de conexión con el mundo espiritual, lo cual podía tener cualidades de sanación.

Otro conjunto de características fundamentales es el amplio conocimiento de la naturaleza, especialmente la botánica. El curandero muestra un gran respeto por su entorno natural, ya que está muy conectado, junto al interés por los tratamientos holísticos. Se entiende por tratamientos holísticos a los enfoques de la salud y el bienestar que abarcan a la persona en su totalidad, física, mental, emocional y espiritualmente.

En resumen, la noción central es que todos estos elementos influyen en la vida del individuo y, por ende, en su bienestar. En consecuencia, un enfoque holístico no solo tiene en cuenta los síntomas de una enfermedad, sino las raíces de la misma, además de contribuir al equilibrio y a la salud en general del paciente.

Y, sobre todo, están dispuestos a las prácticas rituales basadas en la fe. Los sanadores suelen ponerse a otros niveles de comunicación, donde aseguran lograr diversos contactos divinos, como la Virgen, los santos, las santas e incluso los difuntos propios o del paciente. Al igual que en el momento de su muerte, suelen informar quién va a recibir sus conocimientos, bien entregando su obra de anotaciones, fórmulas de herboristería o plegarias secretas que utiliza, aunque también afirman que será en espíritu, como una reencarnación de sus poderes.

Tengo unas conclusiones que pueden servir para añadirlas al perfil más característico de los curanderos, poniendo de límite una fecha que han estado ejerciendo hasta 1990 en las provincias de Valencia, Castellón y zonas de Castilla La Mancha, aunque podían ser extrapolables a todas las regiones. Es mi resumen personal al cotejar historias y datos.

La mayoría no posee estudios, no de medicina, sino educativos, ni durante la dictadura franquista con su rígido sistema educativo ni tampoco un solo atisbo de la desaparecida Educación General Básica (EGB, Ley 14/1970). Esto es debido a su aislamiento en su medio rural y las dificultades de su tiempo, ya que la mayoría de los sanadores proceden de entornos rurales. Su formación ha llegado de sus antecesores, pues, a menudo, ha existido un curandero, yerbero o comadrona entre sus parientes más cercanos. Quizá este motivo de ausencia educativa radica en el pretexto de que no existe, en términos generales, un registro de sus pacientes, escritos de sus experiencias, anotaciones, aportes de otra índole…

El analfabetismo era patente en muchos curanderos que ejercieron hasta la década de 1970, muy pocos sabían escribir y leer correctamente.

Muchos de ellos han sufrido enfermedades graves o accidentes que casi les cuestan la vida y se recuperaron milagrosamente. Pese a ello, pocos conservan esa prueba de enfermedad o del accidente. Motivo que reforzaron su fe religiosa, puesto que creen que la divina providencia fue quien les ha salvado su vida, por ello están convencidos de que son intermediarios y canalizadores entre el paciente y un ser divino. Ese personaje celestial puede ser Dios, pueden ser ángeles, puede ser la propia Virgen de su localidad o incluso seres de otras dimensiones, desde difuntos familiares o, aunque suene extravagante, hasta presencias extraterrestres. Esto último es algo extraño para muchos, puesto que piensan que no son seres divinos quienes se manifiestan a ellos y al resto de curanderos y quieren ayudar con sus conexiones energéticas. Hay casos como el del alcoyano Rafael Civas, que contactaba con alienígenas de Andrómeda, o un conocido curandero de Torrent, Francisco Ramón Jiménez, más popularmente conocido como Paquito, que en este caso contactaba con seres de Ganímedes y sanaba comunicándose a través del código Morse. Estos le concedieron un poder de energía vital para sanar incluso a través de la telepatía y en menos de un minuto.

Entre sus prácticas usan elementos esotéricos, como varillas, péndulos, cristales y minerales. Incluyen variedades de masajes usando aceites naturales o la imposición de las manos, que se conoce actualmente como reiki. Esto no es de antaño, sino de unas épocas recientes, ya que muy pocos conocían el uso de estos elementos y se limitaban al uso del rosario. Prácticamente todos los sanadores usan alcohol etílico al natural o en preparados con romero, lavanda, tomillo, eucalipto o aloe vera.

Lo más llamativo es que ningún curandero o curandera puede curarse a sí mismo. Posiblemente sea por la implicación emocional que puede ocasionar, ya que incluso en sus creencias lo ven como una falta de respeto a las virtudes donadas por las entidades divinas. Aunque esto parece algo confuso, ya que ciertos sanadores se aplicaron a sí mismos los remedios naturales. Por ejemplo, un conocido curandero de Móstoles (Miguel Piquera) asegura que se curó él mismo de úlceras de estómago en varias ocasiones y de «azúcar» (se supone que es diabetes). En este último punto, utilizan a menudo un argot popular para identificar diversas dolencias y enfermedades.

Respecto a otros factores relacionados con los pacientes y sus nexos, muchos de ellos pueden llegar a tener más de 60 pacientes al día si alcanzan cierta notoriedad en su zona, y no suelen cobrar directamente con tarifas, sino por la voluntad, siendo muchos de ellos denunciados en alguna ocasión por algún médico por competencia desleal o prácticas ilegales desde el punto de vista del colegio médico oficial.

La mayoría de los pacientes que han pasado por su consulta llegan con dolores de artrosis, reumatismo, lumbalgias o indisposiciones gástricas. Paralelamente, acuden pacientes que han pasado sin éxito por muchos médicos y diversos tratamientos farmacológicos.

Entre esos dones que poseen los curanderos, existen otras facetas curiosas y extravagantes que hay que añadir, en este caso entre mujeres, las «mamantonas». Mujeres que hicieron de su profesión succionar los pechos de las mujeres que acababan de dar a luz y que, por diversas causas, no eran capaces de dar leche materna a su recién nacidos. Es lo que se conoce como «nodriza», aunque esta última es más una dedicación exclusiva en familias que económicamente estaban mejor y se podían permitir el lujo de contratarlas y sin ninguna virtud mágica «curanderil». Las mamantonas, dentro de ese abanico de dedicaciones a la salud, eran especialistas en ello y conocían algunas facetas de artes sanadoras, especialmente para neonatos. Por supuesto, también estaba entre los hombres, aunque quedaba más reducido, muy alejados de las prácticas de sanación, y lo ejercían por su cuenta sin más recursos de salud, eran conocidos como «mamadores». Esta función no solo era de succionar los pechos que tuvieran problemas para amamantar los retoños, sino que podían succionar heridas e incluso venenos provocados por animales, práctica peligrosa y con riesgo enorme para los curanderos que a veces suelen realizarlo, pero que gracias a esa virtud mágica de estar protegidos no suelen pasar ningún problema.

Lo más llamativo que atañe a los antiguos curanderos es su práctica y arte de hacer masajes terapéuticos, tratar lesiones de toda índole o dolencias musculares. Es difícil encontrar una academia que enseñara estas prácticas en décadas anteriores, solo puede quedar la opción de aprenderlo por educación de otros sanadores anteriores, la observación de los animales en la naturaleza o el aprendizaje particular de observar los cadáveres humanos, aunque esto no puede sustituir el estudio anatómico riguroso. Recordemos que estaba totalmente prohibido durante la jurisdicción de la Inquisición, que podía tener consecuencias que iban desde la excomunión hasta la ejecución. En muchos países europeos, se promulgaron diversas leyes para regular el acceso a los cadáveres. Por ejemplo, en el Reino Unido, el «Anatomy Act» de 1832 daba licencia libre a los estudiantes de Medicina y permitió el uso de cadáveres para su estudio y disecciones de personas fallecidas en hospitales o prisiones o que no tuvieran reclamación familiar. Esto legalizó una práctica que previamente estaba rodeada de controversia, supuestos ritos de nigromancia y de otras prácticas clandestinas, es posible que hayan tenido algún contacto los curanderos populares con algún cadáver para su observación, pero serían muy escasos y complicados, pues, además de surgir esa posibilidad, debieron contar con el visto bueno de su presencia como meros observadores durante algún estudio.

Es evidente que faltan muchos detalles en estas conclusiones personalizadas, pero creo que son las destacadas en este oficio que se vive como una inspiración. ¿Debemos darle una oportunidad para que mejore nuestra salud y niveles emocionales?

VIII. PLEGARIAS MÁGICAS Y TAUMATURGIA RELIGIOSA

Un proverbio popular de esa España de la fe y la creencia en las supersticiones dice así: «Dios da salud a quien cree, no al que reza». Posiblemente existe algo que no funciona en el universo del curanderismo, como la curación por la palabra, a través de unas plegarias. No se busca legitimar, sino que deseo mostrarlo como una práctica visible. No conviene olvidar que los ensalmos ocupan parte importante de sus procesos de sanación.

Las plegarias han formado parte del ser humano desde las primeras etapas en que surgen las tendencias religiosas, y se han utilizado como un medio para poder comunicarse con lo divino, pedir deseos, expresar miedos e incluso agradecer las mediaciones celestiales.

Una plegaria es una forma de comunicación verbal o también mental con el mundo espiritual o divino. Su uso está enfocado normalmente para los rituales religiosos, aunque existe la posibilidad de usarlo como parte de la vida cotidiana para pedir protección y acción de gracias o de agradecimiento.

La palabra «plegaria» proviene del latín *precaria*. Aunque seguramente nos vienen a la mente las plegarias cristianas, muchos ignoran que no son de las más antiguas, ya que existen diversas rogativas por todo el planeta, siendo una de las más antiguas plegarias la conocida hasta la fecha como *Sub tuum praesidium*. Es el himno que se conserva como alabanza a la madre de Dios, según datos de expertos, que aparece escrita por primera vez en un texto griego del año 250 de nuestra era.

Aunque debo hacer un aporte: no es la plegaria más antigua, ni mucho menos. Están los himnos del *Rigveda*, que son prácticamente plegarias en sánscrito a diversas deidades y datan del 1500 a. C. Incluso más antigua es la plegaria a Ra, el dios del sol en el antiguo Egipto, que lo datan sobre el 2400 a. C. Siguiendo en tierra de faraones, se dispone del papiro Ebers, que es un tratado mágico de medicina que incluye plegarias y conjuros a las diosas Isis y Sekhmet, ambas vinculadas a la medicina y la curación.

¿Por qué se usa en el curanderismo?

Primero sería correcto responder en qué momento se comenzó a usar en el curanderismo.

Aunque se usaban desde tiempos mucho más antiguos, aplicando oraciones de índole pagana a ojos de la Iglesia, puedo citar reminiscencias de origen visigodo basado en el arrianismo, incluso otras culturas algo más anteriores como la celtíbera, que realizaban oraciones a Ataecina (diosa de la sanación) o Endovélico (dios de la salud). Posteriormente, durante el Imperio romano, está presente el culto a Ceres (diosa de la agricultura y la fertilidad).

Cuando se aferra con fuerza esta práctica es durante el proceso de sincretización de todas las culturas no cristianas para adaptarse a la nueva tendencia religiosa en la Península. Lo que sí es cierto es que cada plegaria de sanación varía en cada región y estaban enfocadas a la protección contra enfermedades, la fertilidad y la buena fortuna, las buenas cosechas y, posiblemente, invocando las fuerzas del Sol y la Madre Tierra.

Existía un razonado temor a la Inquisición desde el momento de su implantación, incluso mucho antes, cuando se denominaba Justicia Civil. Esto forzó al mundo del curanderismo a una adaptación significativa para el uso de sus ritos, especialmente durante la práctica de sanación, donde las plegarias tradicionales se reformularon para encajar en el cristianismo, permitiendo la supervivencia de muchas prácticas antiguas bajo una nueva apariencia.

Muchas plegarias se transformaron inicialmente en oraciones a la Virgen María, para sustituir a las diferentes deidades femeninas y a san Benito por su influencia en la lucha contra el mal y su poder para el exorcismo.

Incluso se modificaron ciertas oraciones de san Cipriano, que desde mi punto de vista es una adaptación cristiana de antiguos ritos de magia protectora, de un hechicero que lo convirtió al cristianismo. Os cito un ejemplo de cómo han añadido elementos cristianos:

Oh, glorioso san Cipriano, bendito siervo de Dios, que conociste los secretos de la magia y la brujería, y después te convertiste a la fe cristiana. Te imploro que me protejas de todo mal y me libres de las malas lenguas, de la envidia, del mal de ojo y de cualquier hechizo o embrujo. Con tu poder intercede ante Dios para que ningún mal pueda tocarme. Amén.

Posiblemente, esta oración era muy diferente, pero es complicado localizar la original plegaria precristiana. Si observan, lo invocan como siervo de dios convertido, y conservan elementos contra el mal de ojo, brujería y hechizos. Mi propuesta sería que la plegaria primigenia invocase a las fuerzas de la naturaleza, energía cósmica o seres espirituales benignos.

Con la evolución, especialmente a partir del siglo XII en adelante, se intensificó la persecución de cualquier práctica que fuera considerada herética o pagana. Esto forzó a muchos practicantes de curanderismo a adaptarse en todos los sentidos para evitar la persecución. Entre esos oficios de sanación estaban las matronas, barberos, sangradores, hechiceras, sacamuelas o componedores de huesos, entre otras prácticas vinculadas con la salud tanto en seres humanos como en el ganado. Cada labor debió adaptarse, y aquellos que no pudieron hacerlo o se negaban a esa evolución no acabaron bien: las hogueras y las torturas estaban listas para usarlas hasta extremos inimaginables.

En resumen, las invocaciones, diferentes para cada tipo de intervención, en las que aparecen citados Dios, Jesús, la Virgen y diferentes santos, piensan muchos que tienen su origen en el momento que mandó sus apóstoles por el mundo a difundir su palabra y oraciones. Sin embargo, los antropólogos e historiadores plantean la hipótesis de que se trata de ritos más antiguos que los que citan las Sagradas Escrituras, que se remontan a los primeros druidas de la edad del Bronce (aproximadamente el 3300 y el 1200 a. C.).

En el momento de los juicios por brujería, dado que algunas de las personas sospechosas poseían oraciones supuestamente curativas, la terminología pagana fue reemplazada por deidades cristianas por razones de seguridad. Aquellos que no aceptaron ese cambio eran los que más complicado lo tenían frente a la temida Inquisición. Es una de las hipótesis planteadas por expertos.

El uso de plegarias por parte de las personas que ejercen el mágico acto de sanar o mejorar la dolencia produce, según palabras de los curanderos que consulté, una «transferencia de la gracia» al enfermo, que facilitaba y despejaba el camino para que pudiera salir ese desarreglo del cuerpo afectado. Incluso durante esas plegarias, han llegado a acontecer algunas curaciones asombrosas que la medicina convencional califica como milagrosas e inexplicables. Posiblemente, sea un milagro, sea también la virtud extraordinaria del sanador o quizá el problema de salud era inexistente, ejerciendo como efecto placebo, que activa una respuesta fisiológica de su cuerpo. O bien esa enfermedad, como he citado, era inexistente a causa de un diagnóstico erróneo, o bien no era tan grave la dolencia como se pensaba.

No conviene olvidar que muchas oraciones y plegarias son transmitidas oralmente, en determinadas fechas sagradas, por lo que muy pocas han sido comunicadas de forma escrita.

Por este motivo abundan casos en la interpretación de las plegarias que puedan distorsionarse por la mala memoria de los recitantes y el receptor, que ha supuesto que algunas partes de las oraciones quedan relegadas en el olvido, frases de las fórmulas o incluso una mala comprensión de la palabra.

Las novenas también eran usadas, siguiendo las normas específicas que manda el canon religioso. El paciente debe usarlas durante nueve días y en momentos determinados que recomienda el curandero. Esto forma parte del oportunismo del curandero, pues es consciente de la ignorancia de quienes le piden ayuda y, cuando detecta un fanatismo religioso, aprovecha para buscar un remedio místico que pueda ayudar en su convalecencia a las personas que realmente no tienen ninguna enfermedad, tan solo esa crisis psicológica del hipocondríaco que se trata con buena dosis de terapias mentales y cognitivas.

21. *Curandera nauha, invocando a través de plegarias.*
Fuente archivo Universidad Autónoma de México (UAM).

Es un factor psicosomático: las plegarias, las novenas y las oraciones pueden ayudar a aliviar la ansiedad y el estrés a los que está sometido el paciente. Y esto la ciencia lo sabe bien al día de hoy, pues proporciona una excelente terapia de esperanza, control de emociones, sosiego mental… Y es interesante recordar que en los grandes recintos hospitalarios de la actualidad suele existir una capilla para orar. Un espacio entregado a la ciencia, a la tecnología, deja un ámbito para el poder de la mente. Ante estas situaciones, la fe es importante para ambos protagonistas (curandero y paciente). El curandero debe tenerla con sus convicciones más profundas, su entrega total a sus creencias, mientras que el paciente ya la carga de forma instintiva acudiendo a su consulta, se abre a la posibilidad de un hecho prodigioso y emocional.

Las oraciones o plegarias a menudo pueden ser personalizadas que muchas de ellas han logrado llegar a todos los sanadores de la geografía española, no exentas de ciertas controversias con la Iglesia de su tiempo. Aunque no hubo una prohibición, por parte de Franco, generalizada del curanderismo, se vigilaba y en algunos casos se penalizaba a los curanderos, que se consideraba que ponían en peligro la salud pública o competían con los médicos oficiales. A menudo, los curanderos eran acusados de intrusismo profesional si practicaban actos que se consideraban exclusivos de la medicina oficial (diagnósticos, tratamientos complejos, etc.), pero también se los podía castigar si sobrepasaban los límites, ya fuese a través de plegarias, invocaciones o ritos mágicos, de modo que podían enfrentarse a sanciones. La conocida «Ley de vagos y maleantes», que estuvo vigente desde 1933 hasta 1970, permitía la persecución de prácticas consideradas impropias o peligrosas. Aunque estaba enfocada principalmente en el control de la delincuencia y el comportamiento social, también se aplicó para vigilar y castigar a aquellos que ejercían el curanderismo y otras prácticas no autorizadas. Eran tiempos convulsos y complicados, había que hilar fino para no molestar al Gobierno y la doctrina católica.

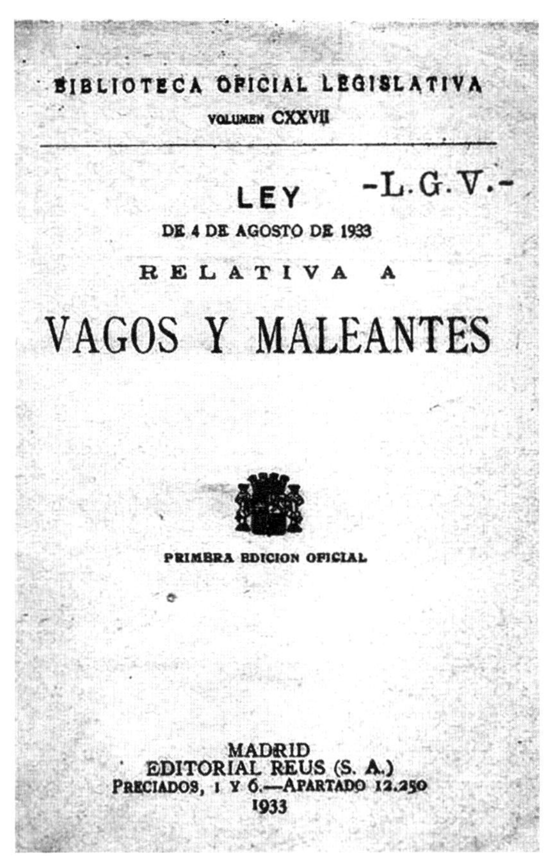

22. Ley de vagos y maleantes.

Un detalle habitual de la España de la posguerra consistía en que, en aquella época, era complicado conseguir una buena alimentación, así que el hambre estuvo presente durante décadas. A causa de ello, los cuerpos estaban bastante delgados y su estómago se veía bastante reducido. Si comían un poco más de lo habitual, se producía un pequeño desorden biológico en el proceso de la digestión, lo que producía un incómodo malestar.

La receta era sencilla y ecuménica: hervir en agua limpia una parte de romero, ruda y hierbabuena. O bien podía ser la sencillez de la manzanilla.

La receta en sí debería bastar para notar un alivio en esas molestias estomacales, pero falta el efecto místico, aplicar la carga divina a la fórmula junto con la acción sanadora que aplicaría (un masaje, señal de la cruz sobre el punto de dolor…) y la demostración de uno de los poderes secretos de un curandero: la plegaria.

Y esta era la oración más recurrida en general:
Madre de Dios, quita el dolor donde lo toco yo.
Dios es muy alto, Dios es muy bajo.
En el nombre del Padre, el Hijo y el Espíritu Santo.
Amén.

O bien pueden recurrir a la siguiente oración:
Jesús, José y María: pon tu mano donde yo pongo la mía.

Otra alternativa similar a este rito es la siguiente jaculatoria:
En nombre de Jesús y María,
pon tu mano antes que yo la mía.
La Virgen María entró en Belén encinta.
Salga el mal y entre el bien.

Si observamos, en las oraciones es necesario que el curandero ponga la mano sobre la zona dolorida para continuar el proceso. Estas plegarias no solo eran útiles para las incomodidades de vientre, sino que se podían usar para cualquier tipo de dolencia general y con gestos como llevarse la mano izquierda al corazón mientras recitan su plegaria.

Prácticamente todos los curanderos emplean oraciones y rituales durante su labor y creen en el poder de la palabra, sin olvidar que, al acabar con cada ensalmo o plegaria, se rezaba un padrenuestro y un avemaría, siempre en números mágicos, que podían ser tres o nueve veces. Tres porque la tradición nos lleva a la Santísima Trinidad (Padre, Hijo y Espíritu Santo) o nueve porque, supuestamente, se refiere a las novenas religiosas, o bien podían referirse a la invocación de los ángeles, que eran nueve coros según la biblia, que se dividen en tres jerarquías.

En mis observaciones, existen tres tipos de orden de palabras que suelen aplicar algunos curanderos: palabra escuchada, palabra dicha y, finalmente, palabra contenida.

En la primera, son las dichas por el propio paciente, es una forma de pedir súplica al curandero como mediador ante la divinidad para conocer su problema y diagnóstico. Para el curandero, es importante que lo solicite con fe y esperanza a su sanación, tanto física como espiritual. La segunda es la dirigida a Dios, la Virgen o los diversos santos que pueda manejar el sanador; normalmente, son palabras secretas que cita el curandero, rara vez el paciente entiende lo que está rezando. Y, finalmente, está la «contenida», aquello que no se dice pero que tiene un efecto dentro de la persona.

Suponen que, cuando las palabras de una plegaria se pronuncian de manera adecuada, con fe y con el propósito bien enfocado, tienen el poder de influir por completo en la salud de una persona. Siempre la plegaria va acompañada de contacto físico con el paciente, al que se le va aplicando un suave masaje sobre la zona a tratar o bien se le aplica la imposición de las manos, práctica que está inspirada en la figura de Jesús en la Biblia (Mateo 8:5-13 y Lucas 7:1-10).

Otra oración que tengo repetida en mi bitácora de plegarias para sanar al paciente de heridas cotidianas como un corte profundo, herida de arma blanca, etc. es apelada por diversos sanadores, incluso comadronas que también ejercían de curanderas. No hay una zona geográfica específica, ya que la citan en aldeas del Maestrazgo castellonense, algunas localidades de la comarca valenciana de L´Horta e incluso un sanador de Teruel, que también la citó con alguna palabra variada, aunque en su conjunto era la misma plegaria:

Santo el día,
santa la hora,
santa la herida,
santo lo que digo.
Yo te conjuro,
no debes sangrar,
ni hincharte,

ni entumecerte,
ni causar dolor.
En nombre de la Santísima Trinidad,
Del Padre, del Hijo y del Espíritu Santo.
Amén.

No obstante, el uso de la palabra no es exclusiva del cristianismo. Como he citado antes, en otras culturas ya se venía usando el poder de la palabra y la oración, como en China, en las tradiciones budistas o en el islam con la *ruqyah*, que son recitaciones del Corán para tratar enfermedades tanto físicas como espirituales. Muestro un ejemplo de oraciones islámicas como el versículo del trono, *Ayat al-Kursi*, que se utiliza comúnmente entre todos los adeptos de esta fe. Su uso está enfocado a la protección contra el diablo, el infortunio y el mal de ojo.

Otra oración basada en el Corán cuyo objetivo no es otro que la sanación absoluta a través de la fe podemos observarla en la sura 26:80:

Y cuando yo caigo enfermo,
Él es quien me cura.

La palabra u oración con la que se dirigen a las diversas divinidades se denomina «plegaria», y esto lo saben bien muchos sanadores a la hora de iniciar sus labores como curanderos. Durante la citación de plegarias, ellos se consideran un simple medio, un elemento de la curación porque Dios los guía, no son ellos quienes erradican la enfermedad. La magia de la palabra a través de invocaciones, oraciones, etc. transfiere una energía positiva y mágica al enfermo, y esto facilita que mejore.

Había que acertar el tipo de oración, pues no todas están enfocadas a Dios, muchas de ellas apuntan a diversos santos. Por citar un ejemplo muy recurrido, estuve indagando con curiosidad en la «folkmedicina» en el balneario de Benassal, famoso lugar para las infecciones de orina. Allí existe una oración a san Liborio, patrón de los urólogos. A este santo se lo representa con un libro en la mano y tres piedras sobre él: son las piedras de riñón, cálculos biliares y en número místico y simbólico de tres. Por este motivo se ha convertido en santo referente cuando se invocan sus plegarias para sanar infecciones de riñón, haciendo posteriormente la señal de la cruz sobre la zona dolorida.

A menudo se toma como alternativa esta otra plegaria inspirada en las tres piedras de los cálculos biliares:

La Virgen María ponga su mano
Antes que yo la mía.
Estaba la Virgen pura en su aposento
Con nueve ovillos de lana.
Con tres urde.
Con tres trama.
Con tres cura
las vejigas de tu cara.

O para los dolores de garganta también existía su correspondiente plegaria, en este caso apuntaba la invocación de san Blas. Aunque no sufrió ningún mal en su zona de garganta, según la leyenda salvó la vida de un niño que se estaba ahogando con unas espinas de pescado clavadas en su pequeña garganta. Esta es la plegaría tradicional que los curanderos usaban tras hacer el signo de la cruz o imponer sus manos sobre el cuello:

Oh, glorioso san Blas,
a ti acudimos en busca de protección
para nuestras gargantas, ruega por nosotros
y por aquellos que sufren
de dolencias de la garganta…

Prácticamente en todas las plegarias se debe hacer un «signo». Es un universo poco estudiado, pues cada curandero tiene un gesto mágico que aprendió a través de diversas herencias. Podía ser la sencilla señal de la cruz o un dibujo imaginario realizado con los dedos sobre el cuerpo del paciente, habitualmente suelen hacer un gesto de espiral o haciendo un ocho. Estos signos que aplican no solo sirven para (supuestamente) la sanación física del enfermo, sino también para proporcionar una sensación de protección y bienestar espiritual al entrar en contacto con el paciente.

Algo tan común como un dolor de muelas, encías o dientes es recurrir a las plegarias a santa Apolonia (fallecida en el año 249), que fue martirizada arrancándole todos los dientes. Su herencia de oración es la siguiente:

Bendita santa Apolonia, que por tu virginidad y martirio mereciste del Señor ser instituida abogada contra el dolor de muelas y dientes, te suplicamos fervorosos intercedas con el Dios de las misericordias, para que esta criatura sea sanada.

Señor, accede benigno a la súplica que te dirigimos. Amén.

Tras la oración se hace el signo de la cruz (+) tres veces, normalmente en la parte afectada, siempre en múltiplo de tres y untado en aceite. A partir de este punto, las prácticas varían frente a esta dolencia, como escupir tres veces al suelo si hay luna llena, chupar una «piedra mágica» (una sencilla piedra de río) o recomendar el uso de ciertas plantas como el clavo, que tiene un componente antiinflamatorio que es la clave de su uso: el eugenol.

Los curanderos a menudo se ofrecían para extraer esa parte dental que era recomendable extraer. Para ello utilizaban herramientas simples como pinzas o unas tenazas para agarrar y extraer la muela afectada. Muchos de ellos son instrumentos creados por ellos mismos, en forma de gancho o garfio. Este método era muy rudimentario y excesivamente doloroso, ya que no era habitual contar con una anestesia adecuada. Sin embargo, a pesar de ser una auténtica tortura, había que sumar lo peligrosa que era esta operación si no existía una esterilización adecuada de esos instrumentos, pues la infección estaba garantizada y podía suponer un riesgo de salud o incluso perder la vida tras ese proceso infeccioso.

Son innumerables la cantidad de oraciones diversas que se usaban dentro del santoral cristiano. Pero muchos de ellos esconden secretos, plegarias que apenas nadie conoce, personalizadas, que cuando las citan apenas son imperceptibles para el paciente o balbucean unas palabras de difícil comprensión, quizá para dificultar escuchar o que se apropien de esa virtud mágica del poder de la palabra.

No solo había oraciones para activar la sanación, también para proteger durante un parto. En un mundo donde antaño se hacía difícil encontrar un médico o una asistencia hospitalaria, se recurría a las matronas locales o a mujeres que tenían unas nociones básicas para dar a luz, todo ello a cambio de algo de ropa, unas pocas monedas o algo de comida. Nacer era un trance complicado, pues existían numerosos problemas y podían fallecer, no solo por incidencias del parto, sino por las diversas enfermedades que iban circulando en un mundo rural que estaba alejado de las mejoras sanitarias. Incluso hay aportes de localidades del interior de Murcia y Castellón que han llegado a dar luz dentro de cuevas, ya que consideran que tiene una connotación mística y sagrada.

La oración que han utilizado con más frecuencia en estos lances es la siguiente invocando a san Ramón Nonato, considerado el patrón de las mujeres embarazadas y los recién nacidos. Su relación con los partos se debe a su leyenda, pues la madre de san Ramón falleció durante el parto y el bebé fue extraído del útero materno mediante una cesárea de emergencia realizada por un cirujano, algo inédito en su época (nació en 1204) y un gesto extraño de manipular un cadáver. Su madre estaba muerta, por lo que la manipulación del cuerpo de un fallecido sería un acto de violación de las leyes, según las costumbres funerarias de su tiempo, que exigían un trato respetuoso de los muertos sobre todo alejado de prácticas mágicas e impuras. Esta cirugía excepcional salvó la vida del niño, lo que llevó a que Ramón fuera llamado «nonato» o «no nacido»:

San Ramón no fue nacido,
ni su madre lo parió,
que a los tres días

de estar muerta
por un costado salió.

Eso es uno de los mejores secretos que protege el curandero y todas las mujeres que también ejercen la virtud de sanar. Esto también forma parte de esa denominada «gracia», heredar los conocimientos u oraciones de sus padres, abuelos e incluso otros familiares cercanos, especialmente si están muy cerca del momento de su muerte o como una última voluntad poco antes de expirar.

El poder sanador radica, según las propias creencias de estos, en que solo es posible oralmente, bien en esos instantes antes de su fallecimiento, bien por voluntad propia del sanador, que desea compartir el secreto de sus remedios. Pero en este último caso solo tiene efectividad traspasarlas en una fecha determinada.

Esas fechas no son nada extrañas, ya las he citado y coinciden con días muy sagrados en la fe cristiana: periodo de Semana Santa (normalmente suelen elegir Jueves o Viernes Santo); el Día de san Juan es otra fecha importante, tanto desde el punto de vista de los que creen que es la noche de las brujas como en cuanto al cambio del solsticio; y, finalmente, durante el periodo de Navidad.

Se debe citar siete veces la plegaria, que quien la recibe debe memorizar. Si no consigue el objetivo, se pasa a otra plegaria que pueda recordar con facilidad.

La magia de esa oración se perdería para siempre si no logran retenerla o si las circunstancias del aura espiritual de esa persona que las recibe no son las apropiadas. Incluso si la revela sin motivo alguno a otra tercera persona, la plegaria que han mantenido en secreto durante generaciones podría perder el don de sanar, lo que significa que el curandero que la ha citado perdería también su poder de ser el mediador y quien la recibe tampoco podría usarla. Como podemos ver, las plegarias las cuidan, aunque sean parte de una parafernalia, un efecto placebo o, quién sabe, el verdadero secreto del curanderismo ancestral.

Tan poderosas son las plegarias y oraciones que no solo los curanderos de la Península estaban interesados en mantener el secreto o era algo exclusivo y privilegiado. Si nos adentramos un poco en la historia, y sin ir muy lejos, existieron movimientos que pretendían difundir el poder de la palabra y la oración, tenemos el ejemplo de *Christian Science*, que fue fundada por Mary Baker Eddy. En ella trataba de convencer a la sociedad de que la oración espiritual facilitaría la curación de todas las enfermedades, tanto físicas como espirituales, todo ello debido a su propia experiencia personal, pues en 1866 Mary sufrió un terrible accidente que dañó prácticamente toda su columna vertebral, no lograba mejorar ni calmar el dolor con los remedios médicos de su tiempo, y se dedicó a la plegaria y la oración cristiana, que según su historia logró sanarse gracias a esto.

Podíamos considerarlo un auténtico milagro, pero ella no era una mujer que se resignaba a su destino, sino que aprendió, era adepta a los encuentros espiritistas e incluso uno que sería su futuro esposo, Phineas Parkhurst Quimby (1802-1866), era un hipnotista mesmerista, además de curandero al que conoció antes de su grave accidente, pues ella tenía ataques de índole epiléptica. Quizá en ese velo de misterio podríamos encontrar el enigma de su sanación, y no en la oración cristiana, ya estaba siendo tratada por un curandero y aprendió mucho de P. Quinby, aunque existieron numerosas discrepancias entre ambos respecto a sus métodos.

Es posible que cuando salió más reforzada la práctica de la plegaria para sanaciones sea motivada por momentos que se vivieron en épocas de desastres humanitarios, como una epidemia. Por citar un ejemplo, durante la pandemia de la gripe española (1918-1919) se realizaban numerosas misas de plegarias para pedir intercesión de la Virgen para acabar con la terrible epidemia y sus consecuencias, actos de los que muchos curanderos pudieron tomar en un maravilloso efecto de fe. O, algo más cercano a nuestro tiempo, la plegarias del padre Pío (1887-1968), famoso por sus estigmas y visiones místicas, quien conseguía sanar diversas heridas y enfermedades con oraciones y rogativas, según numerosos testimonios y fieles seguidores de este religioso canonizado por Juan Pablo II en 2002.

La fe y la creencia en la eficacia de la taumaturgia pueden jugar un papel decisivo durante los procesos de sanación. Muchas personas que son pacientes de un curandero confían en la intervención divina a través de su mediación, y esto es visto como un mecanismo psicológico que proporciona una evidente mejoría y genera cierto bienestar.

Cuando un paciente recurría a un curandero con unas molestias focalizadas (por ejemplo, de vientre o de cabeza), se aplicaban los remedios más recurridos y prácticos de los que se disponía en la consulta. En ocasiones no existe mejoría, y puede suceder una serie de opciones. Una es que lo remita a un facultativo oficial, dado que no consigue ningún resultado. Otra opción es remitirlo a un curandero con conocimientos superiores para sanar su dolor o patología. La otra opción es la que tratamos: si finalmente no responde a los tratamientos de sus terapias, se acudía a invocar al santo o santa que estaba vinculado con esa enfermedad. Si alcanzaba ese milagro de sanarse o no, dependía en buena parte de la fe de cada uno, el convaleciente y el curandero. Por estas causas, en ermitas o recintos religiosos consagrados, se pueden encontrar numerosos exvotos para agradecer su intercesión.

Algunos casos de sanación por taumaturgia han evidenciado una notable mejoría debido a esos misteriosos procesos de autosanación, lo que significa que el cuerpo humano tiene una capacidad inherente para sanarse a sí mismo, haciendo de la taumaturgia un catalizador, un modo de conectar con las energías sutiles o espirituales.

Se piensa que la taumaturgia puede activar la gnosis humana y se puede interpretar desde diferentes perspectivas, desde la esotérica hasta la mística espiritual o la psicológica.

«Taumaturgia» es un término de origen griego que procede de la palabra *thaumatourgos*, que significa «hacedor de maravillas» o «persona capaz de hacer milagros». Y en ello confían muchas personas a través de los curanderos que ejercen de mediador o canalizador para invocar a ese mágico personaje religioso implicando rituales, oraciones, símbolos sagrados y otras formas para esa conexión con lo divino y que puedan proceder a su sanación.

Esto no es una idea o costumbre de los curanderos, pues en el Concilio de Trento (1545-1563) ya animaban y recomendaban la veneración de santos:

Es bueno y útil invocar a santos, que juntamente con Cristo dominan y ofrecen a Dios sus plegarias en pro de los hombres y recabar de ellos en sus oraciones, su poder y ayuda, con objeto de conseguir de Dios beneficios por intercesión de su hijo Jesucristo, nuestro señor, nuestro único redentor y salvador.

La Virgen María es la principal invocación de estos santos sanadores que recurren. Su causa es comprensible, ya que es la más cercana a Jesús, al margen de ser su madre, y según las escrituras teológicas es reina de todos los santos.

Curiosamente, nunca fue considerada una sanadora de enfermos hasta el siglo v. Según indica el historiador Salaminio Hermias Sozomeno (400-447), muchos enfermos acostumbraban a pasar por la iglesia de Anastasia (Bizancio), ya que durante las noches solía aparecerse la Virgen María y los curaba, bien por contacto o indicándoles un remedio que los ayudaría a sanar. Posiblemente este sea el origen de sus invocaciones generalizadas para poder mediar los curanderos en la sanación de sus pacientes. Del mismo modo que dirigían sus plegarias las parteras a la Virgen de la Buena Esperanza, una tradición que viene desde hace siglos, cuya imagen representa a María embarazada.

Se realizaban las rogativas a esta Virgen para tener un buen parto. Hoy en día sigue la tradición en una figura tras el ábside de la Catedral de Valencia, donde muchas mujeres le rezan a la figura de la Buena Esperanza.

Hasta el siglo XVI, en Valencia era muy tradicional dedicarle oraciones y procesiones a la Virgen de la Buena Esperanza por los embarazos acaecidos en la familia real.

Una divinidad muy invocada por las parteras cuando acudían muchas madres a dar a luz o buscaban ayuda durante la gestación.

La figura de María, como componente taumatúrgico, se extiende en la cultura popular medieval hasta llegar al siglo xx en algunos ritos, como el de los niños herniados durante la Noche de san Juan.

Es frecuente entre sanadores un rito enfocado en los niños «quebrados» (herniados) en la Noche de san Juan, que consiste en pasar al menor entre una oquedad de un árbol, normalmente un roble. Si no había un hueco natural en el árbol, el procedimiento implicaba abrir uno sin separar el tronco, y hacer pasar al niño a través de la abertura mientras se recitaban oraciones o plegarias a San Juan y la Virgen María. ¿Qué relación tiene la Virgen María con el rito de curación de niños herniados durante la Noche de San Juan? El origen de esta práctica es un enigma, desconozco el momento de su uso, es algo difuso. En algunas creencias precristianas como las célticas, ya realizaban este paso usando árboles considerados sagrados y que poseían poderes curativos, pero la Inquisición persiguió este rito al considerarlo impropio de su fe y pagano. Pero, como bien sabemos, las costumbres ancestrales se transforman en ritos cristianos. En este caso consideraban la oquedad del árbol como el órgano sexual femenino, y el niño al atravesar ese hueco «renace» a través de la mediación de la Virgen María. Algunos curanderos me sugieren que representa el órgano sexual de la propia Virgen María. Eso sí, antes de atravesar ese hueco, el niño debe pasar de mano en mano por personas que se llamen Juan o María, mientras el curandero pronuncia la siguiente oración en cada pase de manos (las oraciones pueden variar según zonas geográficas o costumbres locales):

Tómalo, Juan; tómalo, María. Buenos días, María, buenos días, Juan, aquí te entrego a este niño quebrado para que me lo des curado.

Existe otra variación más extensa que se cita durante la Noche de san Juan y con el mismo procedimiento de pasarlo por la oquedad del árbol:

Oh, Santísima Virgen María, madre de nuestro Señor Jesucristo y madre nuestra, te pedimos humildemente tu intercesión divina para la sanación de este niño/a (nombre del niño/a) herniado/a.

Así como en la Noche de san Juan, donde la naturaleza renueva su fuerza, pedimos que renueves la salud de este pequeño/a.

Por tu infinita misericordia y amor, alivia su dolor y restaura su bienestar, como madre amorosa que siempre atiende a sus hijos.

Te rogamos, querida Madre, que escuches nuestra súplica, y que tu manto de protección envuelva a (nombre del niño/a), para que recupere su salud y crezca fuerte y sano/a.

En el nombre de tu Hijo amado, Jesús. Amén.

Otra jerarquía de invocación de los curanderos en san Miguel. Según parece, su veneración comienza por el siglo III en Frigia (actual Turquía), aunque quizá cuando su figura adquirió más popularidad teológica fue en el momento en que Justiniano I ordenó construir una iglesia y hospital consagrado a san Miguel Arcángel (actualmente no existen), pues consideraba a esta entidad divina como un intercesor muy poderoso en asuntos de salud y bienestar.

Al relacionarlo con la salud, se ha erigido en una entidad recurrida por la mayoría de los practicantes del curanderismo cuando se le necesita para intervenir en esa enfermedad a través de plegarias, no solo a nivel de salud, sino también porque ayuda a nivel espiritual incluso en ritos contra el mal de ojo o posibles ataques de demonios, lo cual es un elemento usado como herramienta de exorcismos. San Miguel facilita un entorno seguro y libre de energías negativas. Realizar invocaciones a san Miguel es una forma poderosa de conectar con lo divino e influir en el paciente con sus plegarias.

San Roque es otro de los santos más citados durante una terapia de curanderismo, especialmente durante las épocas pasadas que la peste arrasaba ciudades y pueblos casi al completo.

Este santo de origen francés vino al mundo con una mancha en su pecho. Esa marca era roja y en forma de cruz, motivo que sus padres consideraron como un designio divino y podía ser una futura santidad.

23.La prueba del «mal de ojo», según curanderos, basta con unas gotas de aceite para saber si se está influenciado por malas energías o vibraciones. Imagen: A. Beitia.

San Roque enfermó de peste mientras estuvo en Piacenza. La cosa se complicó mucho, puesto que nadie quiso ayudarlo y optó por aislarse. En ese bosque donde se refugió comenzó su leyenda, cuando un perro se acercaba diariamente a lamerle las heridas y le traía un trozo de pan, de ahí su representación iconográfica, con un perro a su lado y un pan. No es mi intención contar toda la vida de prodigios de este personaje del santoral, simplemente trato de explicar el porqué de su elección taumatúrgica como uno de los santos referentes de los curanderos. Esto procede de cuando estuvo san Roque en la cárcel de su Montpelier natal, pensando que era un espía al servicio de los italianos y, en esa prisión falleció sin olvidar su sanación de la peste dejando un escrito en la pared. Esta nota es algo confusa, ya que varía en las tradiciones populares. Las leyendas citan lo siguiente: «Quien se vea atacado de la peste y recurra a Roque, obtendrá amparo en su enfermedad».

De ahí su vínculo con la sanación de enfermedades contagiosas y las plegarias que enfocan los curanderos.

Ya hemos citado que el curanderismo tiene ciertos vínculos con la brujería y la hechicería, por ello se recurre a estos sanadores para eliminar el mal de ojo, ya que son considerados como intermediarios entre el mundo espiritual y el físico, así como sus conocimientos en la influencia de energías negativas, y saben trabajarlas para neutralizarlas por completo.

Previamente realizan un clásico rito muy popular generalizado en toda la geografía, que es la prueba del aceite, donde el «hechizado», tras untar su dedo índice derecho en aceite, dejará que se desplacen tres gotas sobre un cuenco o vaso, preferentemente trasparente, con agua, lo más pura posible o procedente de las iglesias (agua bendecida). A veces no es necesario, según datos de los que dispongo, empapar el dedo, basta con coger la botella de aceite y dejar caer el paciente tres gotas en ese recipiente. Según se comportan las gotas de aceite en el agua, la tradición nos dice que, si las gotas se disuelven rápidamente o se dispersan, puede ser interpretado como una señal de que la persona está afectada por el mal de ojo.

En caso contrario, si las gotas de aceite permanecen flotando juntas en el recipiente sin dispersarse, se intuye que la persona no está afectada por el mal de ojo ni tiene ningún embrujo.

Para actuar en caso de ser embaucado en esas artes de la envidia o que tiene energías negativas en su cuerpo causadas por los hechizos, utilizan un huevo, que lo pasará por el cuerpo de la persona sin romperlo, para que cargue de su energía. Una vez completado el recorrido, se debe romper el huevo en un vaso de agua y observar su contenido. Según la apariencia del huevo en el agua, informa de lo siguiente:

Burbujas o manchas, puede indicar que había presencia de energía negativa o mal de ojo.

Si se observa como hilos o líneas, este efecto informa de que es víctima de envidias o maldiciones más severas.

Si la apariencia es normal, no había un problema significativo ni mal de ojo.

Podía existir otra práctica que he podido observar a los sanadores espirituales de mi zona levantina, y era usar un plato hondo (algunos sugieren que debe ser de barro), unas tijeras abiertas en forma de cruz en su interior como símbolo de «corte» para cortar el maleficio, una copa de agua, que representaría la purificación, y si posible que esté bendecida, luego puede acompañar a este conjunto un rosario, crucifijo personal o estampa.

Una vez logrados estos elementos, se aplicaba el ritual de las gotas de aceite en la copa. A menudo podía ser que se llenase el plato de agua, donde se arrojaban unas cerillas encendidas al agua. Si flotaban, estaba libre de maleficios el paciente; si se hundían, estaría bajo algún hechizo o mal de ojo. En este último caso, recomendaría el curandero dejar tanto el plato como la copa donde se arrojaron las cerillas en la habitación donde descansa el afectado, para poder absorber toda la mala energía, y al día siguiente debería lanzarse el agua por la ventana.

Por supuesto, la plegaria no faltará para eliminar definitivamente el hechizo. El curandero, como buen mediador entre la divinidad y la espiritualidad, tiene varias personalizadas que nunca suelen revelarla a nadie, rodeadas de secretos y silencio.

24. *Tijeras, rosario, aceite y agua bendita contra*
el mal de ojo. Imagen: A. Beitia.

Solo se transfiere en momentos adecuados a otros adeptos de curanderismo. Sin embargo, he podido localizar en publicaciones de grimorios religiosos contra este tipo de males espirituales una oración contra el mal de ojo:

Dos te miraron,
tres te han de sanar.
Santa Ana parió a María.
Santa Isabel, a san Juan.
Estas palabras son dichas,
son dichas muy de verdad
y todo el mal que tuvieres
hoy te deseo quitar.
Si es la cabeza, santa Elena;
en los ojos, san Antonio;
en los brazos, san Ignacio.
Si es el cuerpo,

el Divino Sacramento.
Si es en los pies,
el bendito san Andrés.
Con sus ángeles treinta y tres,
Jesucristo vive,
Jesucristo reina,
Jesucristo te defiende
de todo mal que tuvieres.

En esta última oración debo indicar un detalle: el número dos que cita se refiere al número de ojos que miraron al afectado. Aunque existe una diversidad cultural de estas oraciones contra el mal de ojo, no podemos olvidar que es sumamente complicado obtenerlas, es un secreto personalizado que solo pueden pasarlo en una determinada fecha sagrada del calendario y a personas que vean con cualidades de proteger el misterio del poder de la oración. Aquí un ejemplo más de oración mágica para hacer frente al aojamiento, y es popular en la región sur de Albacete:

Antes fue Cristo
que el mal de ojo se hubiese visto.
Muera el mal de ojo y viva Cristo.
Dos te lo han hecho,
tres te lo han de quitar,
que son las personas santas
de la Trinidad:
Padre, Hijo y Espíritu Santo.
Si te lo han hecho por la mañana,
que te lo quite la Virgen Santa Ana;
si te lo han hecho por la tarde,
que te lo quite la Virgen del Carmen;
si te lo han hecho a medio día,
que te lo quite la Virgen María;
si te lo han hecho por la noche,
que te lo quite san Roque.

Los curanderos con sus plegarias han dejado un mágico legado de sabiduría ancestral. No podemos negar que sus capacidades de conectar con los niveles espirituales han facilitado consuelo y sanación a muchas personas que buscaban soluciones y alivio a sus males espirituales. En nuestro tiempo, en que estamos rodeados de tecnologías, desconectados de su entorno natural, indiferentes y sin dogmas de fe, nos invitan a recordar que debemos volver a esa conexión humana con la naturaleza. Esta predestinación nombrada como «mal de ojo» o «aojamiento» por los curanderos y las rezadoras se ha creado un universo propio de ceremonias y rezos para prevenir su presencia y su propagación (en las que, por cierto, en la actualidad seguimos creyendo muchas personas).

El curandero, en ocasiones, ha necesitado la fuerza de otras personas para erradicar algunas enfermedades más letales como el cólera o tifus. Normalmente era complicado que el enfermo acudiera a su consulta por la debilidad y padecimiento de estas enfermedades que causaron una gran mortandad en diferentes épocas en España. Suele presentarse en casa del necesitado, y necesita que los presentes oren en voz alta una plegaria a san Roque para expulsar el sufrimiento, en un alarde de superstición, devoción y confianza en la taumaturgia:

Glorioso san Roque, que por amor a Dios y al prójimo te consagraste con admirable caridad a asistir a los enfermos de la peste, y por este heroico sacrificio mereciste ser singularmente escogido por Dios como protector contra esta terrible plaga: míranos aquí, postrados humildemente ante tu imagen, implorando tu poderosa intercesión para ser preservados de toda enfermedad contagiosa.

Líbranos de todo mal, san Roque, protégenos con tu amor y bondad, y ruega a Dios para que la enfermedad se aparte de nuestras vidas y seamos fortalecidos en la salud del cuerpo y del espíritu.

Así, como el Señor te concedió la gracia de hacer milagros en favor de los enfermos, escucha nuestras súplicas y concédenos por tu intercesión alivio en nuestros males, paz en nuestras almas y confianza en la voluntad divina.

San Roque, protector nuestro, ruega por nosotros. Amén.

No termina su labor con esta oración a capela entre los presentes, recomendaba quemar diversas prendas del enfermo (por ejemplo: pañuelos, ropa interior, camisas…), ya que en su acervo cultural pensaban que alejaría su contagio. No es más que un acto simbólico, se sabía que no bastaba ni era suficiente para sanar. Era un rito para generar calma en el entorno familiar y un poco de fe, un soplo de magia al corazón, como en todas las plegarias.

IX. METODOLOGÍA Y RECURSOS

En términos generales, observando las memorias de curanderos del pasado y los que ejercieron durante las décadas de 1960-1990, no tienen interés en destacar dentro de la sociedad. Lo más importante para los que ejercen esta función es que los clientes reconozcan su trabajo realizado, pues ellos son la mejor publicidad, ya que pueden ponerlo en los altares como un sanador divino o singular. De lo contrario, puede caer en un vacío o en un abandono total por parte de toda la localidad e incluso de su comarca. Por eso es muy importante amar sus vínculos, ganarse el respeto, el calor humano y la empatía de la persona a la que va a tratar, esa es una de las primeras normas y metodologías que tiene apuntado en la bitácora el curandero rural. No importa si ha sanado o no, la impresión y el trato recibido es esencial para su imagen en el exterior.

Los curanderos y curanderas saben bien que la medicina oficial ha ido caminando hacia un sistema deshumanizado, donde existe la sensación de querer cronificar la enfermedad en lugar de sanar o paliar el dolor, incluso se ha convertido en un burdo negocio en dolencias cuando pueden solucionarse con remedios naturales muy económicos, accesibles para todos y con el máximo respeto a la naturaleza.

Esto último es innegable, pues existen muchos intereses de incentivos de mercado y hacerse con patentes dentro de la farmacopea, especialmente desde la implantación del seguro obligatorio de enfermedad en 1942 durante el régimen de Franco, para mejorar la asistencia de los trabajadores y sus familias. A su vez, ya hay mención de alejarse de las prácticas de curanderismo, al considerarlas como fraude. Desde 1995, el artículo 403 del Código Penal ya sancionaba el intrusismo profesional, incluyendo la práctica de una profesión que afecte al bienestar público sin tener el título correspondiente, lo cual afecta a los curanderos.

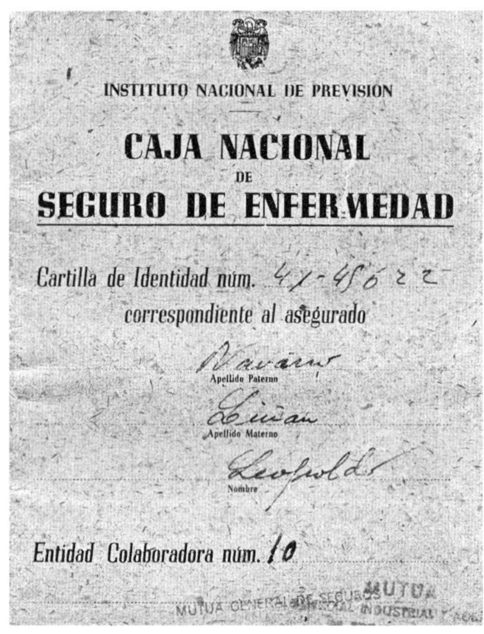

25. *Cartilla Seguro Obligatorio de Enfermedad.*

Sin embargo, he podido observar que en las localidades que he visitado para indagar un poco y recopilar aportes, han tenido su propio personaje o mujer para los menesteres de salud hasta la llegada de un servicio médico decente por parte del Estado. Se acercaban a aquellas personas que tenían unos conocimientos básicos y, sobre todo, que tuvieran buenas referencias del uso de la botánica medicinal (y, si tienen un historial milagrero, mucho mejor).

Se presume de que la salud pública ha mejorado gracias a la medicina moderna, y es una verdad a medias. Se ha avanzado gracias a la tenacidad de la inteligencia artificial, los avances informáticos, las mejoras de tratamientos…, pero realmente lo que dio un verdadero impulso a la salud ha sido la higiene personal (aseo y limpieza personal) y la higiene exterior (alcantarillado, recogida de residuos, control de plagas…). Si no fuera por estas normas, os aseguro que seríamos muy vulnerables a muchas infecciones y diversos virus, por mucha tecnología y avances medicinales que nos pongan sobre la mesa. Diversos aportes de estudios de historia farmacéutica nos sugieren que (resumidos los apuntes) «la industrialización cambió las condiciones de vida de los trabajadores que, de artesanos, oficios rurales al aire libre, pasaron a ser obreros y vivir en peores condiciones debida al trasladarse de su medio rural a la ciudad. La mortalidad aumentaba a medida que descendía en la clase social». Esto nos indica también una de las causas de recurrir a curanderos debido al bajo coste y las causas que originaron enfermedades.

No trato en estas líneas de quitarle méritos a la medicina actual, que, por supuesto, ha contribuido en su buen porcentaje a la mejoría de la salud pública, ni tampoco sumarles méritos a los curanderos, que fraudes en este mundo abundan, como también la mala praxis médica.

Sus métodos no cambian, siguen siendo y seguirán el mismo camino, salvo la fórmula que puedan dispensarle al paciente, si fuese necesario y aconsejable para mejorar el problema por el que lo han atendido.

Aunque el paciente suele indicar su complicación o malestar físico, la forma de diagnosticar al paciente es por el toque de sus manos sobre el cuerpo, bien apoyando sus palmas sobre la zona o apretando suavemente los dedos. Mientras están en ese proceso, la mayoría tienen, gracias a esos dones adquiridos, una sensitividad, perciben señales desde ese punto del cuerpo. Un calor extraño, o bien sienten que es una zona fría respecto al resto del cuerpo, inclusive un hormigueo. Otros, por su alto nivel de clarividencia y capacidad extrasensorial, perciben señales basadas en la luz: sienten oscuridad en el punto que supuestamente necesita sanar, aunque esto último genera cierta controversia.

No todos poseen ese privilegio en sus manos para detectar un área de carga negativa en el cuerpo del interesado. Esto requiere, al margen de esa «gracia» divina, mucha práctica y percepción, es comparable al *reiki*, que busca su canalización de energía. Si no la poseen, recurren a una alternativa popular: péndulos, varillas de radiestesia, cristales y piedras energéticas o algo más llamativo: el bastón atlante, aunque este uso procede del auge de la llamada Nueva Era (1980-1990), y no hay ninguna constancia de su uso general en épocas anteriores. Es una varilla de unos 20/30 cm de largo con un mineral insertado en uno de sus extremos, el cual luego se usa pasando por el cuerpo del interesado, como si fuera algo parecido a un pincel.

26. Masajes terapéuticos con minerales y cristales, una nueva tendencia que no tiene respaldo científico concluyente.

Ese calor que a menudo citan los pacientes es algo extraño, pero no se cita lo que sucede previamente a este método. Muchos de ellos aplican diversos tipos de ungüentos que contienen una alta cantidad de alcanfor, planta que conocían bien los curanderos desde la época medieval y que era conocida como «raíz del diablo». Algunos apuntes sugieren que era una planta que la Inquisición tenía en el punto de mira incluso con prohibiciones, pero no hay evidencia de ello. Si un herbolario o un curandero era acusado de usar plantas supuestamente vetadas (mandrágora, ajenjo, belladona…) en rituales considerados mágicos o heréticos, ellos y sus prácticas serían perseguidos, pero la planta en sí no era sancionada. El uso del alcanfor hace también ese efecto de calor al producirse la friega inicial antes de ese mágico rito de imponer las manos, aunque no debemos olvidar que la sugestión juega un papel importante en este acto, pues siempre les informa que sentirán un cierto aumento de temperatura corporal en el punto donde acercan las manos. Esto es lo que se conoce como «efecto placebo». Incluso los sanadores saben que sus manos emiten un ligero aumento de calor que puede ser percibido por el paciente, sobre todo cuando están en un momento de relax.

Entre sus métodos está incorporar diversos rituales y extravagantes ceremonias que estaban más cerca de una liturgia cristiana en un templo. Podían utilizar agua bendita, genuflexiones ante una representación religiosa que albergaban en su casa o ante su propio altar y uso de sahumerios. Esto último es importante, ya que crea una atmósfera agradable y suele verse como un excelente purificador del ambiente, que hace limpieza espiritual y ayuda a concentrarse al curandero para invocar ciertas entidades que pueden ser percibidas a través de experiencias místicas y visiones. También son posibles las entidades psíquicas, que en este caso suelen percibirse a través de otras experiencias como sueños, meditación o introspección.

Un detalle curioso en la metodología de los curanderos es que, a la hora de realizar señales de la cruz, aplicar compresas impregnadas de diversos aceites y plantas aromáticas o repetir procesos con el paciente, deben hacerlo siempre en un número determinado que está basado en la numerología bíblica. Por ejemplo, cuando una persona es mordida por un animal de cualquier índole o tiene una herida abierta, tras las correspondientes plegarias (si las usan), aplican sobre la misma unos emplastos o gasas que suelen aplicar una cantidad de aceites vírgenes, de lavanda o romero, por citar los más habituales. Curiosamente, se suelen poner en número de tres, en referencia a la Santísima Trinidad. O, si algunos ven que tienen una herida más amplia, se van al número nueve, lo que representa a una clásica novena. Incluso realizan la señal de la cruz tres veces.

27. *Una de las virtudes sanadoras de un curandero es ser buen masajista o reponedor de huesos. Figura: Centro Francés de la Documentación e Investigación sobre Masajes (Musée CFDRM).*

Esta práctica basada en números la usan con asiduidad las mujeres curanderas, especialmente si utilizan los ensalmos que las mencionan en un número concluyente que tenga relación con la creencia cristiana. O bien utilizan palabras que solo conocían quienes practicaban el curanderismo y las repetían siete veces, numero relacionado con la creación del mundo y la plenitud. Por ejemplo, para eliminar verrugas, aunque supongo que antes aplicaban algún emplasto o aceite sobre ellas, aunque era frecuente usar previamente el látex del higo (irritante en la piel) e incluso polvo de azufre.

Todos conocían diferentes recetas contra el mal de orina o cálculos renales, y esto formaba parte de sus métodos: sugerir diversas plantas medicinales en infusión.

Hace décadas existían diversas enfermedades que en la actualidad está controladas, pues existen tratamientos farmacológicos como los antibióticos y numerosas terapias heterogéneas. Sin embargo, en aquellos tiempos en que imperaba el desconocimiento generalizado, el tratamiento para algunas enfermedades por las que se recurría a un curandero era realmente morboso.

Durante los duros tiempos de tuberculosis en España (finales del siglo xix y principios del xx), las consultas a curanderos y sanadoras eran constantes cuando existía la desesperación ante la enfermedad, hasta que los doctores Selman Waksman y Albert Schatz descubrieron la estreptomicina en 1940 y pudieron comenzar su control.

Mientras tanto, se aferraban a la magia y conocimientos de estos personajes tocados por la varita de la divinidad y el conocimiento. Las cataplasmas de harina y mostaza bien calientes sobre el pecho eran habituales, pero la receta de hacer un guiso de un perro recién nacido y dárselo de comer a los niños hasta la edad de 10 años, era «infalible», o bien colocar un sapo vivo sobre el pecho, fijado para que no escape, e incluso inhalar los vapores de uno hervido.

Podía recomendar el sanador de turno que tomase el enfermo por tuberculosis un vaso de sangre y que comiera carne cruda de animal, asegurando que aportaría vitalidad. Sin olvidarse de invocar a santa Rita, san Roque o san Sebastián, trío de santos taumatúrgicos, una contra causas perdidas y el resto para enfermedades contagiosas y plagas.

Sin embargo, encuentro otros recursos curiosos en sus métodos para sanar. No es muy frecuente, pero citan que «lo similar se trata con lo similar».

Puedo ofrecer unos ejemplos que a menudo hemos escuchado, sin evidencia científica. De este modo, se cree que comer corazón de animales ayuda al corazón, así como el hígado o pulmones. O usar ciertas plantas como el ciclamen, por el parecido de sus hojas a la oreja, aplicando una hoja, ayuda a los dolores de oído. Con enfermedades como la ictericia, que destaca por la palidez y el amarillismo de la piel, se usan plantas que tengan ese color.

28. El charlatán de aldea, escena costumbrista pintada por Francesco Sasso (1750). Museo del Prado.

Una receta para combatir las lombrices intestinales (ascariasis), tiene en cuenta su proceso: «Se hacen secar lombrices y se hace polvo con ellas, y se ponen en la sopa, caldo o vino y se sirve para curar los gusanos del cuerpo».

Esto último es una muestra más de sus recursos más extraños o recurrir a usar la sangre menstrual, evidentemente, no se utilizaba este recurso en las últimas décadas, pero los tabúes que rodeaban a la menstruación facilitaron numerosas charlatanerías sobre ello, la propia sangre se utilizaba como remedio terapéutico para tratar la hipermenorrea.

Su uso puede parecer más una receta de brujería que de una curandera, pues, a su vez, se usaba como un elemento mágico para apasionar a un hombre o atraer el amor. De esto saben mucho las antiguas mujeres llamadas «celestinas»; no obstante, era un recurso poco habitual.

Aunque no tan frecuente, siguiendo esa teoría de tratamientos, también recurren a «lo contrario se trata con lo contrario». Por ejemplo, cuando se está en estado febril, el cuerpo se sobrecalienta y es necesario aplicar una fuente de frío. Son principios arcaicos que Galeno (siglos II-III) recomienda, es decir, que la enfermedad debe tratarse logrando un equilibrio de estados ánimo.

Entienden y saben manejar perfectamente la picaresca con sus clientes. No es una estafa el procedimiento, sino algo de sentido común, ya que la mayoría tienen una vida sedentaria en términos generales y les visitan por problemas de sobrepeso, molestias en las articulaciones, cansancio general…, y para ello usaban la magia del agua. No disponían de ella en su consulta, sino que les hacían diariamente acudir temprano a una fuente que estuviera a cierta distancia y, si era posible, que proviniese de algún manantial o estuviese cerca de algún punto de índole religiosa, pues consideraban que estas aguas estaban magnetizadas por el poder divino y recomendaban que bebieran una vez que llegasen. Al mismo tiempo, deberían llenar algún cántaro u objeto con dicha agua y regresar a la consulta para poder bendecirla el propio curandero. El recipiente debería durarles tres días. Pero ¿qué tiene de mágico ir a por agua y bendecirla? Simplemente, es un truco psicológico, un efecto placebo inteligente: es ejercicio físico, les hacía andar distancias largas, idas y venidas, todo a primera hora de la mañana para activar el cuerpo del doliente, que estaba inactivo por una vida sedentaria. La falta de una actividad mínima produce un aumento de peso, además de que se pierde masa muscular, hay menor resistencia cardiovascular y aeróbica, y se produce un posible riesgo de descontrol de la insulina, lo que puede acabar en una diabetes.

Una receta fácil y sana solo consiste en andar en ayunas de madrugada a por agua. Este simple gesto ayuda a la larga a mejorar la condición física y mental del paciente.

En las prácticas contra los problemas de visión, son más reducidos (al menos en la zona que recorrí y por la que indagué). Al margen de sus plegarias a santa Lucía y soplar sobre ellos o untar previamente con su saliva «divina», usaban las infusiones de manzanilla empapando una gasa y aplicándola al ojo afectado e incluso recomendaban comer hígado o vísceras de determinado animal. Ambas fórmulas tienen un pequeño plus de efectividad, pues la manzanilla ayuda a limpiar el globo ocular (aunque difícilmente ayudará a mejorar la visión), mientras que comer hígado aporta vitamina A, muy útil para combatir la ceguera nocturna. Tras recomendar estos usos, debían regresar y aplicarse sobre ambos ojos o el afectado una piedra, normalmente de río o de algún manantial que consideraban sagrado o que era procedente de algún santuario mariano.

Todas las fórmulas aplicadas a la vista recurren a la imposición de manos sobre ellos, ningún curandero de mi bitácora aseguró tratar de operar o recordar que lo hiciera alguno de sus ancestros que le enseñaron el curanderismo. No estaba en su poder esa «gracia» mágica de recuperar la vista o mejorarla.

X. CUANDO SE APRECIA EL FRAUDE EN EL CURANDERISMO Y LOS EFECTOS PLACEBO

Es evidente que el fraude abunda en este mundillo de la sanación con actividades realmente obsoletas y absurdas.

Esto no es nuevo, pues desde hace siglos ya existía el timo respecto a servicios de salud con panaceas realmente insólitas con elementos imposibles, y es un debate con sus controversias constantes incluso hoy en día, con los escasos curanderos que aún estén ejerciendo.

Uno de los problemas que nos podemos encontrar es la falta de argumentos científicos que corroboren esa sanación, un informe o analíticas del paciente al que ha tratado el curandero. Siempre muestran el informe médico con el que diagnostican una determinada enfermedad o problema, pero existe un vacío documental en la sanación, así como en su evolución posterior.

El curanderismo consigue buenas noticias en las zonas rurales, donde pueden explotar la ignorancia de sus habitantes por una ausencia de educación escolar generalizada y una dejadez por parte de los servicios sanitarios. Con este apunte no me refiero a las últimas décadas, sino a las anteriores a 1980, en que aún existían localidades sin apenas servicios. Afortunadamente, vivimos en una época en que la comunicación es más fácil, pero insisto en esa España rural que está hundiéndose en el olvido y dejadez en la actualidad, perdiéndose unas tradiciones y antropologías únicas.

29. *Las noticias sobre curanderos siempre han sido habituales en la prensa de hace décadas. Figura: Diario Crítica, de Buenos Aires.*

Otra faceta que puede facilitar la confusión al paciente es la buena disposición a las teorías conspirativas de la medicina por parte del curandero, que, a menudo, hace desconfiar del médico titulado y seguir sus propias pautas como curandero. Para ello recurre a sus dotes de psicología casera, es decir, empatía, agudeza de escucha, labia…

Un cirujano militar, Alonso Argüello, publicó en 1796 unas notas que ayudarían a diversificar a los curanderos de los lenguaraces curanderos que son más charlatanes y timadores que otra cosa. Sus apuntes pueden ser útiles en nuestro tiempo:

Los que aseguran conocer un remedio que sirve para curar todas las enfermedades.

Los que andan vendiendo elixires orviétanos (contenían las mismas virtudes que la famosa triaca[3]) y quintas esencias a los que atribuyen grandes propiedades para determinadas enfermedades.

Los que resucitan antiguas recetas peligrosas abandonadas hace mucho tiempo por malos resultados y, cambiándoles el nombre o la denominación, las presentan como propias.

Los que, una vez conocido el diagnóstico del médico, instan al enfermo a cambiar lo recomendado por otros remedios que ellos saben y consideran mejores.

Los que aseguran ser capaces de curar determinadas enfermedades con un don de Dios, con especial interés en las sanaciones de huesos y la esterilidad.

Los que, dentro de la misma cirugía, arruinan la carrera de compañeros haciendo correr el rumor de que tienen «malas manos».

Los boticarios que se meten a médicos echando mano de lo que dicen las farmacopeas.

Son puntos que hoy en día pueden servir y podemos aplicar, como se ha podido observar de este conjunto de principios.

La crítica, la presión social y la persecución por parte de los medios de comunicación, entre otros, pueden causar un serio problema a las virtudes de una persona que ejerce el curanderismo, ya que el miedo y la desconfianza la atenazan y hacen que fracase en sus remedios. Este detalle me lo sugieren unos retirados sanadores de las localidades valencianas de Guadassuar y Massalavés.

Estos mismos, ya octogenarios, piden erradicar los curanderos que solo engañan a las personas para sacarles cantida-

---

3　Triaca: era un antiguo antídoto usado desde la época grecorromana hasta el siglo XVIII como medicamento contra la fiebre, envenenamientos, enfermedades crónicas… Su composición era compleja, pues contenía diversos tipos de plantas, veneno de animales, opio y minerales en polvo.

des muy altas de dinero en una sesión o en unas pocas sesiones, o bien alargando lo máximo posible el número de las visitas que deben hacer para controles o terapias de sanación para seguir sacando beneficios.

Sin embargo, también he podido recopilar en numerosos medios de comunicación escrita de hemeroteca (*Levante-EMV*, *Las Provincias*, *Estampa*, *La Verdad* y *Pueblo*, entre otros) que, debido a las presiones por parte del Colegio Oficial de Médicos y sus denuncias por intrusismo, que ellos (los facultativos) también se equivocan a menudo, que también existen médicos religiosos, galenos radicales, etc., y pocas veces se actúa contra ellos desde su entidad, salvo que el propio paciente los denuncie por mala praxis médica.

Jueves, 4 de abril de 1985

COMARCAS

Oració i fe popular

El Dijous Sant es tramet la curació de les malalties

El Dijous Sant és una data important per al curanderisme popular en les comarques valencianes. Durant aquest dia, i segons la tradició, es poden trametre algunes oracions amb la finalitat de curar les nostres malalties, que van de pares a fills.

VICENT CLIMENT

Dins el món del curanderisme i la medicina popular, el **Dijous Sant** és una data clau, ja que és en aquest dia quan, segons la tradició, es poden trametre algunes oracions que remeien les nostres malalties.

Presa d'aire, hepatitis, presa d'ull, enfit són algunes de les malalties que poden curar-se mitjançant aquestes pràctiques. Són, generalment, pràctiques basades en el rés d'oracions de caire religiós. I en definitiva tot depén de la fe que pose el malalt en la seua curació i de la gràcia que tinga la persona qui cura. Sabem de persones que, preocupades per l'estat físic o «anímic» del seu cavall, han buscat remei per mig d'una persona que sabera l'oració contra la presa d'ull. En aquest cas poca fe podia posar l'animal malalt; tot depenia de la gràcia del curander.

Presa d'aire

La presa d'aire és un dolor a les juntes dels ossos, produït per una corrent d'aire fred. Aquesta afecció apareix ja al «Tirant lo Blanc», quan al capítol CXVIII el protagonista de la nostra gran novel·la afirma: «E jo no tinc altre mal sinó de l'aire de la mar que m'ha tot comprés». La nostra medicina popular compta amb una oració per curar-la:

Airada si és pel matí / valga'm Déu i Sant Martí, / si és pel migdia / valga'm Déu i la Verge Maria / i si és pel vespre / valga'm Déu i Sant Silvestre. / Maligne, on vas? / A trencar-li els ossos a... (nom del malalt). / Puix, no iràs pas, / perquè et lligaré / amb les cordes del gram / i t'enviaré a la muntanya de Sant Julivert / a menjar herbes amargues.

El text arreplegat a **Alfarb (Ribera Alta)** és d'una gran bellesa i d'una riquesa lingüística remarcable, conservant la forma verbal **iràs** i la partícula negativa **pas**.

Enfit, hepatitis

L'**enfit**, produït per una gran menjada, és trenca amb una pràctica molt estesa per les comarques valencianes. Es tracte de prendre mida amb una llista de tela, a l'avantbraç i la mà de la persona desenfitadora, durant tres vegades, fent-la aplegar al ventre del malalt. Alhora va dient-se una oració: **Salve, María; / Salve, Madre de Dios, / cuando llegue a tu aposento / espérame en el Señor.**

Si la tercera vegada que es pren mida la cinta no arriba al ventre del malalt, no hi ha dubte, aquest està enfitat.

L'hepatitis, coneguda popularment com l'aliacrà, té també un remei en la medicina popular, pel mig del rés d'una oració:

Eixos ulls són els que t'han mirat, / tres són els qui t'han de defensar, / Pare, Fill i Esperit Sant. / El Nostre Senyor nasqué el dia de Nadal / i morí el Divendres Sant. / Un parenostre i una ave maria a Sant Gil / perquè aquest aliacrà siga secat.

En Pego encara hi ha qui «trenca l'enfit».

30. Noticias de sanadores y curanderas. Imagen: Diario Levante, 1985.

Es cierto que existen curanderos que rozan lo absurdo, que abusan de la ingenuidad de las personas e incluso pueden provocar la muerte involuntaria, a veces en un exceso de paranoia. Tenemos los casos extremos del exorcismo en el barrio granadino de Albaicín en 1990 o el terrible caso a una niña en Almansa (septiembre de 1990) fallecida en manos de una curandera que, lamentablemente, era su propia madre y extirpó sus órganos internos desde la vagina de la niña. O tratamientos que resultan perjudiciales para el paciente. Entonces nos surge una pregunta: ¿y los testimonios de que han sanado?

Aquí es donde está el debate dentro de nuestra sociedad actual. Si pudiéramos dar un salto en el tiempo y plantarnos en 1960, por ejemplo, abundarían numerosas sanaciones de todo tipo, dando fe los clientes de su mejoría, pero ¿seguro que estaban enfermos? ¿Cómo fueron sus tiempos posteriores?

No voy a añadir los problemas de lesiones, contracturas, torceduras y demás, dado que no las considero enfermedades y son fácilmente reparadas si se tiene un mínimo de conocimiento del cuerpo humano a nivel articulatorio y muscular. Eso no lo considero una sanación, pero admiro esa facilidad manual tan mágica que tienen los curanderos o los denominados «componedores de huesos» para tratar estas lesiones sin tener formación académica, tan solo experiencia, paciencia y capacidad de observación.

En la actualidad esto sería inadmisible, pero existen casos de curanderismo en décadas anteriores que han llegado a diagnosticar como cáncer de pulmón lo que en realidad era una fuerte gripe, ya que a menudo suele doler y existen dificultades para seguir con una respiración normal, además de una alta fiebre. Ya sabemos que no son los síntomas que presenta un cáncer de pulmón, son muy diferentes, se trata de un dictamen erróneo y, si lo hacen intencionadamente, es para aprovecharse de la ingenuidad del paciente y curarle en pocos días. El resto de la historia ya saben cómo termina: paciente feliz por acabar completamente con el cáncer, difundir las manos milagrosas del curandero y demostrar que está completamente sanado.

Encontré una referencia curiosa de 1918 que cita un dosier titulado *Curanderismo y muerte en Moratalla* (Jesús Navarro), donde se indicaba que más de dos millones de personas acuden a psicoterapias, poniendo en riesgo las vidas de aquellos que usaban las recetas suicidas de ciertos curanderos que aconsejaban tomar cloro o agua con una dosis de lejía. Estos aseguraban que curaba el autismo e incluso el cáncer. Me vino a la memoria un moderno sanador de Cataluña que, en nuestro tiempo, insistía en usar dióxido de cloro contra muchos males, entre ellos el cáncer o el COVID-19 y otras enfermedades de difícil tratamiento. Acabó en los juzgados por delito contra la salud pública.

*31. «Las hierbas y sus aromas han sido elementos esenciales
en el curanderismo tradicional, utilizados para limpiar
energías, aliviar dolencias físicas y promover el bienestar
espiritual.» Imagen: Elsa Olofsson en Unsplash.*

A menudo, muchas enfermedades más simples se confundían fácilmente y se las consideraba otras muy graves, de ahí que sanasen con el paso de los días. Por ejemplo, una simple gripe (influenza) podía confundirse con un proceso de tuberculosis o una neumonía. Este temor viene arrastrado por el miedo que produjo la denominada «gripe española» de 1918, que hizo activar todos los recursos médicos y remedios populares. Cuando había migrañas, molestia que con frecuencia se consideraba un tumor cerebral, para ello recurrían a diversas infusiones como la manzanilla, menta o unos aceites cuyo componente esencial era la lavanda, con el que se daba un masaje en las sienes.

Su olor tan característico aportaba una excelente sensación de calma, relax y bienestar, y esto se conoce en la actualidad como «aromaterapia». Por supuesto, dado su diagnóstico inexacto, cuando se consideraba una clásica migraña como un tumor maligno dentro del cuerpo, se hacía necesario recurrir a las dotes mágicas del curandero para interceder ante las divinidades y realizar diversas plegarias. Incluso una anemia la podían catalogar como leucemia u otro tipo de enfermedad grave de la sangre, lo que sugería realizar posibles sangrías para eliminar esa «sangre mala», o el uso de un conjunto de hierbas como la ortiga, el regaliz o comer hígado de res. Como detalle para reforzar la terapia de utilizar las hierbas medicinales, aseguran que las recogían citando una oración que solo conocen ellos para reforzar su calidad y virtud sanadora.

A estos ejemplos no les veo fraude, sino una falta de acceso a tecnologías o recursos para analíticas, pues las enfermedades o dolencias que cito no eran tan graves, y su curación es relativamente sencilla, lo cual conocemos su posterior fin a estas historias: el milagro de curar un tumor cancerígeno o una enfermedad muy grave que iba cavando la tumba del paciente y que, gracias al maravilloso «don» o la «gracia» del curandero, ha logrado curar del todo. Esto se resume, a menudo, en efecto placebo, de ahí surgen numerosas historias de personas que han sanado de un supuesto cáncer o enfermedad letal. Tan solo un ínfimo porcentaje tiene el beneficio de la duda.

El efecto placebo es sugestivo, pero estos efectos son muy eficaces porque el paciente confía en el curandero, incluso en su médico convencional, siendo más eficaz que la propia medicina. Esto no es nuevo, conocen bien esta derivación, en todos los ámbitos han llegado a ofrecer auténticas panaceas de salud contra todas las enfermedades, cuyas composiciones no son más que tabletas de lactosa o glucosa y sin ingredientes activos o el uso de soluciones salinas que no tienen efectos terapéuticos. Hasta agua del grifo han llegado a ofrecer a sus pacientes.

Sin embargo, cuando no actúa el efecto placebo, se produce la tragedia, bien porque el paciente así ha decidido dar un paso a lo desconocido y mágico, desafiando la ciencia, y el resultado es su propia muerte, como ocurrió con un joven enfermo de leucemia en Valencia[42]. Fue un caso trágico, ya que el joven valenciano decidió dejar de recibir el segundo ciclo de quimioterapia y ponerse en manos de un naturópata, aunque este nada tiene que ver con el curanderismo cotidiano. Es un claro ejemplo de lo que puede suceder en casos realmente graves, cuyas denuncias pueden quedar en papel mojado, ya que la decisión fue del propio paciente, nadie lo obligó a nada, y la justicia puede eximir de responsabilidad al pseudomédico o curandero.

Realizar algo de escenificación, rituales y gestos ceremoniales también ayuda a ese efecto placebo, aumenta la expectativa de sanación y ese ritual debe tener un significado cultural y religioso.

Un ejemplo frecuente es el ritual del «empacho» o *l'enfit*, como popularmente se conoce en tierras de la Comunitat Valenciana. ¿En qué consiste este efecto placebo de ritual de *l'enfit*?

---

4   Este caso es la muerte de Mario Rodríguez, quien, con solo 21 años, decidió dejar la quimioterapia y falleció a los pocos meses en julio de 2013. El naturópata (José Ramón Llorente) ha sido absuelto por la justicia, pese a no tener licencias médicas, ya que el paciente lo aceptó todo bajo su propia libertad y decisión.

Primero hay que explicar qué es *l'enfit* o empacho: se trata de una incomodidad de vientre, mala digestión, exceso de comida, pesadez…, es decir, lo que se entiende en general como un trastorno digestivo común.

En la región valenciana era muy frecuente acudir al curandero con estos síntomas, sobre todo en épocas de grandes celebraciones como las Navidades, la celebración de eventos festivos en las localidades o un banquete imprevisto.

No solo era un exceso de comida, pues había un problema muy amplio en la España de la posguerra, ya que la falta de alimentos se traducía en hambre, en especial en las localidades más profundas y aisladas, donde, cuando surge la oportunidad de comer de forma abundante, esos cuerpos, a menudo, no están acostumbrados a grandes ingestiones de alimento, surge un cambio brusco en el ritmo de su aparato digestivo y se produce en muchas ocasiones el llamado empacho. A menudo, el paciente habitual es un retoño. La madre, ante la tendencia de darle pecho en excesivo debido a un constante llanto y calmarlo, pensando que es hambre, es lo contrario, existe una sobrealimentación del pequeño y le produce muchas incomodidades digestivas. Aunque a estos no suelen hacerles rito, sino que ordenan para la lactancia, por un día, masajear el vientre con miel o algún bálsamo popular para facilitar el proceso digestivo, sumando algún pellizco sin causar dolor al retoño, eliminando los retortijones o posibles flatulencias. Los de edad pueden ser aptos para el ritual.

Para ello acuden a *trencar l'enfit* (romper el empacho) al curandero, aunque normalmente este ritual lo ejercen las mujeres.

Para este remedio ancestral se necesita un pañuelo preferentemente de seda, bien grande y, si es posible, de color negro. De no tener ese pañuelo, puede sustituirse por una cinta también de seda y, en este caso, el color preferente sería rojo.

Previamente, para que ese pañuelo o cinta tenga una carga mágica, se recomendaba que estuviera toda la noche bajo algún pedestal de un santo local de la iglesia más próxima o bien estirarlo en el suelo durante la procesión de la Semana Santa, para que pudiera pisarlo el paso de la cofradía con su representación religiosa. Tanto la primera opción como la segunda solo son válidas en Jueves Santo.

Para realizar el popular rito de *l'enfit* o empacho, el paciente sujeta un extremo del pañuelo grande o la cinta a la altura de su estómago; y la curandera, situada en el extremo opuesto, mide tres veces la distancia a codos, al tiempo que se persigna y reza una plegaria secreta en voz muy baja. Esa oración solo la conoce ella, y solo puede transmitirse en Jueves Santo o Viernes Santo, ya que, si informa de dicha oración, pierde su «gracia». Tras este rito, aseguran que dicha pesadez o estreñimiento desaparece. Pero no es más que una sobreactuación mágica, para demostrar que tienen poderes, «gracia», junto con la capacidad de sanar por plegarias que solo conoce ella. Es un efecto placebo, porque previamente se pueden realizar unos masajes suaves en el vientre del afectado, lo cual produce una excelente sensación, y ese masaje va acompañado de aceite de oliva, miel, ceniza o incluso la propia saliva de la sanadora. Esto nos trae a la memoria una vieja profesión conocida como «saludadores», curanderos que sanaban el ganado y a veces a muchas personas con su saliva o aliento.

Antes de estos masajes, se pone en marcha el efecto psíquico del paciente, puesto que se hace la señal de la cruz tres veces sobre el vientre, acompañado de una oración clásica como un padrenuestro. Esto activa los mecanismos del paciente que pueden liberar en el cerebro neurotransmisores como la dopamina. Además, tras el rito recomiendan (la mayoría) un día de ayuno, comidas blandas, infusión de manzanilla o agua con zumo de limón. Si la cosa se ponía difícil y las molestias continuaban, estaba la opción de una lavativa (evidentemente, el agua se bendice haciendo la señal de la cruz tres veces). Como se puede observar, el relajante masaje previo y la receta final son los verdaderos motivos de la franca mejoría de ese empacho, y el rito es solo una parte mística para acentuar el remedio. El origen de este ritual no está muy claro, pero posiblemente se trate de una amalgama de diversas culturas del Mediterráneo, desde la hebrea hasta la egipcia. No obstante, Enrique de Villena (1384-1434) ya citaba en su *Tratado de fascinación o aojamiento*, publicado en 1425, el rito de «pasar cinta», aunque, curiosamente, está enfocado en el mal de ojo: «[…] e medían su cinta a codos o a palmos, y si viene une vez larga e otra corta, de aquella variación tomaban señal del daño […]».

No solo está este rito de efecto placebo para el empacho, hay otros que varían según la geografía. En zonas del norte, por ejemplo, es habitual ponerse un pescado fresco sobre el vientre, mientras que en varias zonas rurales del interior optan por verter sobre el abdomen la sangre caliente de un conejo sacrificado. Son prácticas que no entran en motivos para confiar en una sanación directa por esta ceremonia.

*Nota del autor: Si desean conocer un rito del *enfit,* pueden acceder a través del código QR a este vídeo de YouTube del antiguo canal valenciano Canal 9:

XI. ¿DE VERDAD ERAN EFECTIVOS SEMEJANTES PROCEDIMIENTOS?

Este capítulo tiene más tintes de robarnos una pequeña sonrisa o quizá de hacernos arquear las cejas por la incredulidad ante diversos métodos de sanación que utilizaban y continúan usando algunos curanderos para sorpresa de todos.

Son recetas asombrosas y rituales que hasta bien entrado 1980 se habían realizado con asiduidad. Huelga decir que ya he citado en algunas líneas ciertos procedimientos de los curanderos. Sin embargo, existe una lista extensa de formas extravagantes, especialmente usando animales e incluso insectos.

El uso de insectos era habitual en las consultas. En los pueblos más profundos de España y, sobre todo, por Castilla la Mancha, era muy recurrido utilizar arañas que guardaban en pequeñas bolsitas de tela para evitar que escapasen, y que luego se ataban en algunas partes del cuerpo del afectado para poder sanar la enfermedad. Confiaban en que la araña tenía la virtud de absorber las malas energías y expulsar algunas enfermedades. Incluso ofrecían saltamontes, bien tostados al fuego y convertidos en polvo, ya que se recomendaban para tratar heridas superficiales. Incluso los podían mezclar con miel y hacer ingerir como un tratamiento contra el asma o la tos crónica.

Los sacrificios de animales, quizá influidos por las creencias religiosas que también lo ejercían, han formado parte del manual de los usuarios del curanderismo. No han tenido reparos ni dudas en aplicarlo y los pacientes asimilaban que era lo mejor para ellos, dada su ignorancia y la fe que le profesaban al sanador.

Aunque la práctica de uso de un animal ha caído en desuso, el acto de un sacrificio animal tiene un significado que busca establecer de alguna forma su conexión espiritual, liberar de alguna forma las energías positivas o, como es evidente, influir en el proceso de sanación. Esto es herencia de viejas creencias ancestrales, ya que, en las culturas americanas, africanas o asiáticas, sacrificar animales forma parte de numerosas prácticas para sanar.

No era necesario sacrificar, a menudo bastaba con tocar o «restregar» por el cuerpo del doliente un animal o un reptil adecuado para su problema de salud.

Para las dolencias gastrointestinales era frecuente verter sobre el vientre del interesado una gran cantidad de sangre de palomo, que previamente se había destripado y, ubicadas esas pequeñas entrañas del ave, se dispersaban sobre la panza del enfermo. Dependiendo de la fauna local, por ejemplo, hay constancia de que ciertos sanadores de las localidades de la franja del lago valenciano de L'Albufera dan un mismo uso para remedios de vientre, como utilizar en este caso la sangre de una anguila recién pescada en el día. O bien se podía dar el caso de colocar un pescado fresco mediano sobre el vientre para rebajar molestias e incluso para bajar los síntomas de calenturas.

Una receta que roza la morbosidad era usar el corazón de una golondrina: «El corazón de golondrina se parte por la mitad y se da al niño; con la otra mitad se hace una sopa y se le da en cucharadas. El niño crecerá con gran juicio».

Es una receta que me relató un testimonio nonagenario de Guadassuar, quien aseguró que la tomó en varias ocasiones, aunque ignora o no recuerda si sus efectos fueron beneficiosos. En este caso, yo observo un claro simbolismo con la golondrina, y posiblemente sea un recurso ancestral que ha perdurado desde hace siglos. La golondrina simboliza cierta inteligencia y memoria, por su gran capacidad de movimientos migratorios y su orientación.

32. A menudo, cualquier animal, anfibio o insecto era útil para sus extrañas recetas. Calcografía de Giuseppe M. Mitelli (1634-1718). Fondo Corsini, Bolonia.

La sangre protagonizaba diversos remedios, ya que desde tiempos ancestrales se la consideraba como portadora de fuerza vital, protectora contra enfermedades e incluso una gran barrera defensora contra diversos ataques del llamado «mal de ojo», que se debía beber sin más o mezclada con diversas plantas medicinales como salvia, ajenjo, menta, manzanilla o romero. Existía otra opción más retorcida y desagradable: bañarse en sangre, aunque esto era algo raro y extraño. Es algo improbable este método, aunque nos recuerde a los míticos y terribles baños de sangre de la condesa Erzsébet Báthory para mantener su eterna juventud (si bien parece que su historia se ha exagerado).

Ignoro la causa y motivo de su origen en un remedio, pero, durante la época del Imperio romano, se creía que beber sangre de gladiador curaba la epilepsia, lo que fomentó un curioso mercado macabro de esta codiciada sangre[5]. Esta actividad terminó en el año 404 d. C., cuando se prohibieron por completo los combates de gladiadores por orden del emperador Honorio. Entonces los romanos recurrieron a los ejecutados, bien por crucifixión o decapitados, aunque estos últimos eran los preferidos, ya que su sangre se recogía de un modo mucho más eficaz.

Había que extraerla, así que, cuando alguien estaba enfermo o tenía «sangre espesa», fiebre, hipertensión o alguna inflamación, se recurría al conocido sangrador, que ejecutaba un perfecto corte en una vena del enfermo y este sangraba durante un tiempo (o, según pudiera observar el sangrador, unos 1200 ml, aunque esto es una especulación).

Existía otra práctica para extraer sangre «nociva», que era el popular uso de sanguijuelas, aunque esta práctica sí tiene ciertos avales científicos, pues ayudan de forma óptima en algunos procesos de cicatrización o varices, por ejemplo, y, en general, en el campo de la cirugía reconstructiva y la medicina vascular.

A menudo se pueden encontrar sorpresas desagradables y con final trágico. Dispongo de un curioso documento del siglo XVII procedente del Archivio di Stato di Venezia: se trata del proceso de Mare Radolovich. Aunque se lo acusó finalmente por realizar pactos diabólicos y prácticas de brujería, realmente su objetivo era sanar un dolor de garganta a una niña.

---

5   Según citan en sus obras, por ejemplo, Plinio el Viejo (*Historia natural*) y Celsus (*De medicina*).

Era sanadora, y quiso aplicar una técnica de sangría diferente a las conocidas. Quizá estaba instruida en experiencias vampíricas, ya que ella procede de las regiones de Istría (Croacia), así que absorbió la sangre de aquella niña por el cuello a través de un pequeño corte en sus venas faciales. Estuvo succionando durante un largo rato hasta hacerle perder el conocimiento a aquella pobre chiquilla, que perdió la vida.

Otro remedio insólito que se ha usado hasta bien entrado el siglo xx es el uso del estiércol. Aunque parece ser que aún lo utilizan en ciertas zonas muy profundas y con poco acceso educativo en Sudamérica.

Es cierto que no es idea propia de los curanderos de nuestros últimos tiempos, sino un método ancestral, ya que desde el antiguo Egipto o incluso en la China de la cultura Longshan (3000-2000 a. C.) ya se hace mención del uso del estiércol como remedio medicinal. Dependiendo de la procedencia del estiércol (vaca, cabra, buey, camello…), se podía usar contra inflamaciones de las llagas y eliminación de verrugas o incluso de quemaduras.

A menudo se aplicaba mezclada con otros componentes como harina, cenizas, vinagre, vino o aceite. Se creaba una cataplasma y se aplicaba en la zona afectada. Pero es un peligro tremendo recurrir a esto, puesto que los patógenos, las bacterias y otros parásitos pueden causar una enfermedad muy grave.

Algo similar sucede con el uso de la orina, pues existen testimonios y recursos de curanderos que han llegado a usar la orina animal e incluso humana para sanar ciertas dolencias.

Especialmente se aplicaba sobre las infecciones cutáneas o eccemas de piel, y era muy frecuente utilizar orina para eliminar verrugas. Algo más extravagante es recomendar hacer gárgaras para aliviar el dolor de garganta o infecciones bucales. Normalmente, se recomendaba la propia del paciente, y este dato es llamativo, puesto que algunas evidencias personales de mi zona han mencionado este recurso (evidentemente, sin resultados óptimos). En otras regiones, como en la zona sur de Levante y áreas más meridionales de

Albacete, he podido constatar que se usaba excremento de gallina para sanar la garganta, usándola como un emplasto. El riesgo de infección y otras patologías bacterianas estaban a la orden del día.

Aunque no lo crea, se realizan sangrías en la actualidad, pero de forma muy limitada y con seguridad, solo en casos de porfiria cutánea o hemocromatosis, pero nada que ver con el uso de antaño, que era muy peligroso y nada mejoraba al paciente. Su uso procede de las teorías de los humores de Hipócrates y Galeno, cuyas conclusiones resumo aquí: «la sangría tiene la función de eliminar un desequilibrio humoral, un exceso de sangre que determina la aparición de enfermedades» (Fuente: De Venesectione, Galeno).

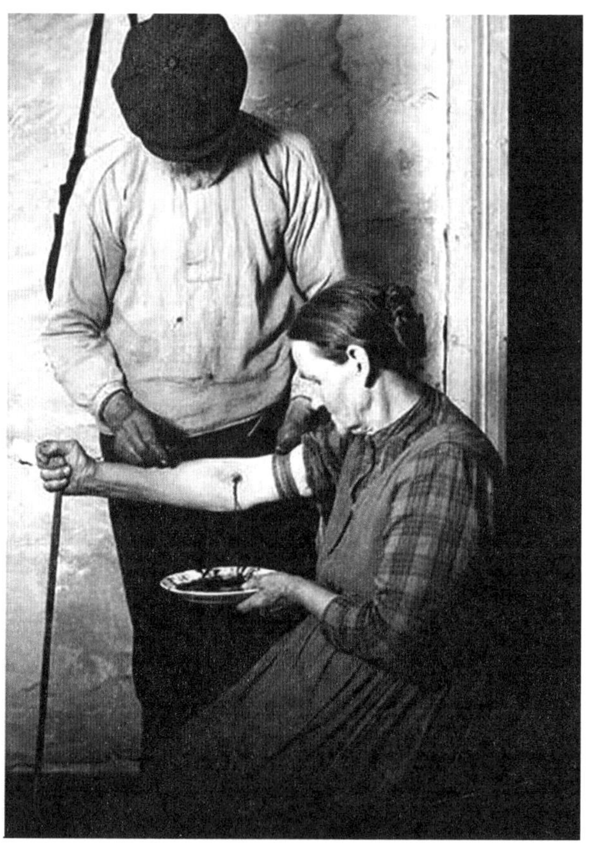

33. El recurso de las sangrías era habitual en el curanderismo. (1935).

No todos eran aptos para aplicarles la sangría. En una visita a la biblioteca de Ca´Foscari (Venecia), a la que suelo acudir siempre que viajo, encontré un interesante ejemplar titulado *Regola sanitaria salernitana* (F. Gherli, 1959), donde ya en los siglos XII y XIII se cita que «el hombre debe tener más de 17 años para ser apto para una flebotomía [...] cortar la vena hace que las luces sean muy claras y purga el cerebro y la mente [...]».

Algo más rústico era poner una simple cruz hecha con dos palos o ramas sobre el lugar doloroso, lesión o infección. Esta práctica es cierta, pude recoger esta curiosa nota de curanderos con sus remedios populares por la Italia más rural, concretamente en la localidad piamontesa de Biella, incluso ha llegado a un tribunal por su ineficacia. En junio de 1858, un médico italiano, el Dr. Piero Gracis, presentó una denuncia contra Lorenzo Gariazzo. Este personaje no se limitaba a dispensar medicinas supuestamente milagrosas, sino que practicaba un rito de religiosidad basado en su propio poder obtenido por la «gracia».

El curandero había intentado curar a la enferma haciéndole beber leche a la que añadía unas gotas de agua bendita y, posteriormente, colocándole trozos de madera cruzados en el cuerpo en forma de cruz. La paciente, que era una niña, falleció por esa infección que no pudo curar. Tampoco era efectivo ante la cantidad de personas que acudían por un dolor a causa de una lesión, a quienes colocaba unas varillas haciendo forma de cruz sobre el lugar que molestaba y recitaba una oración (normalmente era el padrenuestro); evidentemente, ninguno mejoró sus dolencias. Sin embargo, los vecinos de su alrededor confiaban y seguían acudiendo a su curanderismo particular. Este caso es un ejemplo del abuso de muchos personajes que se dedican a conseguir beneficios a costa de la ignorancia y el bajo nivel cultural.

Se ha hablado muchas veces de la llamada «piedra de bezoar», una acumulación orgánica que se forma en los tractos digestivos de los animales rumiantes de las ganaderías (normalmente, cabras, ovejas y vacas), unos sedimentos de material que no ha podido ser digerido por los ganados, como pelos, diversas fibras vegetales, semillas y otros elementos no digeribles, y que son muy valorados en el curanderismo tradicional, por sus supuestas propiedades curativas y mágicas. No se crean que esperan a una deposición, sino que la encuentra dentro de los estómagos de los animales muertos, tras abrirlos durante un despiece o sacrificio. Esa piedra de compuestos orgánicos se conservaba y se raspaba una porción en agua, vino o leche, cuyos beneficios atribuidos eran óptimos para los síntomas de envenenamiento, dolores de estómago o cólicos, sin olvidar que llevar colgado o en una bolsita un trozo de piedra de bezoar era útil para protegerse de cualquier influencia negativa y de diversos maleficios en los que creía el folclore local, como las brujas, duendes malignos o posibles anomalías espectrales.

34. Piedras de Bezoar. German Pharmacy Museum.

La aromaterapia no es un fraude en absoluto, pues se ha demostrado que ayuda a reducir el estrés o la ansiedad y facilita el sueño. Pero ni mucho menos debe ser considerada como una panacea de salud ni para curar dolencias, pese a asegurarme un experto y comercial de aromaterapia que puede sanar ciertos cánceres (no cito el nombre para evitar un posible linchamiento). Si bien puede relajar o estimular el bienestar emocional, jamás lo sanará.

Sin embargo, se ha utilizado como un elemento más dentro del vasto catálogo de recursos y terapias de curanderismo como un alivio sintomático. Por ejemplo, recurrir a los vapores de eucalipto para ayudar a aliviar la congestión nasal y facilitar la respiración. Hay otras opciones, realmente de dudosa eficacia, para aliviar ciertas dolencias o infecciones. Así, contra el herpes se usaban castañas inhalando el vapor producido por la ebullición de estas en una cazuela con agua. Es cierto que las castañas tienen unas propiedades antisépticas en forma de cataplasmas o que comerlas ayuda al sistema cardiovascular, pero, a pesar de ello, sus vapores carecen de valor.

Antaño siguieron los consejos de uno de los grandes referentes de la historia de medicina, Hipócrates, con el uso del incienso. En sus remedios, cita que prescribía tratamiento para las enfermedades de la mujer, donde la paciente debía ponerse a horcajadas sobre esos humos que desprendía y facilitar que entrasen las emanaciones por la vagina. No solo es incienso, podía contener otros elementos como estiércol de vaca, cuerno de cabra, ciprés seco…

El uso del incienso es bastante habitual en el recetario del curandero. Al margen del anterior y extraño consejo, solían recomendarlo para reducir molestias intestinales, flatulencias, irritación de garganta… y, especialmente, para mantener alejadas las malas vibraciones o aojamientos.

Tan cotidiano es que alguien te diga: «Tengo anginas o estoy resfriado». Y tan extraños son ciertos remedios frente a estos síntomas cotidianos del ser humano.

Se recomendaba ponerse una moneda de cobre atada con un pañuelo en una de las muñecas para eliminar las anginas. O bien disponían de un socorrido recurso de hacer diversos tipos de emplastes, cuyas recetas tienen variedad de componentes que dejaría a más uno sorprendido, ya que pueden tener desde ceniza hasta diversas plantas y excrementos de vaca, de oveja y no se descarta que de humano. El barro es un componente que no faltaba en la mayoría de los emplastes, así como el polvo de huesos. Esto se aplicaba en una friega por el pecho para erradicar las molestias pectorales y la mejora del resfriado, aunque lo más seguro es que hubiera empeorado debido a alguna infección por esa «magistral receta».

En algunas localidades del País Vasco y Navarra, el uso de friegas o emplastos de ortiga era bastante habitual, incluso aún siguen usándola a nivel personal, y los resfriados se trataban con esta planta. Se hacía un ramo con esas plantas recogidas y se restregaba bien por la planta de los pies hasta la altura de las rodillas. Evidentemente, la reacción alérgica o el picor estaban asegurados, dado que sus compuestos, como la histamina, ácido fórmico y acetilcolina, provocan esa reacción irritante en la piel. Sin embargo, algunas teorías sugieren que facilitan la circulación sanguínea y ayudaba a una rápida recuperación de los síntomas. A menudo, suelen frotarse la espalda con la ortiga, para después darse una friega con vinagre, pues aseguraban que despeja las vías respiratorias y mejora notablemente los catarros.

Si existieran molestias intensas en la garganta, era factible que recomendaran, como cito al inicio de este capítulo, hacer gárgaras con orina. Esa orina podía ser la propia o ajena, y se recomendaba que fuera de los niños, al ser más pura. El uso de la orina no es propio del curanderismo popular, ya viene de siglos esta práctica, que se utilizaba hasta para tratar problemas de visión, tratamientos contra quemaduras e incluso contra picaduras de diversos anfibios o insectos.

No olvidemos que el alto contenido amoniaco en la orina de una persona hacía blanquear los dientes, de ahí que se usara desde los tiempos de Grecia y Roma como un elixir bucal y antiséptico. Todo supuestamente «efectivo y sano», así que ni de broma se les ocurra probar estas prácticas.

O, cuando las cosas se complican para un sanador y no sabe cómo ofrecer un servicio para su sanación, realizar diversas oraciones, rituales purificadores o «tomar el aire». Esto último era un recurso muy útil cuando el doliente presentaba mareos, pero ese aire debe ser por la naturaleza, lo cual proporcionaba un plus de bienestar mental o una mejora de la hipoxia (falta de oxígeno). En este aporte hay que tener en cuenta que era muy frecuente la consulta por mareos, ya que se utilizaba antiguamente el brasero como recurso de calor en los días fríos, e incluso para cocinar. De sobra es conocido que, sin las precauciones correctas, produce intoxicación el humo, siendo muy peligroso. Por ello, siempre ventilaban la estancia, de ahí un excelente recurso aplicado por el curandero ante mareos por humo.

Desde mi punto de vista, el uso de estos remedios con escasa o nula efectividad y absurdos, tenga sus motivos a causa de la desesperación del paciente y la falta de acceso a la medicina moderna, no me refiero a prácticas de hace siglos, sino durante gran parte del siglo xx, donde los diversos sanadores populares llenaban este vacío científico ofreciendo soluciones asequibles a la economía del paciente y basándose, a menudo, en las tradiciones.

Hay unos tipos por los pueblos cuya vida es una perfecta historia de copla, que debía contarse así en el mal romance de los ciegos, para darle todo un carácter popular y campesino e ilustrarse con los garabatos pintarrajeados del cartelón.

Tal la historia de este pastor - curandero, llamado Eustoquio Antón, sin más apodo que su mismo nombre —*el tío Ustoquio* le llaman—, natural y vecino de Quintanar de la Sierra, con ochenta y cinco años de edad, cuarenta de práctica y muchas leguas a la redonda de fama, de buena y merecida fama de curandero.

Este arte de curandero ha quedado por las aldeas como una reminiscencia de las milagrerías y ungüentos prodigiosos del medievo. El curandero es el Merlín degenerado, atoscado, y casi perdido que queda en nuestros días.

Su *ciencia*, que es como él llama justamente a su intuitivo saber sin necesidad de profanar la palabra técnica, le viene de lo maravilloso y espontáneo. Sus diagnósticos son como recitaciones de iluminado. Sus recetas no suelen pasar por la botica. Todas estas estupendas circunstancias son las que mantienen la fe y atraen la romería de los campesinos.

A casa de este buen Eustoquio Antón, que vive en la parte más vieja y más alta del pueblo, como corresponde, no pasará día que no llegue un doliente, porque "tampoco hay día que no tenga su

El pastor-curandero de Quintanar de la Sierra, con su familia.

HISTORIA DE UN PASTOR-CURANDERO

tormento", como dice él mismo con raras y filosóficas palabras.

—¡Y cuántas veces irme a buscar al campo, y venir y encontrarme esperando buena cola!

Le hemos encontrado precisamente con las manos en un herido. Un mozo de Soria, que, camino de una romería, se ha caído de la bicicleta y se ha magullado el b r a z o. Le acompañan muchas gentes condolidas: mozos y viejas, que ponen cara de sufrir por él.

—Dicen que aquí no se le puede curar — dice uno.

—¡Dejará! — exclama una mujer—. ¡Pues no tié arte el tío *Ustoquio!*

—¡*Na* de arte!— dice él modestamente, m i e n tras zarandea el brazo del paciente—. ¡El conocimiento de poner los huesos a tope, y ya es bastante!

Mientras venda el brazo, haciendo extraños nudos por el pescuezo, y colocando un tremendo almohadillado, nos da su buena lección de medicina casera.

El curandero practicando con un paciente el conocimiento de poner los huesos a tope...

—D'aquí, de la osamenta, es de donde depende to el funcionamiento... Las heridas más importantes son las de costao... Algo vale que a este mozo no le ha cogido más que el hueso, pero aquí ha habido endividuos que venían escalabraos y han salido por su pie...

El coro de aldeanos que asiste a la cura rivaliza en contar casos prodigiosos:

—Cuando lo María la *Mema*...

—¡Y el de Arnedillo, catorce meses sin poder andar y venir aquí y echar a correr que *to* fué uno!

—Sí, y aquél que llegó de Pampliega a la posada de Zenón, después de haber *estao* tres meses en el hospital.

Sin dejar su labor, el tío *Ustoquio* nos va explicando los casos.

—A la *Mema* se le había salido la mandíbula de la misma quijada. El médico y el *ministrante* le pusieron una servilleta y se la subieron *pa* arriba y no podía tomar ni leche... Pero yo le busqué el mecanismo, se lo puse en su sitio y de seguida se puso a hablar.

Sus descripciones parecen leyendas de esos cuadros que colocan como ex votos en las ermitas milagrosas. El mismo reniego de la medicina, igual tono dolorido, exacto final solucionado.

—Y a ése de Pampliega que dicen éstos le habían puesto once metros de vendaje; casi no se podía mover. En *cuanti* que vino le aligeré el arropo, le puse el hueso en su lugar y marchó *pa* casa a los ocho días...

El secreto está, según este magnífico saludador, en saber dónde se hallan los huesos y cuál es su mecanismo. El se los tiene bien estudiados en sus

35. El mundo rural es rico es testimonios y presencia de curanderos. Imagen: La Estampa 1934

XII. MEMORIAS DE CURANDEROS

Es importante recordar algunos personajes que se dedicaron a la práctica del curanderismo, sin entrar en debates sobre si era un verdadero sanador o no. Su presencia, sus anécdotas, sus milagros o sus formas de aplicar remedios fueron importantes para mantener viva esa fe en la magia del curandero, así como la mística que rodea su entorno. Muchos de estos nombres los anoté en mi bitácora, tras indagar en diferentes aportes históricos locales, estudios de medicina popular, informaciones exteriores, etc., para recordarlos en estas líneas de forma concisa y breve, que nos sirve para comprobar, en general, que siguieron las mismas pautas ancestrales para ofrecer sus remedios basados en la botánica. Después cada uno tiene y aplica, a menudo, su particularidad a la hora de realizar diferentes ritos de efecto placebo a sus clientes. Por supuesto, existen algunas rarezas en los curanderos, que pueden ser apariciones, herencias genéticas o simplemente la decisión de seguir sus instintos.

Lo que sí puedo afirmar es que los curanderos activan una serie de mecanismos inconscientes de autosanación en los pacientes, y eso hace que puedan surgir los casos de curación espontánea o paulatina. Pero no todos son capaces de activar esa señal, dada la escasa fe, desconfianza o solo porque acuden a probar «a ver qué pasa». La mente es poderosa, no hay duda. Ese es uno de los grandes enigmas que debemos resolver: ¿hasta dónde alcanza el poder de nuestra mente?

Es evidente que no podemos abarcar a todos en estas páginas, seguramente le vendrá a la memoria otro personaje más conocido, pero confío en que sean de interés estas referencias.

EL CURANDERO DE LA SERRA D´EN GALCERAN

José Vicente Agut (1900-1982), más conocido como el «tío Vicent», era el curandero más popular de la aldea castellonense de Mas de Montino, un lugar donde están los hogares diseminados por diferentes senderos, rodeados de algarrobos y olivos.

36. Jose Vicente Agut.

Cuando recorrí esa zona, pude observar que aún perduran las costumbres ancladas a décadas anteriores, aún siguen confiando en las virtudes de la naturaleza, en la etnobotánica, y ese personaje que siempre ha sido referencia en este valle de fríos inviernos, donde sus aguas poseen numerosas virtudes para mejorar el organismo, ha sido un referente en la mayoría de los posteriores curanderos que aún siguen de forma encubierta por las localidades de Els Ibarsos, Els Rosildos o Els Pujols.

Vino al mundo un señalado Jueves Santo de 1900. Nació con algo primordial para su futuro y la señal de ser una persona elegida para algún designio divino: envuelvo en la membrana, conocida como «tela» o «manto». Una señal que sus padres, Jaime y Társila, interpretaron como que José Vicente había nació con «gracia».

Sus progenitores eran agricultores, pero tenían buena cultura, ya que su padre sabía leer y escribir, algo que era primordial y de una mentalidad privilegiada para aquellos tiempos. Conocimientos que no le sirvieron para ayudar a uno de sus hijos, que perdió a causa del cólera, y tenía dos hijas más.

Lo morboso y llamativo de su caso era esa membrana con la que vino al mundo: es primordial conservarla, debían llevar el llamado «manto» a la iglesia local de inmediato, el mismo día del nacimiento, sin que la autoridad religiosa lo supiera, y allí debía estar oculta, pero no en cualquier rincón del recinto sagrado, sino debajo de la sacristía o en su interior, y debía estar nueve días para no perder esa bendición recibida. El riesgo salió bien, nadie se percató y su pericia parece que dio resultado.

Recordemos que esta aislada pedanía se ubica a los pies de la Serra d´en Galceran. En esos periodos que la membrana estaba en la iglesia, aunque no citan qué templo, seguramente sea la iglesia de Benlloch, a dos horas andando entre sendas, o bien está a la misma distancia la de Els Ibarsos, aunque sería más sencillo el plan en la ermita de san Miguel. Según la creencia del arraigo cultural de la comarca, mientras esa membrana estaba oculta, hasta recuperarla, no se podía sacar absolutamente nada de su hogar, ni siquiera la basura producida, ni tampoco atravesar ningún producto a la casa, ni siquiera un cántaro de agua. Así debería seguir esta norma durante tres días, desde el Jueves Santo que nació hasta el Sábado Santo. Fechas de mucho interés místico entre los curanderos, saludadores, matronas…

Aquellos escasos habitantes que aún recuerdan a este curandero, aunque casi todos por referencias de sus padres y algunas personas ancianas de las localidades cercanas, aseguran que tenía una gran sabiduría y conocimientos para sanar. Quizá su nacimiento fue un regalo de la providencia, lo necesitaban en aquellos años que comenzó a curar a muchos habitantes de aquella agreste sierra castellonense con apenas 11 años y no dejó nunca de hacerlo hasta el día de su muerte.

Dislocaciones, lumbago, molestias musculares, torceduras… era algo habitual en la zona, y sabía cómo reparar esas típicas lesiones. Sin embargo, también era un auténtico curandero rural, era muy avezado en el tratamiento de diversas enfermedades como la ictericia (conocida en la zona como *aliacrana*), infecciones del tracto intestinal, diversos casos de tos ferina, problemas de la piel y paludismo.

De manera extraña, llegó a tratar esta última enfermedad a más de 300 personas, según crónicas locales y fuentes orales, con un misterioso rito de cuya efectividad difícilmente sabremos el porqué, quizá era un efecto placebo o una mera actuación teatral, porque se ignora si le daba posteriormente algún medicamento natural, como la quinina, ajenjo o hierba de San Juan, muy útiles para las infecciones.

Su extraño y misterioso rito consistía en colgar o atar un sapo vivo de la rama de un árbol, a la que realizaba una plegaria y citaba el nombre del enfermo; y, a medida que iba agonizando el sapo atado en la rama de aquel árbol, mejoraba el paciente.

Él respetaba los límites éticos de la enfermedad, así que, si el paciente debía operarse para su mejoría, remitía al enfermo a la autoridad sanitaria.

Hasta sus últimos días, estaba al servicio de la zona, caminando entre masías y pedregosos caminos, cuyo precio era la voluntad del paciente o de las familias que lo buscaron.

Nunca se separó de la naturaleza, supo elegir bien las plantas que lo ayudaban a curar —conocimientos que adquiere de forma autóctona y por las tradiciones locales—. Esas plantas eran espliego, ruda, tomillo, hierba de San Juan (artemisa) y las diversas variedades del *crespinell*, entre otras. Aún perdura en la memoria de los más mayores una receta de José Vicente Agut, que se preocupó de difundir en la zona para mejorar la salud de todos. Según las deducciones del curandero, la receta «refuerza al débil, limpia el nervio, aclara el corazón y los bronquios», y su fórmula es la siguiente:

3 yemas de huevo.
1 cuarto de coñac.
1 cuarta parte de azúcar.
El zumo de 5 limones.
Todo crudo, removido y bebido.
«Con dos dedos de brebaje, hasta medio día no tendrás hambre».

Ignoro si alguien la sigue tomando, pero algunos vecinos de estas masías la conservan anotada en algunas libretas o notas sueltas del puño y letra de sus antepasados. No saben si era efectiva, si ayudaba en algo, pero de lo que no hay duda es que confiaban en su sanador local, ya que tenía la «gracia», y eso ya es más que suficiente para confiar en él.

La ciencia y la superstición aún coexistían en aquel tiempo entre sombras. Mientras tanto, los curanderos continuaban su labor en silencio, casi de incógnito por esos solitarios caminos rurales, repartiendo esperanza y la panacea de la salud a los suyos.

EL TOQUE REAL

En esta parte agrupamos varios nombres históricos.

Existen diversas representaciones de reyes europeos, especialmente ingleses y franceses, que nos muestran al soberano de turno en el acto de aplicar sus manos sobre una persona enferma, cuya inscripción nos dice: «El rey te toca, Dios te cura».

El concepto de que un rey o reina pudiera sanar diversas enfermedades puede parecer un suceso sensacional en nuestro tiempo; sin embargo, desde que se tiene constancia en archivos, Eduardo el Confesor (rey de Inglaterra en los periodos de 1042 a 1066), tenía ese «don» de curar con la imposición de sus manos sobre los enfermos.

Este tipo de sanación se hizo popular, y su costumbre, junto con el rito, se trasladó a otros lugares como Francia. Una cura indolora, instantánea y milagrosa. La práctica de «tocar» se consideraba un ejemplo del derecho divino de los reyes, una manifestación de la autoridad que se creía otorgada por Dios. Tan importante era el llamado «toque real» que Luis XIV de Francia tocó a nada menos que 1600 personas durante un Domingo de Pascua. Carlos II de Inglaterra, mientras estaba exiliado en los Países Bajos en la década de 1650, tenía tal demanda que varios pacientes que esperaban ansiosamente su imposición de manos, entre multitudes, murieron aplastados por la avalancha humana en las prisas por ser curados por las manos mágicas del que fuese rey de Escocia entre 1660 y 1685, antes de que la Restauración lo convirtiera también en rey de Inglaterra e Irlanda.

En esas ceremonias siguió también una costumbre heredada de su ejecutado padre Carlos I (que fue decapitado en 1649): entregar una moneda perforada y con una cinta atada, con la imagen plasmada del arcángel Miguel venciendo al dragón, moneda que luego se llevaba colgada como talismán protector.

37. Carlos II de Inglaterra (1630-1685), cuyo «toque real» era esperado para sanar diversas dolencias. Imagen: Wikipedia.

La costumbre de esta moneda parece que procede de los siglos XV y XVII. Estos pretendientes también recibían como regalo una moneda de oro laminada, conocida como «ángel». Esta curiosa moneda fue introducida en Inglaterra por el rey Eduardo IV en 1465, siguiendo el modelo de una moneda similar acuñada en Francia, llamada *ange* o *angelot*.

La muerte de la reina Ana en 1714 marcó el fin de esta ceremonia de sanación en Inglaterra. Aunque el fin definitivo fue a causa del avance de la ciencia, lo que dejó en el olvido esta característica, supuestamente sanadora, que aportaba la esperanza a su pueblo.

William Shakespeare describió el «toque real» en su obra *Macbeth*:

Se llama el mal.
Obra sumamente milagrosa de este buen rey,
Que muchas veces desde mi aquí permanezco en Inglaterra.
Le he visto hacerlo. Cómo solicita el cielo,
Él mismo lo sabe mejor,

A lo largo de la historia, muchos gobernantes han reclamado la aprobación divina para establecer la legitimidad de su monarquía y ha sido parte integral en el desarrollo de muchas culturas. En la China antigua e imperial, se utilizaba la tradición de un mandato del cielo, como voluntad del universo o ley natural, para justificar la posición del gobernante. En el Imperio inca, el *Sapa Inca* era considerado descendiente del dios Sol, y en esa capacidad se le debía conceder poder absoluto sobre el pueblo, incluido el control y destino de la salud. En Europa las monarquías afirmaban gobernar por voluntad divina y, hasta el día de hoy, el servicio de coronación británica incluye una unción sagrada del nuevo rey o reina, como hemos visto recientemente con la coronación de Carlos III de Inglaterra, aunque este último no ha ejercido ese toque mágico de salud, que ya quedó en el olvido y obsoleto por ser inútil en términos generales.

La creencia mágica y curativa del «toque real» está relacionada por la causa de que los reyes eran ungidos por Dios y, por lo tanto, poseían un carácter sagrado. Se realizaban en fechas señaladas, como la coronación del monarca, o en festividades religiosas, lo que añadía un aspecto ceremonial y solemne al «toque real».

Este gesto de sacralización de la monarquía otorgaba a los reyes un estatus casi divino, con poderes sobrenaturales, espirituales y místicos, entre los cuales estaba el poder de sanar. En mi opinión, era más un efecto placebo ante la enfermedad, e incluso no descarto la teatralización del acto para demostrar el poder divino del rey. Esto puede ocurrir en las clínicas de los curanderos del siglo XX, donde, a menudo, existe un paciente que ha sanado de un cáncer o una enfermedad crónica sin remedio médico, solo con las virtudes del curandero visitado, propagando su milagrosa sanación en la sala de espera o bien difundiéndolo por la zona a través de la palabra.

El poder divino del «toque real» tiene sus orígenes en el siglo XI, cuando se creía que Eduardo el Confesor, último de los reyes anglosajones, poseía poderes para curar a los enfermos mediante alguna forma de imposición de manos.

La enfermedad que solían sanar era la llamada «escrófula» (científicamente conocida como «linfadenitis cervical tuberculosa»), una dolencia terrible que se manifestaba con llagas dolorosas, una variedad de tuberculosis. ¿Por qué esta enfermedad era la más reparada? Simplemente, por la alta asiduidad de esta enfermedad en tiempos medievales, ya que existía un alto contagio por diversas causas, desde un aire contaminado e infectado por la bacteria hasta la falta de higiene, la mala calidad y la defectuosa conservación de los alimentos. Raro sería que la imposición de manos fuera efectiva.

JAN MIKOLÁSEK, UN CURANDERO
DE TODOS Y PARA TODOS

Una interesante biografía sobre un conocido curandero originario de la desaparecida República de Checoslovaquia es un ejemplo de curandero que reúne prácticamente todo: herboristería, don de sanar por unas virtudes, apariciones celestiales…, no difiere en exceso de los curanderos de la Península.

Se trata de Jan Mikolásek. Fue una celebridad que sanó de ciertas enfermedades a altos funcionarios durante la ocupación nazi y después a los comunistas, tras la caída del Ejército alemán. Motivos suficientes para que numerosas personas confiaran su salud en Jan; de hecho, cientos de personas hacían cola en la puerta de su casa.

Lo llamativo de sus virtudes era diagnosticar las enfermedades de cada paciente con tan solo observar la orina a simple vista, sin usar ningún artilugio científico de analíticas u otros medios de estudio e investigación de la medicina moderna, virtud que aseguró el propio Jan de atender al rey de Inglaterra, Jorge VI, aunque no existe una constancia oficial o al menos creíble.

Jan nació en el seno de una familia que se dedicaba exclusivamente a la jardinería, profesión que fue clave en el desarrollo de sus conocimientos en la medicina basada en la herboristería y el conocimiento de las plantas.

Tuvo el tiempo suficiente para escribir unos diarios de su vida, donde antes de ejercer como sanador/curandero un gitano le predijo, tras observarle detenidamente las manos y las facciones, que curaría a las personas a través de las virtudes de la naturaleza.

No solo este personaje de la etnia gitana vaticinó su porvenir, sino que una vieja curandera de 85 años a la que Jan Mikolásek acudió, le entregó su orina a la anciana para una revisión y posteriormente le preguntó: «¿Quién eres? Tienes una mirada extraña. Vas a ser sanador».

Curiosamente, se convirtió en aprendiz de esa curandera llamada Josefa Mühlbacherová, con la que aprendió diversas formas de curanderismo rural, remedios de herboristería y, sobre todo, analizar la orina a simple vista. La fama llamó a su puerta tras sanar a su propia familia: a su hermano, de nefritis, enfermedad que afecta al riñón con inflamaciones; y, además, pudo curar una infección en la rodilla que casi amputan la pierna a su hermana, sanaciones que fueron de boca en boca en su región, y abrió las puertas a su futuro como curandero.

En su biografía anota que conoció a Valentín Zeileis, otro famoso curandero que, según crónicas, atendió a más de 14 000 personas usando la electrofisioterapia. Zeileis era un ocultista que conocía el pasado de la Atlántida y del antiguo Egipto. Según los informes, se consideraba como un gran sanador que utilizaba tanto el magnetismo como la terapia con piedras; sin embargo, todo parecía ser un fraude, de nada servían sus habilidades.

*38. Jan Mikolásek, curandero checo que sanó a nazis,
comunistas y toda ideología política. Imagen: Wikipedia.*

La noticia de estas milagrosas sanaciones realizadas por
Jan Mikolásek se difundió por las localidades de la región
de Pilsen, donde Jan había nacido en 1889 en la ciudad de
Rokycany. Era muy religioso y las notas biográficas afirman
que sus poderes eran un regalo de Dios, añadiendo que fue
el séptimo hijo de los trece que tuvo su madre, un detalle
mágico y místico que reforzaba su posible futuro como
personaje importante dentro de la sociedad, pues, según
las supersticiones, el séptimo hijo tendría virtudes, aunque
este detalle es más propio de la zona de Europa occidental,
mientras en la oriental se enfoca como algo más pernicioso,
que puede ser portador del algún mal, incluso se le aplicaba
algún exorcismo o ritual local para alejar esas malas energías; aun así, conservaba esa aura mágica y poderes especiales. ¿Cómo fue ese regalo que cuenta?

Asegura que un día soñó con la llegada de un ángel, mientras echaba una siesta en un campo de flores, llevando un

mensaje bien claro que marcaría su vida: «Recolecta, trabaja, piensa y no creas nada más que en ti mismo».

Le causó tanta impresión el sueño y mensaje que ordenó realizar una figura a tamaño humano de un Cristo, ante el que solía arrodillarse y rezar casi a diario.

Se casó en 1929 con la viuda de un jardinero en Dobruska, una localidad fronteriza con Polonia, ya con la agitación de la invasión nazi. Allí comenzó a recibir pacientes y, con sus dones, pudo mejorar la salud de numerosos vecinos y personas procedentes de localidades limítrofes, hasta el punto de que cada vez tenía más gente y comenzaban a acumularse enormes filas para poder hacer consultas y terapias de sanación. Esto dio lugar a problemas judiciales por ejercer sin licencia médica.

Curiosamente, las autoridades policiales que intentaron detenerlo eran pacientes suyos, y no entendían la orden, siendo ellos testigos de sus mejorías. Realmente era la envidia y los celos de los médicos académicos que no toleraban competencia desleal.

Su matrimonio no duró en exceso, apenas siete años. No por desavenencias ni trifulcas, sino porque, según teorías, era homosexual, pues no tenía una relación muy romántica ni emocional. Posiblemente, estaba más interesado por el jardín heredado de su difunto marido que otra cosa, al margen de su supuesta homosexualidad, que, quizá trató de ocultar.

Ya en 1939, con la presencia de los nazis en su zona, pudieron observar que existía una considerable presencia en su domicilio y, tras indagar en los cargos, le ordenaron que acudiera a una cita para analizar, como tal suelen hacerla Jan Mikolásek en sus consultas a sus pacientes, nada menos que 29 pequeños frascos con orina y diagnosticar las enfermedades.

la Semana Santa en Valencia no solo es un viaje de fe y tradición, sino también un encuentro con lo inexplicable, donde el misterio y la devoción caminan de la mano en cada rincón de la historia.

39. Imagen de Josefa Mühlbacherová, con quien aprendió a diagnosticar enfermedades a partir de la orina de los pacientes.

Con suerte o no, Jan Mikolásek pasó la prueba con éxito baja la mirada atenta de los agentes de la Gestapo y la Sicherheitsdienst (servicio de inteligencia), que solo le informaban con dos datos: la edad del paciente y el sexo. Sus aciertos no tardaron en llegar a los cargos superiores, puesto que se interesaron por sus métodos numerosos funcionarios alemanes, entre ellos Martin Bormann, uno de los asesores de Adolf Hitler, que le curó de cálculos renales y gracias a ello recibió la protección.

Tras la caída de Alemania, Jan fue arrestado por el Gobierno comunista, acusado de colaborar con nazis. Pero durante su presidio no dejó de aplicar sus curas entre el resto de los presos y, entre esos beneficiados de sus dones, estaba el vicepresidente de la Asamblea Nacional y que tiempo después se convirtió en presidente de Checoslovaquia, Antonin

Zápotocky, cuya gangrena pudo curar y evitó la amputación con el uso de plantas medicinales y unas compresas. Este comunista, como en el pasado bajo control nazi, lo protegió de la prensa, de las críticas y de desprestigios hasta que falleció en 1957 el mencionado presidente y quedó Jan muy desprotegido. Entonces comenzaron a considerarlo como un vulgar sanador rural, charlatán y timador, incluso se lo acusó de hacer fraude fiscal y blanqueo de capitales, pese a atender a más de cien personas diarias en su domicilio.

Jan Mikolàsek fue detenido, encarcelado y finalmente puesto en libertad en 1964, pero nunca volvió a ser el mismo, se refugió en casa de un médico amigo suyo que estuvo conviviendo con él hasta su muerte en 1973.

Su cuerpo descansa en el cementerio de Praga (Olsany), donde un epitafio resume magníficamente el significado de su vida como sanador o curandero: «Respetaba y amaba las hierbas. Con su ayuda daba salud a la gente».

Posiblemente, la vida de este personaje no ha cautivado en exceso al lector, pero lo más importante es demostrar que existen los mismos patrones que en la España más profunda: conocedores de herboristería, apariciones de ángeles o vírgenes, el don de sanar, paroxismo de pacientes en busca de una sanación o esperanza, personajes de poder interesados en ello, denuncia de galenos oficiales, detenciones… ¿Pero cómo empieza todo esto, el mundo del curanderismo mágico que nada tiene que ver con la evolución académica de la medicina? ¿Qué factores son los que hacen a un curandero?

Este personaje, que me llamó la atención por su disposición a sanar sin mirar las ideologías políticas, su curiosa forma de analíticas y su visión a través de los sueños que lo alentaban a seguir su camino de mejorar la salud de los demás, hizo que recordara a muchos que se dedicaban, de manera similar en sus prácticas, a comparar las características que existen en común entre estas personas afortunadas de poseer un privilegio mágico procedente de supuestas divinidades o bien a través de sus herencias familiares.

NATALIA CAPILLA, LA DESCONOCIDA VALENCIANA

En el pasado 2023, publiqué en una obra en coautoría una breve reseña acerca de una desconocida curandera valenciana: Natalia Capilla. Indagando un poco más en su vida como curandera, es realmente llamativa. Y creo que merece recordarse su memoria, aunque si curaba o no es complejo, dada la escasa información documental, y sus datos proceden de antiguas noticias de hemeroteca local y la memoria de los más ancianos de ciertas localidades donde Natalia ha actuado.

Se hizo bastante popular en Valencia y su nombre ya estaba en boca de muchos medios del resto de España, a pesar de las numerosas denuncias y multas recibidas que pagaba Natalia sin problema gracias a su numerosa clientela, que dejaba buenos beneficios que ni siquiera un ingeniero de su época podía ganar. Realmente quien denunciaba a Natalia no era el Colegio de Médicos, sino el de Farmacéuticos, por competencia desleal en venta de productos, como cita la noticia del *Eco de Cartagena* en junio de 1928:

> En Valencia, el subdelegado de Medicina ha denunciado a la curandera Natalia Capilla, que hace tiempo venía recibiendo en su clínica diariamente a unos ochocientos enfermos. El día de San Juan se presentó en la playa haciendo cruces sobre el agua que la gente recogía en cántaro. Por tal motivo ha recibido limosnas por valor de 5000 pesetas. El juez le ha tomado declaración no habiendo adoptado aún ninguna resolución.

Ejercía su labor a finales de 1920 en el Huerto del Santísimo (frente a los actuales Jardines de Monforte de Valencia), llegando a formar unas largas colas de pacientes con la esperanza de sanarse o curarse de sus enfermedades. Incluso personajes de la alta sociedad no escatimaban en gastos para poder conseguir su cita y preferencia de atención.

Vino al mundo en la localidad de Alginet en 1886, la cual también tiene un buen pasado de sanadoras contra enfermedades de piel y problemas estomacales, cuyo rito del empacho era muy habitual en su localidad. Pero, antes de alcanzar su fama en la ciudad de Valencia, comenzó a ejercer como curandera-hierbera en su domicilio, que estaba junto al puente de Catarroja. Ella vivía en una de las primeras casitas que daban acceso a la localidad de Massanassa.

Los escasos recuerdos del paso de Natalia por esta última localidad dejan su memoria local como una buena curandera que comenzaba a tener cierto prestigio y se trasladó pronto a la capital levantina (en concreto, al barrio de Ruzafa).

40. Natalia Capilla. Diario Estampa (1928).

Poco se sabe sobre los orígenes de sus virtudes sanadoras, sus mentores o posibles señales místicas para ejercer esta práctica. Quizá fue una mujer inteligente que supo imponerse a la ignorancia de aquellas personas con sencillos rituales como bendecir agua (algo que denunció también la Iglesia valenciana a esta mujer por su práctica, que está vetada: la bendición) y recomendar diferentes remedios basados en el uso de infusiones, beber agua o algún emplasto natural.

Su figura causaba respeto entre los presentes, vestida de negro riguroso, seca y con facciones marcadas, con un aspecto más de mujer de acercarse a los abismos de la muerte que de ofrecer luz a los presentes. Tuvo tanto éxito en Valencia como curandera que su esposo decidió cerrar una lucrativa taberna para dedicarse a la gestión de reservas y atención al público.

Tras una última denuncia, un reconocimiento psiquiátrico en su época y vigilancia intensiva a su actividad, desapareció sin dejar rastro, tras un breve lapso continuando su curanderismo.

¿Qué ocurrió realmente? Los médicos de su tiempo no ejercieron presión a ella, puesto que muchos de ellos acudían a la consulta de Natalia Capilla, según las crónicas de la época.

41. Intervención de las autoridades a Natalia Capilla.
Imagen: Archivo de la Biblioteca Valenciana.

CIRUJANOS PSÍQUICOS

En este caso, son un conjunto de personas que están señaladas por el fraude, pero no deja de ser curiosa su historia y merece ser recordada, principalmente para que no vuelvan a suceder semejantes casos, puesto que, hasta el momento de descubrirse toda la parafernalia que rodeaban sus expertas manos en cirugías psíquicas, muchas personas confiaban en sus prodigiosas manos y habilidades.

Desde los inicios de la humanidad siempre se han realizado diversas cirugías, usando cuchillos de obsidiana (por ejemplo) para hacer diversos abscesos o sangrías e incluso trepanaciones.

En este morboso acto de operar para erradicar un tumor o solucionar diversas dolencias, existen nombres que aplicaban estos hechos y que son conocidos por muchos de nosotros, como el extraordinario cirujano brasileño Zè Arigó o João Teixeira de Faria (João de Deus), todos los cuales fueron un fraude colosal que destaparon los conocidos James Randi y el religioso español Óscar González Quevedo, más conocido como «padre Quevedo», cuya obra es imprescindible para entender y conocer el mundo del curanderismo, especialmente acerca de los cirujanos místicos.

A este grupo de charlatanes se unen los cirujanos de Filipinas, siendo conocido el caso de Tony Agpaoa, que tuvieron su momento de gloria, hasta que se fueron descubriendo todos los trucos que empleaban en sus teatrales operaciones. Tanto los brasileños como los filipinos aseguraban que sus manos no operaban, sino que eran guiados por espíritus de diferentes personas que se apoderaban de sus manos. Por ejemplo, el mencionado Joao Texeira estaba bajo el influjo espiritual del médico Bezerra de Menezes. O la popular chamana mexicana Bárbara Guerrero, más conocida como «Pachita», que en sus operaciones y sanaciones aseguraba estar poseída por el espíritu del Cuauhtémoc, una intervención mística que le permitía y facilitaba hacer diversos milagros de sanación. Pese a ello, esta mujer tiene un aura de misterio de la que aún queda mucho por resolver, empezando por la desaparición de un hombre que se centró en narrar su vida, Jacobo Grinberg, aunque el escritor Carlos Castaneda dejó un excelente trabajo sobre su vida. Personas como el mencionado Grinberg y Salvador Freixedo aseguraron haber sido testigos de las curaciones de Pachita, donde operaba sin instrumental, llegaba a abrir partes del cráneo, vientre, pulmones…, lo que añade un plus de credibilidad a la curandera mexicana. Sin embargo, siguen existiendo, desde la aparición en su momento hasta hoy, diversas opiniones escépticas, ya que notan una falta de información más concisa y científica. Pachita adquirió una fama nacional en México, no solo por sus extraños e inusuales métodos, sino por la clientela de alto nivel que solía atender a diario. Se dice que importantes políticos del momento, empresarios acaudalados y figuras importantes del ámbito cultural acudían a ella en busca de curación y alivio para sus males. Entre sus pacientes más notables se menciona a personajes como el expresidente mexicano Luis Echeverría y su esposa Esther Zuno, así como otros funcionarios del Estado y con alto rango.

Todos los que aplicaban la cirugía sabían esconder en sus manos y bolsillos unas bolsitas con trozos de vísceras de animal (normalmente, de pollo) y otras con sangre, a veces escondidas en el centro de una esponja que luego apretaban para romper esa frágil protección e impregnarse de sangre, distribuyendo la misma sobre la zona que estaban, supuestamente, operando. Tenían, todos, el arte del disimulo, habilidad y prestidigitación que parecía tan real las extracciones de tumores malignos de los pacientes y sin instrumental médico. Y de usar los instrumentos de forma pomposa y sin esterilizar, lo cual significaba un alto riesgo e incidencia en contagios.

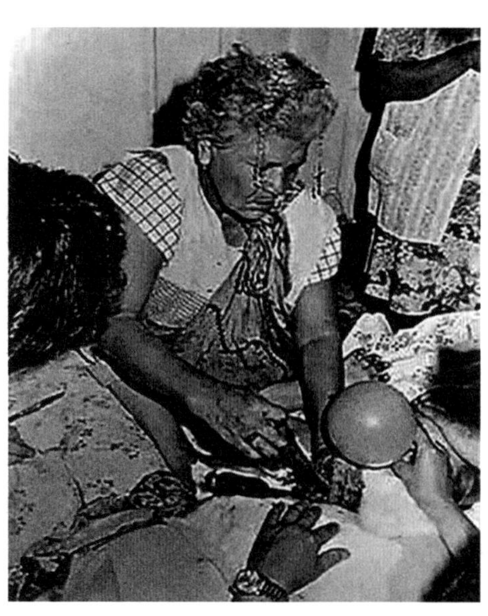

42 . Pachita, en una de sus icónicas intervenciones.

En muchas investigaciones se destaparon los fraudes y negocios que existen en estos ritos de curanderismo al analizar la sangre usada, que es cierto que era humana en muchos casos, pero donde el Rh de la persona operada no coincidía y estaba cargado de anticoagulantes para que pareciera más fresca a la hora de usarse sobre la operación y con más impacto visual de cara a los que presenciaban la operación y el paciente. La sangre humana la conseguían en los bancos de sangre tras unas negociaciones previas y clandestinas.

Un mundo turbio basado en el fraude, la corrupción y el blanqueo de capitales.

«EL BALDAET», CURANDERO Y ESPIRITISTA

José Cerdá Baeza, más conocido en Alacant como «El Baldaet», fue un peculiar curandero-espiritista de finales de las últimas décadas del siglo XIX.

Aunque su historia sea algo superficial, pude conocerla en una vieja publicación espiritista en la Biblioteca Pública de Alacant. En esta publicación era habitual ver colaborar a la popular Amalia Domingo, una pionera del movimiento espiritista en España, pensamiento que era parte del curandero que tratamos, se consideraba un médium y un espiritista, facultades que usaba para sanar a través de «fluidos».

«El Baldaet» fue denunciado en 1879 por ejercer como médico sin poseer titulación. La causa es proveer a sus pacientes fórmulas personalizadas cuando ya se dispensaban en las farmacias locales, acusación que siempre ha negado.

El apodo le viene de su poco agraciado físico, pues no era atractivo, y la prensa de su época lo tacha de feo, con joroba, el brazo izquierdo no tenía apenas movilidad, quizá sea motivado por esclerosis o isquemia, un impedimento que solo hacía tener el brazo derecho como útil y lo usaba para sus magnetismos. Carecía de estudios y no tenía facilidad de palabra, usaba solo unas pocas locuciones y tartamudeaba a menudo.

Solía poner ese brazo sano sobre la boca las botellas llenas de agua para magnetizarlas o, si fuera algún recipiente más amplio como un cántaro, insertaba los dedos de la mano derecha para agitarlos y realizar el mismo efecto de magnetización del agua que, posteriormente, recomendaba beber o hacer paños empapados de esta agua bendecida por José Cerdá sobre los puntos dolorosos.

Los más de cien pacientes diarios que se agolpaban en su domicilio confiaban en su palabra, aunque no era habitual pagar por sus servicios, ya que se ofrecían gratis.

Esto facilitó que muchas madres llevasen a sus pequeños retoños a las manos de «El Baldaet» para la sanación de las enfermedades infantiles, que, por lo visto, no eran más que trances típicos del desarrollo: llorar, comer poco, problemas de lactancia indisposiciones gástricas… Pocos estaban infectados o aquejados de alguna enfermedad grave. Acudir a este afamado curandero alicantino era una alternativa habitual.

Lo más curioso era su poder de sanar enfermedades a distancia, visualizando al enfermo, su habitación, la enfermedad… e incluso de resucitar a una mujer que estaba muerta y llevaba ocho horas en estado de cadáver, y ya estaban preparando la mortaja y el correspondiente cortejo fúnebre.

¿De dónde proceden esos conocimientos y habilidades?

No existe una información concisa, no ha tenido presencias místicas ni traspasos de conocimientos de curanderismo entre familia, todo parece que se debe a la profesión de su padre: era herrador, oficio que le facilitó convivir con animales de ganadería y equinos. Pudo aproximarse a conocer de forma autodidactica a la veterinaria, como, según relata la publicación espiritista *La Revelación* (enero de 1878), pasaba sus manos sobre los animales para hacer sus diagnósticos, aunque no acertaba la enfermedad, pero lo ayudó a sentir el cuerpo, las articulaciones y las palpitaciones, y esto lo llevó a la práctica, posteriormente, con las personas, como cita el medio: «[…] le venía del aprendizaje que le había supuesto el hecho de haber sido hijo de herrador […]. Cuando intentaba hacer diagnóstico manoseaba con tanta intención al animal, […] le hacía estremecer y con esto, muchas veces, acertar donde estaba el mal […]».

Aunque no hay unos datos muy fiables, estuvo un tiempo en la denominada «ciudad de los curanderos»: Villena, lugar donde aprendió el espiritismo, la mediumnidad y los magnetismos. Nunca aprendió a leer del todo, de ahí que fuese parco en palabras. Un clásico del curanderismo alicantino.

FRANCISCA ROMERO, SANAR COMO LOS VAMPIROS

En este punto, la muestra sería para una conocida andaluza, considerada como la última hechicera de Huelva: Francisca Romero. Fue juzgada por el Tribunal de la Inquisición que inició sus pesquisas en 1804 hasta 1807 y se alargó hasta 1814 a causa de la invasión napoleónica. Parece un caso más cercano al mundo de la brujería o hechicería, que se le acusó de ello precisamente, una persecución que perdió a su hijo en ese proceso, que se negó a informar a los inquisidores de su paradero cuando fueron a buscarla, que los ahorcaron allí mismo, en el jardín de su casa.

Pero los testimonios que estuvieron presentes durante los juicios dejaron claro que era una auténtica sanadora, todo ello bien documentado en el Archivo del AHN Inquisión (legajo 3731, exp. 148).

Curaba a numerosos enfermos o con dolencias chupando la sangre tras dar un bocado a su cuerpo, pues así podía extraer la «sangre maligna», como cita el testigo Rafael Guerra: «Que le mandó tender en la cama y le sacó de la espalda con la boca tres buchadas de sangre, lo que por ser mucha le pareció no podía ser de las encías. Que así le curó por cuatro o cinco veces» (AHN Inquisición, legajo 3731, exp.148).

También cita un nuevo testimonio Francisca Pabón, le solicitó ponerse boca abajo su cuerpo y hasta tres veces le extrajo sangre: «[...] con su boca sacándola sangre negra [...]».

Francisca también estaba dispuesta a ayudar a quien lo necesitase, sin importar el objetivo. Podía realizar diferentes conjuros para propiciar el mal o bien intentar solucionar con otros remedios las infidelidades de los matrimonios.

Tenía buena fama, le llegaban de todos los puntos de la Andalucía más rural para acercarse a ella e intentar sanar sus dolencias, que también aplicaba diferentes remedios de herboristería que sus elementos primordiales parece ser que usaba sal, aceite y romero.

Lo llamativo de esta curandera es su peculiar recurso vampírico de chupar la sangre de los enfermos. Ignoro de dónde aprendió este método tan morboso y peligroso, tanto para el paciente como para ella.

LOS TRES SANTOS DE JAÉN

La senda de los milagros, que cubre principalmente las comarcas jienenses de Sierra Mágina y Sierra Sur, en unos tiempos en que existía una pobreza notable, ausencia de servicios y caminos difíciles de transitar y nos lleva a recordar a tres personajes vinculados entre sí. Es uno de los ejemplos más importantes de la antropología del curanderismo rural basado en la fe y la confianza en la «gracia» que reciben las personas privilegiadas, incluso tras su muerte, pues sus tumbas son veneradas todavía y se producen diversas peregrinaciones. Esta zona es rica en historias mágicas, de taumaturgia, de leyendas con sus manantiales de agua milagrosa, de curanderos y mujeres con el don de sanar que datan del siglo xv, sin olvidar los numerosos fenómenos inexplicables que podemos encontrar, como las populares «caras de Bélmez de la Moraleda», hasta hipótesis vinculadas con la legendaria Atlántida de Platón.

43. Santo Luisico, uno de los grandes curanderos de la sierra de Jaén.

Todo comienza con Luis Aceituno Valdivia, conocido posteriormente como «santo Luisico». No hay una fecha exacta de su nacimiento, pero es seguro que nació a principios del siglo xix y su muerte aconteció en 1912. Sus restos son un misterio y se ignora el paradero.

Según parece, mientras pastoreaba de pequeño por los cerros de esas mágicas sierras, ya tenía encuentros celestiales y comenzó a curar gracias a esa «gracia» recibida. Sanaba por imposición de manos y sus recetas eran papel de fumar. En dicho papel realizaba un garabato casi ilegible, era difícil de entender lo que quería escribir o representar. Los pacientes, tras unas largas esperas de muchas horas a la puerta de su casa, lo tomaban como una píldora: bien hacían una bolita de papel que se tragaban con agua bendecida por el propio Santo Luisico, bien lo fraccionaban a trocitos pequeños que ingerían a lo largo de unos días seguidos, también con el agua consagrada.

Tras su muerte, la «gracia» se la traspasó a Ángel Custodio Pérez de Aranda (1885-1961), conocido comosanto Custodio.

Siendo adolescente, le gustaba visitar a Luis Aceituno. Al parecer, se convierte en su mejor alumno y se vislumbraba que sería su sucesor en el futuro, puesto que los vecinos y enfermos que acudían al Santo Luisico le besaban la mano como señal de respeto y superioridad. Sin embargo, han visto como santo Luisico no se permitía ese gesto con Ángel Custodio, sino que era el propio Luisico quien besaba su mano como signo de respeto y reconocimiento.

No tardó en aumentar su popularidad, pese a tener muchos elementos en contra y ser denunciado. A pesar de ello, nunca pudieron aplicarle una condena en firme, aunque lo acusaron de estafador algunos vecinos de Noalejo (su localidad natal) y algunos médicos de la comarca. Sus curaciones y milagros eran numerosos.

El santo Custodio curaba frotando la espalda de las personas, a quienes realizaba el signo de la cruz con los dedos húmedos de agua bendecida por él mismo y lanzaba soplidos al signar. Posiblemente sea la herencia ancestral de los llamados «saludadores», personajes ya extinguidos que se dedicaban la mayoría a sanar los animales de ganadería con la saliva y el aliento, que posteriormente se unieron con sus virtudes a sanar a las personas. Y, siguiendo lo habitual de su antecesor, entregar las «recetas» en papel de fumar con los mismos procedimientos sugeridos por el santo Luisico. Según su biografía, a los 25 años tuvo la hierofanía de la Virgen María, que le encomendó sanar. Esto es fruto de su profunda fe y oración constante, que solía realizar en una pequeña gruta cerca de una ermita consagrada a la Virgen de la Cabeza, la misma cueva que se albergaba el pastor que fue protagonista de la manifestación sagrada de la mencionada Virgen en 1227.

Tras su muerte, la mágica y misteriosa «gracia» la heredó Manuel Cano, que sería conocido como el santo Manuel (1912-1983). Un personaje muy reservado, que se dedicó como los anteriores a sanar espiritualmente, a bendecir y dar consejo.

El santo Custodio, antes de morir, dijo que, cuando él desapareciera, en la aldea de Los Chopos (localidad donde nace y vivía Manuel) aparecería su sucesor, como así fue. Manuel estaba desempeñando su profesión cuidando su humilde granja y, de repente, empezó a comportarse de forma extraña, empezó a irradiar bendiciones a todos, empezó a hablar de una forma muy espiritual que nunca se le conoció esos conocimientos (ninguno de los tres santones tuvo educación alguna). Su familia pensó que se había vuelto loco y decidieron llevarlo a un hospital psiquiátrico en Jaén, donde estuvo lo necesario para que los médicos le dictaminasen que no deliraba ni tenía trastorno mental, por lo que regresó a su pueblo y empezó su labor de sanador. Los vecinos de las aldeas cercanas aceptaron inmediatamente que el Santo Manuel era el heredero de aquellos curanderos que iniciaron esta trilogía: santo Luisico y santo Custodio.

Tras su muerte en 1983, nadie sabe quién ha heredado esa virtud, nadie conoce quién pudo ser el discípulo o persona que quiso cederle el privilegio divino.

En la actualidad, se veneran dos tumbas: la de santo Custodio y la de santo Manuel (se ignora el lugar de reposo de santo Luisico), y se reverencian de una forma realmente curiosa, lo que muestra las herencia y riqueza ancestral de nuestro pasado mágico. Es una herencia musulmana, un rito similar a los cultos sufíes que habitaron en siglos anteriores.

Ninguno de estos tres santos de las sierras de Jaén cobraba por sus servicios, aunque no negaba cualquier donativo honesto y acorde a las situaciones de cada paciente.

Probablemente sea uno de los mejores ejemplos de los últimos rasgos de la España rural y mística, donde confiaban en la «gracia» recibida por estos personajes.

El Dr. Manuel Amezcua, en su obra *La Ruta de los Milagros*, describe y narra en una fantástica labor de estudio del misticismo popular de esta comarca y sus tres milagrosos curanderos que han traspasado las fronteras provinciales incluso en algunos países.

SANADORAS Y REZADORAS DE CANARIAS

En el archipiélago canario, las curanderas y rezadoras han tenido un papel muy importante en la historia popular, actuando como guardianas de tradiciones ancestrales que combinan espiritualidad, medicina natural y conocimientos que se han transmitido de generación en generación. Estas mujeres, vistas como sabias en sus comunidades, eran fundamentales para la salud física y espiritual de las personas, especialmente en épocas en las que el acceso a la medicina formal era escaso o incluso inexistente.

Las curanderas empleaban remedios naturales hechos con hierbas autóctonas como el poleo, la ruda o el tomillo, aprovechando las propiedades curativas de la flora canaria. Preparaban infusiones, ungüentos y cataplasmas para tratar problemas como el mal de ojo, el empacho o dolores musculares. Su conocimiento iba más allá de la botánica; también incluía rituales de sanación que fusionaban elementos cristianos con tradiciones prehispánicas, reflejando la rica herencia cultural de las islas.

45. Imágenes de archivo local de Canarias, Seña Lugina y usando la cruz de madera cornical sobre un paciente. Imagen: Centro Popular Cultura Canaria.

Por otro lado, las rezadoras se enfocaban en aliviar el sufrimiento espiritual. Como he citado en páginas anteriores, a través las de oraciones y plegarias, estas mujeres canalizaban creencias religiosas para ayudar a quienes enfrentaban enfermedades, *malestares* o momentos de angustia. Se les atribuía la habilidad de interceder ante lo divino, y su presencia era solicitada en momentos cruciales como nacimientos, enfermedades graves o incluso en los últimos días de vida de una persona. Sus oraciones, muchas veces transmitidas de forma oral, tenían un carácter casi místico y eran vistas como una conexión directa con lo sagrado.

Quizá la más popular en las Canarias sea doña Eloísa Expósito, más conocida como Seña Lugina (1887-1980). Una santiguadora que unía las tradiciones indígenas con las influencias del catolicismo. Con el devenir del tiempo, aprendió el uso de oraciones para ayudar a los enfermos a recuperar su salud y liberarse de sus dolencias con el uso de una cruz de madera cornical, un objeto utilizado tradicionalmente en las Islas Canarias en prácticas de curanderismo y rituales de sanación. Está hecha con la madera del cornical (*Periploca laevigata*), un arbusto típico de las zonas áridas y costeras del archipiélago canario, se cree que posee unas propiedades protectoras y curativas que se utilizaba para trazar cruces en el aire o sobre el cuerpo del enfermo mientras se recitaban oraciones destinadas a aliviar dolencias físicas o espirituales. Lugina, al margen de sus conocimientos como yerbera, era buscada en la zona de Anaga como partera, sanar pulmonías, dolores renales... Una mujer que no recibió educación escolar, sus conocimientos se basaban en saber las propiedades medicinales de las plantas de su zona así como también las virtudes protectoras contra el «mal de ojo».

XIII. HISTORIAS DE HOY DE PACIENTES Y CURANDEROS ANÓNIMOS

No podía cerrar esta labor de recuperación de unas prácticas llamativas sin indagar en los escasos curanderos, sanadoras, parteras, hueseros…, aunque estén retirados o fallecidos o sean parientes cercanos de estos curiosos protagonistas. Siempre está la posibilidad de recordar su pasado, incluso recuperar alguna práctica, aunque obsoleta, para conocer el cómo y el porqué de su uso.

Por supuesto, no es fácil en mi entorno más cercano, quizá era más numerosa la presencia en el barrio valenciano de Nazaret por un motivo: en el pasado, era una zona muy vinculada a las labores portuarias, de ahí la numerosa presencia y testimonios repetitivos de hombres y mujeres que se dedicaban a la tarea de recuperar lesiones corporales, distensiones, lumbalgias, dislocaciones…, es decir, lesiones típicas de los rudos hombres de su tiempo, que se dedicaban a cargar y hacer un notable esfuerzo sin las tecnologías y las facilidades mecánicas de nuestro tiempo.

Cuanto más me adentraba en los núcleos más alejados de las grandes urbes, más facilidad existía de presencia del curanderismo más variado y remedios basados en la botánica y con diversas anomalías como, por ejemplo, manifestaciones marianas, espirituales y oníricas.

Unos eran populares en su pueblo, con notable reputación, otros ejercían en clandestinidad o incluso los repudiaron por sus abusos o estafas, por no mencionar el alto ritmo de vida que lograron algunos gracias a las voluntades de sus clientes.

Pocos testimonios relatan o recuerdan alguna sanación de un cáncer, una ceguera o una enfermedad grave que haya salvado su vida por las manos mágicas de un sanador. Eso sí, son numerosos los casos de personajes, tanto masculinos como femeninos, que se dedicaban a recuperar de diversas lesiones corporales, migrañas, molestias gástricas o alguna erupción cutánea, como son las verrugas. Nadie de los aportes que recogí hizo referencia al mal de ojo. Por lo visto, no había tanta malignidad o quizá tenían algo de timidez poder relatarlo, ya que es un asunto rodeado de un aura esotérica, de recursos inspirados en las artes más nefastas.

Las conversaciones han sido coloquiales, no un interrogatorio judicial o médico, buscaba la naturalidad, para facilitar el diálogo y los recuerdos, puesto que los testimonios provienen de personas con más de 65 años, y tuvieron que hacer un gran esfuerzo por buscar en su memoria o lo que les contaban sus padres y abuelos por estos lares, así como sus anécdotas y experiencias.

Un recuerdo presente aún perdura en la localidad de Catarroja: al parecer, hubo una época en que la presencia de mujeres dedicadas a la sanación era algo cotidiano, gracias a Mikèla Segarra, una vecina que tiene por costumbre buscar las historias locales de su pueblo desde fiestas y comuniones hasta la colocación de una simple farola. Una de ellas trata de la curandera Isabel Ramón, que en la calle Colón tenía ubicada su consulta. Todos los vecinos cercanos recuerdan las largas colas que había en su calle entre finales de 1970 y principios de 1980, incluso no era normal que esta zona sea donde más tráfico de vehículos existía, había numerosos vehículos aparcados de diferentes matrículas (recordemos que entonces se distinguían por las iniciales de provincia) y se hacía complicado andar por las calles colindantes. Eran de diversos orígenes: madrileños, alicantinos, de poblaciones cercanas de Cuenca, Albacete e incluso familias de Extremadura, que se acercaban para confiar en sus dones de sanación. Cualidades que iban desde sanar enfermedades cotidianas como gripes hasta infecciones de piel o problemas articulares y musculares.

Según me citan algunos otros testimonios de esta misma localidad, Isabel Ramón tenía la capacidad de contactar con difuntos, por lo que supongo que era una médium, así como que sus virtudes se basaban a menudo en masajes en la espalda, siempre tras realizar unas oraciones e invocar a la Virgen.

Durante otra consulta a un nuevo alegato (esta vez hay que desplazarse a la localidad de Alcàsser), nos cuenta lo siguiente:

> [...] hubo una mujer de Alcàsser que se llamaba Angela Tello Torres, esta mujer nació en 1850 aproximadamente, tenía la costumbre de subirse al tejado de casa y hacía como que cogía algo y lo lanzaba y la gente cuando le veía le decía: «Pero ¿la Angelita qué hace?», cuya respuesta nos dejará sorprendidos: «Es que aquí estoy recogiendo las animitas que estaban perdidas» [...].

Ángela se dedicó a sanar de diversas enfermedades y ese mismo testigo nos relata el suceso que tuvo su abuelo cuando acudió a ella, lo que nos deja una muestra más de la magia de las llamadas «signaturas», es decir, hacer señas en el cuerpo, bien puede ser la señal de la cruz o un movimiento ancestral que ha heredado o conocido:

> [...] estaba fatal entonces, a su abuelo le acercó su dedo a su mejilla sin tocarlo y empezó a hacer círculos con alrededor como si estuviera haciendo una espiral y al hacer esto el tumor le reventó y empezó a chorrearle el pus y la sangre, pudo sanar de esa infección casi al instante [...].

Ángela, inexplicablemente, perdió su «don» de sanar. Según parece, al final de su vida algo no hizo bien, posiblemente no cumplió alguna promesa que suelen tener los curanderos, como la prohibición de poder curarse a sí mismos o desvelar remedios u oraciones fuera de los momentos designados.

Una de las localidades que aprecio por su historia, cultura y patrimonio es Carcaixent, que no está exenta de numerosos personajes curanderos y mujeres que se dedicaban a los mismos menesteres de la salud. Sin embargo, es llamativo que la mayoría de estos usaban y recetaban un ungüento llamado *ungüent del mes de maig* («ungüento del mes de mayo»»).

Un bálsamo que se utilizaba y se sigue usando en la actualidad para diferentes golpes, alguna erupción cutánea en la piel, irritaciones… Posiblemente, tenga el origen por el siglo XIX, cuando fusionaron la trementina, cera virgen con el aceite de oliva junto con diferentes plantas locales. Una receta que ha sido secreta durante muchas generaciones y ha pasado de madre a hija, con cuya evolución han ido añadiendo alguna variedad de planta para darle mejores cualidades según las necesidades de la enfermedad, que podía ser el romero, flor de pastor o hipérico. Todo depende de la intuición de estos sanadores, que basaban muchas esperanzas a la farmacopea natural de su entorno, no descartaban la naranja y su flor: el azahar.

En mi búsqueda de huellas y memorias de curanderos, opté por recorrer Catarroja, de la que tengo varias referencias cercanas de mujeres que se dedicaban a esto y era habitual que visitasen a algún que otro curandero. Sin embargo, me llevé una sorpresa cuando en uno de estos casos unimos fenómenos paranormales, videncia, premoniciones, maldiciones y sanaciones.

Esta calle la conocen los más ancianos de esta localidad valenciana como «de las bombas» (carrer Galicia), ya que durante la Guerra Civil cayeron algunos artefactos explosivos.

Nuestra testigo (Ana), relata que nuera e hija fallecieron por la explosión de una de esas bombas que cayó en su casa (actualmente reformada y recuperada).

Durante mucho tiempo ha vivido intranquila, pues no se sentía segura en ese nuevo hogar, ya que existía una extraña presencia invisible que solo se dedicaba a hacer ruidos extraños de procedencia desconocida, por lo que recurrió a una famosa curandera de Sedaví para pedir ayuda ante esta curiosa situación y le solicitó que fuese a «inaugurar» [*sic*] su casa (bendecir o limpiar el hogar).

El consejo recibido fue que, cuando se encontrara a solas en la casa, se armara de valor y, sin miedo, se dirigiese a esas presencias extrañas de casa y les preguntara qué era lo que querían y qué hacían allí. Ana asegura que, al formular esta pregunta, experimentó un frío intenso en su cuerpo y los ruidos cesaron poco a poco.

El consejo de la curandera llamada Mari Cruz parece que hizo efecto. Pero no acaba la historia de Ana ahí, pues, durante una consulta en su domicilio, la curandera la trasladó a otra estancia de su consulta, donde había colgado un cuadro con la popular representación de Jesús y el sagrado corazón, una imagen religiosa muy habitual en las consultas de curanderismo, a la que Mari Cruz le hizo mirar para que observara si notaba algo extraño en él. Por su propia virtud de intuición, videncia y captar vibraciones de las personas, Ana, tras un instante mirando fijamente el cuadro, dio un salto atrás y un grito de sobresalto al observar que las manos de ese cuadro del sagrado corazón se movían. Los dedos tenían vida milagrosamente, algo que Mari Cruz tuvo que darle una explicación a este fenómeno: solo había otra persona, aparte de la propia curandera, que era capaz de ver este milagro. Un prodigio que solo las personas con virtudes especiales o bendecidas pueden ver.

Curiosamente, Ana, mi testimonio, me invitó a su casa para que pudiera ver un cuadro similar, y continuó su relato. Ese cuadro que domina su salón tiene más de cien años, no es suyo. Es una imagen que la regalaron hace décadas tras el derribo de una casa en Catarroja que estaba olvidada, un cuadro traslúcido del que se ve la pintura. Cuadro que, tras esa experiencia con la curandera Mari Cruz, se dispuso a hacer lo mismo, observarlo fijamente, con paciencia, y observó el mismo fenómeno que aconteció durante su visita al domicilio de esa misteriosa curandera. Sin embargo, esa manifestación de retrato de Jesús llevaba un aviso inesperado: poco después su esposo sufre un infarto.

Tras el susto que padeció por el infarto, Ana decide acudir con su esposo a la consulta de Mari Cruz, para que cuide de él. Sus remedios eran la imposición de manos. Tras su meditación y unas oraciones personales, le ponía las manos en la cabeza, y asegura que no tiene problemas desde entonces.

El mismo cuadro volvió a manifestarse inexplicablemente en su hogar, cuando el sagrado corazón de Jesús cayó al suelo, pero tengo que explicar el misterio que rodea a este momento. Delante del cuadro hay una gran mesa de comedor, apoyada casi sobre la pared, así que lo lógico sería que, si la imagen se cae, sería sobre la mesa o al menos dejaría sobre la tabla alguna marca de su desprendimiento. Nada de eso. Es como si hubiera salido disparado, pues se lo encontró a una distancia considerable, sin roturas, ni siquiera el gancho de esa sacra imagen tenía defecto. Como si alguien lo hubiera descolgado y arrojado al suelo. Cuando esto ocurrió, ella entraba a su casa y escuchó el ruido del golpe, y al acceder al salón pudo ver el cuadro en el suelo. Imposible que hubiera entrado o salido alguien. No hay más salida que su puerta. No consideró este fenómeno como un aviso, tras la experiencia de su marido, ni tampoco por su hijo, puesto que padecía cáncer desde hacía tiempo.

Las videncias de la curandera se amplían con este testimonio: Ana le enseñó una foto de la novia de su hijo, para que pudiera verla tras una conversación amistosa, de familia, hijos, trabajo…, pero al ver la imagen, la rechazó, se asustó, se santiguó asegurando que tenía una mala aura, que tenía la percepción de estar realizando brujería.

Parece que era cierto, la novia tenía un pequeño negocio y en la trastienda realizaba algún que otro conjuro. Ana cree que debió de realizarle cierto ritual o filtro de amor a su hijo, puesto que le entraron muchas dudas antes de casarse. Finalmente, pasaron por el altar, y esta chica cuida de su hijo con cáncer en la actualidad. Curiosamente, de este hijo le habló a la curandera Mari Cruz, puesto que su hijo notaba una sensación extraña en su trabajo, es abogado fiscal y muy escéptico en estos temas; sin embargo, la curandera, tras santiguarse, le dijo que dejara lo más pronto posible aquel bufete de abogados en el que trabajaba, puesto que le habían realizado a esa empresa un «trabajo de mal de ojo», por envidias, y estaba bien hecho el encargo. Incluso sería lo mejor para él. Consejo que aceptó, así que dimitió de su puesto, y poco se sabe del bufete que abandonó. Ahora asesora a grandes corporaciones a nivel internacional y con mucho éxito.

En la localidad de Alginet, recorriendo su casco viejo, buscaba los testimonios de aquellas personas que tuvieron dificultades para encontrar una mejoría de salud. Me acerqué al Hogar del Jubilado, allí donde se unen para recordar el pasado personal y disfrutar de una clásica partida de truc[6]. Me derivaron a un anciano señor que vivía cerca del elegante y modernista centro de mayores ubicado en la calle Almàssera.

Deogracias era su nombre. Me costó convencerlo de que me contara la historia que cuentan sus vecinos y conocidos, era reacio a ello. Pensé que tenía poco más de 70 años, por su mente tan fresca, viva y una agilidad física impropia de su edad; pero, para mi sorpresa, me aseguró que tenía 88 años[7].

La breve entrevista/conversación fue suficiente para conocer su historia como una persona que estaba al borde de la muerte tras diagnosticarle un cáncer de colon. Se lo diagnosticaron en 1979, cuando la medicina no estaba tan avan-

---

6   Juego popular de la baraja española.
7   Dato aportado por el testimonio en noviembre de 2023. Nota del autor.

zada como hoy en día, solo la cirugía y unas quimioterapias agresivas eran lo único que podían ofrecer en su momento. Tuvo que dejar su empleo de recolector de naranjas, toda una vida entre localidades como Carcaixent (donde también existe un crisol de curanderismo y medicina popular), Alzira y su localidad, Alginet.

—Me encontraba mal, fatal —me dijo—. Conforme iban pasando los días, los tratamientos no me servían de nada. Me operaron poco después, y nada pudieron hacer. Me recomendaron que me preparara para irme al otro barrio, me trataban en La Fe.

Era evidente que aquellos tiempos era bastante complicado el periodo posoperatorio, solo se basaban las esperanzas en uno de los fármacos que se utilizaban para tratar este tipo de cáncer: el 5-fluorouracilo, introducido en la década de 1950. Sin embargo, en esa época no era el recurso habitual ni definitivo y la efectividad de este tratamiento estaba limitada a los pacientes con enfermedad muy avanzada o metastásica, donde la cirugía ya no era viable, como fue el caso de Deogracias.

No tenía nada que perder, así que, como se negaba a aceptar su destino, recurrió a diversos curanderos. Para ello fue primero a Massalavés, en compañía de su hija, donde una sanadora que le había sugerido un conocido suyo de la localidad albaceteña de Almansa, ya que ella tenía otra virtud que no era para curar enfermedades, sino terapéuticas y de tratamientos contra dolores articulares, poco podía hacer para mejorar o curar el cáncer. No obtuvo mejoría tras visitarla, perdió peso, cada día observaba cómo se iban apagando sus fuerzas. Le aplicó un masaje terapéutico mientras recitaba unas plegarias e invocaba al arcángel san Miguel y le ofreció unas bolsas con diferentes infusiones: ortiga, cola de caballo y manzanilla. Tras esta sesión, le recomendó acudir a una dirección de Villena, según relata el anciano:

—A donde estaban los mejores curanderos de España, que era su maestro de no sé qué, quien le traspasó la gracia y muchos secretos de salud. Allí me trató un señor mayor, recuerdo que vivía cerca del castillo, me puso unas cataplasmas sobre mi vientre y después sobre mi ano. –Le costó indicar dónde se lo puso, algo avergonzado, con divertidos gestos—. Después lo cubrió con unas hojas de col. No sé lo que hizo, no dejaba de cantar, de rezar, de llamar a la Virgen, de pasarme por el cuerpo un rosario… Pero me curó, no sé cómo. No tengo nada tras aquella visita.

Es cierto que genera duda el relato al lector, y a mí también. Según ciertos vecinos que lo conocen, es cierta su historia, pero ¿y si fuera un diagnóstico equivocado? ¿Y si sanó por el tratamiento previo del hospital, y el cuerpo respondió positivamente de forma inesperada?

Quizá estamos ante un caso en el que restamos la virtud científica y se la damos a la práctica popular. Ignoro si continúa con algún resto de aquel cáncer que puso al límite su vida, pero, al escuchar su testimonio y ver su aspecto, parece que no hay rastro, salvo las dificultades propias de la edad.

No disponía de ningún documento que acreditara su enfermedad, lo cual hace complicado afirmar con rotundidad su sanación en manos de aquel enigmático curandero. Tampoco ningún informe que pueda corroborar su historial clínico. Sin embargo, dejo la puerta entreabierta para que discurra el misterio que rodea al mundo del curanderismo y los posibles milagros de sanación, que sabemos que abundan, sean creíbles o no. Demos una oportunidad al misterio de las sanaciones en manos de curanderos mágicos y fascinantes.

Tan fascinantes eran los «hueseros» que, en la localidad de Castellar, hasta principios de la década de 1990, ejercían diversos especialistas en lesiones. Incluso se llegó a percibir cierta tensión entre ellos por pura competencia, me pregunto si había una extraña carrera para ver quién sanaba más y más rápido, sin importar el resultado final del paciente, pues al parecer bastaba con una sencilla sesión. Un simple paseo conversando con los vecinos de esta pequeña localidad demuestra que guardan muchas experiencias con sus visitas a los diferentes masajistas-sanadores, y grabé algunas conversaciones a pie de calle a algunos de ellos:

—Acudían por este pueblo numerosos jugadores del Valencia CF y del Levante, solo para darse un masaje y recuperarse de lesiones, se los disputaban por tenerlos en su casa. Sí —continuó—, yo acudí a uno de ellos, pero en Horno Alcedo [localidad próxima a Castellar, nota del autor], me quitó unos dolores de espalda con una sesión, utilizaba imanes.

Me imagino que se refiere a una práctica de dudosa efectividad desde mi punto de vista, ya que aseguran los sanadores que pueden equilibrarse los campos magnéticos del cuerpo y mejora la circulación sanguínea, y en esto no existe un estudio concluyente que respalde las posibles sanaciones por el uso de imanes.

Pese a ello, los curiosos masajistas supieron hacer caja:

—Un curandero se hizo rico, tanto que tiene varios pisos y casas aquí. Había que coger turno con mucha antelación, no sanaba nada, pero te quitaba el lumbago o esguinces con mano de santo.

Las diversas conversaciones obtenidas son casi idénticas, cada sesión de estos personajes y creo entender que había una cierta competencia entre estos terapeutas sin título ni estudios, nadie tenía formación, es un recordatorio de cómo sus manos se convierten en herramientas de conexión, aliviando tensiones, dolores e incomodidades que nos surgen a lo largo de la vida. Cada sesión de estos masajistas es recordar el poder del tacto, de escuchar a través de las manos, y cada movimiento es un gesto mágico de cuidado.

XIV. BREVE DICCIONARIO DE LA JERGA DEL CURANDERO PARA DENOMINAR LAS DIFERENTES ENFERMEDADES

A menudo nos encontramos con denominaciones de ciertas enfermedades o dolencias con una jerga rural o exclusiva de los curanderos. No es siempre así, todo depende de la zona, pero en este caso he optado por añadir estas denominaciones que, habitualmente, suelen usarse en la vertiente levantina, Castilla La Mancha y parte de Murcia. Muchas enfermedades, dolencias o infecciones tienen varias denominaciones.

Seguramente, se acordará de otras denominaciones, pero esta jerga es la más conocida entre los pacientes de antaño y los sanadores que solían buscar los remedios para ello. El uso de esta jerga era muy útil para el curandero, pues facilitaba la conversación con el doliente y la comprensión de qué tipo de enfermedad o infección se debía tratar. Una maravillosa perspectiva antropológica que aún se sigue usando incluso en las consultas médicas, farmacias y hospitales, es una herencia ancestral de este mundo de la «folkmedicina» rural.

Te animo a ti, que tienes este libro entre tus manos, a averiguar en tu zona cómo llamaban las diversas enfermedades o dolencias en la jerga de los curanderos.

Los curanderos no solo trataban cuerpos, también los escuchaban, y lo hacían en el idioma que entendían los pacientes, en su lenguaje local. De fácil aprendizaje, de verborrea de campo, de pueblo. Eso lo denomino como el «idioma de la compasión», ya que cada malestar es nombrado con delicadeza.

44. *El mundo rural ingenió una jerga para entender las enfermedades y dolencias con los curanderos. Imagen: Diario Estampa (1929).*

TÉRMINOS

ALIACÁN: Ictericia.

ANGINAS: Amigdalitis.

BICHO MALO: Cáncer en general.

BUBAS: Viruela.

CARBONCA: Carbunco.

CARNE *CORTÁ*: Esguince o distensión muscular.

CULEBRILLA: Herpes zóster.

DESIPELA: Erisipela.

DOLOR DE AZÚCAR: Diabetes.

DOLOR DE PIEDRAS: Cálculos en la vejiga.

DOLOR DE PUENTE: Pleuresía.

EMPACHO O *ENFIT* (Zona de la Comunidad Valenciana): Exceso de consumo de alimentos, molestias gastrointestinales, hinchazón abdominal.

ESTAR QUEBRADO: Hernia.

FLORES: Difteria.

FUEGO EN LA BOCA: Herpes labial.

FUEGO DE SAN ANTONIO: Ergotismo, cornezuelo, aunque en algunas áreas también lo citan para señalar el herpes zóster.

GARROTILLO: Difteria.

HÍGADO HINCHADO: Hepatitis.

HINCHAZÓN DE SAPO: Inflamación de una parte del cuerpo.

JAQUECA: Dolores de cabeza en general, incluida la sinusitis.

LLOMADURA: Lumbalgia, ciática.

MAL *COLORAO*: Sarampión.

MAL DE CORAZÓN: Epilepsia.

MAL DE AIRE: Cólera.

MAL DE ESPANTO: Enfermedad causada por un trauma mental.

MAL DE MISERERE: Apendicitis, obstrucción intestinal, peritonitis.

MAL DE OJO: Creencia de maldición provocada por la envidia u otros actos de hechizos.

MAL DEL REY: Escrófula.

MAL DE SAN VITO: Epilepsia.

OJO DE SOL: Insolación.

ORINA DULCE: Diabetes.

ORINA EN LA CAMA: Incontinencia renal.

PÚSTULAS: Varicela.

SANGRE GORDA O ESPESA: Colesterol.

SOPLO DE ORINA: Cistitis.

SUSTO: Pérdida de personalidad, trauma…

SUBIDA DE SANGRE: Erupciones en la piel.

TABARDILLO: Tifus.

VERRUGAS: Lesiones cutáneas.

EPÍLOGO

Que esté leyendo estas últimas páginas supone para mí una pequeña satisfacción, pues significa que ha seguido con interés cada palabra, cada capítulo.

Además, estoy seguro de que ha llegado a una conclusión personal y que incluso por momentos lo he trasladado a épocas anteriores, rebuscando en su memoria algunas situaciones con diversos sanadores que lo atendieron personalmente o bien a unas conversaciones de recuerdos con nuestros mayores contando las anécdotas, virtudes, los milagros de sanación o situaciones inexplicables durante un proceso ritual del curandero. Que haya sanado o no es un debate que dejaré abierto. Quizá exista algún caso de sanación en manos de un curandero, cuya vida dependía del uso de sus prodigiosas manos, de sus plegarias, mediaciones divinas o ungüentos con los componentes más insólitos que podemos observar.

Hoy en día es complicado encontrar un curandero de antaño, de aquellos que sanaban rodeados de estampas religiosas y otras parafernalias. A pesar de ello, el rol del curandero ha caído en desuso, pero algunos han evolucionado como mejor consiguieron adaptarse a los avances, las leyes y los pensamientos actuales, y en ciertos lugares siguen siendo una figura importante en su comunidad, especialmente las rurales o las zonas más alejadas de la civilización, donde la medicina tradicional y espiritual sigue teniendo una implantación con arraigo.

En la actualidad tiene que superar unas perspectivas y desafíos, la globalización del siglo xxi ha facilitado unos intercambios de medicina científica y una evolución que ya están manejando la inteligencia artificial, y esto supone desacreditar e incluso marginar las prácticas de los curanderos, ya que se topan con un serio problema: legitimar sus conocimientos y sanaciones. El paciente confía cada vez más en los avances del futuro.

No solo se enfrenta a esos gigantes de la farmacéutica y las más avanzadas técnicas hospitalarias, se encuentran en un marco de leyes que impiden a menudo poder seguir sus prácticas de curanderismo, sobre todo si incluyen sustancias medicinales o recetas particulares que no están aprobadas por Sanidad o las normativas del Colegio de Farmacéuticos.

Si nos centramos en sus tradiciones, costumbres ancestrales, etc., las nuevas generaciones nos están por la labor de conservar este pasado.

Muchas prácticas y rituales se han basado en los conocimientos transmitidos oralmente de generación en generación, y esto se diluye con el cambio de estilo de vida y la pérdida de interés entre los jóvenes, lo cual pone en riesgo la transmisión de este saber popular, sumando a ello la desconfianza total ante unos ritos desconocidos que se vilipendian en términos generales.

El futuro de los escasos curanderos va a depender de la capacidad de adaptarse a los cambios sociales, a la colaboración con la medicina de nuestro tiempo con sus conocimientos de herboristería atávica.

Ellos, los curanderos, son los testigos de una fragilidad humana y del milagro cotidiano de la vida, cuando ellas (las parteras, en este caso, que eran las primeras en oír el primer llanto de la vida), con su compasión, nos ofrecían una esperanza de futuro. Sus prácticas, por muy extrañas y rocambolescas que hayan sido, eran el refugio de los anhelos humanos cuando la ciencia no tenía respuestas para sus sanaciones.

Recordemos a estas personas que nos daban un suspiro de vida cuando todo se asomaba al abismo de la muerte y la desesperación.

ÚLTIMA NOTA DEL AUTOR

Cuando cerré este libro tras casi dos años de estudio y análisis, sucumbió a las pocas horas mi localidad ante una de las fuerzas más salvajes de la naturaleza: el agua.

La mortal riada de octubre de 2024 será difícil de olvidar. Ni los mejores médicos ni los mejores curanderos van a lograr sanar esta herida emocional que permanecerá en nuestros corazones y nuestra memoria. Esta tragedia también se llevó por delante algunos domicilios de curanderos locales y, con ellos, sus recuerdos y testimonios.

Con todo mi afecto a mis vecinos y vecinas de Alfafar, que sufrieron las consecuencias desastrosas de la terrible DANA.

Alfafar, 29 de octubre de 2024.

BIBLIOGRAFÍA Y FUENTES CONSULTADAS

Alamillos, Rocío. *Hechicería y brujería en Andalucía en la Edad Moderna. Discursos y prácticas en torno a la superstición en el siglo XVIII*. Publicaciones de la Universidad de Córdoba.

Amezcua, M. *La ruta de los milagros*. Ed. Index Narrativa.

Amezcua, M. «Prácticas y creencias de los santos y curanderos en la Sierra Sur». *Gaceta de Antropología*.

Arazo, M.ª Ángeles *Gente del valle de Ayora*. Ed. Prometeo.

Arries, Javier. *Chamanes, señores del fuego*. Ed. América Ibérica.

Barandiarán, José Miguel. *Mitología vasca*. Ed. Txertoa.

Beitia, Ángel. *Valencia misteriosa*. Amazon Books.

Bove, Emilio. *Fu la peste: maghi, ciarlatani, taumaturghi, guaritori*. Ed. ABE.

Caro Baroja, Julio. *Las brujas y su mundo*. Ed. Del Prado.

Caro Baroja, Julio. *Las formas complejas de la vida religiosa*. Ed. Sarpe.

De Corgn, Christian. *Los sanadores filipinos*. Ed. Martínez -Roca.

De Dios Ramírez, Juan. *Nosotros los gitanos*. Ediciones 29.

De Villena, Enrique. *Tratado de fascinación o aojamiento*. Ed. Índigo.

Ehrenreich B. y English D. *Witches, Midwives, and Nurses: A History of Women Healers*. Ed. The Feminist Press Cuny.

Eliade, Mircea. *El chamanismo y las técnicas arcaicas del éxtasis*. Ed. Fondo de Cultura Económica.

Elworthy, Federick T. *The Evil Eye: The Classic Account of an Ancient Superstition*. Ed. Dover.

García Barbuzano, Domingo. *Prácticas y creencias de una santiguadora canaria*. Ed. Centro de la Cultura Popular Canaria.

García Ballester, L. *Historia social de la medicina en España de los siglos XIII al XVI.* Ed. Akal.

Gherli, F. *Regola sanitaria salernitana.* Ed. Sarturnia.

Grinberg-Zylberbaum, Jacobo. *Pachita.* Ed. Penguin Random House.

González Quevedo, Óscar. *Los curanderos.* Ed. Sal Terrae.

Granata, Tiziana. *Almanaco di remedi popolari.* Ed. Programma.

Haeger, Nkut. *Historia de la cirugía.* Ed. Raíces.

Jiménez del Oso, F. *Los curanderos: ¿iluminados, superdotados o farsantes?* Ed. UVE.

Jung, C. G. *La dinámica de lo inconsciente.* Ed. Trotta.

Laín Entralgo, P. «La curación por la palabra». *Revista de Occidente,* 1968.

Mann, Edward. *La Inquisición.* Ed. Humanitas.

Nardon, Franco. *Benandanti e inquisitori nel Friuli del Seicento.* Ed. Universidad de Trieste.

Neuville, Pierre. *Ur le chemins de la guerison.* Ed. Agència Parisienne.

Pazzini A. *La Medicina popolare in Italia: Storia, tradizioni e leggende.* Ed. Stargatebook.

Osuna, José M.ª. *Los curanderos.* Ed. Aula.

Pedrós Ciurana, M.ª Luisa. «El tribunal de la Inquisición de Valencia y los procesos por delitos de superstición en el siglo XVIII: la problemática en torno a la documentación». *Revista de historia moderna,* n.º 37.

Pertierra, Miguel Ángel. *Milagros médicos.* Ed. Luciérnaga.

Perwhels M. H. *Brujos, sacerdotes, médicos y curanderos.* Ed. Gaviota.

Rojas, Fernando. *La Celestina.* Ed. Cátedra.

Rodríguez, Pepe. *Curanderos.* Ed. Temas Hoy.

Ruíz, Dolores. *Historia de las matronas en España.* Ed. Guadalmazán.

Sacks, Olivier. *Musicofilia.* Ed. Anagrama.

Sánchez C. y López Neira, F. *Las otras medicinas.* Ed. Lyder.

Sánchez Pérez, J. A. *Supersticiones españolas.* Ed. Saeta.

Segado-Uceda, M. J. *La España mística.* Ed. Almuzara.

Seijo, Francisco. *Curanderismo y otras medicinas.* Ed. Biblioteca Alicantina.

Vicens Carrió, J. *Los curanderos ¿curan?* Ed. ATE.

Vilarrasa, Josep. *Santas y santos sanadores: Historia, leyenda, gozos.* Ed. Mediterrània.

Wiley, Andrea S. y Allen, John S. *Medical Anthropology: A Biocultural Approach.* Oxford University Press.

OTROS ARCHIVOS Y CONSULTAS

Archivo UAM Universidad Autónoma de México (Fondo fotográfico)
Archivo de la Diputación de Valencia: *Manual dels Consells.*
Archivio di Stato di Venezia: Varios archivos y procesos.
Biblioteca Pública de Alacant: *La revelación* (1878-1879).
Biblioteca de la Universidad Ca´Foscari (Venecia).
I.N.E. (Instituto Nacional de Estadística) Anuario estadístico de educación 1940-1980
Varios autores: *Revista española de investigaciones quirúrgicas,* vol. XIII, 2010.
Revista Folklore (varios números entre los años 1986-1990).
Hemeroteca Provincial de Valencia:
ABC.
Ideal.
Diario de Cartagena.
Diario de Jaén.
Estampa.
Eco de Cartagena.
El valenciano.
La hoja del lunes.
Las Provincias.
Levante.
Pueblo.

«Dios no ha puesto ninguna enfermedad en la tierra sin
antes haber puesto el remedio en la naturaleza».
Paracelso